Wilderness Comes Home

Middlebury Bicentennial Series in Environmental Studies

Christopher McGrory Klyza and Stephen C. Trombulak, *The Story of Vermont: A Natural and Cultural History*

Elizabeth H. Thompson and Eric R. Sorenson, *Wetland, Woodland, Wildland: A Guide to the Natural Communities of Vermont*

John Elder, editor, *The Return of the Wolf: Reflections on the Future of Wolves in the Northeast*

Kevin Dann, *Lewis Creek Lost and Found*

Christopher McGrory Klyza, editor, *Wilderness Comes Home: Rewilding the Northeast*

Terry Osborne, *Sightlines: The View of a Valley Through the Voice of Depression*

Stephen C. Trombulak, *So Great a Vision: The Conservation Writings of George Perkins Marsh*

WILDERNESS COMES HOME

Rewilding the Northeast

Edited by
Christopher McGrory Klyza

Middlebury College Press

Published by University Press of New England ❧ Hanover and London

Middlebury College Press

Published by University Press of New England, Hanover, NH 03755

Printed in the United States of America   5   4   3   2   1

Library of Congress Cataloging-in-Publication Data

Wilderness comes home : rewilding the Northeast / edited by Christopher
McGrory Klyza.
p.   cm. — (Middlebury bicentennial series in environmental
studies)
Includes bibliographical references (p.   ).
ISBN 1–58465–101–6 (cloth) — ISBN 1–58465–102–4 (paper)
1. Wilderness areas—Northeastern States. 2. Nature
conservation—Northeastern States. I. Klyza, Christopher McGrory. II.
Title. III. Series.
QH76.5.N96 W56 2001
333.95'0974—dc21   00–012160

To Caroline, Isabel, and the missing wolverine

Contents

Illustrations and Tables

Figures

Graphs

Maps

Tables

Preface

Wilderness Comes Home: The Rewilding of the Northeast is the fifth volume
in the Middlebury Bicentennial Series in Environmental Studies. This series, a joint effort of Middlebury College and the University Press of New
England, seeks to focus attention on the interplay between nature and
culture in the rural and wild landscapes of New England, and the Northeast more generally. The landscape of this region of the country has un-
dergone tremendous change since the arrival of European colonists in the
seventeenth century. The original forests were almost entirely cleared for
agriculture and by logging, and many of the larger species of wildlife were
extirpated or greatly reduced in number throughout the region. Since the
middle of the nineteenth century, however, the forests and wildlife in the
hinterlands of the Northeast began to return as agriculture declined and
human population growth slowed or stopped. The pace of this recovery
accelerated with proactive conservation efforts that themselves accelerated
through the twentieth century. Today, the Northeast is perhaps the most
complex and interesting conservation story in the nation, a place where
there is more forestland than one hundred years ago, a place where animals such as beaver and moose and fisher—and perhaps even wolves—
are returning. The books in this series seek to explore the landscape of
this region from a wide variety of angles, yet always looking to the connections of nature, culture, and time.

Wilderness Comes Home seeks to fulfill three main themes within this
broader mission. First, the volume serves as a survey of wilderness in the
Northeast at the beginning of the twenty-first century. Second, the volume seeks to provide an eastern voice in the national conversation on
wilderness. This conversation has been almost exclusively a western one,
both in terms of where wilderness has been designated and in terms of
what were perceived as the relevant questions for debate. And third, the
volume offers a model for wilderness in the twenty-first century based on
the Northeast. This model focuses on recovered and restored lands rather
than pristine ones; on interwoven private and public lands rather than
just public lands; and on a landscape of wilderness and sustainably man-

aged farmland and forestland rather than wilderness alone. We do not argue that this model is any way superior to the western model; rather, it is a different model for a different landscape with a different history and different land ownership patterns.

The contributors to this book are among the leading thinkers and practitioners of particular pieces of this larger model, working in areas ranging from documenting old growth in the Northeast to ecological reserve design to land trusts to sustainable forestry. I am thankful to each of them not only for their contribution to this book, but more importantly for their contributions to the northeastern landscape. In recognition of their contributions, and of the need for much more work on the ground, all royalties from this book will be split between Buy Back the Dacks, working to protect wilderness in the Adirondacks, and Vermont Family Forests, a leader in efforts to make sustainable forestry work in Vermont.

Let me now turn to a more specific set of thanks. John Elder's chapter "A Conversation at the Edge of Wilderness" originally appeared in *Wild Earth* (Winter 1998/1999). I thank editor Tom Butler and the Cenozoic Society for permission to reprint it in this book. Figure 5.1 originally appeared in *Wild Earth* (Special Issue 1992) as well. Thanks again to Tom Butler and the Cenozoic Society, as well as to Reed Noss, for permission to reproduce it in this book. The maps in the book were created by Northern Cartographic in South Burlington. Figure 8.1 was created for Sweet Water Trust. The photographs in the book are by John Knuerr, Gary Moore, Susan C. Morse, Jeffrey P. Roberts, Tim Simmons, and Barbara Slaiby. One photo appears courtesy of the Woodstock Historical Society. The beautiful linocuts and wood engravings that appear between the different sections of the book are by Suzanne DeJohn. I am grateful to each of these mapmakers, photographers, and artists for their work.

The Trustees and administration of Middlebury College provided the time and resources necessary to undertake this book series and my editing of this volume. Even more importantly, they have nurtured a campus where environmental studies has taken root and grown to include a diverse and stimulating group of students, faculty, and staff. Conversations within this community are reflected in this book. More specifically, over the years my thinking on wilderness has been most importantly shaped by conversations—frequently in the woods of the Northeast—with David Brynn, Tom Butler, John Davis, John Elder, Nan Jenks-Jay, Leanne Klyza Linck, Bob Linck, Steve Mylon, Jamie Sayen, Jared Snyder, David Sousa, and Steve Trombulak. Most importantly, I thank my wife Sheila McGrory-Klyza. All of my work is built on the foundation of her insight, support, and love. My daughters Isabel and Caroline have given my interest in northeastern wilderness an added depth and perspective. It is to them, and to the wolverine that I hope can one day return to share this landscape with them, that I dedicate this book.

Middlebury, Vermont   C.M.K.
March 2000

Part I

TAKING STOCK

CHAPTER I

An Eastern Turn for Wilderness

CHRISTOPHER McGRORY KLYZA

"IN WILDNESS IS the preservation of the World." With these words, Henry David Thoreau began serious discussion about the place of wild lands in the American landscape. The wild that Thoreau writes of in his 1862 essay "Walking" is the western United States. Ever since Thoreau wrote these words—in the Northeast—American wilderness, in both theory and practice, has centered on the towering mountains, vast plains, and rich forests of the West. It is time, however, for Thoreau's native Northeast to make significant contributions to America's engagement with wilderness and the place of humans in nature in general. Just as the forests and moose are returning to their homes in the landscape of the region, so too should the wilderness discussion return to the home of its first advocate and the country's first protected wilderness areas in the Adirondacks and Catskills of New York.[1]

The Northeast and the West offer stark contrasts when it comes to wilderness (see map 1.1).[2] One fundamental difference between them is how the land has been managed since European settlement of North America. At one time, historians and conservationists spoke of a pristine nature throughout North America at the time of European arrival. More recently, due to the work of anthropologists, ecological and environmental historians, and geographers, we have a better understanding of how Native Americans across the continent manipulated the landscape for their needs, primarily through the use of fire and their hunting, gathering, and fishing. This is an important and useful corrective. However, the difference between a pristine landscape and a humanized landscape is not quite so simple. Rather than selecting between the two, we need to think in terms of a continuum. In some parts of pre-Columbian North America, population densities and the use of fire were relatively high, and the effects of the native people on the landscape were significant. In other parts, population densities and fire use were low, and it makes little sense to speak of these landscapes as humanized compared to places with high

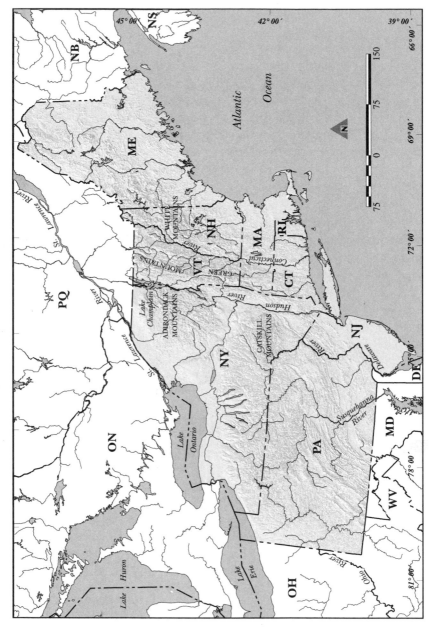

Map 1.1. The Northeastern States.

4

population densities and fire use, not to mention the humanized land-scapes of today.[3]

This contention between those who perceive 1492 North America as a pristine continent versus those who perceive it as a humanized continent is central to today's debate over western wilderness. The Wilderness Act, the 1964 law establishing the National Wilderness Preservation System on federal lands, defines wilderness as a place "where the earth and its community of life are untrammeled by man, where man himself is a visitor who does not remain." Leading critics, such as William Cronon, argue that this focus on pristine, untrammeled wilderness gets us back to the wrong nature. "Far from being the one place on earth that stands apart from humanity," he writes, "it is quite profoundly a human creation." We focus too much of our attention on big, (mythically) pristine, distant wilderness and too little attention on sustainably living on the middle ground of home. "We need to embrace the full continuum of a natural landscape that is also cultural," Cronon states, "in which the city, the suburb, the pastoral, and the wild each has its proper place, which we permit ourselves to celebrate without needlessly denigrating the others." A turn to the East can help us to do this; to concentrate on both wilderness and managed lands.[4]

There is no mistaking the Northeast today for a pristine landscape. Forests covered well over 90 percent of this region in 1492. The forest was manipulated to greater or lesser degrees in different areas. In the coastal plains of southern New England and New Jersey, Native Americans made frequent use of fire. This coastal region supported much larger human populations than the interior regions. In these interior regions — northern New England, the Adirondacks, and parts of the Allegheny Plateau in New York and Pennsylvania — the effects of the Native Americans on the landscape were much more limited. In Vermont, for instance, no evidence has been found of the widespread use of fire by the Abenaki. Anthropologists estimate their population in 1600 to be six to eight thousand. Although such a hunting-gathering-fishing people affected the landscape by hunting and gathering certain species and clearing small areas for farming, it is hardly useful to describe the landscape as humanized in the same way that we describe the much more heavily populated and manipulated southern New England regions.[5]

There is no argument about the degree that the northeastern landscape was humanized from the seventeenth century through the present. As settlers arrived in coastal regions and moved up the rivers, the forests were cleared for farms. Settlers put other pressures on the forests as well: for fuelwood to heat homes, cook food, and propel trains; for charcoal to fuel iron and lime kilns; for lumber and pulp for the growing country; for tannin to process leather; and for room for the growing urban areas of the Northeast. This forest clearing reached its peak in the middle to late nineteenth century. By this time, the original forests were almost completely gone. Old-growth forest in the Northeast today covers 400,000 to 500,000 acres, less than one-half of 1 percent of the landscape (see chapter 3). Gone, too, were many of the wild animals that lived in the Northeast in pre-Columbian times, such as the mountain lion and timber wolf. Even species common today, such as the white-tailed deer and wild turkey, had virtually disappeared from the region (see chapter 2).

The contingencies of history soon combined to restore the forests of the Northeast, with some explicit help from humans. Two factors were most responsible for this return of the forests. First was the decline of agriculture throughout the Northeast, primarily due to the region's competitive disadvantage compared to the Midwest and Great Plains. As marginal farms throughout the Northeast were abandoned, forests reclaimed fields and pastures. The migration of the timber industry to the relatively uncut forests of the Great Lakes, the Southeast, and then the West was the second factor. Although the logging of forests in the Northeast peaked again in the late-nineteenth and early twentieth centuries, primarily due to the building of logging railroads into previously remote regions, the forest products industry thereafter went into significant decline, recovering to some degree in Maine and parts of northern New Hampshire, northeastern Vermont, the Adirondacks, and central Pennsylvania. Helping at the edges of this reforestation was the rise of conservation in the region, namely forestry with its emphasis on fire fighting, reforestation, and sustained yield.[6]

Although there has been, in the words of Bill McKibben, "an explosion of green" throughout the East during the twentieth century, most of the forests of the Northeast at the beginning of the twenty-first century are quite different in terms of composition, structure, and age from the forests of four hundred years ago (see table 1.1). Indeed, the Wilderness Act designated only three wilderness areas in the East, one in New Hampshire and two in North Carolina. When eastern supporters wanted more wilderness designated in the East, the Forest Service responded that virtually no wilderness remained in the East, since these forests had already been completely cut over; they had been wholly trammeled by man. Responding to Forest Service intransigence, Congress passed the Eastern Wilder-

Table 1.1

Percentage of Forest Cover in the Northeastern States over Time

State	Percent forested, 1500	Percent forested, 1900	Percent forested, ca. 1990
Connecticut	95	39	59
Maine	95	79	90
Massachusetts	90	52	64
New Hampshire	95	58	87
New Jersey	90	43	42
New York	90	39	62
Pennsylvania	95	51	59
Rhode Island	95	40	60
Vermont	95	43	77

ness Act in 1975, designating sixteen wilderness areas in the East (including one in New Hampshire and two in Vermont) and preparing the way for future eastern expansion.[7]

This expansion could not go too far, however, because of the second great difference between the Northeast and the West when it comes to wilderness: land ownership. The federal government conservation and natural resources agencies—the Bureau of Land Management, the Fish and Wildlife Service, the Forest Service, and the National Park Service—control over half of the land in the thirteen western states, almost all of it federally owned since these lands became part of the United States. It is on these public lands that the grand western wilderness areas exist—the Wrangell-St. Elias in Alaska, the Frank Church-River of No Return in Idaho, the Bob Marshall in Montana, the Gila in New Mexico. The great bulk of the wild lands in the West not legally designated as wilderness is also located on these federal lands. In the nine states of the Northeast, these agencies manage only 2 percent of the land (see chapter 4). Given the small amount of federal land, it is not surprising that there is little wilderness or wild land in the Northeast. If all eighteen wilderness areas in the region were combined, their total of nearly 205,000 acres would only constitute a single medium-sized wilderness area by western standards.[8]

The one great exception to this difference is in the Adirondack and Catskill mountains in New York, home to the nation's first protected wilderness. In 1885, New York State established the Adirondack Forest Preserve and the Catskill Forest Preserve. All state-owned land—at this time and in the future—in these two regions would be part of these preserves, which were incorporated into the Adirondack Park in 1892 and the Catskill Park in 1904. More importantly, in 1894, constitutional convention delegates added the "forever wild" clause to the New York Constitution. Still part of the state constitution, the clause reads:

> The lands of the state, now owned or hereafter acquired, constituting the forest preserve, as now fixed by law, shall be forever kept as wild forest lands. They shall not be leased, sold or exchanged, nor shall the timber thereon be sold, removed or destroyed.

This clause protects over two and one-half million acres of land in the Adirondack Park (nearly half of the park lands) and close to three hundred thousand acres in the Catskill Park (over 40 percent of the park lands). Five wilderness areas in the Adirondacks exceed one hundred thousand acres; the largest wilderness in the Catskills is nearly fifty thousand acres. The combined wild lands in these two forest reserves are over twelve times the federally designated wilderness in the Northeast. Furthermore, the Adirondacks played a formative role in the thinking of wilderness leaders Robert Marshall and Howard Zahniser.[9]

These two fundamental differences—more intense and widespread land manipulation since European arrival and far less federally owned land—in the Northeast compared to the West, suggest the need for different approaches to wilderness, for different paradigms. The northeastern approach described here, however, is not meant to supplant the western paradigm (see chapter 12). I fully support the idea of protecting landscapes on federal lands that have been dominated by natural forces for hundreds of years. But such a paradigm cannot be forced on landscapes without large-scale federal ownership or on lands that have recently been affected significantly by human actions. In the Northeast, we need a different paradigm for a different place with a different landscape history.

My vision of northeastern wilderness is land that has recovered its ecological integrity or has the potential to do so, although it may at one time have been significantly altered by human actions. It is land where natural processes dominate; where the influences of humans are minimized. There is no development, logging, mining, or use of mechanized vehicles on the land. It is home to healthy populations of native species, including top-level predators. Northeastern wilderness areas are primarily located on federal and state-owned lands, are part of a connected regional and continental wild-lands system, and are embedded within a matrix of sustainably managed private lands.

This northeastern paradigm incorporates three core components:

1. The primary purpose of wilderness areas should be as ecological reserves for the survival of other species and the continuation of evolution. Although such wilderness areas may continue to segregate humans from nature, as some critics argue, such segregation is necessary until a transition to a more sustainable society occurs. Without these reserves, many species will go extinct.

2. The wilderness idea should be applied in temporally and spatially specific ways; that is, wilderness in Vermont, Alaska, and Indonesia may be implemented in different ways, just as wilderness is implemented differently in areas relatively pristine today (such as Alaska) than in areas that have been greatly manipulated by humans yet are on their way to recovering their wildness (such as many areas in the northeastern United States).

3. The wilderness idea and its supporters must be clearly and actively connected with those improving human management of non-wilderness land. The development of ecologically sustainable management schemes—in agriculture and forestry especially—must be fully connected to wilderness. This can help to reconnect humans with nature, to make us better understand that islands of wilderness cannot survive unless the surrounding lands are better managed, and to demonstrate that wilderness proponents care greatly about the fate of humans as well as other species.

Before elaborating on these core components, I close this introduction by offering the Green Mountains of Vermont as a metaphor for a northeastern conception of wilderness. Just as the forest that covered these mountains when the Europeans arrived was cut and has returned, so too the Green Mountains likely topped 20,000 feet before erosion and glaciers wore them down. These mountains and forests are more ambiguous than the young, rugged western mountains and their old-growth forests. What seems clear in the West is cloudier in the East. That doesn't make one landscape better, just different. And just as we use different tools to farm different kinds of land, and wear different kinds of clothes in different climates, so must we tailor our idea of wilderness to the different landscapes and different histories of our places.

Wilderness, Biodiversity, and Ecological Reserves

I take infinite pains to know all the phenomena of the spring, for instance, thinking that I have here the entire poem, and then, to my chagrin, I hear that it is but an imperfect copy that I possess and have read, that my ancestors have torn out many of the first leaves and grandest passages, and mutilated it in many places.

—Henry David Thoreau

The rationale for wilderness as expressed in the Wilderness Act of 1964 was almost wholly human-centered, or anthropocentric. The justifications for such wilderness ranged from its importance for spiritual recharge to its role in helping humans develop a sense of humility to its significance in American history. A minor theme at the time was the need to preserve lands to protect biological diversity and ecological functions, as well as to protect nature because of its inherent value, that is, the concept that nature and its component pieces have a right to exist independent of their value to humans. This branch of wilderness thought has grown significantly in importance during the thirty-five years since the Wilderness Act passed. Over this time, we have seen the rise of concern about endangered species, an accelerating rate of human-caused extinction, and the general decline of biodiversity.[10]

Society has responded to these concerns in a number of ways. Most notable have been the passage of the Endangered Species Act and the development of the new field of conservation biology. The former seeks to protect species at risk of global or local extinction with a suite of legal and administrative tools: determining which species are endangered or threatened, protecting their habitats, protecting the species through regulations, and implementing recovery plans. Conservation biology seeks to protect, maintain, and restore biodiversity through scientific research, and then to share and apply the knowledge gained. A major focus of conservation biology is the design of ecological reserves to protect biological diversity in landscapes across the world (see chapter 5).[11]

Briefly, research has demonstrated the importance of systems based on core areas, connectivity, and buffer areas. Core areas would be managed (or not managed) primarily to protect and restore biological diversity, with the long-term goal in the core areas to minimize any human management and to let natural processes, such as predation and ice storms, determine the composition and structure of the landscape. Connectivity focuses on the need for seasonal movements of some species of animals; the importance of genetic interchange when small populations are present in core areas (for example, large predators) and of providing corridors for dispersal of plants and animals, especially crucial if a particular core area is decimated by a disturbance, such as disease or fire; and the potential need for species to shift ranges in response to global climate changes. The last piece of the design is the buffer areas. Such areas would be available for ecologically sensitive human uses, such as sustainable forestry, agriculture, and recreation. These areas would ameliorate problems that arise when an animal leaves a reserve and enters developed areas, such as a wolf preying on livestock, as well as problems that move from heavily developed regions into ecological reserves, such as roaming domestic cats and dogs and reckless motorized vehicle use.[12]

Given the history of significant and total landscape disturbance in the Northeast, as well as the relative lack of public lands, can this model of cores, connectivity, and buffers be of any use in this region? The answer is an unqualified yes. In some ways, this reserve design system is even more important in the Northeast. Existing wilderness areas will serve as the first set of core reserves. Only in the Adirondacks, however, where New York State owns over two and one-half million acres of protected wild lands, will existing wilderness land be anywhere close to sufficient for core reserves. Elsewhere, the logical choice is to examine all other public lands—state and federal—for their potential role as core reserves. State lands can play a major role, especially in New York and Pennsylvania, where each state owns millions of acres. However, Pennsylvania and the other northeastern states need to establish wilderness programs for their lands. Since wilderness lands will not be managed for profit, it is unlikely that many private landowners would be willing to declare their lands reserves. Furthermore, since the protection of biological diversity is a compelling public interest, it seems only logical that public lands should play the central role in its protection, restoration, and continuation. Existing public lands will need to be augmented, though. The lands are distributed unevenly throughout the northeastern states and among natural communities.

The size of such cores will vary depending on the relevant natural community, target species, and disturbance regime. Some natural communities, such as cobble shores and talus woodlands, covered very small amounts of land at the time of European contact. Such communities typically are found in rare, localized settings, such as along rivers or at the base of cliffs. These natural communities can often be protected—and many already have been protected—through small public or private reserves. Although small in size, sometimes-rare natural communities are crucial parts of the landscape, often home to significant biological diversity located only in these particular landscapes. At the other end of the continuum are the very large reserves, hundreds of thousands of acres (see chapter 6). Such reserves are of primary importance for the restoration of large native mammals missing from all or parts of the Northeast, such as bison, elk, moose, and the top-level predators—mountain lions, timber wolves, wolverines. Such large reserves are also necessary for the establishment of large stretches of old-growth forest, which covered an estimated three-quarters of the pre-Columbian landscape. In such large reserves, plants and animals can interact and evolve relatively insulated from the major human activities that have wrought havoc on their natural communities. The large size of such core reserves also ensures that these landscapes can withstand the natural disturbances that have traditionally affected the varying locales of the Northeast, including disease, fire, hurricanes, insects, and windthrow.[13]

For the buffers that surround the cores, the key is to make sure that the activities that take place within them are compatible with the mission of the cores—protecting and restoring biological diversity. Among the activities that could take place in these buffer areas are sustainable agriculture and forestry (discussed below); low intensity, nonmotorized recreation (such as cross-country skiing, fishing, hiking, and hunting); and either tightly clustered human settlements (such as traditional New England villages) or very low-density houses. One central component of all of these uses is the need to limit habitat fragmentation. This means limiting road density, clearcuts, and subdivisions. Such buffer zones can be created most easily on public lands adjacent to, yet not suitable for, core wilderness reserves. Due to the lack of public lands in the Northeast, however, other lands will be necessary. A most promising avenue here is to work with land trusts that primarily have been protecting managed farmland and forestland in the region for decades. The land trusts purchase, or receive a donation of, conservation easements to land that stays in private ownership, and the conservation easements can be designed in a manner to achieve buffer land-management goals (see chapter 8).

Once such reserve systems have been designed, they can be used to guide management of existing conservation lands and the purchase of future conservation lands, with priority going to core and connectivity lands. For areas already conserved that studies determine are crucial for cores or connectivity, management should be geared to eliminating roads, cutting trees only if necessary as part of a restoration plan, and managing exotic species as needed. Federal and state governments are constantly buying conservation lands, as are some nonprofit groups such as the Nature Conservancy. Adopted reserve designs should serve as a guide to prioritizing land purchases for such groups. Furthermore, the vibrant land trusts of the Northeast should also follow such reserve designs to guide their acquisitions of easements—in some cases for cores and corridors, but in most cases for buffer areas. Such an approach has already been adopted in a number of places, most successfully to help guide land purchases for Florida Preservation 2000, a program begun in 1990 that has spent $3 billion to purchase well over one million acres of land for conservation and recreation purposes. In 1999, the state continued the program for another decade as Florida Forever, funded by an additional $3 billion.[14]

In sum, wilderness designation in the Northeast should be driven by the need to protect and restore biological diversity. Although this represents something of a change in the rationale for wilderness, it does not represent a change in what uses will and will not be allowed. The wilderness land should be "affected primarily by the forces of nature," with no roads, timber cutting, or human habitation. Wilderness cores and most connective corridors will be owned by federal and state governments. Buffer lands will include public lands, private lands protected by conservation easements, and other private lands managed in ecologically sensitive ways (such as green-certified forests or predator-friendly agricultural lands). How much land will such a reserve system entail? This will vary from place to place, and depend on how land is managed. Perhaps one-quarter of the landscape, perhaps one-half. We must remember, though, that assembling such reserves will take many generations. The reserve systems will provide an evolving conservation blueprint for hundreds of years to come. As a society we will make a big mistake if we get stuck today fighting about how many acres will be protected in 200 years. What is obvious is that we need to protect more land, and that we should get to work.

Wilderness Specific to a Time and a Place: Rewilding and Restoration in the Northeast

The ghost map of this place is reasserting itself: the bear and the turkey and the moose reclaiming their place, the trees growing up around the million stone walls.

— Bill McKibben

As the idea of wilderness continues to evolve, to become more focused on enhancing, protecting, and restoring biological diversity, our applied definition of wilderness needs to become more sophisticated, complex, and contingent. More specifically, we need to develop more nuanced spatial and temporal understandings of wilderness. By spatial, I mean that wilderness in the East and Midwest—often wilderness in recovery—is something different than wilderness in the West, where large parts of the landscape have been minimally affected by humans (except by fire in certain regions). By temporal, I mean that we need to understand more about what these landscapes looked like in the past in order to inform our thinking about wilderness today and into the future. Land heavily logged in the Northeast one hundred years ago may very well be worthy of wilderness, thanks to the abundant precipitation and the resilience of the ecosystems here. Similar land in the forests of much of the West, given its slower recovery and the relative abundance of less disturbed lands, is likely disqualified as wilderness there.

Since virtually the entire northeastern landscape has been significantly manipulated over the last few hundred years, wilderness of any kind in the Northeast is restored or rewilded wilderness. As soon as we begin to speak of restoration or rewilding, we need to specify what it is that we are holding up as our model. What does it mean for the land to be restored? What has to return for land to be wild again? It is important at the outset to understand that we cannot restore the landscape to some pre-Columbian mythic climax forest in the Northeast. Such static climax forests really didn't exist; rather the landscape consisted of constantly shifting mosaics affected by natural disturbances and, in some places, anthropogenic disturbances. Furthermore, the activities of the colonists and their successors wrought massive changes to the landscape. Although we cannot return to a pre-Columbian landscape, taking stock of what that landscape was like provides us with a necessary benchmark for restoring wilderness (see chapter 2). Ecological history, using a variety of tools— written materials, maps, photographs, land surveys, statistical series, studies of old-growth forests, archeological evidence, pollen analysis, and lake sediment studies—is crucial to this task. Although we cannot produce a fine-grained portrait of the past, we can create a rough sketch of it.[15]

Most significantly, although forests have returned to cover over two-thirds of the Northeast in the 1990s, and the tree species and the general boundaries of the major forest types are basically the same, the structure and composition of these recovering forests are significantly different from the pre-Columbian forests. The most pronounced change in the Northeast is the decline of beech, from more than 40 percent at sites in New York, Pennsylvania, and Vermont in 1800 to 5 to 13 percent in the 1960s. Ecological historian Emily Russell summarizes these forest differences:

These young or recovering stands are growing on soils that have a history of disturbance, lack of old mound and pit topography, increased air pollution, high levels of carbon dioxide and available nitrogen, non-native diseases and pests, high levels of herbivory, absence of such formerly abundant species as passenger pigeons and large chestnut trees, and other changed conditions known and unknown. That they are as similar as they are to precolonial forests suggests the critical, basic role of species availability, climate, topography, and some essential soil characteristics, all of which are amenable to conventional forest modeling. Most important tree species in this region are, however, already under the onslaught of disease or pests: gypsy moth, chestnut blight, beech bark disease, Dutch elm disease, and most recently hemlock wooly adelgid, among others.

Significant portions of the other major terrestrial ecosystem type of the Northeast, wetlands, have been destroyed, and continue to be altered. Scientists estimate that the area has lost over one-third of the wetlands present circa 1500, almost entirely due to human action. Over half of the wetlands of Connecticut, New York, and Pennsylvania are gone.[16]

As European settlement spread across the Northeast, and beyond, the settlers affected wildlife in four basic ways: (1) The larger quadrupeds (e.g., deer, bear) disappeared due to habitat loss and overhunting; (2) the changes to the landscape favored open area and edge species (e.g., raccoon), and forest interior species (e.g., pine marten) declined dramatically; (3) the populations of many species of freshwater fish declined substantially due to water pollution, dams, overfishing, and the introduction of exotic species; and (4) the Europeans introduced exotic species, both knowingly and unknowingly, which established themselves throughout the region. More specifically, gone forever from the Northeast are four species of birds (Carolina parakeet, great auk, Labrador duck, and passenger pigeon), the silver trout, and potentially seven species of insects and three species of plants. A number of widely distributed vertebrate species are extirpated from the Northeast (Eskimo curlew, greater prairie chicken, mountain lion, timber wolf, wolverine, and woodland caribou). There are even more extirpations specific to states in the region (bison from New York and Pennsylvania; Henslow's sparrow from Connecticut and Rhode Island; lynx from Massachusetts, New York, Pennsylvania, and probably New Hampshire and Vermont; timber rattlesnake from Maine and Rhode Island; and a trout-perch from Massachusetts and New Jersey). A far larger number of invertebrates and plants are extirpated from the Northeast and the nine states individually. Northeastern states have lost 1 to 5 percent of their plant species (ranging from 131 plants believed to be extirpated from Pennsylvania to more than 50 in Massachusetts), most frequently those at the edge of their range or those confined to restricted habitats. It is likely that a number of species, especially invertebrates and plants, have disappeared that we don't know about.[17]

With this sketch of the pre-Columbian natural landscape of the Northeast and the changes European settlement induced, some things become strikingly clear. Some species are lost forever. We will never know the sky-darkening flocks of passenger pigeons. Nor will these birds play their major ecological roles of transporting seeds and providing massive fertilization of the forest at their roosting sites. Gone, too, are the tremendous runs of native salmon and shad throughout the region, along with their significant ecological effects. The top tier of the region's predators, though not extinct, is still absent.[18]

Nevertheless, substantial restoration—both active and passive—has already taken place in the Northeast over the last one hundred years. Thoreau wrote in 1856 that "when I consider that the nobler animals have been exterminated here,—the cougar, panther, lynx, wolverene [*sic*], wolf, bear, moose, deer, the beaver, the turkey, etc., etc.,—I cannot but feel as if I lived in a tamed, and, as it were, emasculated country." Since that time, deer, turkey, and beaver have returned, flourishing through much of their former range; moose are expanding their range throughout northern New England and the Adirondacks; and bear populations are stable throughout the region. It is only the large predators—the cougar or panther, the wolverine, the wolf, and, in all but small pockets of Maine, the lynx—that are still missing from Thoreau's list. Much of this restoration has been passive rather than active. As McKibben writes, "So far we can claim neither humility nor wisdom; our good fortune is mostly accidental." Changes in our economy and society are largely responsible for the return of the forests of the Northeast and the creatures that live there (see chapter 11).[19]

Another fundamental change to the northeastern landscape is that other species have migrated into new regions since European arrival, often with the indirect help of humans. In New England, for instance, coyotes were not native in 1600. They have since migrated from the west to establish themselves as part of the native fauna, with the indirect help of human extermination of the timber wolf. This raises questions for restoration. As we seek to restore native ecosystems in New England, where does the coyote fit in? Should we attempt to exterminate it since it was not part of the native fauna in 1600? Should we treat it as a new native to be protected like all other native species? Should we simply let natural processes take their course after the return of the wolf to the Northeast? Similarly, turkey vultures are a recent arrival to the area, being practically unknown in Vermont prior to the late 1930s. Their spread into Vermont is most likely caused by an increase in the number of animals killed on roads and an increase in white-tailed deer mortality from overpopulation. What conservation policy should we adopt toward these birds?[20]

We now need to think more consciously about the recovery of this landscape and how we can aid in it. Our goal should not be to eliminate any traces of human use or effect to the restored and rewilded wilderness of the Northeast—this is impossible. Instead, our goal should be to re-store the primacy of natural forces to a particular landscape and to favor the flourishing of native plants and animals. Mostly, in those places we designate as wilderness, we need to let the land rewild, to let natural processes dominate the land: natural disturbances, species interaction, the development of old-growth forests. However, at least two issues require at least the discussion of more-active human involvement. First, for cer-tain small, rare ecosystems, human management may be necessary, in the form of prescribed burns or removal of exotic species, in order to protect particular native species and natural communities. Second, and an issue of much larger consequence, what do we do about the absence of locally and regionally extirpated animals?

It seems clear that the Northeast will not be healthy or whole without the return of its top-level predators: the mountain lion, the timber wolf, and the wolverine. The deer and beaver are back, but without their pred-ators they are wreaking ecological havoc in many places. One fundamental question is how these predators might return. Although sightings of mountain lions are common in the Adirondacks and northern New En-gland, it is unlikely that a viable breeding population remains in the Northeast or eastern Canada. The nearest significant populations are in the Black Hills of South Dakota and the Florida Everglades. Hence, it's not likely that mountain lions will return to the Northeast on their own. The same is true for wolverines; the closest populations are in far-northern Quebec and Labrador. Wolves, on the other hand, are abundant in On-tario and Quebec and may have the capability to disperse naturally to northern New England and the Adirondacks. Reintroduction—trapping animals and releasing them elsewhere—is an extremely active form of hu-man management (see chapter 7). Such reintroductions, at the least, lead to trauma for the individual animals. Many of the reintroductions fail (roughly one-third), and the animals die. Reintroductions in the North-east have been quite successful for beaver, deer, fisher, peregrine falcon, and wild turkey. They have been unsuccessful for caribou in Maine, elk in New Hampshire, and lynx in New York. In the western United States, wolf reintroduction has been spectacularly successful in Greater Yellowstone and central Idaho. Other ongoing reintroduction projects, such as the wolf in Arizona and New Mexico and the lynx in Colorado, have been much more problematic. The reasons for the failure of reintroductions are complex; some reasons are primarily social (e.g., humans killing released wolves because they don't want them back), some primarily biological (e.g., inadequate habitat or prey base). What is clear is that the intentional reintroduction of any extirpated species is not to be done without significant study and preparation. Even though such efforts may take time, plenty remains to be done to further rewilding in the interim — namely protecting land.

Rewilding and restoration in the northeastern landscape, then, should proceed through a series of steps. We should work to make sure that the rewilding that has occurred by good fortune is allowed to continue. This means protecting more land. On this land, we should favor natural processes as much as possible, even though we know that this will not return the landscape to its pristine pre-Columbian composition and structure. A rewilded landscape might look significantly different from the landscape of 1500; but it will be a wild landscape, home to wild creatures, a place for evolution to continue its unending journey relatively free from human constraints. We should strategically protect land for cores and connectivity (as discussed above) as the keys for rewilding. And, finally, when biological and social conditions are fitting, we should reintroduce those species missing from the Northeast. The mountain lion, the wolf, the wolverine — when these natives return to the Northeast, wilderness finally will have come home. It might be decades before they are thriving here again. But we mustn't rush. Like building a wilderness ecological reserve system, this process will take generations, as it took us generations to fundamentally alter this landscape. Too often we expect results immediately; our vision is five, ten, or perhaps twenty years. Our vision must be lengthened. We must learn patience and the ability to view events from the perspective of centuries. Over time, even though we may still cross stone walls and see the scars on trees along old skid trails in the rewilded and restored wilderness of the Northeast, these lands will meet the standards of the legal definition of wilderness in a very meaningful sense; they will be places "affected primarily by the forces of nature."

Making the Connection that has to be Made: Wilderness and
Sustainable Farming and Forestry

You really cannot specialize the work of conservation. You cannot save the land apart from
the people or the people apart from the land. To save either, you must save both . . . To
save both the land and the people, you need a strong rural economy.

—Wendell Berry

Although my focus in this chapter—and that of this volume generally—
is on fostering wilderness in the Northeast, the use of lands for farming
and forestry is a crucial part of this discussion for three reasons. First, we
rely on the land to supply us with essential needs such as food, fiber for
clothing, and forest products for building, fuel, and paper. Although we
can certainly reduce our consumption of some of these products (such as
paper and wood for pallets), there is no escaping our need for these basics.
Second, sustainably managed lands will play an important role as buffers
in the ecological reserve architecture described above. Wilderness advocates have a responsibility to support the development of viable sustainable agricultural and forestry practices if we seek their use over wide
ranges of the landscape. And third, wilderness will not survive as islands
in an ocean of exploitative land management practices; nor will it flourish
unless the dominant paradigm of unending consumption and economic
growth is changed. A central part of changing the dominant paradigm
involves creating an alternative model based on healthy, sustainable human and natural communities (see chapter 9).[21]

With a global population approaching 6 billion people and a United
States population of 270 million people, all of whom consume food, fuel,
and fiber (indeed, vastly disproportionate shares of these goods), it is
irresponsible for wilderness advocates to focus only on protecting wilderness without thinking about where we will get the resources we are using.
It does us no good to protect wilderness in the Northeast if it means
exporting ecologically damaging activities to Oregon or Indonesia. We
must seek to consume less and reduce human population, and as we make
this transition we must also make the production of food, fiber, and forest
products more sustainable. Furthermore, the involvement of conservationists in such work connects us to people economically tied to the land;
it can help us to form necessary alliances rather than creating opponents
who block and slow the needed shift to sustainability.

Buffers will play a crucial role in ecological reserves. Conservationists must play an active role in determining what takes place in those areas. What does sustainable agriculture adjacent to wild lands look like? How large can fields and pastures be? What practices should be used to protect livestock from predators? How will we try to minimize the spread of exotics into adjoining wild lands? How close to streams and lakes can trees be cut? How many snags per acre should be left standing after a timber cut? What road density is acceptable in buffers? What human population density is acceptable? The answer to each of these questions will significantly affect the integrity of wild lands and the success of ecological reserves in enhancing and protecting biological diversity.

Two individuals who most clearly make the case that wilderness is not viable unless we change how we think about the entire landscape are Wendell Berry and Wes Jackson. As we move in new directions, Berry writes,

> We also need to make sure that we don't carry over into our efforts at conservation and preservation the moral assumptions and habits of thought of the culture of exploitation . . . The most persistent and the most dangerous of these is the assumption that some parts of the world can be preserved while others are abused or destroyed. As necessary as it obviously is, the effort of "wilderness preservation" has too often implied that it is enough to save a series of islands of pristine and uninhabited wilderness in an otherwise exploited, damaged, and polluted land. And, further, that the pristine wilderness is the only alternative to exploitation and abuse. So far, the moral landscape of the conservation movement has tended to be a landscape of extremes . . . the conservationists' program is embarrassingly incomplete. Its picture of the world as either deserted or desertified landscapes is too simple; it misrepresents both the world and humanity. If we are to have an accurate picture of the world, even in its present diseased condition, we must interpose between the unused landscape and the misused landscape a landscape that humans have used well.

Such a well-managed landscape will feature "the small owner or operator, farmer or forester or both, who lives with a securely placed family and community, who knows how to use the land in the best way, and who can afford to do so." In other words, sustainably managed land will be cared for by small landowners firmly connected to place in a society where sustainable management makes it possible to earn a living from the land. In his recent collection of essays, *Becoming Native to this Place*, Jackson makes the same point: "to treat wilderness as a holy shrine and Kansas or East Saint Louis as terrain of an altogether different sort is a form of schizophrenia. Either all the earth is holy or none is. Either every square foot of it deserves our respect or none does . . . It is possible to love a small acreage in Kansas as much as John Muir loved the entire Sierra Nevada. This is fortunate, for the wilderness of the Sierra will disappear unless little pieces of nonwilderness become intensely loved by lots of people."[22]

Just as wilderness has spatial and temporal characteristics, so does sustainable management of agricultural lands and forestlands. Sustainable farming practices in New York will be different from those in Kansas or California to accommodate different soil types, climate, and marketing opportunities; sustainable forestry in Pennsylvania will differ from that in Washington or North Carolina to accommodate different tree species, climate, and topography. We in the Northeast need to develop models that work best for this region. Many groups are already doing this, including the Northeast Organic Farming Association and a variety of forestry groups.[23]

One alternative for agricultural lands and forestlands that won't work is the effort in the Northeast—and elsewhere—to preserve the status quo, the so-called "working landscape." We can't do this; we can't save the status quo. Consumer changes (such as the substitution of coal and then oil for wood as the main source of heat), ecological changes (for example, the loss of mature chestnut due to chestnut blight), economic changes (such as the decline in the price of milk due to increased supply), and technological changes (such as the introduction of whole tree harvesters)—all of these changes are unpredictable. Furthermore, the pace of such change has accelerated with the globalization of the economy. Placing easements on lands to protect them from development does not guarantee that the lands will remain in agriculture or forestry; this depends on a vast array of interactions that today occur at the global level. Indeed, only one hundred years ago, many people in northern New England were similarly focused on this idea of a working landscape. As historian Richard Judd writes, "This immutable preindustrial vision—a working landscape frozen in time—offered a solid anchor for those adrift in the confusing world of urban-industrial development." But efforts to freeze such a landscape in time did not work then, and we need not repeat the same mistake. Moreover, the status quo has not served the natural or human communities of the region well. A working landscape implies that a wild landscape is not working. Nothing could be further from the truth. Wild landscapes—forests in the Northeast—clean our air, supply clean water, help control floods, provide recreation, and serve as home to fish and wildlife. In addition, using one phrase to describe all managed farmland and forestland greatly blurs the significant distinctions among the variety of management practices used on those lands. A working landscape of selective logging and small, organic farms is far different from a working landscape of clear-cutting and aerial herbicides, of factory poultry farms and dairy herds pumped full of antibiotics and bovine growth hormones. Human communities, too, have often been poorly served by this generic working landscape. In many parts of the Northeast, dairy production is up while the number of farms and number of farmers is down. Similarly, paper industry employment in northern New England has declined by thirty thousand jobs in the last three decades. In Maine, millions of acres of land have been changing hands annually in the 1990s, leaving workers and communities to continually worry about their future.[24]

The effort to save the working landscape alone is just as much a dead-end as efforts to protect wilderness alone. Just as wilderness as a series of unconnected islands in "an otherwise exploited, damaged, and polluted land" will not survive over the long run unless we change how we live on the rest of the land, the working landscape won't survive unless we change an economic system that makes it increasingly difficult for small-scale farmers and forestland owners to earn a living by managing the land sustainably. Without such economic changes, easements on the working landscape run the risk of becoming a way to protect the views of people who don't earn their living on the land. For example, farming in Vermont is overwhelmingly concentrated in dairy. This concentration makes Vermont farmers vulnerable to consumer changes in demand for dairy products, to midwestern dairy farm productivity, and to the political machinations in Washington, D.C., where the Northeast Interstate Dairy Compact—passed in 1996 to help northeastern dairy farmers—nearly expired in the fall of 1999 at the hands of politicians from other regions.

Important and exciting projects are underway in the Northeast involving the development of truly sustainable, economically viable agriculture and forestry. The most exciting example is David Brynn's work with Vermont Family Forests (VFF), the topic of chapter 10. Briefly, this forest-landowner network centered in Addison County combines green certification of forestland with improved economic opportunities for landowners, loggers, and others involved in the value-adding process. Green certification both documents sustainable management on the ground and, by differentiating VFF products, gives landowners a price premium in the marketplace. VFF seeks to connect local landowners with local wood-product users, keeping more money in local communities. Rather than taking the existing economy as a given, VFF seeks to alter aspects of the forest-products economy to make improved environmental management of forestlands economically feasible.[25]

As we move in the Northeast to restore and rewild more and more of our landscape, we must work closely with those people and organizations who are developing and advocating sustainable agriculture and forestry in the region. Such managed lands can supply us with needed resources rather than allowing us to irresponsibly import our resources and export our problems. In many places, these sustainably managed lands will form the matrix in which wilderness is embedded. Working closely together, wilderness and sustainability advocates can help create a natural and political landscape that is conducive to old-growth forests and timber harvesting, to cows and wolves, and to humans in nature rather than alienated from it. Working together, we can build a better world for our communities, both human and natural.

Conclusion

One of our major tasks as educators is to expand the imagination about our possibilities.
— Wes Jackson

It may seem radical to propose creating a system of connected wilderness reserves in the Northeast and embedding such a system in a landscape of sustainably managed farmland and forestland at the beginning of the twenty-first century. Yet, paradoxically, in many ways the proposal is conservative. It is about conserving nature, about conserving ways of living on the land, and about conserving a meaningful, balanced way of life for humans in a natural setting. It is in the recovered and rewilded landscapes of the hinterlands of the Northeast that a model for healthier human and natural communities applicable to wide areas of the globe can arise. The Northeast is a place where humans have significantly modified nature and that has a relatively large human population. Nevertheless, thanks to a resilient natural world, the contingencies of history, and some wise policy decisions, significant rewilding and recovery has occurred. We need to act to protect these positive changes, and to make sure they can continue to unfold. Such changes may not be as difficult to achieve as one might think.

Indeed, a number of positive conservation trends in and around the Northeast support the expansion of wilderness in the region.

- In March 1999, Ontario proposed the creation of 378 new parks and protected areas, covering nearly 6 million acres (increasing the amount of land closed to logging and mining to roughly 23 million acres, 9 percent of the province). In the Maritimes, Nova Scotia recently designated thirty-one areas covering over 700,000 acres as wilderness, and New Brunswick has proposed wilderness protection for twelve sites covering nearly 750,000 acres.

- Serious discussions of wolf recovery and reintroduction in northern New England and the Adirondacks are underway, with the U.S. Fish and Wildlife Service soon to begin work on a recovery plan for the region.

- The people of the Northeast are ready to move ahead. In a 1995 Forest Service survey, 94 percent of Vermont respondents supported the protection of remaining undisturbed, unroaded land in the Green Mountain National Forest; 86 percent wanted to see clearcutting banned on the forest; 64 percent supported the establishment of more wilderness (with an additional 25 percent undecided). A survey in New Hampshire discovered similar attitudes.

- President Bill Clinton proposed the protection of remaining roadless areas on national forests in October 1999. With the Forest Service still taking comments on the Draft EIS in the summer of 2000, how this will affect northeastern national forests is still unclear. Also, in October 1999, a coalition of the Appalachian Mountain Club, Conservation Law Foundation, and Wilderness Society released a report calling for the protection of a total of 500,000 acres of roadless lands in the White Mountain National Forest (including already designated wilderness).

- Both the federal government and state governments in the Northeast proposed significant funds for land conservation in 1998 and 1999. The Clinton administration's $1 billion Lands Legacy Initiative proposed spending $442 million for federal land acquisitions in fiscal year 2000. The Northern Forest region is one of five priority areas listed in the proposal. The Forest Legacy Program, which provides funds for the purchase of easements on forestlands primarily in the Northeast, would receive $50 million. In Maine, voters passed a referendum in November 1999 establishing a $75 million fund for land acquisition. In June 1999, New Jersey Governor Christine Todd Whitman signed legislation to fund a ten-year, $1 billion program to protect one million acres of land in the state, approximately 60 percent for parks and forestland, 40 percent for farmland.

- Conservationists recently have completed a number of significant land conservation purchases. Nearly 300,000 acres of Champion International lands in New Hampshire, New York, and Vermont were acquired in December 1998. Of this land, New York State acquired approximately 30,000 acres in the Adirondacks that will be protected as forever wild. In Vermont, the U.S. Fish and Wildlife Service acquired 26,000 acres and state agencies 22,000 acres. The remainder of the lands in these two states has been sold, with conservation easements for forest management in New York and forever logging easements in Vermont. In Maine, conservationists purchased 185,000 acres in late 1998, and the Pingree family agreed in March 1999 to sell conservation easements on over 750,000 acres of its forestlands to the New England Forestry Foundation.
- Green-certified forestland, which, although rife with problems, is generally a move in the direction of sustainable forestry, is expanding across the region—including over a million acres of private land in Pennsylvania.
- Demolition of the Edwards Dam on the Kennebec River in Maine took place in the summer and fall of 1999. This was the first time the federal government has ordered a dam breached against an owner's wishes. The dam removal will allow the return of salmon, sturgeon, shad, and other anadromous fish to the upstream reaches of the river.[26]

Two crucial things, however, are missing from these stories: the protection of more wilderness and the evidence of an overarching conservation framework for the Northeast. Less than 2 percent of the region is protected as wilderness. We simply must have more wilderness in the Northeast. This fundamental need means that we must take better advantage of opportunities such as the Champion lands purchase to establish wilderness. Less than one-tenth of that land—all in the Adirondacks— will be protected as wild lands. Without more wilderness, we will miss our opportunity for fully recovered natural communities. Without such flourishing natural communities, we will miss our opportunity for healthy, vibrant, and sustainable human communities. The choice is not between wilderness and sustainable farmland and forestland; we must have both. We need to weave these conservation strands of the Northeast together. Rather than have our future landscapes determined by accident, chance, and uncoordinated conservation policies, we need to think holistically and for the long term. This is the challenge to the people of the Northeast. Can we follow through on our chances for more wilderness and can we weave that wilderness into a beautiful new tapestry of nature and culture? The authors in this book think we can, and the chapters that follow can help us begin to see the design we need to follow.

CHAPTER 2

"Remote, Rocky, Barren, Bushy Wild-woody Wilderness"

The Natural History of the Northeast

ALICIA DANIEL AND THOR HANSON

EUROPEAN COLONISTS FIRST encountering the forest of the northeastern seaboard suffered biological culture shock. By 1594, the shortage of wood in western Europe had grown so severe that French bakers were firing their stoves with brush.[1] A walk through typical countryside would have revealed a landscape dominated by pasture with a few hedgerows of trees and small coppiced woodlots, which were managed by cutting main stems of trees and growing "crops" of branches. Compared with trees of western Europe, the size, straightness, abundance, and diversity of the forest trees in North America stretched the imagination and caused an outpouring of reports that in turn stretched the credulity of people "back home."

Primeval forests were, for most western Europeans, the stuff of legend, gone from their landscapes for nearly three hundred years. When naturalist Wilson Flagg described the forests of Maine, he had never seen anything like them. "One of the conditions most remarkable in a primitive forest," he writes, "is the universal dampness of the ground. The second growth of timber, especially if the surface were entirely cleared, stands upon a drier foundation. This greater dryness is caused by the absence of those vast accumulations of vegetable *debris* that rested on the ground before it was disturbed. A greater evaporation also takes place under the second growth, because the trees are of inferior size and stand more widely apart. Another character of a primitive forest is the crowded assemblage of trees and their undergrowth, causing great difficulty traversing it."[2]

The abundance of animal life also defied European experience. According to Edward Forbush, there were probably more wildfowl in North

America at the time of European arrival than there had ever been anywhere in the world.³ William Wood writes "If I should tell you how some
have killed a hundred geese in a week, fifty ducks at a shot, forty teals at
another, it may be counted impossible though nothing is more certain."⁴
John Josselyn reports of walking knee deep through stranded herring
across a quarter mile of beach.⁵ Others tried to temper such reports: "I
will not tell you," Captain Christopher Leveritt wrote, "that you can smell
the corn fields before you see the land, neither must men think that corn
doth grow naturally, (or on trees,) nor will the deer come when they are
called, or stand still and look on a man until he shoot him, not knowing
a man from a beast: nor the fish leap into the kettle, nor on the dry land
. . . which is no truer than that the fowl present themselves to you with
spits through them."⁶

Even if the forests of Europe had been more intact, the richness of the
northeastern flora and fauna would have stood out. The woods of Pennsylvania and southern New England were open and park-like, full of oaks,
chestnuts, and hickories, while the woods of northern Maine were spruce-
fir forests covered with lichens and mosses. How did they come to be so
diverse and beautiful? The richness and diversity of the flora and fauna is
based on a complex history of interactions among climate, geology, soils,
and disturbances, such as wind and fires.

Initial European contact with North America was largely limited to
coastal areas and inland waterways where a maritime climate extended the
growing season relative to the interior forests. Additionally, the colonist
and visitor accounts are dominated by reports from the spring and summer seasons when most people, and mail, crossed the Atlantic. So at first
blush, the climate did not seem so different from Europe. However, as
settlers were soon to discover, the climate of most of the Northeast is
continental, not maritime, with more arctic winter weather patterns.
While cattle could be pastured successfully in the British Isles year around,
the short 100- to 150-day average growing season in the Northeast quickly
put animal husbandry to the test. "Although snow falls occasionally in
winter [in England] it usually remains no longer than three days," wrote
Swedish naturalist Peter Kalm.⁷ The climate in the northeastern United
States could swing from the high summer temperatures of southern Italy
to the lows of Sweden in the short span of three months.⁸ This climate
creates a confluence of plant species that overlap at the northern and
southern limits of their ranges. Hickories and oaks thrive in southern New
England and survive on the warm rocky ridges of the northern states,
while boreal spruce and fir forests swing down into the northern half of

New York, Vermont, and New Hampshire. The harsh winter climate also pushes treeline lower on eastern mountains than on western mountains such as the Rockies, so an alpine flora persists at 4,000 feet in these states as well.

Bedrock in the Northeast contributes to the diversity of species in several ways. Much of the bedrock of western New England formed in a shallow, tropical ocean along a continental margin that rested near the equator five hundred million years ago. This variety of depositional environment gave rise to a rich palette of sediments from calcium-rich muds and sandy beach and delta deposits to off-shore muds, all of which were changed to stone and thrust up to form the Green Mountains, Taconics, Berkshires, and Appalachians as North American, African, and European continental plates (and various island arcs) collided. Adding to the mix, the White Mountains of New Hampshire are granite that upwelled during the collision phase and the Adirondacks are basement rock from the ancient, Precambrian Canadian shield. The bedrock exposed at the surface of the Northeast contains dozens of rock types, whose time of formation spans over a billion years.[9]

Not only do these rock types give rise to different soils, but their topography, with its north/south orientation, conveyed a distinct advantage to native flora and fauna during the last Ice Age. While the plants and animals of North America could shift their ranges to more hospitable southern refuges in front of the advancing ice, European species ran into an insurmountable east/west barrier: the Swiss Alps and the Carpathian Mountains. It is estimated from the pollen record analysis that several European tree species went extinct in their former range during the Ice Age.

From about two million up until about 12,500 years ago, glaciers advanced over the Northeast several times, scraping away at the bedrock and leaving behind a veneer of mineral soil containing particles of all sizes. Where calcium and magnesium carbonates remain in these soils, the soils are rich and fertile. Glaciers also dammed previous river drainages and gouged U-shaped valleys, creating new lakes. Some of these persist today, including the Finger Lakes of northern New York; others have drained, leaving behind fertile valleys. The cooler post-glacial climate enhanced the diversity of soils by slowing decomposition rates in these new basins, creating extensive wetland complexes, including bogs and fens, which are habitat for some of the region's rarer plants and animals.

Since the last Ice Age, a gradual warming period peaking about five thousand years ago allowed oaks and hickories to expand their ranges and dominate the Northeast. During that period, Woodland Indians hunted bison in these drier forests. Their descendants harbored an intimate knowledge of wild animal husbandry. "Wherever villagers expected to find the greatest natural food supplies, there they went," writes historian William Cronon. "When fish were spawning, many Indian families might gather at a single waterfall to create a dense temporary settlement in which feasting and celebration were the order of the day; when it was time to hunt in the fall, the same families might be found scattered over many square miles of land."[10] While it is beyond the scope of this chapter to address the complexity and diversity of indigenous cultures in the Northeast at the time of European settlement (New Hampshire alone had seventeen tribes from the Amariscoggins in the north to the Squakheags along the coast), it is useful to note ways in which Native Americans acted to maintain and enhance wildlife diversity.[11] The Native Americans had a remarkable knowledge of breeding habits and food requirements of wild game. The indigenous Americans actively managed the forests for game by selectively managing for trees with good mast crops of nuts and berries. The fall burning of oak and chestnut forests not only kept "vermin" like fleas at an endurable level, it also ensured abundant forage for turkey, passenger pigeons, bear, and deer. The use of fire as a management tool varied from region to region. Burning was practiced most commonly in southern New England and New Jersey and less commonly in northern New England and interior New York and Pennsylvania.[12]

Finally, the convergence of sea and land in rich estuaries gave rise to the legendary fish populations that first drew Europeans to this continent. It is no accident that fish, the most abundant and sought-after resource, are (after large carnivores) the most threatened of the wild riches of the new world.

Clearing the Land: 1600–1880

In fewer than twelve generations of European settlement, the vast northeastern forests once termed "infinite" and "seemingly boundless" by early colonists survived only in dwindling patches and inaccessible mountainous terrain.[13] Where travelers once remarked on "the twilight that prevailed in these woods even at high noon," they now encountered an open landscape of endless hillside pastures, coppiced woodlots, and small valley farms.[14] By the mid-nineteenth century, up to 80 percent of southern New England was devoted to agriculture, and chronic firewood shortages forced cities such as Boston to import nearly all their wood from northern Maine.[15] Pioneering conservationist George Perkins Marsh decried the loss of forest in 1848, describing the rocky, denuded hills of his native Vermont as "barren and unsightly blots, producing neither grain nor grass, and yielding no crop but a harvest of noxious weeds."[16] In the 1850s, Henry David Thoreau counted three generations of stumps in the forests of Concord, Massachusetts, and lamented the landscape as "a maimed and imperfect nature."[17] Such warnings, however, came too late and went largely unheard in a pioneer atmosphere founded on the notion of limitless resources, with a vast, unexploited continent stretching away westward. Ultimately, less than sixth-tenths of one percent of the Northeast's original forest would remain untouched.[18]

To describe changes in the region's flora during this period is to trace patterns of settlement and land use as the colonists moved inward from the coast. Agriculture, logging, and the growth of a market economy led to rapid alterations of every vegetation community, from salt marshes to boreal forest. Since virtually no large tracts of original vegetation remain, those reconstructing pre-settlement conditions must rely on a combination of early travelers' accounts, land survey data, and inference from modern analogues. Of these, the land survey information may be the most valuable. County and township boundaries were systematically marked with blazes on the trunks of nearby trees. Surveyors recorded species information and other descriptive notes so that these "witness" trees could be located again. Where early travelers often wrote promotional tracts, exaggerating the best features of the landscape to encourage settlement, witness tree data provides a relatively unbiased sample of the primary forest.[19]

Reliable observers described a dense woods of large, old trees festooned with epiphytes, where fallen trunks and other detritus crowded the mossy, humid understory.[20] Open, park-like forests along the coast and in southern regions reflected the long history of regular burning by Native Americans. Where European incursion interrupted this practice, thick undergrowth soon reclaimed the woods. Abundant fallen debris and the pit-and-mound topography still evident in remnant stands point to wind as the major natural disturbance in the original forest. Regular storms and the occasional, devastating hurricane or tornado maintained a range of disruptions, from individual tree-fall gaps to large blowdowns. Insect pests and disease also played a role, as did natural fire on dry ridgetops and sand plains, helping keep the forest in a dynamic state of constant renewal.

The sheer diversity of plant life that so stunned early European arrivals precludes a simple description of northeastern landscapes. Forest dominated throughout, but local variations in geology, soils, climate, topography, and disturbance resulted in a patchwork of wooded communities spread and intermingled across the landscape. Several broad categories, however, outline the major vegetation zones and provide a framework for discussing change. Boreal balsam fir and red spruce forest dominated far northern New England, as well as high altitude areas further south. American beech, yellow birch, and sugar maple, often associated with hemlock, characterized a broad zone of diverse northern hardwoods, while the southern half of the region gave home to a forest of chestnuts and oaks, interspersed with hickory. White pine was abundant on sandy soils in the lower elevations. Red and pitch pines occurred on well-drained, sandy sites or on those subject to frequent fire cycles throughout the region, but rarely dominated large tracts in the pre-settlement forest.

Colonists often chose their farm sites based on the presence of trees known or suspected to indicate good soils. "Selectmen," community leaders who scouted and assigned settlement locations, looked for basswood, hickory, and other species associated with fertility and calcium richness.[21] These rich forest communities, as well as any natural fields or openings, may be the least well known today, since they disappeared first and were rarely left to regenerate. Like the Native Americans before them, colonists concentrated their agricultural activities first in fertile river valleys and rich upland sites. Coniferous woods, red maple swamps, and other areas with poor or saturated soils survived longer, but eventually fell to the demands of a growing population.

In New England, the model community consisted of a central meeting house and village green surrounded by growing rings of croplands and pasture.[22] Many rural towns still reflect this historic design. Pennsylvanian and more southerly farms were larger and scattered, with an early emphasis on commercial agriculture.[23] In either case, one precept held true: "agriculture required the elimination of the forest."[24]

Faced with the prospect of farming a country "verie full of Woods and Wildernesses," settlers devised efficient means for ridding their land of trees.[25] Girdled trunks could be left standing to rot away in place, with crops or livestock raised in the cleared land below. For a faster route to the plow, trees felled in late summer fueled huge slash fires the following spring, their ashes providing a flush of nutrients for the new field's first harvest. Both methods involved a tremendous waste of wood. Only the finest oaks or white pines might be saved for timber, while the largest proportion of the forest burned or rotted in a mad rush to clear land for planting.

For newly arriving colonists, northeastern America's abundance of forest and sparsely settled land represented an overwhelming resource. Long centuries of dense habitation in Europe and England had spawned a landless peasantry and constant shortages of wood. Farming and forestry practices sought to maximize yields from small plots; firewood was expensive; and hunting privileges were usually reserved for the rich. In America, any settler could expect to own several hundred acres of land, with no restrictions or regulations on its use. Such liberty led to prodigal exploitation, but the waste was grounded in what, for the times, were sound economic decisions. As one historian summarized, "Europeans labored to save their scarce land. Americans spent their land to save their labor."[26] By clearing more and more forest, settlers could regularly shift their crops to new, fertile fields, avoiding the intense effort required to fertilize and manage a small plot for the long term. Cleared land also brought a premium on the growing real estate market; recent arrivals always paid more for fields ready to be planted. So long as ample land remained unsettled, no incentives existed for the conservation of resources. Efficient land use meant working harder and losing money.

Economics also played a role in the accelerating pace of forest destruction. Records from the mid-eighteenth century show that the amount of cleared land suddenly increased at a rate disproportionate to population growth alone.[27] The difference represents a shift from subsistence agriculture to production for new urban markets, as well as export abroad. Livestock, either sold in urban markets or traded with Caribbean plantations for sugar, brought easy profits.[28] Set loose in the forest, pigs and cows flourished, denuding the understory and sowing non-native grasses that would proliferate when the land was cleared. Pasture soon dominated all but the best agricultural lands, and in some places, livestock outnumbered people by a factor of ten.[29] Rising urbanization and industry also created new markets for wheat, corn, and several important byproducts of forest clearing. Surplus hardwoods could be reduced to potash, a valuable chemical for the production of soap, gunpowder, flint glass, linen bleach, and wool scour.[30] Hemlock and black oak bark contributed tanning acids for the leather trade, while iron smelting drove local charcoal industries throughout the region. With so much to be gained, clearing the land became a lucrative occupation in and of itself.[31]

Throughout the settlement period, the impact of logging in the Northeast increased steadily as new markets developed and transportation improved across the region. Initially, only exceptionally valuable trees warranted the high cost of moving logs to market, and river transport further limited trade to buoyant softwood species. Of these, one tree dominated the early timber industry. Measuring up to 8 feet in diameter and more than 200 feet in height, eastern white pines towered above their neighbors and provided excellent wood for all types of construction. Before independence, the British Royal Navy attempted to claim all large white pines as future ship masts; they were the only species big enough to power their immense "man of war" vessels. Agents marked the chosen trees with an arrow-shaped blaze, but the edict proved impossible to enforce, and pines disappeared rapidly from their preferred habitat in the Northeast: sandy riparian floodplains and steep ravines protected from wind and fire.[32]

While white pine garnered the most attention, other species supplied a wide range of forest products. Local sawmills provided white oak for building and barrel staves, rot-resistant black oak for ship hulls, and red and white cedar for shingles and clapboard. Export to urban markets in North America, the Caribbean, and Europe gradually increased the rate of cutting, but the real boom for logging came with steam-powered mills and the advent of railroads in the nineteenth century. Cheap transportation suddenly increased the profit margin for hardwoods and other secondary species, and opened up previously inaccessible stores of white pine. By 1880, logging had replaced agriculture as the region's major source of forest clearing.[33]

The cumulative impact of agriculture and logging on northeastern forests ranks among the most rapid and dramatic ecological shifts in recorded history. Botanists estimate that between 1 and 5 percent of the original flora disappeared in the transition from forested wilderness to farmland.[34] The structure and species composition of remaining and regenerating habitats differed considerably from the original forest. In 1821, Timothy Dwight observed, "the pines for nearly a mile were many years since entirely cut off, and in their place has sprung up a forest of oaks. Such a change in vegetation is not uncommon."[35] Patterns of regeneration varied widely, reflecting the ecology and specific land use history of a given site. Dwight's pine forest, for example, might have burned soon after clearing, eliminating any fire sensitive seedlings while favoring the stump-sprouting capability of oaks (which were probably a minor component of the original pine grove). Plowing or grazing the same land could have led to different associations. In spite of such local variation, travelers' descriptions, witness tree data, and ecological inference reveal several general trends within the major forest communities.

Throughout the oak forests of southern New England, Pennsylvania, and New Jersey, settlers often managed second-growth woodlots for firewood production. Stump-sprouting species such as chestnut and the various oaks became even more numerous, at the expense of hemlock, hickory, and other species that sprouted from seed. Coppiced oaks and chestnut produced poles large enough for fuelwood on a rotation of twelve to fifteen years, and repeated cutting kept them in a constant state of arrested development. Fireweed, goldenrod, and other disturbance colonizers replaced the original herbaceous layer, while a dense tangle of ericaceous shrubs eventually dominated the understory.[36] These scrubby young forests accounted for as much as 70 percent of the area's woodlands in the nineteenth century.[37] Over time, fire suppression in second-growth areas led to increases in black cherry, sugar maple, white pine, and other species long held in check by Native American burning practices.

At least two canopy trees suffered severe declines in the northern hardwood zone. The ecologies of both American beech and eastern hemlock give them a dominant role in undisturbed forest, but leave them vulnerable to major habitat changes. Beech trees propagate largely by root sprouting, a strategy that allows several individuals to form dense stands over long periods of time. When clearing and plowing or grazing destroy those root systems, it may take centuries for them to reestablish their dominance. As one of the most shade tolerant species in the region, hemlock also flourish in old-growth situations, but suffer when the land is repeatedly disturbed. They recover more quickly than beech, however, as long as the regenerating woods create a shady, closed canopy. Hemlock populations actually increased in some undisturbed second growth, since livestock find their saplings unpalatable and mature trees have little value as timber or firewood. Studies suggest that sugar maple took the place of declining beech and hemlock, while birch and other disturbance colonizers saw at least a brief increase in numbers.[38]

Changes in the boreal forest occurred later in the settlement period, when heightened logging activity and subsequent slash fires began to affect large areas in northern New England. The proliferation of newly cleared sites led to a dramatic expansion of white birch and aspen, opportunistic pioneers with abundant, wind-dispersed seeds. Balsam fir, faster growing than its co-dominant red spruce, may also have increased proportionally in the second-growth forest.

Microclimate and habitat conditions in the altered landscape differed substantially from old growth. As noted earlier, naturalist Wilson Flagg described the change in 1872: "One of the conditions most remarkable in a primitive forest is the universal dampness of the ground. The second growth of timber, especially if the surface were entirely cleared, stands upon a drier foundation."[39] Communities dependent on the moist old-growth environment included complex lichen, moss and fungi associations, as well as groundcover and understory species ranging from goldthread, yew, and mountain maple to various orchids. All disappeared or were severely reduced in the second growth forest.[40] Other habitat types suffered as well. Draining swamps, channeling waterways, and the decline of beaver led to a dramatic loss of wetlands throughout the region, taking whole plant communities with them. Natural grasslands or "intervales" along the major rivers were replaced by cropland or by European grasses and clovers better adapted to grazing.

Massive erosion accompanied declining forest cover and the rise of intensive agriculture, threatening watersheds and affecting natural communities across the region. Flooding increased in frequency and severity, small streams filled up with silt, and the deposition of sediments on floodplains and in lakes and bays rose anywhere from four to one hundred times the pre-settlement rates.[41] The port of New Haven, Connecticut, extended its wharf over 3,900 feet between 1765 and 1821, just to keep ahead of the growing mud flats.[42] George Perkins Marsh drew attention to the crisis in several of his speeches and books:

> The suddenness and violence of our freshets increases in proportion as the soil is cleared; bridges are washed away, meadows swept of their crops and fences, and covered with barren sand . . . and there is reason to fear that the valleys of many of our streams will soon be converted from smiling meadows into broad wastes of shingle and gravel and pebbles, deserts in summer, and seas in autumn and spring.[43]

While the loss of wilderness went largely unmourned aesthetically and ecologically, people responded to the threats of erosion that rutted fields, speeded soil exhaustion, and led to noticeable declines in water quality. Protecting water supplies became the rallying cry of many early conservation efforts, including the creation of New York's Adirondack Forest Preserve in 1885.

Social and political events in the mid-nineteenth century brought fundamental changes in land use throughout the Northeast. Tens of thousands of able-bodied men left their farms and fields to fight in the Civil War, and many never returned. At the same time, railroads and the Homestead Act opened the vast prairie for settlement. With cheap land suddenly available elsewhere, northeastern farmers with played-out fields, or those frustrated by harsh winters and rocky, hilly terrain, deserted their landholdings in droves and headed for the flat, deep topsoil of the American Midwest. The nation's breadbasket had migrated, and agriculture would never regain its former stature in the Northeast. Throughout most of the Northeast, industrial logging shifted control from individual landowners to large corporations managing huge tracts for lumber and pulp production. The population of rural areas declined sharply and trees began to reclaim thousands of abandoned farms and pastures, setting the stage for a recovery nearly as dramatic as the forest's initial demise.

Wildlife in the Northeast

Greg Streveler, an Alaskan naturalist, has called animals "whispers of thought through the forests of time."[44] By the late 1800s in the Northeast, all large native mammals had grown quite scarce. As Europeans settled the Northeast and beyond, the settlers affected the wild animals in the landscape in four major ways: (1) the larger animals such as moose and mountain lions disappeared because of habitat destruction and overhunting; (2) landscape changes favored open area and edge species, such as skunks; forest interior species, like the pine marten, disappeared in most areas; (3) many freshwater fish populations declined sharply in response to water pollution, dams, overfishing, and the arrival of exotic species; and (4) the Europeans brought with them many exotic species, intentionally and unintentionally, that became widespread throughout the region.[45]

It is hard to imagine that deer were virtually gone from these forests less than one hundred years ago. In 1853, Zadock Thompson wrote that "notwithstanding all that has been done for their preservation, their numbers have been constantly diminishing within the state [Vermont], till they have become exceedingly scarce, except in a few of the most unsettled and woody sections."[46] Today, hiking anywhere in the northeastern forests one encounters copious deer scat in all but the most rocky or frigid terrain. In Vermont and upstate New York, deer are browsing tree seedlings and saplings to the ground in places and entire generations of trees are being lost; ecologists are convening conferences on the effects of deer browsing on forest regeneration. As Aldo Leopold described in his celebrated essay "Thinking like a Mountain," each winter is followed by the "starved bones of the hoped-for deer herd, dead of its own too-much."[47]

That deer populations have swung from near zero to an overabundance in much of their suitable habitat is just one example of the oscillations set into motion by European settlement and subsequent "management" practices.

The precipitous decline of deer and their hoofed relatives, the moose, elk, caribou, and bison, began early in settlement history. Massachusetts enacted the first closed season on deer in 1694, indicating a realization that the resource was limited. Hunted for their meat, the white-tailed deer was one of the few species that declined *before* the forests were cut.[48] While Native Americans traded in buckskins and used them for clothing, settlers mostly saw deer as tasty prey. Moose ranged throughout the Northeast from Maine to Pennsylvania (see map 2.1). Conspicuous and easy targets, they were also hunted out of most of their range by the 1900s. New Hampshire native Nathan Caswell killed ninety-nine in one winter in the late 1700s.[49] Caribou, seasonal residents in Maine, New Hampshire, New York, and Vermont, also disappeared. Their little-understood migration patterns added to the confusion about their decline until it was too late. An 1896 report from the Maine Commissioners of Inland Fisheries and Game listed 239 caribou killed in the season. By 1904, the commissioner's report stated "there is no indication that the caribou are returning or will ever return." A closed season was enacted in 1905 that prohibited the killing of caribou before October 15. The report for 1906 briefly stated: "There are no indications of any caribou in the state."[50] While the extirpation of deer and their relatives was brought on by overzealous hunting, the current explosion of deer in suitable habitat can be traced in large part to the disappearance of other animals: wolves and mountain lions.

Unlike wolves, ungulate populations were not targeted for elimination as "noxious predators." For these large predators, settlers employed techniques such as animal drives, in which hunters converged upon their prey in an ever-tightening circle, sometimes covering an area thirty miles in diameter. Colonel H. W. Shoemaker described one drive in Snyder County, Pennsylvania, in 1760 intended to rid the area of noxious predators: "41 Panthers, 109 Wolves, 112 Foxes, 114 Mountain Cats, 17 Black Bears, 1 White Bear, 2 Elk, 98 Deer, 111 Buffaloes, 3 Fishers, 1 Otter, 12 Gluttons [wolverines], 3 Beavers and upwards of 500 smaller animals" were killed.[51] The extermination story is also written in the laws of the day. Even while legislation was being enacted to protect deer, bounties were established on wolves. Bounties rose from a penny per wolf in the early 1600s to $20.00 in Vermont by 1853. Wolves were gone from Con-

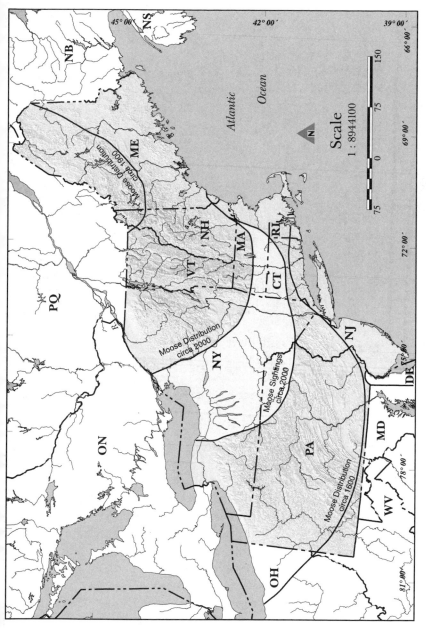

Map 2.1. Historic Moose Distribution in the Northeast. Approximate range of moose populations at pre-settlement, late 1800s, and 2000. Shaded area indicates multiple sightings of individuals. Southern distribution of moose is controlled by temperature, specifically heat. In summer coats, moose experience stress at temperatures of 59°F or higher. Eastern distribution of moose in Connecticut and Massachusetts is limited by road density.

Figure 2.1. Mountain lion. *Photo © Susan C. Morse.*

necticut by 1837, New Hampshire by 1895, the remote regions of the Adirondacks by 1899, and Maine by 1909.[52] Once one of the most widely ranging land mammals on earth, wolves were reduced to 5 percent of their range in the lower forty-eight states, none of that range in the Northeast.[53]

In 1638, King Charles I decreed the compulsory use of beaver pelts in felt and fur hats. By the time the beaver hat went out of fashion at the beginning of the 1800s, the beaver was virtually extinct east of the Mississippi. In 1743, just *one* port in Rochelle, France, received the pelts of 127,080 beaver, 30,325 martens, 1,267 wolves, 12,428 otters and fishers, 110,000 raccoons, and 16,512 bears. These pelts were taken exclusively from the northeastern United States and southeastern Canada. In 1831, John Godman wrote in *American Natural History*, "In a few years, comparative speaking, the beaver has been exterminated in all the Atlantic . . . whelmed in the fathomless gulf of avarice."[54]

The *coup de grace* for wildlife populations occurred during an intense period of exploitation at the end of the nineteenth century, when fish and wildlife were extracted from the nation's forests, rivers, and grasslands to supply a growing urban market.[55]

Recovery and Change: Return of Native Forests and Animals

Since deforestation peaked in the mid-nineteenth century, regenerating woodlands have steadily reclaimed much of their former range in the Northeast. Forests now cover 90 percent of Maine, 87 percent of New Hampshire, and more than 75 percent of Vermont, a near-complete reversal from the height of the agricultural period, when uninterrupted expanses of croplands and pasture prompted one observer to muse that "the forests are not only cut down, but there appears little reason to hope that they will ever grow again."[56] Bill McKibben has heralded this renaissance of green as "the great environmental story of the United States."[57] Many scientists and environmental thinkers view the reforested landscape as cause for hope, and as an opportunity to reexplore the relationships between human communities and the natural world.

The story of the Northeast's recovery begins with farm abandonment. Nineteenth-century farmers moving westward left behind countless untended fields and empty pastures, setting the stage for the growth of new forest communities. Local environmental conditions and the proximity of different seed sources led to a variety of successional patterns, but any trees successful at colonizing open ground found limitless habitat to exploit. Birch proliferated on exposed mineral soils, sugar maple did well in wooded pasture, and white pine grew vigorously in grassy pastures and hayfields. For the pines, colonizing old fields marked a dramatic change in habitat from the pre-settlement forest. Where they once inhabited river valleys and formed occasional ridgetop groves, a cleared landscape gave them access and advantage in upland sites. Stands of even-aged white pine soon covered large areas of abandoned farmland, and fueled a brief logging boom when they reached harvestable size at the turn of the century. The hardwood saplings that grew up in their shade survived to dominate much of the modern forest.[58]

A shift in white pine habitat was far from the only change in the post-agricultural forest. Like coppiced woods or other secondary growth, the species composition, microclimate, and understory communities of recovering pastures differed significantly from original forest. The same general trends held true, with fewer late-successional trees such as beech and hemlock, and a drier environment that favored different herbaceous species and bryophytes. In central and southern New England, where over three-quarters of the landscape was devoted to agriculture, abundant stone walls and rusty barbed wire crisscross the woods, a clear sign that abandoned fields form the backbone of the modern forested land-scape.[59]

With the increase in forest cover, wildlife long since extirpated from the region began to return. The deliberate reintroduction of deer, beaver, martins, fishers, turkeys, and lynx aided the natural repopulation of the forests (see chapter 7). A number of widely distributed vertebrate species, though, remain extirpated from the Northeast: Eskimo curlew, greater prairie chicken, mountain lion, timber wolf, wolverine, and woodland caribou. Gone forever from the Northeast and the world are four species of birds (Carolina parakeet, great auk, Labrador duck, and passenger pigeon) and the silver trout, along with an estimated seven species of insects and three species of plants. The original diversity, abundance, and distribution of some invertebrates and plants is a dark mystery and it includes the possibility of disappearances that went undocumented.[60]

While the return of forests and fauna marks an encouraging trend, the Northeast remains a highly altered landscape. Four centuries of intensive land use have brought permanent changes and new realities, including a human population over two hundred times greater than the population estimates for pre-colonial times.[61] Growing urban centers fragment the landscape and bring new pollution threats, while international trade and travel have introduced hundreds of new species to local ecosystems. High demand for forest products has spawned a new era of industrial logging and management, particularly in the boreal forest region.

Just as railroads and portable mills opened up the last stands of north-eastern old growth forests to logging in the late nineteenth century, recent changes in the paper industry created a vast new market for forest products in the late twentieth century. New processing technology allowed wood pulp to replace cotton and linen rags as the primary raw material for papermaking. The long wood fibers found in conifers make particularly strong paper, putting intense pressure on the remaining spruce-fir forests of northern New England.[62] This sudden demand for wood pulp not only increased the rate of logging, but also introduced new techniques and management practices. Where traditional timber harvesters sought primarily the mature, straight-trunked trees, wood pulp could be processed from anything larger than a sapling, and clear-cutting soon became the dominant method of harvest. Competition and consolidation spawned large corporations that could effectively manage the boreal forest industrially, using herbicides, pesticides, and short rotations to maximize yields from even-aged stands of spruce and fir. Corporations still control large areas in the northern part of the region and the landscape remains mostly

Figure 2.2. Moose. *Photo © Susan C. Morse.*

undeveloped, but its young, heavily managed forests bear little resemblance to the pre-settlement forest. Birch, aspen, and balsam fir have all increased at the expense of the slower-growing red spruce that once dominated the area. But unlike other secondary forests, frequent clear-cutting and herbicide applications have altered the natural patterns of regeneration in northern timberlands. Dense, even-aged stands lack structural diversity and never develop the understory microclimate and accompanying shrub and herbaceous communities of ancient forests. Logging in other parts of the Northeast continues on a more selective basis, having less impact on the forest as a whole, but making large specimens of valuable hardwoods such as black cherry uncommon throughout their range.

From the first European colonists to the latest shipments of trade and tourists, people and products arriving in the Northeast have not traveled alone. Stowed away in ballast, livestock fodder, pant cuffs, and personal luggage, hundreds of foreign species have also made the trans-oceanic journey. Exotic plants now constitute a full 30 percent of the region's flora, including the state flowers of Vermont (red clover), New Hampshire (purple lilac), and New York (rose).[63] Non-native animals range from Norway rats and house mice to the common earthworm and the honeybee. Whether introduced accidentally, for cultivation, or for nostalgic reasons, these species are now an indelible part of the northeastern landscape, and a small portion of them — the ones that become truly "invasive" — have the power to reshape whole ecosystems.

Invasive species — those exotics that multiply unchecked and displace local communities — are second only to habitat loss as a threat to worldwide biodiversity.[64] In the Northeast, the first invasives may have been European pasture grasses and clovers, which quickly replaced native species less adapted to grazing.[65] The list has grown through the centuries to include representatives in virtually every habitat. Zebra mussels, a Eurasian bivalve introduced accidentally in ballast water, now threaten local shellfish and other plankton feeders in lakes and waterways throughout the region. Purple loosestrife, brought from Europe as a garden ornamental, has overrun thousands of acres of prime wetlands, while alien buckthorns, honeysuckles, and green-briar are spreading just as rapidly through many upland forests. Attempts to control these and other invasive species have met with little widespread success. Because of their unpredictability (a small population of an invasive species may lie dormant for decades before suddenly exploding in numbers) and the increase in global travel and trade, the impact of invasive species is expected only to grow in the years ahead.

Furthermore, exotic insects, fungi, and other pests have also had devastating effects on a number of native northeastern species. In 1900, the American chestnut accounted for one out of every four trees in the Northeast, and for as much as 70 percent of the forest's basal area.[66] When an Asian fungus known as chestnut blight arrived in a nursery shipment to New York City in 1904, it found a population of trees with no natural resistance to its attack. Within five decades, the American chestnut had disappeared from its entire range. Thirty years after the chestnut blight arrived, American elms met a similar fate at the hands of another fungal invader, Dutch elm disease. Currently, white pine, eastern hemlock, American beech, flowering dogwood, and butternut all face threats from specific and, most often, alien pathogens. The disappearance of a species affects everything from forest structure to soil biology, and in the case of chestnut and beech, the myriad animals and birds dependent on their once-abundant nut crops. Like other invasives, the number of pests and pathogens is thought to be rising.

Northeastern forests have recovered dramatically over the past century, but the region is home to one of the densest human populations on the continent and faces the growing threat of urban sprawl. More than the effects of agriculture or logging, the spread of cities and towns marks a permanent change in the landscape. Development replaces natural areas with pavement, buildings, and a patchwork of small woods and landscaping that offer little habitat for native flora and fauna. Urban and suburban areas present a foreign landscape to most species, with a fundamentally altered hydrology, microclimate, and ecology. Additionally, human activities have introduced a wide range of damaging pollutants that effect ecosystems on both a local and regional scale. Notable examples include acid precipitation, which has caused the decline of many lakes and red spruce forests, and the sewage and agricultural runoff that has caused the eutrophication of countless waterways. The rebirth of northeastern forests may present an opportunity to reexplore human interactions with a natural landscape, but in many areas that process will have to begin with restoration.

On a larger scale, increasing urbanization and industrialization around the world have introduced another factor into the northeastern landscape: global warming. Climate models predict the greatest change in northern forests at the boundary between hardwoods and boreal conifers, a transition that bisects the northeastern region.[67] At the doubled levels of atmospheric carbon dioxide expected in the next century, spruce and fir could disappear from the Northeast entirely, replaced by mixed hardwoods on productive soils, and by oaks and pines on poor sites.[68] Hemlock may also suffer in a warming climate, while the implications for herbaceous, faunal, and microbial communities remain largely unknown and unstudied.[69] Without a concerted international effort to control greenhouse gas emissions, the next great environmental transformation in the Northeast will be part of a larger story: worldwide ecosystem responses to a changing global climate.

Conclusion

The landscape of the northeastern United States continues to change in response to both human and natural pressures. Any efforts at its rewilding must consider changes in the land over time, and define the level of wilderness to be restored. The forested ecosystem first encountered by European colonists was the result of a complex geologic, glacial, climatic, and biological history. Small populations localized and minimized human effects so that the land appeared pristine and largely untrammeled. Over the past four hundred years, the original forests have been cleared, wildlife has been depleted, rivers have been blocked, and land has been subjected to intensive farming and grazing. Exotic species and pests have altered natural communities, while urbanization, pollution, and global warming introduce new threats to the region. Recovery of the forest and the return of wildlife in this century show the ecosystem's great resilience, giving hope for a new balance between wilderness and human society. Species such as the American chestnut and passenger pigeon, and undocumented communities like the original riparian grasslands, may be gone forever, but the opportunity still exists to reestablish mature habitats populated by the full complement of extant biodiversity.

CHAPTER 3

Old-Growth Forests of the Northeast

ROBERT T. LEVERETT

THIS BOOK IS about wilderness restoration in the Northeast for the twenty-first century. The original wilderness is long gone and enters our collective thinking more as a reverie than as a concrete memory. Any new paradigm that we forge that is based on restoring wilderness must necessarily take shape within our technology-glutted society and among a runaway human population, an explosive combination that elsewhere has been eliminating wilderness at a frightful pace. Many restoration advocates want the new paradigm to incorporate the charismatic, wide-ranging megafauna of the Northeast, including wolves, mountain lions, bears, lynxes, and moose. But given our dense human population, it will not be possible to restore these animals in sizable geographical areas, so that the emerging species mixes will not constitute a resurrection of the past, regardless of the historical ranges of the megafauna. The species distribution will be more area-specific than in historical times. This distribution probably will apply to the flora as well as the fauna. Are there any common denominators in these localized wilderness areas? For all restored areas, the inescapable element must be forest, the natural land cover of almost the entire Northeast.

To comprehend what might be the nature of these futuristic wild woodlands, it seems axiomatic to consult the past. The forests of pre-settlement America appropriately fit our notions of wilderness. We typically think of the pre-settlement forests as "virgin" in the sense of not having been shaped or disturbed by European Americans. This, in turn, suggests a role for the surviving "old-growth" forests of the Northeast, which are as close as we can come to virgin. However, when we begin to move beyond discussion to implementation, we encounter problems. We lack consistent definitions for both wilderness and old growth. These terms are bandied about as though there were a consensus as to their meanings, but in truth there is no consensus. Even deeper probing can raise questions about the very root concepts, particularly as they might be applied to the settled northeastern landscape of the twenty-first century.

Even for those who firmly believe in the raw concept of wilderness, important questions remain to be answered. Is wilderness across the northeastern landscape defined by the absence of human presence and human support structures? Does wilderness require the presence or absence of particular species? Is there a minimum physical size requirement for an area to be designated as wilderness? Are the larger tracts of old-growth forests synonymous with wilderness? Do we agree that examples of wilderness still exist in the Northeast, such as the designated wilderness areas of New York State's giant Adirondack Park? Do the logged-over, but unsettled parts of northern Maine qualify as wilderness? Do politically designated wilderness areas within our national forests qualify as real wilderness? Would we agree among ourselves that wilderness had returned to a specific region? With respect to the wilderness/old-growth connection, if nature doesn't produce old growth sufficiently fast, can we artificially create old-growth conditions to satisfy a tenet of the paradigm? Even if we could, should we?

These questions are not just academic. Bizarre experiments have been conducted for a number of years by, not too surprisingly, the U.S. Forest Service, to speed up the development of the physical characteristics commonly associated with old-growth forests. The motives of the Forest Service are hardly benign. Forest Service priorities have never been driven by a preservation ethic, but rather by the intention to make logging more palatable to the public. Quickly restoring wildlife habitat is one way to ease the pressure. Hunters jump to your side. Even with hidden Forest Service agendas, wilderness restoration implications of designer old growth cannot be completely ignored. In the final analysis, is wilderness in modern America more a state of mind than a physical reality?

Any serious investigation of wilderness dictates that we explore all these issues. Furthermore, if we are to relate the larger remnant old-growth forests in the Northeast to wilderness, then we must agree on what constitutes an old-growth forest in biological terms as opposed to political decrees. This may eventually lead us to challenge historically recognized old-growth sites, and precedents do exist for that. The Cathedral Pines of Cornwall, Connecticut, is a stand owned by the Nature Conservancy. It was virtually destroyed by a tornado-like microburst in July 1989. The pines were well known and much admired and the stand was often classified as old growth, and sometimes called virgin. However, despite their physical impressiveness, almost all the Cathedral Pines were colonial-aged regeneration—what foresters commonly call old field pines.

If the task of defining wilderness itself seems daunting, we can at least take pride in our progress toward understanding the evolution of our northeastern forests. Today, we know more about the processes that shaped our forests than at any time in the past. It is a safe bet that no lost caches of knowledge on old-growth forests remain to be rediscovered from the writings of the scientists and foresters of the last century or even the first half of this century. The past research on old growth is sufficiently well preserved and available to current-day researchers. We are in our best position ever to evaluate different ecologically based definitions and concepts of old growth and to fit forests that are in their old-growth phase into a new wilderness paradigm applicable to the next millennium.

Concurrent with our development of the new wilderness paradigm, we should frequently look backward into time to examine the entire wilderness/forest continuum. Science will continue to provide us with the means to understand the evolution of natural forest ecosystems, and consequently, the probable development, composition, and structure of the pre-settlement old growth. As a result, our understanding of the continuum should become ever more accurate. This should allow us to stay firmly moored to the natural environment of the Northeast.

A Working Definition of Wilderness

Even though wilderness and old growth are "floating" concepts, we need a starting point, a wilderness frame of reference that applies to the Northeast. The pre-settlement landscape fits the requirement. It is fair to conclude that wilderness and old growth were synonymous, or at least indistinguishable, for people living in the early 1600s. The howls of wolves in the forest would have ensured that. Regrettably, except for a few jewels and lots of scraps, that forest-based archetypal wilderness is gone. We can read about our ancestral wilderness in the writings of dozens of authors, but historical descriptions often confuse rather than clarify. Europeans who directly observed the original wild woods of the Northeast described them poorly. Their verbal pictures often had more to do with their religious convictions than with the actual plant and animal communities. To early writers, Satan's influences were always at work in the dark woods. Thus, historical descriptions fail to provide a reliable baseline in evaluating progress toward wilderness restoration.

We are not rendered helpless, though, in terms of a conceptual framework. To get around definitional difficulties temporarily, I begin with a simple definition of wilderness:

Wilderness operates at the landscape level and evolves naturally in the long-term absence of concentrations of humans intent on reshaping the environment to meet human needs. Wilderness develops as the direct consequence of natural processes working over long time periods, free from the interference and impacts of self-aware humans. This approach does not require the complete absence of humans; they can be part of the landscape so long as their activities do not significantly alter the surface features of the land or the species mix. Viewed across a time continuum, wilderness does not have to remain constant in terms of species mix and indeed it hasn't.

There is not much here to chew on for those who revel in deep intellectual explorations of a subject developed from armchair comfort, such as one gets in Simon Schama's *Landscape and Memory*.[1] Regardless, an important corollary to this definition should not be allowed to escape our notice. The dominant vegetative cover of the Northeast still consists of trees. If left to strictly natural processes, cleared land quickly develops a dense regrowth of trees. This cover is a natural consequence of the northeastern region's abundant rainfall and moderate temperatures. So by the above definition of wilderness, which includes the requirement to minimize human impact, and the ecological reality of northeastern forests, I would argue that naturally evolved woodlands, by default, become an integral part of a wilderness classification. The inclusion of old-growth forests as a part of real wilderness follows from the fact that forests in the Northeast, left to nature for a sufficiently long time, will include a significant proportion of old growth.

Bonding Old Growth Securely to Wilderness

From the foregoing, I believe the ecological tie between wilderness and old-growth forests is secure. But if we still need more assurances, we can invoke images of the past, if for no other reason than for the sheer romance of it all. The early eastern woodlands contributed handsomely to our frontier folklore. The tales of Paul Bunyon, James Fenimore Cooper's accounts of the eastern frontier, Washington Irving's "Legend of Sleepy Hollow," and Henry Wadsworth Longfellow's poems replaced puritanical ideas of eastern forests as a "howling wilderness"—not something to be reconstituted. Romanticizing can reinforce our need for archetypal forests. Rutherford Platt, a well-known author of numerous books on American forests, has referred to the woodlands of the eastern United States as the Great American Forest. The mere use of this phrase raises our expectations.

But if we are left only with romanticized descriptions of those early American forests, we are in danger of basing the new wilderness model on mythology, on a forest existing mainly in the imaginations of current-day humans. To many early European settlers, eastern forests were dark and foreboding, a wilderness filled with demonic beings. Their self-righteous task was to cut down the forest, kill the large predators, and clear the land for pasturage, agriculture, and settlement. Oh yes, and rid the land of its original human inhabitants. By contrast, nineteenth-century European Americans such as Henry David Thoreau, looking at an abundance of fields and a paucity of forests, bemoaned the loss of the latter and wrote longingly of the forests. Portrayals of the early forests turned romantic. Forests were mentally transformed into friendly, cathedral-like places, filled with game, and of legendary extent. I still read descriptions of the pre-settlement woodlands as extending in one unbroken swath from the Atlantic Ocean to the Great Plains. European Americans today, looking to escape the stress of daily life, find the romantic wilderness model appealing, and often idolize Native Americans.

The original forests were not so extensive as romantic descriptions portray. Consequently, it is even more miraculous that scattered pockets of old-growth forests still survive on both public and private lands. I contend that the new wilderness paradigm dictates that we protect the remnants. But who do we turn to for information on them and insights about them? Scientists? Naturalists? Forestry professionals?

We might begin with the science-based profession of forestry. Foresters often manage the public lands that contain the old-growth remnants. In the public mind, foresters know about old growth. It sounds reasonable, but I have found it rarely to be true. It is a matter of economics. Foresters are interested in working forests. They make no money from trees they cannot cut. Old trees are seen as a waste of natural resources. Forestry professionals who do value old-growth usually do so from a historical perspective. I am frequently reminded of a visit to Michigan's famous and well-designed Hartwick Pines State Park. A logging museum stands within the boundaries of a small, surviving stand of stately old-growth white pines. A lumber company donated the stand. The collocated logging museum is meant to be educational, but I cannot help thinking of it more as a tribute to the lumberman who cut all but the tiny stand. Today, the surviving pines silently stand like spared trophies that, in irony, have outlived their captors.

If foresters cannot teach us about old growth, who can? We must turn to those who have no vested economic interests, the naturalists and scientists who embrace the thinking of such visionaries as Henry David Thoreau, John Muir, Aldo Leopold, and David Brower. These naturalists and scientists recognize old-growth forest remnants as a window to a vast wilderness past. Even in their current diminutive status, the old-growth remnants make important ecological contributions. At the least, we know that our old-growth forest remnants add to biological diversity, function as genetic reserves and refugia for at least a few species, and serve as baselines for the evaluation of climatic and environmental changes.

Current-day Old-Growth Forests in the Northeast: An Historical Perspective

Prior to the 1990s, the number of widely acknowledged old-growth stands in the Northeast was quite small. For example, a 1983 report prepared by the state of Maine lists only thirteen sites as traditionally recognized old growth for the entire New England region.[2] Oddly, none of the thirteen sites listed are in Maine. However, the authors identify 104 potential old-growth sites in Maine and conclude that sixty-eight are examples of old-growth forest. Prior to the 1983 report, old-growth sites in Maine went largely unacknowledged by state officials. Many more candidate sites have been identified in Maine since this report.

In terms of officially acknowledged old-growth sites, Massachusetts faired only slightly better. Of the thirteen sites listed in the Maine report, one was in Massachusetts, an old-growth reserve in the central Berkshires on the Cold River. However, a few other sources have identified pockets of surviving old-growth in Massachusetts. An Audubon field guide lists Ice Glen in Stockbridge as a remnant virgin hemlock stand.[3] Oddly, the far more significant Cold River site is not listed in the Audubon guide. Chesterfield Gorge is included in the same Audubon guide, but no mention is made of an old-growth stand in that gorge. That claim is made elsewhere. I know of no popular source published prior to 1990 that lists more than four old-growth sites for Massachusetts. Currently, my colleagues and I have identified thirty-nine sites in the Bay State and we know that we have not located them all.

Literally dozens of other examples of hit or miss (mostly miss) old-growth identifications could be cited for every state in the Northeast. The inescapable conclusion is that no single source accurately lists old growth in the Northeast. This lack would be more understandable were we entering the twentieth century as opposed to leaving it. However, the absence of comprehensive state-by-state listings of old-growth sites has not

Figure 3.1. Old-growth hemlock grove, Monterey, Massachusetts. *Photo by John Knuerr.*

been entirely a result of lack of interest. The biggest reason has been a general lack of recognition of old growth. Based on what we know about forests today, this seems paradoxical. But when we examine the growth of our forest-based understanding from a historical perspective, the reasons become clear.

Today's residents of the Northeast are the human inheritors of a land that was covered by an immense ice sheet some fifteen to twenty thousand years ago. Calculations suggest that the ice cover exceeded a mile in thickness in places. The ice sheet completely eliminated the forest cover of much of the Northeast and bulldozed the landscape, leaving a variety of geological formations associated with glaciation. At the time of maximum coverage of the blanket of ice, no trees even grew in the vicinity of the ice. It is a testament to the raw power of nature that the ice formed and that the land rebounded. It is a testament to nature's fecundity that the forests returned.

After the ice receded, the region again gradually became reforested and remained that way for the past nine thousand years, until the middle of the last century, when the accumulative impact of the activities of European Americans reduced the forest cover by 50 to 80 percent, depending on the geographical area. As a direct consequence of the clearing, several generations of European Americans came to know a landscape less wild and far less forested than today. In fact, wild lands and wilderness were largely abstractions, tenaciously held in the minds of an elite few.

People studying history are often at first surprised to learn that the New England of Henry David Thoreau was largely a landscape of small, towns and villages separated by a patchwork of fields and farms. The nature and extent of the original forests became more myth than fact. In truth, the original forests were almost as much a mystery to the southern New England farmers of the mid-1800s as was the dark side of the moon. The original forest cover had been reduced to small remnants, that for the most part were unknown to even towering figures of human conscience such as Henry David Thoreau. He believed that one had to travel to the "wilds of Maine" to see even the remnants of the virgin woods.

The vast Allegheny Plateau of western Pennsylvania and New York faired no better. That great hemlock, white pine, and northern hardwood belt was logged mercilessly in the latter half of the nineteenth century. Today, only tiny patches of virgin woodlands remain. New York faired better, with its constitutional protection for the state-owned areas of the Adirondacks (of course, almost all of the land acquired for these forest reserves had been cut over by the timber industry). But with the exceptions of the Adirondack and Catskill Parks in New York, and the upper reaches of Maine and New Hampshire, by the middle of the twentieth century, recognized old-growth stands in the Northeast usually fell into one of three categories.

Publicly preserved, widely spread stands containing the most spectacular trees comprised most of the known old-growth sites that appear on maps. Cook Forest and Hearts Content in Pennsylvania are prime examples. Isolated estates of the rich sometimes contained old growth. The Reinstein Woods of Buffalo, New York, is an example. Colleges often had land holdings that contained small areas of original-growth forest. The College Pines of Durham, New Hampshire, is an example.

Other old-growth areas remained largely unnoticed and undisturbed for a variety of reasons. Small areas were bypassed as a consequence of surveying errors. One sometimes sees small patches of ancient trees on the fringes of county or municipal property. On state and national forest lands, inaccessible areas in the mountains and river gorges were often left unlogged or partially logged. A surprising number of these places remain today, though few have been recognized as old-growth forests and most have little or no protection. The Cold River Gorge and the Mount Grey-lock sites are examples of old-growth areas in Massachusetts that survived because of inaccessibility.

Most residents of the Northeast who have grown up in the vicinity of old-growth stands that have not been specifically identified as such seldom recognize the stands as old growth. No reservoir of indigenous wisdom about the Northeast forests flows from European Americans, and that which existed in Native American culture has been irretrievably lost. Old-growth forests passed out of the minds of the public and forestry specialists alike, so that today, the public's recognition of old-growth in the Northeast is tied to the visually spectacular old-growth icons. Cook Forest State Park, Hearts Content in the Allegheny National Forest, and Ricketts Glen State Park, all in Pennsylvania, are examples. Going into the 1980s, the rule was "if it doesn't carry an official label of old growth, then it isn't."

The decades of the 1980s and 1990s were times of intense discovery or rediscovery of old-growth forest. Many scientists and naturalists, professional and amateur, for one reason or another went forth into the forest in search of the Holy Grail of old-growth. I was a member of this driven group. Many of us followed similar courses without knowing of the efforts of others. We sought early descriptions of the landscape in search of what we believed to have been accurate descriptions of the forest primeval. We eventually came to realize that these descriptions were more valuable for what they revealed about the extant belief systems and state of science than for their accuracy as descriptions of old-growth landscapes. Early observers often mistook woodlands that were managed by Native Americans for a virgin landscape. For instance, Giovanni da Verrazano, an Italian adventurer (1480–1527), described widely spaced, large trees with an understory free of young trees and shrubs. These descriptions match the forest's response to periodic low-intensity ground fires.[4]

A surprise for those of us engaged in hunting old growth was the lack of specific knowledge about forest ecology possessed by public agency resource managers. At the outset of my search for missed scraps, I assumed that federal and state foresters knew a lot about old growth. However, I came to recognize that resource managers usually acknowledge only the densely packed, advanced-aged hemlock and red spruce stands of the Northeast as old growth. The sparse ground cover associated with these conifer stands led these same officials to categorize old-growth forests as places of low productivity and health. Descriptors such as "diseased" and "decadent" were, and still are, applied to old growth. This pejorative assessment was further reinforced by the growing industrial view of a forest as a factory, which became the common mindset. Forestry schools conditioned students to believe that maintaining forest health justified the systematic removal from a stand of trees over eighty to one hundred years in age, unless some compelling historical reason dictated otherwise. This singularly commercial perspective toward old growth went far toward desensitizing an entire profession in recognizing values for stands showing advanced age, values readily embraced by naturalists and scientists. Thus, the professional force responsible for forest inventory on our public lands, and generally the people in the best position to identify potentially valuable old growth, became essentially neutralized. This applied equally on state and federal lands. With the advent of concepts such as ecosystem management, this institutional myopia has been diminishing.

Today, it is a safe bet that the Northeast has between 750 and 1,000 geographically separate old-growth stands. It is not hard to justify this extraordinary number. Massachusetts currently has thirty-nine sites spread over 3,200,000 acres of forest. The Northeast has approximately 70,000,000 acres of forested land. Using Massachusetts as the standard, we can estimate 12.2 old-growth sites per million acres of forest. Projecting this rate over the Northeast's forests yields 854 old-growth sites. Even assuming that the densely populated state of Massachusetts is rich in old-growth sites, it is inconceivable that it would have more than double the number of old-growth sites per million acres compared to the other states. Remembering the thirteen sites referenced in the Maine Critical Areas study for New England, the extent of institutional blindness toward old growth has been monumental.

The estimated 750 to 1,000 old-growth sites translate to an equally surprising acreage, courtesy of the Adirondack Park. Forest historian Barbara McMartin has documented at least 300,000 acres of old growth in the Adirondacks. She believes the figure will eventually be confirmed at 500,000 or more acres. Michael Kudish of Paul Smith's College has documented at least 64,000 acres of old growth in Catskill Park. Bruce Kershner adds 3,000 to 4,000 acres spread over thirty-five sites in western New York State. Given what we now know, my conservative projection of the total old-growth acreage for the Northeast is 400,000 to 500,000 acres. The Adirondacks hold the key to a substantially greater acreage. Using conservative figures, the ratio of 450,000 acres to 854 sites yields an average site of 527 acres. However, this size is misleading, because most sites are between ten and one hundred acres. The large, contiguous swaths in the Adirondacks skew the average acreage per site to a figure well above what it would otherwise be.

Original Definition of Old-Growth Forest

It is fascinating to review the history of the ongoing discussions about eastern old-growth forests, indeed about the very use of the term. The layperson might think that "officials" agree on the term. However, the two groups principally involved with the subject, foresters and scientists, often disagree on the terminology. Decisions about old-growth forests made within the U.S. Forest Service and the executive branches of state government often differ from geographical region to region. Disagreements occur within different divisions of an agency at the same location. The Forest Service's research facilities, which are staffed by scientists, often have a very different view of old growth compared to collocated timber managers. For example, no one definition has been generally accepted among the different national forests of the eastern United States. The same can be said of state-level forestry agencies. In fact, many state and federal forestry officials do not believe that the old-growth phase can be defined. The "old-growth condition" is something to be minimized.

The term "old growth" has its origins in the business-based, applied science of forestry as opposed to the more abstract, pure sciences of botany and forest ecology. The term "old growth", as used by foresters, has an economic origin. Timber specialists usually assume that forests exist to serve people in a materialistic sense. In their view, the highest and best purpose to be served by virtually all woodlands is utilization, albeit wisely, by humans as lumber, wood chips, or pulp. No less a towering figure than Gifford Pinchot, the father of the Forest Service, wrote, "there are just two things on this material earth—people and natural resources . . . a constant and sufficient supply of natural resources is the basic human problem."[5] Pinchot's debates with naturalist John Muir over philosophies of conservation versus preservation are legendary.

The strictly utilitarian view of forests by the forestry profession led gradually to an industrial treatment of forests. Academic forestry, often funded by industry, pushed the technology of plantations stocked with laboratory-bred trees, identical in virtually every respect. All that remained was to dicker over concepts like the average age for stand rotation. It would be grossly unfair not to point out that not every forester bought into this sterile model. But the forestry lexicon remained a vocabulary emphasizing the importance of frequent extraction. Stands of trees past the maximum period of rotation became classified as overmature or "old growth."

For most eastern species of trees, this point of overmaturity is assumed to occur between 80 and 120 years of age. A figure of 150 years has been commonly applied to western species. Whatever the number, tree growth rates are overtaken and eventually overwhelmed by the inevitable processes of decay, and the economic value of these "overmature" trees as a resource for timber declines. When this condition is prevalent, the forest, as a whole, is described as overmature. For laboratory-grown stock, the harvest cycle may be abbreviated to between thirty and sixty years.

By contrast, the ecologist does not use economic criteria in judging maturity. Still, from an ecologist's point of view, there is a compelling statistical validity to placing passage to old growth at between one hundred and two hundred years, since most eastern species have average life spans of two to four hundred years.

Other terms often used synonymously with old growth include original, primary, pre-settlement, primeval, ancient, and virgin, but these terms are unclear in terms of what such forests should look like. Today, the most common use of the term old growth embodies the idea of forests that have escaped large-scale natural and most human disturbance for several centuries, preferably long enough that the species mix stays relatively stable. Do we know what such forests actually look like?

Birth of a New Old-Growth Awareness

In the early 1990s, a movement developed within the environmental community to identify and protect eastern old-growth forests. The movement was led by former Earth First!ers David Foreman and John Davis, who organized the publication *Wild Earth*. Dr. Mary Byrd Davis became the project leader. She called upon groups and individuals all over the East to provide input. The effort resulted in the publication *Old Growth in the*

East.[6] High on energy and enthusiasm, but low on detailed understanding, an increasing number of forest activists pushed to locate previously unrecognized stands of eastern old growth. Organizations such as the Western North Carolina Alliance provided training for old-growth enthusiasts. But more was needed.

In 1992, planning commenced in Massachusetts for a conference that has since evolved into a remarkable series of conferences on old-growth forests, launched with the objective of bringing together the key players. The initial goal was to assemble forestry professionals, government officials, academics, environmentalists not part of the preceding groups, and the public at large. The progression of conferences was: August 1993 at the University of North Carolina in Asheville, Williams College in October 1994, the University of Arkansas in October 1995, Clarion University of Pennsylvania in June 1997, and University of Minnesota in June 1999.

In addition to the five conferences, we have held two limited symposia. On 26 October 1994, a one-day symposium on old-growth forest definitions was convened at Harvard Forest, Petersham, Massachusetts. The objective was to work toward agreement on a definition for old growth. However, the job was not completed. A second seminar was convened to review progress on definitions since 1994. The second symposium was held on 6 November 1998. Theoretical concepts and practical criteria that might be applied by resource managers received equal attention. The general consensus from the two symposia and five full conferences has been that the old-growth forest phase represents an indistinct stage of forest development, succession, or progression, with no clear thresholds identifying passage. An analogy may help. There is no precise moment when a human becomes old; at some point, it becomes obvious to all that senior-citizen status has been reached. We can define old age for social purposes, but from a scientific standpoint, passage into old age cannot be pinpointed. Forest conditions and characteristics represent a continuum. No thresholds can be pinpointed where different stages of forest development become immediately apparent.

Old-Growth Characteristics and Criteria

Some ecologists approach old-growth definitions using a processes approach. They search for processes and functions that shape the composition and structure of the forest across a time continuum—long in terms of human life spans. Predictable changes in species composition, starting with a domination by light-loving species and progressing to species that are shade tolerant, are often viewed as the principal natural processes that determine the eventual composition of a northeastern forest. However, disturbances occur on many time scales and intervals to impede the theorized, inevitable march of the species toward a presumed climax state. Fire, blowdowns, ice storms, insect infestations, and fungal pathogens kill trees. In some cases, entire forests are killed and the process of initiation and succession begins anew. However, when disturbances are minimal for scores of years, forests in the Northeast succeed to dominance by the more shade-tolerant species.

What really foils our understanding is that the combinations of natural processes and events that determine the composition and age of a forest are, practically speaking, infinite. Forests do not progress toward the old-growth phase via a single path. Consequently, there is never a point in time when a forest becomes clearly identifiable as old growth. This is especially frustrating to forest administrators who need yes or no answers. However, barring large-scale disturbance, a forest eventually reaches a level of maturity that makes it clearly recognizable as old to the experienced eye. At the advanced stage, physical characteristics can be qualitatively assessed and some quantification is possible, at least within ranges. Thus, observable physical characteristics form the basis for the most currently useful old-growth definitions.

The following list of physical characteristics generally applies to most northeastern old-growth forest types. Each physical characteristic occurs to a different degree based on the forest type; that is, the degree to which an old-growth characteristic exists in a stand depends on the type of forest and the specific history of the stand. Forest-floor pits and mounds are common in northern hardwood stands, but limited in oak-hickory stands. If an area of forest possesses the physical characteristics listed below, exhibits no obvious signs of human activity, such as old stone walls, cellar holes, and the like, and covers a minimum of several acres, it meets most ecologists' requirements for old growth. I label this class 1A old growth.

- **Advanced tree age for a high percentage of stems**. A common maxim of old-growth wisdom is "no old trees, no old growth." This seems intuitive, but in reality, it is a product of the terminology. The percentage of old stems that often is postulated as a necessary old-growth criterion is that 50 percent or more of the trees that have reached the canopy must average 50 percent or more of the maximum longevity for the species. This criterion applies best to forests such as the mixed mesophytic in Tennessee, Kentucky, North Carolina, West

Figure 3.2. Old-growth white oak, Mount Tom State Reservation, Massachusetts. *Photo by John Knuerr.*

Virginia, and Ohio. The criterion does not fit well in those geographical regions that experience periodic catastrophic disturbance more frequently than the natural longevity of the species and that experience frequent small-scale episodic disturbances, or on sites exposed to gradual but continuous land slippage. Vermont forest ecologist Charles Cogbill argues convincingly that red spruce stands seldom reach average stand ages of two hundred years or more in the Northeast.[7] In addition, other ecologists suggest that to be considered old growth, a stand of trees should meet the preceding age criteria plus be the second generation of trees beyond the last catastrophic disturbance. This approach to defining old-growth focuses on stands of trees that have escaped major disturbance for several hundred years. The condition of old growth becomes tied to nature's roulette wheel. Stringent application of the definition results in areas blinking into and out of "old-growth existence" as natural disturbances knock down or burn down the older trees in an area. In places where disturbances are both episodic and periodically catastrophic, old-growth status becomes increasingly improbable. The degrees and types of natural disturbance tend to push us into a stand-oriented mindset or toward adopting a landscape perspective. At the landscape scale, a shifting mosaic of age structures becomes the norm and exhibits some predictability. It seems natural to many of us to extend the concept of old growth to include patches of forest at different stages of succession as opposed to isolating just the oldest pockets. Good arguments exist for both approaches.

- **Uneven age of forest, resulting in multi-layered vertical structure**. When large-scale disturbances such as hurricanes and microbursts strike a forest, a vast acreage may be affected. Catastrophic winds may knock down every standing tree so that forest succession starts over and for a century or more the recovering forest is even-aged. The recent 4 July 1999 blowdown in the Boundary Waters Canoe Area Wilderness covered a mind-boggling 250,000 acres.[8] Other areas such as the Tionesta area in the Allegheny National Forest have lost most of their old growth due to single-event tornadoes or microbursts. Barring these large-scale disturbances, once a forest matures, single trees topple, creating a random scattering of modest-sized gaps or holes in the forest canopy. Surrounding trees expand their crowns to fill the gaps. But for larger gaps, lateral expansion of canopy trees may not be sufficient to close the gaps, and young trees growing in the gaps reach the canopy. Other young trees, if shade tolerant, continue to bide their time, waiting for the opportunity to reach the canopy via new gaps. Thus the process of individual and multiple tree-falls leads to a multi-aged, multi-tiered forest structure.

- **Single and multiple tree-fall gaps**. The processes described above are natural to all forests, young or old, but when a high level of maturity is achieved, the result is more observable; that is, a patchiness develops, resulting from tree-fall gaps. In some parts of a stand, the gaps will reflect larger disturbances. In others areas, the gaps will be small. As trees mature, areas of forest will become old growth via the age criterion, while disturbances will eliminate the older trees in other parts of a stand. The result is a shifting mosaic of age patterns resulting from the random nature of the disturbances. This lack of stand uniformity is a characteristic of old growth.

- **Standing snags.** When a species such as white pine dies, the individual trees usually do not immediately topple over, but may stand as snags for years. Other tree species fall sooner after death. Sugar maple is an example. In either case, an environment of live and dead standing wood is created, which becomes an old-growth characteristic. However, a high density of standing dead snags is mainly associated with conifer forests and is especially noticeable in spruce and fir forests.

- **Woody debris.** This is just wood on the forest floor in varying stages of decomposition. Once a tree falls to the forest floor, it becomes a log that progressively decays. Its latter stages of decay, when the remains of the log is covered with fungi, lichens, mosses, liverworts, and the like, may not even be recognized by a casual observer as the remains of a tree. The decaying material that is still recognizable as wood usually is called woody debris. Old-growth forests predictably have more woody debris than managed forests. Measurements of amounts from existing studies vary greatly across and within forest types.

- **Dominance of late successional species.** The tree species that make up the forests of the Northeast have average maximum life spans that typically fall between two hundred and five hundred years. Species that recolonize after burns, such as aspen and fire cherry, have shorter life spans. Others, such as white pine, can live very long. A white pine growing in the Nelson swamp, near Syracuse, New York, has been dated to 458 years. Blowdowns are often colonized by the same species. Areas prone to repeated fires are often colonized by pitch pine, and sometimes by red and white pine. However, in the absence of periodic fire or blowdown, northeastern forests move toward a dominance of trees that are shade tolerant. Hemlock, beech, birch, and sugar maple are the primary late-successional species at mid- to lower elevations.

- **Abundance of lichens, liverworts, mosses, fungi.** Nonvascular plant communities such as lichens often develop slowly and require a stable environment to persist. Old-growth forests are havens for these species, which colonize on decaying logs and the trunks of older trees. Studies are starting to show that old-growth forests have double to triple the number of fungi associated with second-growth forests.

- **Macro-porous soils.** An important characteristic of old-growth forests is deep, organically rich soil. These soils are sponges for moisture and keep old-growth forests wetter than their younger counterparts. The large cavities left by decaying trunks and stumps lead to soils that are highly porous and aerated.

- **Well-developed herb layer for forest type**. Acidic soils are often rich in bryophytes, but poor in herbaceous species. Neutral soils are often rich in herbs. Old-growth forests that grow in rich, circum-neutral soils (neither acid nor alkaline) are botanical laboratories.

- **Underground fungal networks that connect members of the same and different species**. Mycorrhizal fungi are special fungi that connect to tree roots, either surrounding them or penetrating them, and work to allow the tree to absorb extra water and nutrients through the networks of fungi. In turn, the tree host feeds the fungi from its sugars. This tree root–fungi association is highly developed in old-growth forests.

- **Advanced root grafting among the same and different species**. Trees compete individually with one another for space, nutrients, and other needs. They also become attached to one another through an extensive network of grafted roots and pass nutrients between one another. A wide difference of opinion exists on the extent and nature of root grafting, but it does occur and may reach a stage in old-growth forests where cooperation is as significant as competition.

- **Conspicuously larger trees free of lower branches**. Large trees are the expectation of most visitors to old-growth forests; such trees are a byproduct of a long growing time. It is to be expected that old-growth will contain a higher density of larger trees than what is commonly seen across the greater landscape of young forests. Trees that reach large girths and great heights provide the most striking contrast between young and old forests. Abundant descriptions of the huge trees that populated the virgin woods can be found in colonial literature. However, in the Northeast, the size differential between the trees in old growth and those typically seen in regrowth forests of one hundred years of age is not as dramatic as one might think. A more striking feature that adds to the psychological perception of large size in old growth is the branch-free trunks that are the hallmark of older trees that developed in a closed-canopy forest. It is the branch-free characteristic that produces the cathedral effect. In addition, old trees develop massive root structures that frequently attract moss and become anchored in their tenuous environment by wrapping around rocks. This anchoring is especially noticeable for yellow and black birch. The combination of large root masses, branch-free trunks, and broccoli-shaped crowns provides the visual cues to recognizing old-growth trees.

Statistical Measures and Old Growth

The age and degree of "naturalness" of a forest are recognizable through physical features that experienced naturalists, scientists, and foresters can recognize, but simple numerical measures seldom capture the essence of old growth. Age and the size distribution of trees, ground cover, imprints of past natural disturbances, and other characteristics create a mosaic that is complex but discernable to an experienced eye. It is natural for us to try to measure this mosaic, and statistical measures have been developed, but these are surprisingly ambiguous in helping us distinguish between old-growth and mature forests. That is, the old-growth characteristics are recognizable, but are not easily reducible to a simple set of statistics or measures. Nonetheless, we continue to try. In 1998, a team of scientists working for the Forest Service released a study on eastern old growth.[9] Data from over eight hundred studies are referenced in this 507-page book. Old growth is characterized by forest type, and statistics are presented for: (1) density and basal area of live trees; (2) average and maximum tree age; (3) maximum tree diameter; (4) average canopy height; (5) percentage of space in canopy gaps; (6) density, basal area, and volume of snags; (7) density and volume of logs; and (8) total volume of course woody debris.

If patterns in the old growth are visible to the naked eye, why can't they be coaxed out of such a wealth of data? The primary reason is that the range of values for each statistic is too wide, both within each forest type and across the spectrum of types, to clearly distinguish the old-growth phase. Consider the density statistic (number of trees per unit area), which is presented in the Forest Service study as number of stems per hectare. Within the collected data, this statistic ranges from 50 trees per acre for mesic northern red oak sites to 1,412 for a sub-boreal spruce and fir stand. This range is so broad that younger stands of trees can comfortably fit within this range. Basal area is no clearer (basal area is the total cross-sectional square footage of all trees four inches in diameter or more, measured at 4.5 feet off the ground). In the Forest Service's data, this statistic varies from a low of 39 square feet per acre to a high of 336 square feet. The maximum diameter for the trees included at study sites varies from a surprising low of 2 inches for one study plot to a high of 78 in another.

These extremely wide variances reveal what the eye quickly discerns. Old-growth forests are structurally diverse places and stand in stark contrast to the homogeneity of cultivated stands. The contrast of 50 to 1,412 trees per acre challenges the imagination. It is equally challenging to imagine a maximum size of a 2 inch diameter in an old-growth stand. This suggests that the study plot was centered in a blowdown. The stand high of a 78-inch diameter is more in keeping with what we expect from old growth. The Forest Service statistics reveal that some old-growth sites are populated with a few very large trees while others are literally crammed with tiny trees. Densities at all levels in between are also found.

Coarse woody debris provides another example. Volumes vary from almost none to a landscape dominated by standing snags and logs in all stages of decomposition. Vertical structures afford still another. The canopy of some northeastern old-growth stands does not rise much above the height of a tall stepladder, while others tower to average heights of 120 feet or more, with individual trees reaching 150 feet. The numbers are literally all over the place.

I have struggled for years with stand measures expressed as aggregate statistics, and I continue to find them useful, but I do not consider any of them to be the defining attributes of old growth. This is true not only for the spectrum of forest types, but within each forest type as well. What the numbers from all the studies truly tell us is that nature-shaped forests are far more diverse woodlands than those manipulated by humans. The complexity of old-growth environments may turn out to be their most important attribute in terms of being self-regulating autopoietic forest systems.

A Sample of Old-Growth Remnants Important to the New Wilderness Paradigm

Old growth, as described above, is a miniscule percentage of the northeastern forests—about six-tenths of one percent. Within this tiny percentage, we are extremely fortunate to have stands of inspiring trees that provide us with examples of what we believe to have characterized the pre-settlement forests. The following is a sample of northeastern old-growth stands that possess real or symbolic wilderness value (see map

3.1). For each, I explain why I consider it to be a contributor to the new wilderness paradigm.

1. **Five Ponds Wilderness, Adirondack Park, New York.** This area is the largest contiguous acreage of primary (never been cut) old-growth forest in the Northeast. It is roughly 50,000 acres in size, and possesses a mix of forest type, including red spruce, black spruce, tamarack, balsam fir, hemlock, white pine, and various northern hardwoods. Emergent white pines provide a primeval scene equal to any in the Northeast. Old trees are abundant. Data from researchers indicate typical basal areas of 125 to 250 square feet per acre. The Five Ponds Wilderness represents the exquisite melding of mountains, forest, lakes, and sky. The remoteness of the region can heighten feelings of vulnerability and exposure. To the extent that we associate an element of danger with wilderness, Five Ponds fits the image. The remoteness of this site, its sheer size (equivalent of 78 square miles), and its diversity justifies its placement at the top of the list.

2. **West Canada Lake Wilderness, Adirondack Park, New York.** In contrast to the Five Ponds Wilderness, the region around Lewey Lake in the central Adirondacks is an old-growth jewel that is very accessible from points along State Route 30. Yet, once into the forest, the area loses nothing and it is large. The contiguous old-growth acreage is almost certainly over 6,000 acres and may well be double that figure. Precise boundaries may never be determined, since delineating the boundaries of such a large areas is time-consuming work. The trees are impressive. I have measured large yellow birch on the side of Lewey Mountain to 12 feet, 8 inches in circumference. Old-growth red spruce and hemlock blend with yellow birch and sugar maple along the Snowy, Lewey, and Cellar Mountain ridge front. The swath of old growth is virtually unbroken for several miles. The clear visibility of the West Canada Lake Wilderness old growth from Route 30 serves as a poignant reminder of how imprecise past researchers have been in identifying old-growth forests and demonstrates the challenge of resolving human ideas and concepts about the natural world with physical realities.

3. **Powley-Piseco Area, Adirondack Park, New York.** The southwestern region of the Adirondack Park is less known to the public than the popular north-central and northeastern regions. The mountains are lower and exhibit fewer striking rock faces. Yet the forests of the southwestern region boast some of the best Adirondack old growth. The area around Panther Mountain near Piseco Lake, and a 6-mile

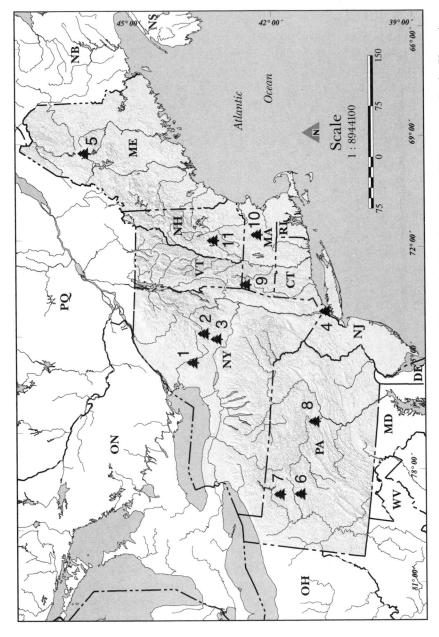

Map 3.1. Old Growth Sites in the Northeast: (1) Five Ponds Wilderness; (2) West Canada Lake Wilderness; (3) Powley-Piseco Area; (4) Mianus Gorge Preserve; (5) Big Reed Pond; (6) Cook Forest State Park; (7) Hearts Content; (8) Tall Timbers Natural Area; (9) Mohawk Trail Corridor; (10) Wachusett Mountain State Reservation; (11) Bradford Pines.

stretch on either side of the Powley-Piseco road offer visitors the opportunity to walk through beautiful mature woodlands containing yellow birch, sugar maple, white ash, hemlock, and red spruce. I measured five red spruce within a short distance of the Powley-Piseco road that were all over 8 feet in circumference. This matches descriptions of some of the best of the Adirondack red spruce that was cut between 1840 and 1890. I also measured three yellow birches on the side of Panther Mountain that are over 14 feet in circumference—remarkable sizes for forest-growth hardwoods in the Northeast. I found sugar maples that measured to 13 feet in circumference and 115 feet in height. This is forest primeval. The principal wilderness value of the Panther Mountain area is its large areas of exemplary primary forest consisting of noticeably large trees. It satisfies an image of an old-growth forest as a forest of stature.

4. **Mianus Gorge Preserve, New York.** Mianus Gorge in Westchester County, New York, was the Nature Conservancy's first acquisition. Working in a volunteer capacity for the Preserve, I delineated about 50 acres of old-growth forest for director Ann French. The Yale School of Forestry has dated individual hemlocks in Mianus to around 330 years old. The diversity of ground plants has been compromised by excessive deer browse and the hemlock wooly adelgid has infested the majestic hemlocks, with no remedy available. Hemlock, tulip poplar, yellow birch, black birch, and chestnut oak all show advanced age in the gorge. The name Mianus honors a Native American who witnessed the end of indigenous societies and the extinguishing of wilderness in southeastern New York and southern New England. For thousands of urbanites, Mianus Gorge serves as at least a symbol of the forest primeval. A mere forty miles from downtown Manhattan, the gorge is symbolic of the region's wilderness past.

5. **Big Reed Pond, Maine.** The Big Reed Pond tract of north-central Maine owes its existence to a foresighted forester who kept it largely hidden from sight. The old-growth acreage, as presently delineated, is approximately 5,000 acres. Dominated by spruce, the Big Reed Pond forest is often cited as the largest contiguous area of old growth in New England. Its location near Mount Katahdin, Maine, makes it especially important as an example of a forest wilderness. The trees in Big Reed are not exceptionally large, but ages exceed three hundred years. Big Reed feels remote because it is remote. It amply fulfills the vision of a somber New England wilderness dominated by water, sky,

and ancient forest. It blends companion images of wildness and remoteness.

6. **Cook Forest State Park, Cooksburg, Pennsylvania.** Cook Forest State Park is slightly less than 8,000 acres of absolutely superlative woods. Of these 8,000 acres, 1,500 are in virgin or near-virgin condition. Hemlocks and white pines dominate the most visually impressive areas of Cook Forest. These two large conifers are often so packed that basal areas exceed 300 square feet per acre. Many of the impressive white pines are between 240 and 290 years old and owe their existence to a past fire. However, pre-burn pines in this area have been determined to be as old as 450 years, which pushes the maximum age for the species. Deciduous species such as sugar maple, red maple, American beech, black cherry, northern red oak, and white ash dominate in other places. Forest ecologists Marc Abrams of Pennsylvania State University and David Orwig of Harvard University's Harvard Forest Research Facility have studied the development of Cook Forest, and they conclude that the current crop of white pines and hemlocks developed together as opposed to pine first followed by hemlock. The stars of Cook Forest are its towering trees. In 1997, Will Blozan, Robert Van Pelt, Jack Sobon, and I measured a white pine, later named the Longfellow Pine, at 179.1 feet, using a combination of laser equipment and a transit. However, big, tall trees are not isolated. The density of white pines over 150 feet is the greatest for any forest in the Northeast. So far, I have confirmed over twenty-five pines at heights between 150 and 179 feet. These are just the trees I've had time to measure. There are many more. Cook is the quintessential cathedral forest. Perhaps the most inspiring story of Cook Forest is the story of conservation activity in Pennsylvania by the Cook family during the early 1900s. Cook Forest is a precursor of today's renewed interest in wilderness. It has had many visitors and supporters. Despite heavy visitation, it remains the icon of old-growth white pine forests.

7. **Hearts Content, Allegheny National Forest, Pennsylvania.** This is a small, 80-acre remnant of the original Allegheny Plateau forest. It has been visited and studied by many foresters and forest ecologists. To many, it is the jewel of the Allegheny National Forest. Blowdowns and the process of forest succession are changing this forest. At one point in time, one-quarter of an acre was calculated to have included 50,000 board feet of timber. As recently as June 1999, I measured nine tall white pines exceeding 150 feet in height. The tallest measured

was 157.7 feet. Other figures have been cited that put the average stand height at 160 feet and individual trees to over 170. These somewhat inflated heights likely result from the measurers having been too close to the tall trees when angle measures were taken.

8. **Tall Timbers Natural Area, Tuscarora State Park, Pennsylvania.** The Tall Timbers Natural Area is not a large place. It serves more as an icon of what the region once grew in abundance. I measured a slender hemlock to 145 feet in height and 8.5 feet in girth. As of this writing, that Tall Timbers hemlock is the hemlock height champion of its species for the Northeast. Hardwood species in Tall Timbers include American beech, red maple, sugar maple, and yellow birch. The value of this stand lies principally in its power to inspire.

9. **Mohawk Trail Corridor, Massachusetts.** Confirmation of old-growth sites in the Berkshires and Taconics of western Massachusetts has repeatedly made news for over a decade. The number of confirmed stands of old growth in western Massachusetts has grown from four or five in the early 1980s to thirty-nine in the late 1990s. The combined area of old growth covers approximately 1,500 acres. Two areas stand out: the swaths of old-growth forest west of the town of Charlemont that lie along the Deerfield River and its tributaries, and the old growth that lies on the Mount Greylock massif. These two areas have most of the state's acreage. However, of greater significance than the modest acreage is the diversity and quality of the Massachusetts old growth and its potential contribution to the new wilderness paradigm. The cool, wet climate of the Berkshires and the relatively rich soils promote excellent tree growth. The result is a forest of exceptional stature for the latitude. The dimensions of individual trees are impressive. In Mohawk Trail and Monroe State Forests, mature white pines, seeded from original old-growth stock, rise to heights of 130 to almost 160 feet and achieve girths of 8 to 12 feet. One pine is 14 feet in circumference. American ash trees rise majestically to heights of 115 to 130 feet and reach respectable girths of 8 to 11 feet. Isolated white ash trees reach from 130 to 145 feet in height and 11 to 14 feet in girth. Sugar maples commonly reach 8 to 11 feet in girth and 110 to 120 feet in height. I have measured a few sugar maples 11 to 13 feet in girth and 120 to 135 feet in height. Other species are comparably large and tall. I have measured hemlocks to 125 feet in height and nearly 13 feet in girth. Red maples, black cherry, American beech, American basswood, and bitternut hickory have all been measured to heights of 100 to 115 feet and girth of 7 to 9 feet. Northern red oaks

have been measured from 8 to 11 feet in circumference and 100 to 115 feet in height. A northern red oak growing in Mount Greylock's Hopper is 13.5 feet in circumference and 102 feet tall. Red spruce on the Cold River have been measured to 114 feet in height and 7.5 feet in circumference, and on Greylock to 127.7 feet in height and 7.6 feet in circumference. These fine trees provide visitors with a visual treat. The wilderness value of the Deerfield watershed and Mount Greylock slopes lies principally in the exemplary forests that clothe the ridge sides. These forests are distinguished from the frequently cut woodlands on adjacent lands.

10. **Wachusett Mountain State Reservation, Massachusetts.** The populous region of central and eastern Massachusetts is an unlikely place to find old-growth forest. No areas of old growth were recognized until May 1995, when a swath of hardwoods and hemlocks around Mount Wachusett was identified as old-growth forest by a team of scientists and naturalists, which included myself. Wachusett is technically known as a monadnock and rises as a rounded dome above the general rolling country of central Massachusetts to a height of 2,006 feet above sea level. The area of old growth has been identified as covering between 130 and 220 acres. The latter determination is the latest. The Wachusett old growth contains the densest stand of old-growth northern red oaks known in the Northeast. Individual oaks and yellow birches have been dated to ages in the range of 250 to 370 years of age. Other species including hemlock, sugar maple, white ash, and beech commonly reach between 150 and 250 years of age. The sage of Concord Henry David Thoreau visited Wachusett Mountain in 1842. Recent attempts to expand a ski resort on the mountain's slopes were thwarted by strong citizen opposition. Rising a thousand feet above the surrounding countryside, the mountain serves as a symbol of New England's wilderness past and offers excellent opportunities for further restoration. Like Mianus Gorge, Wachusett Mountain stands as a symbol of a wilderness past.

11. **Bradford Pines, Bradford, New Hampshire.** This small stand of colonial-aged pines is described as containing New Hampshire's largest white pines. The monarch tree of the stand measures 14.5 feet in circumference at breast height and, when its top was live, measured not less than 144 feet from base to crown. The trunk and limb volume of this tree is close to 1,000 cubic feet. Bradford Pines is an imposing site and provides visitors with a taste of the former glory of the white pine in a region that once had an abundance of Bradford-sized pines.

Figure 3.3. Old-growth sugar maple, Mohawk Trail State Forest, Massachusetts. *Photo by John Knuerr.*

Today's young field-grown pines cannot match the Bradford trees. Little apparent wilderness value remains in this small stand of colonial-aged white pines, except to remind us of what nature produced with no help from modern Americans.

Conclusion

To my mind, it is unrealistic to talk about rewilding the Northeast without simultaneously considering the role of natural forests across the landscape. For me, the two issues are inseparable. If a deforested area anywhere in the Northeast is left to nature, in time it will revert to forest as the natural vegetative cover. Barring human intervention, eventually a sizable old growth component will result. Thus, the tie between wilderness and old growth cannot be circumvented—unless we seek to establish designer wildernesses with avant garde experiments that have more to do with concepts of virtual rather than physical reality. I would hope that we are not aiming toward designer wilderness, for they make no more sense to me than designer old growth. Either would be attempts to recreate a convenient version of what we have destroyed to appease our guilty consciences while concurrently, and characteristically, trying to have it both ways. I believe that those of us who strive to reestablish wildness in the Northeast must accept its old-growth corollary. However, accepting the idea is not tantamount to defining and identifying old-growth forest. This will continue to challenge us.

While the old-growth characteristics discussed above form the basis for practical definitions to be applied in the field, the search for theoretical models that clearly distinguish natural forests from human-manipulated ones must continue. Professor Gary Beluzo of Holyoke Community College in Massachusetts thinks of primary old-growth forests as basically self-regulating systems. He calls them "autopoietic forests" ("self-making forests") and perceives them as evolving through natural selection. Gary Beluzo's old-growth forests are for the most part self-originating, self-perpetuating, and self-regulating. As a consequence, they are dynamically stable. Their controls reside within the system. By contrast, human-managed forests are externally controlled. The idea of internal control through natural selection would then seem central to any wilderness paradigm that is, in fact, not a self-serving exercise in human design and control.

CHAPTER 4

Public Lands and Wild Lands in the Northeast

CHRISTOPHER McGRORY KLYZA

ONE OF THE chief reasons for the differing amounts of wilderness in the Northeast and West, as discussed in chapter 1, is the difference in federal land ownership in the two regions. In the Northeast, the federal conservation and natural resource agencies—the Bureau of Land Management, the Fish and Wildlife Service, the Forest Service, and the National Park Service—control a little more than 2 million acres, roughly 2 percent of the land (see table 4.1 and map 4.1). The Forest Service controls over 1.6 million acres, almost entirely in national forests in New Hampshire, Pennsylvania, and Vermont. The Fish and Wildlife Service owns approximately 180,000 acres in over forty wildlife refuges scattered through all nine states. The National Park Service has over 245,000 acres, with its largest holdings in Acadia National Park, Appalachian Trail corridor, Cape Cod National Seashore, Delaware Water Gap National Recreation Area, Fire Island National Seashore, and Gateway National Recreation Area. The Bureau of Land Management owns nothing in the Northeast. In the West, on the other hand, these four agencies administer over half the land. This difference in ownership patterns helps explain the low total of federally designated wilderness in the Northeast: 205,000 acres. Despite this paucity of federal public lands and wilderness in the Northeast, federal ownership and federal wilderness is significant in parts of the area. More importantly, state conservation lands exceed federal conservation lands in all but two states in the region.[1]

The vast majority of federal lands in the West were carved out of the public domain, land that was already owned by the federal government at the time that it became national forests, national parks, or wildlife refuges. Things are different in the East, where federal lands have been acquired through purchase, and in some cases, through donation. The Weeks Act, passed in 1911, set the precedent for federal acquisition of

Table 4.1
Public Lands and Wild Lands in the Northeast
(acreage and percentage of state)

States	Federal conservation lands		State conservation lands		Federal wilderness		State wilderness	
Connecticut	12,455	(0.4)	209,467	(6.7)	0		0	
Maine	172,163	(0.9)	717,069	(3.6)	19,392	(0.1)	~188,000	(0.9)
Massachusetts	65,315	(1.3)	533,624	(10.6)	2,420	(0.0)	~6,000	(0.1)
New Hampshire	757,378	(13.1)	186,682	(3.2)	102,932	(1.8)	0	
New Jersey	98,778	(2.1)	600,409	(12.5)	10,341	(0.2)	0	
New York	66,839	(0.2)	4,128,534	(13.5)	1,363	(0.0)	1,261,639	(4.1)
Pennsylvania	644,290	(2.2)	3,753,631	(13.0)	8,938	(0.0)	0	
Rhode Island	1,693	(0.3)	58,861	(8.7)	0		0	
Vermont	375,936	(6.3)	309,782	(5.2)	59,421	(1.0)	0	
TOTAL	2,194,847	(2.1)	10,498,059	(10.0)	204,807	(0.2)	1,455,639	(1.4)

Note:

The sums given for state wilderness are based on the following: Maine: the acreage of Baxter State Park minus the Scientific Forest Management Area (~175,000 acres) and two administratively designated remote recreation roadless areas (~13,000 acres); Massachusetts: administratively designated backcountry areas on state forests; and New York: the sum of wilderness, primitive, and canoe lands in Adirondack Park and wilderness lands in Catskill Park.

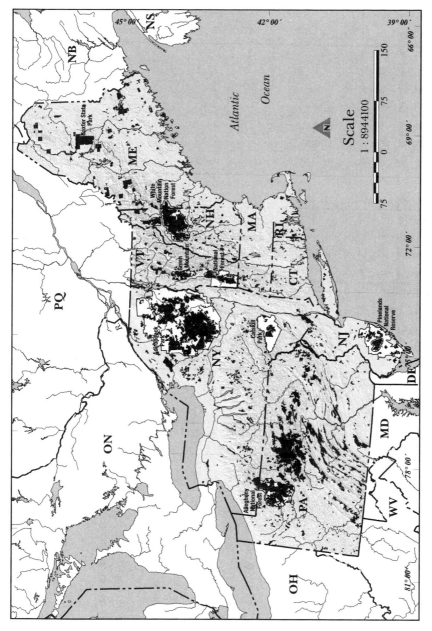

Map 4.1. Public Lands in the Northeast.

conservation lands. It allowed the Forest Service to purchase land for the protection of watersheds of navigable streams and rivers; that is, the Weeks Act meant that national forests could be created east of the Mississippi River. The impetus for this law came from forest advocates in the southern Appalachians and the White Mountains. In New England, these advocates blamed serious flooding along the Merrimack and Pemigewasset rivers on deforestation in the White Mountains. They began calling for the creation of a national forest for the region in the 1880s, a campaign led by the Society for the Protection of New Hampshire Forests after its establishment in 1901. Following passage of the Weeks Act, Congress established the White Mountain National Forest in 1918. Five years later, Congress created the Allegheny National Forest. The language of the Weeks Act limited the scope of these new national forests to protecting the watersheds of navigable streams and rivers (a provision included to make sure the law withstood constitutional challenge, since the Constitution stipulated the federal government's authority to regulate navigation). This limitation changed in 1924 when the Clarke-McNary Act revised the Weeks Act, adding "the protection of timber" as an acceptable rationale for government purchase of forestland. A few years after this change, Congress created the Green Mountain National Forest, the last of the northeastern national forests. These three national forests include three-quarters of the federal land in the Northeast.[2]

Because they were created from lands that were in private ownership, rather than carved out of lands owned by the federal government, these eastern national forests share two characteristics of fundamental importance. First, not all the land within them is owned by the government. Land has been purchased as property came up for sale and as the Forest Service received funds from Congress. Federal ownership ranges from 85 percent in the White Mountain National Forest to less than 50 percent in the Green Mountain National Forest. Since these national forests have been overlaid onto land with a long history of post-Columbian settlement, they also include numerous towns and villages. Second, these forestlands, with some very small exceptions, were all cut over in the past, often a number of times, for farmland and pasture, for timber, and for charcoal and potash. These characteristics make managing these national forests a real challenge, especially for large wilderness tracts, since the forests are often a series of unconnected blocks of lands. Acquisition continues on all of the forests, usually in parcels of hundreds of acres, less often in parcels of thousands of acres.[3]

The characteristics of mixed ownership and formerly cleared lands affected the designation of wilderness in these northeastern national forests. The 1964 Wilderness Act designated only three wilderness areas in the East, only one of which is in the Northeast. When the Forest Service evaluated its other holdings in its roadless area review and evaluation (RARE I), it recommended only three additional wilderness areas in the East. In general, the agency concluded that national forest land in the East was unsuitable for wilderness, since it all showed significant evidence of human occupation and alteration. Such an interpretation, however, proved unacceptable to eastern conservationists. Congress responded by passing the Eastern Wilderness Act. This 1975 law established sixteen new wilderness areas, seventeen wilderness study areas, and generally established a process for designating more wilderness in eastern national forests. The Forest Service undertook RARE II in the late 1970s, and since then, Congress has passed laws designating more wilderness in Maine, New Hampshire, Pennsylvania, and Vermont. Wilderness advocates may have cause for some celebration on national forest lands as the twentieth century draws to a close. In October 1999, President Bill Clinton directed the Forest Service to study its remaining roadless lands with a goal of protecting all such lands. How this will work out specifically on the three northeastern national forests remains to be determined, but it could lead to a substantial increase in protected wild lands in the region.[4]

Yet this lack of federal lands and federal wilderness is far from the end of the public lands story in the Northeast. Here state conservation lands are of the utmost importance. In each of these nine states except New Hampshire and Vermont, more acres are in state conservation ownership than in federal conservation ownership. In each state but Rhode Island, state lands total more than 100,000 acres; Pennsylvania owns over 3 million acres and New York owns over 4 million acres. These state lands are home to significant acreage of protected wild lands in Maine and New York. The most important of these lands are in the Adirondack and Catskill parks in New York, where nearly 3 million acres of state lands are protected by the state constitution as "forever wild." In general, though, these state lands suffer from many of the same problems as the northeastern national forests discussed above. Like the national forest lands, the land purchased for state forests, state parks, and wildlife management areas was generally abandoned farmland and cut-over forestland. State ownership is usually either in small parcels (less than 10,000 acre blocks) or, in larger state forests, mixed with private lands.

This chapter consists of a state-by-state review of public lands and wild lands in the Northeast, focusing on public land holdings larger than

10,000 acres. Special attention is given to the three national forests in the region (the Allegheny, the Green Mountain, and the White Mountain) and the three large state parks in the Northeast (Adirondack, Baxter, and Catskill) as well as the numerous larger state forests. I will also discuss federal or state protected wild lands in each state. Although private reserves are important in most of these states, they are usually small and not managed as wilderness. By not discussing such lands, I don't mean to downplay the importance of private lands in the architecture of land conservation in the Northeast. Indeed, private reserves and land protected by forever-wild easements (as wild cores) and by conservation easements (as buffers), as well as ecologically managed farmlands and forestlands will play a crucial role in a Northeast of healthy, vibrant human and natural communities (see chapters 5 and 8 through 11).

New York

Home to New York City, with federal public lands totaling less than 70,000 acres, with only one federally designated wilderness — and that less than 1,500 acres, one might think that New York State is a lost cause when it comes to wild lands. Nothing could be further from the truth. Thanks to the Adirondack and Catskill parks, and the "forever wild" clause in the New York State Constitution, New York has 1.26 million acres of state wilderness. Only ten states have more designated wilderness. If we include New York's wild forest lands (which cannot be cut or developed, but on which motorized recreation is allowed), the amount of protected wild lands rises to 2.9 million acres, an amount exceeded only by Alaska, Arizona, California, Colorado, Idaho, Montana, Washington, and Wyoming. When we look at percentages, 9.5 percent of New York is protected wild lands. Only Alaska, California, and Washington top that figure. Furthermore, this second-largest wilderness system in the country gives its wild lands the greatest protection. While federal wilderness can disappear through an act of Congress, the wild lands in the Adirondack and Catskill parks are protected by the New York State Constitution. In order for lands to lose their protection, the constitution must be amended, which requires passage of the proposed change by two consecutive sessions of the state legislature and then passage by the voters in a statewide referendum.

Protection for the Adirondacks and Catskills first came in 1885, when New York State established the Adirondack and Catskill Forest Preserves.

Advocates for creating such reserves were supporters of watershed protection for consumption and transportation, hunters and fishers, and resort and estate owners. All feared that continued clear-cutting in these regions would have dire consequences. The 1885 law dictated that all state-owned land in the preserves "shall be forever kept as wild forest lands." At the time the law was passed, the state owned nearly 700,000 acres in the Adirondacks, primarily tax-forfeit lands abandoned after being cut for their timber. Seven years later, the Adirondack Forest Preserve was integrated into the Adirondack Park. More importantly, in 1894, constitutional convention delegates added the "forever wild" clause to the New York Constitution. Still part of the state constitution, the clause reads: "The lands of the state, now owned or hereafter acquired, constituting the forest preserve, as now fixed by law, shall be forever kept as wild forest lands. They shall not be leased, sold or exchanged, nor shall the timber thereon be sold, removed or destroyed." As the state continued to acquire land over the next one hundred years, this clause has come to protect over 2,500,000 acres of land in the Adirondack Park and nearly 300,000 acres in the Catskill Park.[5]

In response to increasing development pressures in the 1960s, the New York legislature passed the Adirondack Park Agency Act in 1971. This law mandated the development of master plans for state and private lands in the park, and created the Adirondack Park Agency to implement the private land use plan. The State Land Master Plan engendered little controversy, since these state lands were already protected as "forever wild" under the state constitution. The plan, approved in 1972, assigned state lands to one of seven categories: (1) wilderness (the state definition is essentially the same as the federal wilderness definition); (2) primitive (these lands are essentially wilderness in character but have certain nonconforming structures, improvements, or inholdings, or are too small—less than 10,000 acres—to be considered as wilderness. The state management goal is to upgrade all primitive areas to wilderness except those areas that are too small); (3) canoe (this designation emphasizes canoeing in a wilderness setting); (4) wild forest (although no timber cutting or development is allowed on wild forests, motor vehicles and snowmobiles can use existing roads and trails in these areas); (5) intensive use (areas for extensive visitor use, such as campgrounds, developed beaches, ski areas, and boat launching sites); (6) wild, scenic, and recreational rivers; and (7) travel corridors. The last two classifications are corridor overlays over other land classifications. Two new classifications, (8) state administrative and (9) historic, were added in 1987. The private land plan, first released in December 1972, was controversial. After much debate and compromise, it was approved the following year. This plan has six categories for private lands in the park (from most restrictive to least restrictive): resource management, rural use, low intensity use, moderate intensity use, industrial use area, and hamlet area. Over half the private land is classified as resource management (which allows one dwelling per forty-plus acres) and one-third is classified as rural use (one dwelling per eight acres). Certain types of development anywhere on private land require a permit from the Adirondack Park Agency. The goal of this private land regulation has been to protect the wilderness character of state lands and to protect private open space in the park. At this time, the Adirondack Park was expanded to its present size of 5,823,367 acres, larger than six states—Connecticut, Delaware, Hawaii, Massachusetts, New Jersey, and Rhode Island.[6]

Development pressures in the Adirondacks and across northern New England rose again in the 1980s, driven in part by the wave of corporate takeovers in the forest products industry and the resulting increase of land for sale. In response, Governor Mario Cuomo established the Commission on the Adirondacks in the Twenty-First Century in 1989. Among the commission's 245 recommendations were state acquisition of over 650,000 additional acres and the creation of a 400,000 acre Oswegatchie Great Wilderness. The commission's recommendations ran into political trouble and did not generate legislative action. Nonetheless, the state has acquired significant acreage in the last decade (including the purchase of 15,000 acres of Whitney Park and 29,000 acres from Champion International). The Adirondack Forest Preserve is currently 2,644,767 acres, with another 226,256 acres protected by conservation easements—an increasingly popular approach in the last ten years (including the 112,000 acre easement that was part of the 1998–1999 Champion land sale).[7]

Sixteen wilderness areas in the Adirondacks total 1,071,590 acres, five of which exceed 100,000 acres. These areas are:
- High Peaks (226,435 acres);
- West Canada Lake (170,530 acres);
- Siamese Ponds (108,503 acres);
- Five Ponds (107,230 acres);
- Silver Lake (105,476 acres);
- Pigeon Lake (50,100 acres);
- Pharaoh Lake (47,085 acres);
- Blue Ridge (45,856 acres);
- Dix Mountain (42,208 acres);

- McKenzie Mountain (37,616 acres);
- Hoffman Notch (36,231 acres);
- Ha-De-Ron-Dah (26,600 acres);
- Sentinel Range (23,252 acres);
- Giant Mountain (22,768 acres);
- Pepperbox (14,600 acres); and
- Jay Mountain (7,100 acres).

An additional 72,049 acres receive virtually the same protection as wilderness in the canoe and primitive classifications. There is one canoe area (Saint Regis, 18,231 acres). There are four major primitive areas:

- Lila-Whitney (22,050 acres);
- Hudson Gorge (16,700 acres);
- Hurricane Mountain (13,768 acres); and
- Valcour Island (1,300 acres).

Remaining lands are classified as wild forest (1.2 million acres), intensive use (14,000 acres), state administrative (1,400 acres), historic (495 acres), and other areas awaiting classification.[8]

The Catskill Park languishes in the shadow of the Adirondacks. Very little has been written about the park or about conservation in the Catskills, yet it is the third-largest state park in the country and features more wild lands than all the federal wilderness in the Northeast. When the state established the Catskill Forest Preserve in 1885, it owned far less land in the region (roughly 34,000 acres) than in the Adirondacks. The 1894 clause added to the state constitution to protect state forest lands in the Adirondack Park as "forever wild" applied to the Catskill Forest Preserve as well. Ten years later, the Catskill Forest Preserve became integrated into the Catskill Park. The park is currently 705,500 acres, with 287,100 acres owned by the state (over 40 percent). Although the Catskills faced pressures similar to the Adirondacks in the 1960s and 1970s, a law analogous to the Adirondack Park Agency Act was not passed for the Catskills. State lands in the park, however, are subject to a master plan similar to that in the Adirondacks that the Department of Environmental Conservation adopted in 1985. Lands are classified as wilderness (118,000 acres), wild forest (155,000 acres), intensive use (5,265 acres), administrative (816 acres), and conservation easements (514 acres). The four wilderness areas in the Catskill Park are:

- Slide Mountain (47,500 acres);
- Big Indian (33,500 acres);
- West Kill Mountain (20,000 acres); and
- Indian Head (16,800 acres).

A final note on the Catskills: The region supplies New York City with much of its water. The city owns significant land in the region to protect its water supply and will be buying significantly more land in the next few decades.[9]

Outside of the Adirondack and Catskill parks, New York owns an additional 1.2 million acres of conservation land in reforestation and multiple use areas (state forests), state parks, wildlife management areas (WMA), and numerous other categories. New York began acquiring abandoned and submarginal farmland for state forests in the late 1920s. The chief management goals of these state forests were to provide wildlife habitat and to support commercial forestry, and they are now managed for multiple use. These state forests total over 680,000 acres, all of which are in parcels smaller than 10,000 acres. Some contiguous areas exceed this acreage, however. The most significant parcels of public lands outside the Adirondack and Catskill parks include:

- Allegany State Park (nearly 65,000 acres adjacent to the Allegheny National Forest in Pennsylvania);
- Harriman and Bear Mountain State Parks (nearly 52,000 acres);
- Frank Jadwin State Forests (over 20,000 acres);
- Brasher State Forests (19,500 acres);
- Sterling Forest State Park (over 15,000 acres);
- Letchworth State Park (over 14,000 acres);
- New Michigan State Forests (nearly 14,000 acres);
- Tug Hill State Forests (over 13,000 acres);
- Lesser Wilderness State Forests (nearly 13,000 acres);
- Eminence State Forests (over 12,000 acres);
- Clarence Fahnestock State Park (over 12,000 acres);
- Minnewaska State Park (nearly 12,000 acres);
- Mongaup Valley WMA (nearly 12,000 acres);
- Deer River State Forests (over 11,000 acres);
- state forest lands in Oneida County (over 11,000 acres);
- Connecticut Hill WMA (over 11,000 acres); and
- Masonville State Forests (11,000 acres).

The Appalachian Trail runs through the Harriman-Bear Mountain and Fahnestock State Parks.[10]

Federal acreage in New York, less than 70,000 acres, is located in a small national forest, ten wildlife refuges (including Iroquois, with nearly 11,000 acres), Fire Island National Seashore (with a 1,363-acre wilderness area), Gateway National Recreation Area (over 20,000 acres in a number of parcels in New York and New Jersey in the greater New York City area), and along the Appalachian Trail corridor. The Finger Lakes National Forest covers over 13,000 acres near Ithaca. The land was originally acquired under a New Deal program to rehabilitate and retire marginal farmland, and managed as the Hector Land Use Project. The Reagan administration's proposal to sell some Forest Service holdings included this land. Congress responded by creating the Finger Lakes National Forest in order to prevent the sale of the land.[11]

The protected wilderness and wild forest in the Adirondack and Catskill parks is the wild heart of the Northeast. Indeed, the combined wild lands in these two forest preserves are over twelve times the total acreage of federally designated wilderness in the nine northeastern states. These wild lands are at the elbow of the potential wild lands system of the Northeast, connecting to northern New England to the east and to Pennsylvania and the Appalachians to the south. Furthermore, through the Algonquin to Adirondack (A2A) Connectivity Zone (see chapter 5), these wild lands can connect to the vast wild lands of Canada. It is clear that these protected wild lands in New York are the foundation for wilderness in the Northeast. As we seek to rewild and restore other lands in the region, it is to New York that we must turn for guidance and inspiration.

Pennsylvania

Pennsylvania, like its neighbor to the north, acquired millions of acres of conservation lands over the last century. The state began to purchase land for the same reasons that New York did. By the end of the nineteenth century, millions of acres of forestland had been cut and abandoned, leading to erosion, fires, and poor quality forests for lumber. Much of this cut-over land, especially in the north-central region, was abandoned and forfeited to the state for lack of tax payment. Other land could be acquired cheaply, since it had little value. In 1898, Pennsylvania began to purchase lands and establish state forests to protect the headwaters of the Susquehanna and Delaware rivers. The state also sought to restore the land to productive forests. Today, Pennsylvania's state forests, organized in twenty state forest districts, total nearly 2.1 million acres. The forest districts with the most significant acreage are located in north-central Pennsylvania:

- Sproul (290,000 acres);
- Susquehannock (nearly 262,000 acres);
- Tiadaghton (215,000 acres);

- Elk (199,000 acres);
- Bald Eagle (196,000 acres);
- Moshannon (nearly 186,000 acres);
- Tioga (nearly 163,000 acres)

Other forest districts that include significant acreage include:

- Rothrock (94,500 acres);
- Tuscarora (91,000 acres);
- Michaux (nearly 87,000 acres, as well as connecting to the Appalachian Trail corridor);
- Delaware (over 80,000 acres);
- Buchanan (over 70,000 acres);
- Forbes (nearly 52,000 acres);
- Wyoming (nearly 43,000 acres); and
- Gallitzin (over 18,000 acres).

In addition to this acreage, in many places state forestlands are adjacent to state parks and state game lands, creating even larger blocks of public land.[12]

Pennsylvania has an administrative natural areas and wild areas program for its state forests. The sixty-one natural areas are places "of unique scenic, historic, geologic or ecological value which will be maintained in a natural condition by allowing physical and biological processes to operate, usually without direct human intervention." These natural areas, totaling nearly 70,000 acres, are typically small—only twelve exceed 1,000 acres and four exceed 3,000 acres. The largest is Pine Creek Gorge, with over 12,000 acres. Wild areas hold the promise of wilderness, but reading the description of these areas indicates otherwise. Such areas are defined "as an extensive area which the general public will be permitted to see, use and enjoy for such activities as hiking, hunting, fishing and the pursuit of peace and solitude. No development of a permanent nature will be permitted to retain the undeveloped character of the area." However, within these wild areas, existing roads may remain open and timber harvesting for forest health and wildlife habitat improvements is permitted. Currently, fourteen wild areas cover over 110,000 acres. All but two are less than 10,000 acres in size. Quehanna (48,186 acres) and Martin Hill (11,596 acres) are the largest areas. Two further wild areas are proposed for designation, including one exceeding 30,000 acres.[13]

The state park system, begun in 1893, has expanded to include over one hundred units and totals over 283,000 acres. The largest of these state parks are:

- Pymatuning (over 21,000 acres);
- Ohiopyle (over 19,000 acres);
- Moraine (nearly 17,000 acres);
- Bucktail (over 16,000 acres);
- Hickory Run (over 15,000 acres);
- Laurel Ridge (nearly 15,000 acres); and
- Ricketts Glen (over 13,000 acres).

The state park system also has a natural areas program to protect areas of "unique scenic, geologic or ecological value." Twenty-two such areas in the state parks cover over 12,000 acres. Five areas exceed 1,000 acres; the largest is 2,845 acres.[14]

The state began purchasing game lands in 1920. Today, the Pennsylvania Game Commission administers nearly 1.4 million acres of game lands in 293 unit blocks throughout the state. Thirty-five of these units exceed 10,000 acres in size, eleven exceed 20,000 acres in size, and the three largest exceed 40,000 acres. These thirty-five larger areas are concentrated in the central portions of the state. The areas over 20,000 acres are located in the following counties (some are in multiple counties):

- Bedford (one);
- Blair (two);
- Bradford (one);
- Cambria (one);
- Elk (three);
- Huntington (one);
- Jefferson (two);
- Lycoming (one);
- Monroe (one); and
- Sullivan (one).

The three largest areas are located in Sullivan and Columbia counties (nearly 50,000 acres), Wyoming and Luzerne counties (44,500 acres), and Dauphin, Lebanon, and Schuykill counties (over 44,000 acres).[15]

Federal lands in Pennsylvania, totaling nearly 650,000 acres, are located in the Allegheny National Forest, three wildlife refuges, the Appalachian Trail corridor (over 13,000 acres), the Delaware Water Gap National Recreation Area (33,000 acres), and nearly 50,000 acres of Army Corps of Engineers lands associated with water projects throughout the state. Allegheny National Forest, established in 1923 in north-central Pennsylvania, includes over 742,000 acres in its proclamation boundary. The Forest Service owns over 513,000 acres in the national forest (69 percent). Rights to the substantial crude oil beneath much of the forest, however, are privately owned. The Allegheny has a pittance of designated wilderness, far less than on the other two national forests in the Northeast. Hickory Creek (8,570 acres) and Allegheny Islands (368 acres) were both designated wilderness in the 1984 Pennsylvania Wilderness Act. Another area proposed for wilderness, Tracy Ridge, was folded into the Allegheny National Recreation Area (23,000 acres) instead. There are two protected areas of old growth on the forest: Tionesta Research Natural Area and Tionesta National Scenic Area (over 4,100 acres) and Hearts Content National Scenic Area (122 acres). Furthermore, thousands of acres of state land are within or adjacent to the national forest.[16]

Pennsylvania has the potential to be a center of wilderness in the Northeast. It has more public land than any state in the region (4,397,921 acres) and is second only to New Hampshire in percentage of land in public ownership (15.3 percent). Although fewer than 10,000 acres in the state are protected as wilderness, state wild area and natural area programs total over 190,000 acres. Making some adjustments in these existing programs is a first step toward bringing substantial wilderness to the state. More wilderness also needs to be designated in the Allegheny National Forest. Such wilderness, centered in north-central Pennsylvania, would be an important hub of large wilderness that could be connected to the wilderness of the Catskills and Adirondacks to the north, and to the central Appalachians of Virginia and West Virginia to the south. So, even though today Pennsylvania is the Northeast's most disappointing state in terms of protected wilderness, it is the state that has the most potential for expanding wilderness on lands already owned by the public.

Maine

Maine is a large state by northeastern standards. It is also 90 percent forested, not far below the percent of land covered by forest at the time of European arrival. Furthermore, much of the northern half of the state is uninhabited, and has been home to few permanent residents since the Europeans displaced the Native Americans of the region. These northern woods, however, are far from wild. They are largely owned by multinational forest products corporations and in family management holdings, which have built 25,000 miles of logging roads in the region. This forestland is the basis for the industrial forestry that dominates northern Maine. The active, large-scale industrial forestry and low population density in the north are key explanations for the relatively small amount of public land in Maine (the lowest percentage of any northeastern state). Although a demand exists among the forest products companies for the land, development pressure on the land has, until recently, been limited; and the large private owners have made the land available for recreation (though increasingly for a fee). These factors have combined to reduce the pressure for public acquisition. The federal conservation and natural resource agencies own 172,000 acres. The major units are parts of the White Mountain National Forest (53,000 acres); nine wildlife refuges, the largest being Moosehorn (over 23,000 acres) and Sunkhaze Meadows (over 10,000 acres); Acadia National Park (nearly 46,000 acres); and the Appalachian Trail corridor in Maine (nearly 29,000 acres). State lands in three categories—public reserved lands, state parks, and wildlife management areas—total 717,000 acres.[17]

Baxter State Park is the largest wilderness in the Northeast outside the Adirondacks. The park, covering nearly 205,000 acres, is home to Mount Katahdin, the tallest mountain in Maine and the northern end of the Appalachian Trail. Maine Governor Percival Baxter purchased the land in the park over time, and began donating it to the state in 1931. Baxter gave the land to the state on the condition that it "shall forever be used for public park and recreational purposes, shall forever be left in the natural wild state, shall forever be kept as a sanctuary for wild beasts and birds, and that no roads or ways for motor vehicles shall hereafter ever be constructed thereon or therein." Baxter changed several of these provisions as he made numerous gifts to Maine for the park over the next thirty years, but he never changed the "forever wild" provision. Not all of the land is wilderness, though. In 1955, Baxter designated nearly 30,000 acres as the Scientific Forest Management Area, to be used for demonstration forestry. Hunting and trapping are allowed in this area, as well as in two parcels elsewhere in the park totaling 23,000 acres. Other wilderness exceptions are the few roads in the park, snowmobile use on parts of those roads and on three lakes bisected by the park border, and motor use on two of those lakes and on two small ponds on the park's southern border. Some controversies have arisen over what management techniques are appropriate in responding to predators, blowdowns, fire, insects, and disease in park forests. Adjacent to the park is the Scraggly Lake unit of public reserved lands (9,000 acres).[18]

The Allagash Wilderness Waterway, in northern Maine, was created by the state legislature in 1964 and added to the National Wild and Scenic River system after it was established in 1968. The nearly 23,000 acres of land adjacent to the river connect with public reserved land along the river's route, including Chamberlain Lake (nearly 10,000 acres), Round Pond (over 20,000 acres), and Telos Lake (nearly 23,000 acres), and almost connect with Baxter State Park in the south. Despite the "wilderness" in its name, the Allagash Wilderness Waterway includes dams on the river, is crossed by logging roads, is used by snowmobiles in the winter, and allows small motors to be used on canoes. Its protective land corridor is narrow, augmented by regulations in a half-mile corridor on each side of the river. Beyond this beauty strip, full-scale industrial forestry is at work.[19]

Other state land holdings exceeding 10,000 acres include fourteen public reserved land sites:

- Nanmakanta (nearly 43,000 acres);
- Bigelow Preserve (35,000 acres);
- Mahoosucs (over 27,000 acres);
- Duck Lake (over 25,000 acres);
- Eagle Lake (nearly 24,000 acres);
- Debouille (nearly 22,000 acres);
- Holeb (nearly 20,000 acres);
- Richardson (nearly 18,000 acres);
- Squa Pan (nearly 18,000 acres);
- Little Squaw (15,000 acres);
- Donnell Pond (over 14,000 acres);
- Seboeis (nearly 13,000 acres);
- Moosehead Lake (over 11,000 acres); and
- Rocky Lake (nearly 11,000 acres);

The Bigelow Preserve, Mahoosucs (with adjoining Grafton Notch State Park), and Nanmakanta connect with the Appalachian Trail corridor.[20]

Federal wilderness in Maine totals less than 20,000 acres. The Caribou–Speckled Mountain wilderness (12,000 acres) in the White Mountain National Forest was established in 1990 by the Maine Wilderness Act. The other wilderness consists of two units in the Moosehorn National Wildlife Refuge (7,392 acres). At the state level, most of Baxter State Park is managed as wilderness (176,139 acres, minus park roads and campgrounds). The main road divides the park wilderness into areas of roughly 120,000 acres and 55,000 acres. Although some snowmobile use of park roads is allowed, as well as some motorboat use on a few designated lakes and ponds, most wilderness in Baxter is protected to the same degree as designated wilderness in national parks (e.g., no pets and no hunting). Maine also has two remote, roadless recreation areas on its public reserved lands, totaling roughly 13,000 acres, that approximate federal wilderness areas.[21]

Maine is so important for wilderness in the Northeast not so much because of the potential for wilderness on its public lands, but rather because of the potential for public acquisition of vast amounts of private land that could become wilderness. The most concrete proposal is for the Maine Woods National Park and Preserve, 3.2 million acres surrounding Baxter State Park. Other areas highlighted for protection by the Northern Forest Alliance include the Androscoggin Headwaters (in Maine and New Hampshire), the Western Mountains, the Upper St. John River Valley, and the Down East Lakes. In their 1989 inventory of roadless wild areas in the United States, Dave Foreman and Howie Wolke describe ten roadless areas in Maine greater than 50,000 acres in size, only three of which include any significant public lands. In contrast, approximately 90 percent of the thirteen areas they identified in New York are publicly owned. A final comprehensive proposal for wild lands in northern Maine, northern New Hampshire, and northern Vermont is the 8-million-acre Headwaters Wilderness Reserve proposal. Millions of acres have been changing hands throughout the region over the last ten years, making the acquisition of large parcels of public land a real possibility (see chapter 6). Some recent purchases in Maine include the Maine Nature Conservancy's purchase of 185,000 acres in the Upper St. John River area in 1998. More land must be purchased, and significant land purchases must be designated wilderness. Northern Maine has the potential to be a core of wildness in the Northeast matched only by the Adirondacks.[22]

New Hampshire

Unlike the other northeastern states, New Hampshire has more federal lands than state lands. It has the highest level of federal ownership of any northeastern state, indeed, the highest of any state east of the Rocky Mountains (over 13 percent). This federal land is comprised largely of the White Mountain National Forest (nearly 725,000 acres in New Hampshire, with an additional 50,000 plus acres in Maine), one of the first national forests established in the eastern United States. Other significant federal ownership is in the Appalachian Trail corridor, in four wildlife refuges, and at several Army Corps of Engineers facilities. The state owns relatively little public land, slightly over 3 percent of the state, the lowest level among the northeastern states.

The White Mountain National Forest (WMNF) includes 908,000 acres within its proclamation and purchase unit boundaries (in New Hampshire and Maine). Unlike most national forests outside the West, the federal government owns the vast majority of the land within these boundaries (85 percent). Furthermore, six state parks and several small state forests totaling 20,000 acres are within or adjoin the WMNF, further increasing the level of public ownership in the area. The four federal wilderness areas total over 100,000 acres in the WMNF, giving New Hampshire over half of the federal wilderness in the Northeast, including the three largest federal wilderness areas in the region. The Forest Service managed the Great Gulf Wilderness (5,552 acres) as a primitive area when the Wilderness Act passed in 1964. Under the provisions of the law, the area was soon reclassified as a wilderness area. The Eastern Wilderness Act established the Presidential Range–Dry River Wilderness (27,380 acres including a 1984 addition). The two remaining areas, Pemigewasset (45,000 acres) and Sandwich Range (25,000 acres), were made wilderness in 1984 in the New Hampshire Wilderness Act. This designation of 77,000 acres of additional wilderness was significantly below the Forest Service's own recommendation of an additional 163,000 acres of wilderness in New Hampshire (from over 260,000 roadless acres studied).[23]

New Hampshire has a well-deserved reputation for being a fiscally conservative state. It has no income or sales tax. This lack of tax revenue means that the state has limited resources for any government program, including public land acquisition. The demand for state-owned lands is also lessened somewhat by the larger federal presence in the state. Total ownership in state forests, state parks, and wildlife management areas is less than 190,000 acres. Only three areas exceed 10,000 acres in size: Nash Stream Forest (nearly 40,000 acres), Pisgah State Park (over 13,000 acres), and Bear Brook State Park (over 10,000 acres). The Mount Sunapee and Pillsbury State Parks total nearly 8,500 acres and are connected by a 2,500-acre conservation easement held by the state. The U.S. Fish and Wildlife Service and state of New Hampshire own nearly 10,000 acres of land on Lake Umbagog on the Maine border. New Hampshire also has a natural areas program with forty-four areas totaling nearly 19,000 acres. Over 13,000 acres of these lands are in the Nash Stream Forest, covering one-third of the forest.[24]

The most likely place for future wild lands protection in New Hampshire is further wilderness designation in the White Mountain National Forest and the protection of private lands to its north. Foreman and Wolke identify four roadless areas over 50,000 acres in the state that are

unprotected, as well as substantial possibilities to expand the Pemigewasset and Sandwich Range wilderness areas. More recently, in October 1999,
a coalition of the Appalachian Mountain Club, Conservation Law Foundation, and Wilderness Society released a report calling for the protection
of a total of 500,000 acres of roadless lands in the White Mountain National Forest (including already designated wilderness). The existing concentration of public lands in northern New Hampshire, as well as 100,000
acres of designated wilderness and the potential for more wild lands, make
this area one of four existing wilderness nodes in the Northeast (along
with the Adirondacks, Catskills, and Baxter State Park). The area will serve
as an anchor for wild lands recovery, and emphasis must be placed on
expanding this wild node as well as on connecting it to wild lands to the
east and west.[25]

Vermont

Like much of the Northeast, the natural landscape in Vermont is in far
better shape today than it was one hundred years ago. Then, substantial
reforestation was just beginning as much of the farmland throughout the
state was being abandoned. Since 1900, forestland in the state has nearly
doubled to cover three-quarters of Vermont. Moreover, significant conservation programs began in the late 1800s. These programs have succeeded to the point that nearly 20 percent of Vermont land is conserved,
with public ownership approaching 12 percent of the state. Federal lands
total over 375,000 acres; state lands are nearly 310,000 acres. Municipal-
ities own over 40,000 acres and private conservation groups own over
55,000 acres. An additional 200,000-plus acres are conserved through
easements. Despite these successes, though, there are still fewer acres of
public lands in Vermont than in New Jersey.[26]

The Green Mountain National Forest (GMNF), established in 1932,
was the last of the northeastern national forests to be created. The proclamation boundaries at first included only 102,000 acres in southern
Vermont. These boundaries would grow over time to 815,000 acres, covering the Green Mountains from the Massachusetts border to the central part of the state and, as of 1990, the southern portion of the Taconic
Mountains in Vermont. The national forest now encompasses 358,000
acres (44 percent of the land within the proclamation boundaries).
Four state WMAs and one state forest directly abut the GMNF, creating
larger public ownership blocks. Six wilderness areas in the GMNF total

nearly 60,000 acres. The Bristol Cliffs (3,738 acres) and Lye Brook Wilderness Areas (15,503 acres, including its 1983 expansion) were established by the Eastern Wilderness Act. Despite Forest Service opposition to any further wilderness in the GMNF, the Vermont Wilderness Act in 1984 created four new wilderness areas and expanded Lye Brook. The new wilderness areas were Big Branch (6,720 acres), Bread Loaf (21,480 acres), George Aiken (5,060 acres), and Peru Peak (6,920 acres). The law also created the 36,400-acre White Rocks National Recreation Area, which includes the Big Branch and Peru Peak wilderness areas. Potential exists for additional wilderness in the GMNF, and wilderness activists are currently preparing a new proposal for the GMNF. Other significant federal land holdings in Vermont include the Missisquoi National Wildlife Refuge (over 6,000 acres) and the Appalachian Trail corridor (over 11,000 acres, which is connected to the Long Trail State Forest, nearly 9,000 acres).[27]

State conservation lands are classified primarily as state forests, state parks, and wildlife management areas. The state forest system, begun in 1909, was originally designed to protect water sources, raise quality timber, and provide examples of quality forest practices. In the 1930s, 1940s, and 1950s, state forest lands became home to downhill ski areas in the state (such as Bromley, Burke Mountain, Jay Peak, Killington, and Okemo). Indeed, state forest land was purchased specifically to found Jay Peak and Killington ski areas. The state forest system continued to grow, reaching thirty-eight units covering over 162,000 acres in 1999. The state park system began in 1924. These parks are primarily small (under 1,000 acres), and are developed for intensive recreation. The fifty-six state parks cover more than 45,000 acres. The eighty wildlife management areas throughout the state total over 95,000 acres. The major state land holdings are:

- Mount Mansfield State Forest (approximately 40,000 acres, including three state parks within the state forest);
- Camel's Hump State Park and State Forest and two adjacent WMAs (roughly 34,000 acres directly north of the GMNF);
- Coolidge State Forest and two adjoining WMAs (over 31,000 acres), which nearly adjoin the GMNF in central Vermont;
- Groton State Forest (approximately 26,000 acres);
- C. C. Putnam State Forest (over 14,000 acres in the Worcester range, across the valley from Mount Mansfield State Forest); and
- three areas in the largely undeveloped Northeast Kingdom: the Bill Sladyk WMA (10,000 acres), the Steam Mill Brook WMA (over

10,000 acres), and Victory State Forest and Victory Basin WMA (21,000 acres).

The Sladyk WMA and Victory Basin State Forest/WMA are adjacent to the recently completed Champion International land deal discussed below.[28]

Although Vermont does not have a wild lands program for its state lands, it does have a natural areas program. These lands, classified as natural areas by the state, meet at least one of three criteria: the lands "(1) have retained their wilderness character, although not necessarily completely natural and undisturbed; (2) may have rare or vanishing species of plant or animal life or similar features of interest which are worthy of preservation for the use of present and future residents of the State; (3) may include unique ecological, geological, scenic and contemplative recreation areas." Currently there are thirty-three natural areas totaling over 18,000 acres in the state. The vast majority are less than 100 acres in size. Three are over 1,000 acres: Camel's Hump (7,404 acres), Worcester Range (4,032 acres), and Mount Mansfield (3,850 acres). Although the current natural areas program is far from adequate to protect state wild lands, it may serve as a useful starting point until a more appropriate law is passed.[29]

In *The Big Outside*, Foreman and Wolke identify one roadless location in Vermont of 50,000 private acres in the Northeast Kingdom, centered on Meachum Swamp. Much of the area was part of the recent Champion land sale. In this sale, announced in late 1998 and closed in 1999, Champion International sold approximately 300,000 acres of forestland in New York, Vermont, and New Hampshire to a coalition of conservation groups and government agencies. The Vermont portion of the sale included roughly 132,000 acres, with 48,000 acres to become public land. The remaining acreage was resold for private forestry with attached easements (including a "forever logging" provision that prevents these lands from being designated in the future as wild lands). The U.S. Fish and Wildlife Service will acquire 26,000 acres as part of the Conte Fish and Wildlife Refuge, with state conservation agencies to own 22,000 acres. Unfortunately, none of this land will be protected as wild lands. Given the lack of wild lands in the Northeast, and the lack of large public acquisitions like this one, this was an unfortunate missed opportunity for the advancement of wilderness in the region. The future for wild lands in Vermont, as in most of the Northeast, requires more public lands acquisition, increased connectivity of those lands, passage of a state wild lands law, and the designation of more federal lands as wilderness.[30]

Massachusetts

Although Massachusetts is densely populated (third ranked) and small (seventh smallest), it is a state with a strong conservation ethic. Nearly one million acres of Massachusetts—19 percent—is permanently protected. The state owns nearly 535,000 acres and federal conservation agencies over 65,000 acres. Only one federal wilderness has been designated in the state, however, less than 2,500 acres in the Monomoy National Wildlife Refuge, an island off the coast of Cape Cod. The other federal land is contained in the Cape Cod National Seashore, the Appalachian Trail corridor, nine national wildlife refuges, and a number of national historic sites. State ownership is concentrated in western and central sections. In these areas, significant potential exists to connect to the Green Mountain National Forest to the north, and to other state lands in Connecticut, New Hampshire, and New York.[31]

State conservation ownership began in 1898 with the establishment of the Mount Greylock Reservation around Massachusetts's tallest mountain. The state forest system began sixteen years later. Over the next one hundred years, over one-half million acres of land has been acquired by the state. The largest parcels in the Taconic Mountains and Berkshire Hills of western Massachusetts are:

- Mohawk Trail-Savoy Mountain-Dubuque Memorial State Forests (over 25,000 acres);
- October Mountain State Forest (over 16,000 acres);
- Mount Greylock State Reservation (12,500 acres);
- Beartown State Forest (nearly 11,000 acres);
- Pittsfield State Forest (10,000 acres); and
- Tolland State Forest (nearly 10,000 acres).

In central Massachusetts, the largest public lands are the Quabbin Reservoir (56,000 acres of land and 25,000 acres of water), the Erving-Wendell State Forests (over 14,000 acres), and the Otter River State Forest (nearly 13,000 acres). In the eastern part of the state are Cape Cod National Seashore (nearly 43,000 acres of federal and state land) and Myles Standish State Forest (nearly 15,000 acres), both surrounded by heavily developed land. Massachusetts also has nature preserve and wild lands programs on its state lands. The wild lands program is an administrative classification on state forest and state park lands. It includes backcountry areas, primarily for primitive recreation, and a representative natural areas program. The backcountry areas total roughly 6,000 acres, mostly in the 1,000-to 1,500-acre range. The representative natural areas are smaller and more numerous. The newer nature preserve program only has one area at present, slightly over 200 acres.[32]

Overall, 40 to 50 percent of the Taconic Mountains, Berkshire Hills, and Worcester Plateau are protected, through either public ownership or conservation easements. It is in these areas that the greatest potential for wild lands in Massachusetts exists. The largest area, the Quabbin Reservoir, supplies water to Boston and other cities and towns in eastern Massachusetts. Acquisition of farmland and forestland in the Swift River Valley began in the 1910s and 1920s, and the last residents of the area moved out in 1928. Since the reservoir filled, the land surrounding it has been managed by the Metropolitan District Commission (MDC) to ensure water quality. The MDC has focused on controlling public access, and despite some timber cutting on the land, the area has substantially rewilded. It is home to deer (far too many), moose, beaver, coyote, bobcat, fisher, and bald eagle, among other species. Hence, this land is ripe for wild lands protection. Management activities inimical to wilderness are timber management, fire control, and the lack of predators to control the overpopulation of deer (now controlled to some degree by hunting). The second-largest block of public—and undeveloped—land in the state is the Mohawk Trail State Forest complex. This could serve as the foundation for a string of connected public land holdings in the western part of the state. These lands in the less-intensively developed part of Massachusetts could more quickly be connected to larger regionwide wild lands in Vermont, New York, and New Hampshire. Crucial to any protected wild lands in Massachusetts, however, is convincing the citizens of the state to enact a state wild lands statute in order to protect these large parcels of public lands for restoration and rewilding.[33]

New Jersey

New Jersey is not a place that brings wild lands to mind to most people. Indeed, as the most densely populated state in the country, New Jersey seems to be far removed from wilderness. Nevertheless, two federal wilderness areas have been designated in the state, and two parts of New Jersey exist where there is significant public ownership and the potential for significant rewilding and wild lands recovery. The Pine Barrens, in the southern half of the state, cover nearly one-quarter of New Jersey, over 1 million acres. This is the largest open space between Boston and Richmond along the East coast. The bulk of these lands are in the 1.1 million-acre Pinelands National Reserve, established in 1978. This reserve is a joint federal-state-local regional greenline planning scheme, including a core preservation area of 368,000 acres, a "semiwilderness preservation area" where little new development is allowed, and an outer protection area of 566,000 acres where more development is allowed. Private land uses in these areas of the Pinelands Reserve are regulated by the state Pinelands Commission, based on a comprehensive management plan adopted in 1980. The remaining land in the national reserve is in the coastal zone, beyond the authority of the Pinelands Commission. The primary role of the federal government is to provide funding for land acquisition.[34]

The rationale for the Pinelands National Reserve, however, was not to protect wilderness. It was to protect open space and to control development, as well as to maintain some relatively intact natural landscapes. People live throughout the reserve, although significant tracts of public lands are uninhabited and other parts of the Pinelands are sparsely settled. Most of the area is less developed than it was a century ago. The Pine Barrens is home to nearly six hundred native species of plants, roughly 70 percent of which are rare, endangered, or threatened. An abundance of animal species live in the Pine Barrens, many at their northern or southern limits. There are almost three hundred species of birds, nearly one hundred of fish, fifty-nine reptiles and amphibians, and a rich variety of insects. Although bear and bobcat are no longer present in the Pine Barrens, they were once common to the region. Many other mammals, including beavers and otters, are present. Unlike most of the Northeast, fire is the main agent of natural disturbance in the pinelands.[35]

Over one-third of the Pinelands National Reserve, nearly 400,000 acres, is in public conservation ownership. The two units of the Forsythe National Wildlife Refuge total over 40,000 acres. Most of the public lands are owned by the state, which undertook significant public land purchases during the 1980s and 1990s. The comprehensive management plan recommended that the state buy 100,000 additional acres in the reserve; by 1990, it had purchased nearly 80,000 acres. The largest units include:

- Wharton State Forest (over 110,000 acres);
- Lebanon State Forest (over 34,000 acres);
- Bass River State Forest (over 25,000 acres);
- Greenwood Forest WMA (nearly 25,000 acres);

- Peaslee WMA (over 22,000 acres);
- Stafford Forge WMA (over 17,000 acres);
- Belleplain State Forest (over 15,000 acres);
- Tuckahoe WMA (nearly 14,000 acres); and
- Colliers Mills WMA (over 12,000 acres).

The only designated wilderness in the Pinelands is the 6,681 acres in the southern unit of the Forsythe National Wildlife Refuge. In 1985, the Sierra Club proposed a 67,000-acre wilderness in the core of the reserve, but nothing came of this proposal. Even if significant wilderness were established in the Pinelands National Reserve, it would be isolated wilderness for the near term. The area is bordered to the north and west by the intensively developed New York–Philadelphia corridor.[36]

The other major area of potential wild lands in New Jersey is in the northwest of the state, referred to as the Highlands or Skylands. There are significant state and federal land holdings in the area, most of them connected or adjacent to the Appalachian Trail. Major public lands in the area include:

- Stokes State Forest (nearly 18,000 acres);
- High Point State Park (over 14,000 acres);
- Wawayanda State Park (over 13,000 acres); and
- Delaware Water Gap National Recreation Area (36,000 acres).

These areas can be connected with other public lands in New York and Pennsylvania over time.[37]

Public conservation lands in New Jersey total 700,000 acres. The great bulk are owned by the state, over 600,000 acres, the third-largest percentage of conservation lands owned by a state in the Northeast. Outside of the Pinelands National Reserve and the New Jersey Highlands, two areas are over 10,000 acres in size: Cape May Wetlands WMA (over 12,000 acres) and Millville (Bevan) WMA (over 12,000 acres). The state also has a natural areas system that includes forty-two sites totaling over 38,000 acres. Thirteen of the areas exceed 1,000 acres. The two largest are Batsto (9,500 acres) and West Pine Plains (3,800 acres), both in the Pinelands. Other federal holdings include four additional national wildlife refuges, including Great Swamp National Wildlife Refuge, which contains the nation's first wilderness designated in a wildlife refuge (3,660 acres). In sum, despite its reputation, New Jersey has done an admirable job in acquiring public conservation land. Although the state lacks any significant wild lands at present, the Pinelands and Highlands hold significant promise for rewilding.[38]

Connecticut

A number of indicators suggest that Connecticut has neither much wild land nor much hope for significant rewilding in the short run. It is the fourth-most densely populated state; it is the third-smallest state geographically; it has a little over 12,000 acres of federal conservation land; and it is one of six states that has no federally designated wilderness. State conservation lands total nearly 210,000 acres in state forests, state parks, and wildlife management areas. Only a few of these are of any significant size: the Pachaug State Forest (nearly 23,000 acres), the Cockaponset State Forest (over 15,000 acres), the Natchaug and Goodwin State Forests (nearly 15,000 acres), the Tunxis State Forest (over 11,000 acres with the adjoining Granville State Forest in Massachusetts), and the Housatonic State Forest (over 10,000 acres). Connecticut also has a small natural areas program, with fifteen sites totaling less than 6,000 acres. These five largest state forests are scattered across the state, surrounded by relatively developed lands. Even these large holdings are far from wild. No place in the Pachaug State Forest, for example, is even a mile from a road. Connecticut holds some potential, however. The Housatonic State Forest, in the northwest corner of the state, could eventually connect to public lands in the Taconic Mountains of New York and Massachusetts, as well as to the Berkshire Hills to the north. The Pachaug State Forest abuts the largest public land holding in Rhode Island. Nevertheless, it is unlikely that the Connecticut landscape will be a significant part of rewilding in the Northeast until major changes occur in our current social and economic systems.[39]

Rhode Island

Rhode Island is a smaller version of Connecticut when it comes to wild lands. It is the second-most densely populated state; it is the smallest state geographically; it has less than 2,000 acres of federal conservation land; and it joins Connecticut among the six states with no federally designated wilderness. Although roughly 9 percent of the state is in public ownership, the parcels are all relatively small. Only the Arcadia complex of a one state forest, three state parks, and two management areas totals over 5,000 acres (the complex is over 14,000 acres). This is adjacent to the Pachaug State Forest in Connecticut, creating an area with public lands totaling over

35,000 acres. Numerous small protected areas, such as those on Block Island, are rich in biological diversity, but these places hardly qualify as wild lands. Indeed, no dry land in the state is even a mile from a road. As with its neighbor to the west, the return of significant wild lands to Rhode Island will require major societal changes.[40]

Conclusion

Despite the common conception of the Northeast as entirely developed, an urban and suburban wasteland as far as wild lands is concerned, significant wild lands exist in the region with the potential for substantial rewilding and restoration. This potential is in the hinterlands of the region. The seaboard from southwestern Maine to Philadelphia and beyond is almost entirely developed, except for the Pinelands of New Jersey. But in an arc from northern New England, through the Adirondacks and Catskills, and down through central Pennsylvania, the chance for large, connected, genuine wilderness is real. Such wilderness will be based on existing pubic lands in the Northeast. As this survey indicates, despite the limited federal conservation lands in the region (2.1 percent), state conservation lands total 10 percent of the region. In every state except Connecticut, Maine, and Rhode Island, total federal and state conservation lands exceed 10 percent. Furthering wilderness in the Northeast requires work on three main fronts.

1. **The federal and state governments need to acquire more land.** Although New Hampshire, New York, and Pennsylvania have significant amounts of land concentrated in particular places, each state needs far more conservation land. Land acquisition requires funds. There are a variety of options: federal funding through direct appropriations, a revitalized Land and Water Conservation Fund, or special initiatives (e.g., the Clinton administration's Lands Legacy Initiative and the Conte National Wildlife Refuge, which plans to protect nearly 80,000 acres of land in the Connecticut River watershed); state funding through bonds, appropriations, and special initiatives (e.g., New Jersey's ten year, $1 billion program to protect 1 million acres of land, Maine's recently passed $75 million fund for land acquisition, and Vermont's Housing and Conservation Fund); nonprofit groups (e.g., the Nature Conservancy, the Society for the Protection of New Hampshire Forests, and the Vermont Land Trust); and private philanthropy. Given the large population and relative wealth of these states, gener-

ating the necessary resources for such acquisition may not be as daunting as it seems at first glance.

2. **We need to develop a regional strategy for land acquisition and protection**. The keys to such a strategy include protecting representative ecological communities, protecting large core reserves where natural processes can largely determine the landscape, creating corridors to connect large protected areas, and focusing the use of easements on areas adjacent to ecological reserves or ecologically sensitive areas where these managed farmlands and forestlands can serve as effective buffer zones. A number of entities are working on plans for protecting lands and creating corridors. Among the most significant are the Northern Forest Alliance's 1997 Wildlands proposal, identifying ten wild areas in New York, Vermont, New Hampshire, and Maine for acquisition and protection; the efforts of the Greater Laurentian Region Wildlands Project; work by conservation groups such as the Nature Conservancy; and numerous state biodiversity or ecological reserve initiatives (see chapter 5).[41]

A major problem with the location of current protected lands is that they are focused in the high elevations. This is analogous to the "rocks and ice" criticism of much of the designated federal wilderness in the West; that is, wilderness is designated primarily in the high elevations of mountain ranges. These lands are very scenic and often outstanding for human recreation; they also are less likely to be in demand for commodity production. Such land, however, is not as important for biodiversity as lower-elevation lands. In the Northeast, given the lower elevations of the mountains, this is not a "rocks and ice" problem, but the issue is essentially the same. A recent study of land protection in the Berkshires in Massachusetts clearly illustrates this: 100 percent of the land above 3,500 feet is protected, 75 percent of land above 3,000 feet is protected, 61 percent of land above 2,500 feet is protected, 44 percent of land above 2,000 feet is protected, 23 percent of land above 1,500 feet is protected, and 15 percent of land above 1,000 feet is protected. Another example is the natural areas system on Vermont public lands. Over 80 percent of the land in this system is in three mountain units—Camel's Hump, Mount Mansfield, and the Worcester Range. The latter natural area consists of all state lands above 2,500 feet.[42]

3. **We need to change how existing public lands are managed**. Currently, public lands in the Northeast are managed primarily for recreation, hunting and fishing, and timber production. The amount of

active management varies from unit to unit, with the most intensive recreation taking place on smaller state parks, the most intensive wildlife management on fish and game lands, and the most active timber management on state forests. We should focus on moving these lands away from a multiple-use focus toward wild lands recovery and the establishment of ecological reserves, especially on the larger parcels over 10,000 acres. Such wild lands will remain open to hunting and fishing in almost all cases, as does federal wilderness. Wild lands advocates should work closely with the hunting and fishing community to increase wild lands protection on these game lands. Given the relatively small amount of public forest land in the Northeast compared to the West, these lands are not major suppliers of forest products. Hence, a move away from timber management on these lands will produce minimal economic problems. Indeed, by reducing the supply somewhat, private landowners may receive increased stumpage for their trees. At the same time, wild lands advocates must support those working to advance ecologically sustainable forestry on private lands (see chapter 10). In order to speed this transition on state lands, we need to establish state wilderness programs. At least eight states have statutory or administrative wilderness programs, but, as discussed above, New York is the only northeastern state with such a program. Administrative programs in Maine and Massachusetts, as well as the large wild lands program in Pennsylvania, are logical starting places in those states. Furthermore, the natural areas programs found in almost all the states are also building blocks for wilderness.[43]

It is clear that the Northeast will not have a wilderness system like the one in place in the western United States for hundreds of years, if ever. One main reason is that the federal government owns very little land in the Northeast. Nonetheless, federal public lands and, even more importantly, state public lands must serve as the wilderness cores in this region. Through purchasing additional lands, designating more federal lands as wilderness, and establishing wilderness on state land holdings, public lands in the Northeast can serve this purpose. In several states, most notably New York, large-scale wilderness is already protected. We have a long way to go, however, and the sooner we can protect more wilderness, the sooner a significantly wild Northeast will return.

Part II

DESIGNING A NORTHEASTERN SYSTEM OF WILD LANDS

CHAPTER 5

Ecological Reserve Design in the Northeast

STEPHEN C. TROMBULAK

CONSERVATION BIOLOGISTS GENERALLY recognize four operational goals as necessary for the protection and restoration of life on Earth. These are (1) representation of all natural communities across their full range of successional stages; (2) representation of viable populations (i.e., able to persist on their own without active human intervention) of all native species; (3) the operation of natural ecological and evolutionary processes with their natural range of frequency and magnitude; and (4) responsiveness to change.[1] All conservation strategies and initiatives focus—or ought to focus—on achieving one or more of these four goals. Taken together, these goals encompass all of the levels of the biological hierarchy: genes (through an emphasis on *viable* populations, since viability is associated with genetic diversity), species, and communities. Further, these goals encompass all three dimensions of biological organization: composition, function, and structure. The composition of biological communities is incorporated by the focus on all natural community types and species, structure by the focus on the full range of successional stages, and function by the focus on processes and adaptability. These dimensions and levels combine to form the full scope of biological integrity, which can be defined as the ability to support and maintain a balanced, integrated, adaptive assemblage of organisms having a species composition, diversity, and functional organization comparable to that of natural habitat of the region.[2]

A growing consensus among conservationists is that one of the most important tools to achieve these goals and to protect and restore biological integrity is the development of a system of ecological reserves within entire regions, and functionally linked to systems in other regions across the continent. Such a system of reserves is broadly characterized as a set of core areas, in which human modification of the landscape is minimal and the primary purpose of management is to protect or restore natural communities, populations, and processes, and which are buffered from human influences that initiate in surrounding areas and ecologically connected to each other to allow for movement of individuals and populations over time. These three components — core areas, buffer zones, and connectivity zones — each offer different benefits that promote the larger goal (see graph 5.1).

Core areas provide two important benefits that cannot be provided by any other form of land management.[3] First, they allow for the persistence of species and ecosystems that cannot persist in the human sphere of influence, and ecological and evolutionary processes that either cannot operate in the face of or are dramatically altered by human disturbance. Among the species that require core areas are those that are especially vulnerable to human disturbance, such as large carnivores; species whose reproductive success is easily disrupted; and species that compete with humans for food or space. Ecosystems that are considered to have little economic value, such as wetlands, also depend on core areas for protection. Processes that are dramatically altered by humans include natural disturbances (such as fire and floods), nutrient cycling, and natural selection. Not all species, ecosystems, and processes require core areas, of course, but without core areas the many that do will be lost.

The second benefit of core areas is that they serve as baselines to help us understand the impacts of our management practices. Core areas are places where nature can operate in its own way in its own time. Many of the natural resource management policies that are practiced today, such as ecosystem management, are intended to mimic natural processes or to be compatible with protection of biodiversity. Ultimately, whether these policies achieve their goals can only be truthfully determined by comparison to areas that are *not* manipulated. Core areas serve both as controls in large-scale experiments in natural resource management and as hedges against our ignorance of how nature can be "managed."

Buffer zones provide similar ecological values as core areas while also allowing for a greater degree of human modification of the landscape to achieve social goals. Thus, buffer zones provide for species and processes that are less sensitive to human disturbance than those that depend on core areas, yet still require some degree of protection from complete habitat destruction. Also, as the name implies, buffer zones serve to moderate the influences exerted on core areas by surrounding human landscapes. Many stresses caused by human actions, such as air pollution and poach-

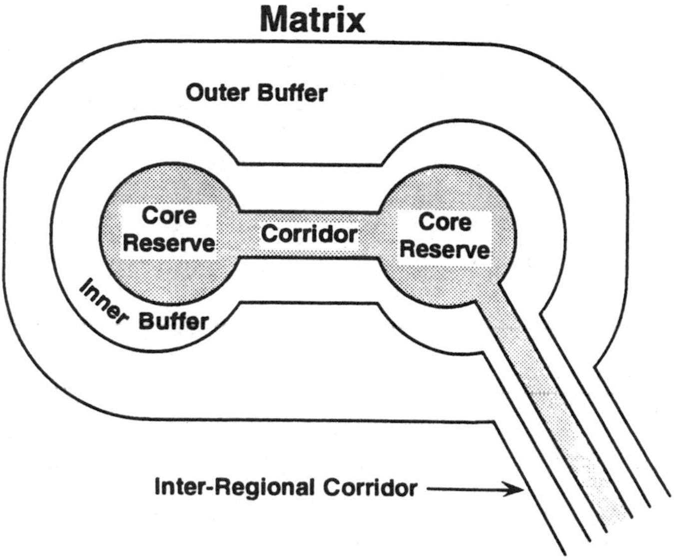

Matrix

Graph 5.1. Ecological Reserve Design. *Reprinted with permission of Reed Noss and Wild Earth magazine.*

ing, do not respect distinct boundaries. Buffer zones provide an extra level of protection for core areas.[4]

Connectivity zones, sometimes referred to as corridors, allow for the movement of individual organisms across a landscape, especially among core areas. Movement of individuals is important for three reasons. It allows for the exchange of genetic material within a population, preventing inbreeding and the subsequent loss of evolutionary fitness. It allows for larger effective populations, making the extirpation of a population by chance events less likely. It also allows for populations to move over time in response to changing environmental conditions; an example would be the latitudinal movements of tree populations in response to climate change.[5]

The system of reserves made up of these three components is implicitly embedded within a larger matrix of land that includes areas that are designated to serve different social and conservation goals than do reserves. These lands would include stewardship lands—such as timberlands and agricultural lands—where growth and harvest of biological resources would be promoted using management principles that provide for sustainability, as well as intensive-use lands, where more intensive human uses of the land would dominate.

An ecological reserve system is not the *only* tool for conservation. Conservation goals are also achieved by protecting individual species (such as by hunting regulations or endangered species laws), promoting sound stewardship of forestland and farmland, and implementing environmental education, for example. But a system of ecological reserves is a necessary part of our overall conservation strategy. Ecological reserves alone will not be sufficient to achieve our goals, but an overall strategy that does not include a system of ecological reserves cannot succeed.

To make its greatest contributions to conservation, ecological reserve systems need to have the following characteristics:

- At least some of the core areas in the system need to be large. This promotes populations of wide-ranging mammals, large-scale natural disturbance regimes, and suites of natural communities that together are necessary for species with complex habitat requirements.
- All of the core areas need to be subject to little if any human disturbance. This promotes the persistence of species that do not fare well under the human sphere of influence and permits the occurrence of ecological processes that are prevented or dampened by cultural influences. Protection of core areas from outside influences is promoted in two ways. First, management practices in core areas would have biological protection and restoration of natural conditions as their central mandate. This would include no extractive uses that degrade the region's biological integrity, no habitat modification that would promote non-native species or communities beyond their natural range of abundance, and removal of biologically disruptive cultural features (such as roads).[6] Second, core areas would be surrounded by buffer zones, where a greater amount of human modification of the landscape would be allowed, but where management practices would still promote ecological health and minimize permanent conversion of the landscape.[7]
- Most, if not all, of the core areas need to be biologically connected with other core areas, both within the region and outside of the region, to allow for the movement of individuals.

Historically, wilderness areas were conceptualized as large areas subject to minimal human disturbance. Therefore, it makes sense to consider the practical relationship between wilderness areas and ecological reserve systems developed to achieve ecological goals. Conservation was not the primary motivation for the original creation of the wilderness system in the United States. The Wilderness Act of 1964 speaks of the importance of land "untrammeled by man, . . . with the imprint of man's work substantially unnoticeable; . . . [with] outstanding opportunities for solitude or a primitive and unconfined type of recreation; . . . and may also contain ecological, geological, or other features of scientific, educational, scenic, or historic value."[8] This highlights the preeminent importance of recreation and aesthetics for the siting and design of wilderness areas. Although the Eastern Wilderness Act of 1975 allowed for the designation of wilderness areas in the eastern United States under the Wilderness Act, it has generally been felt that the original focus of the act on pristine landscapes, recreational isolation, and aesthetic purity made consideration of wilderness areas in the East inappropriate. Yet, with the increase in our awareness of the extent of the biodepletion that is going on today and the rise in our recognition of the importance of ecological reserve systems for dealing with this issue, we now have an opportunity to expand our concept of wilderness, and hence the relevancy of wilderness in the Northeast.

A Brief History of the Design of Reserve Systems

The science of designing ecological reserve systems is young. Reed Noss developed one of the first designs for a system of reserves in the United States for the state of Ohio, building upon the reserve design model promoted by the UNESCO Man and the Biosphere Program in the early 1970s.[9] Noss, working with Larry Harris at the University of Florida, also developed a reserve design for Florida.[10] This early design and the process used to develop it formed the basis for subsequent proposals for a system of reserves in Florida, particularly the Conservation and Recreation Lands (CARL) program now being implemented through public acquisition of lands throughout that state (part of Florida Preservation 2000 and Florida Forever). The CARL program represents an important example of the possibilities for the implementation (as contrasted to the design) of reserve systems. The combined influence of conservation activists, academic biologists, and agency personnel was successful in convincing both the public and the state government to allocate the funds and begin the purchase of lands identified as important in the system's design. To my knowledge, the CARL program is the only effort, at least in the United States, to actually begin the implementation of an ecological reserve system based on the design criteria of interconnected core areas whose primary purpose is to protect and restore biological integrity. Although the CARL program is not perfect, it provides some hope about what may be possible in the future.

A third design, also developed by Noss, was for an ecological reserve system in the Oregon Coast Range.[11] This system emphasized protection of existing stands of old-growth forest and watersheds important as breeding grounds for salmon. Since then, a handful of ecological reserve systems have been initiated or completed, including the Sky Islands-Greater Gila Nature Reserve Network in Arizona, New Mexico, and northern Mexico; the Klamath-Siskiyou Reserve System in northwestern California and southwestern Oregon; the Yellowstone to Yukon Conservation Initiative in the northern Rocky Mountains; and the state of Maryland's Green Infrastructure Strategy.[12] Along with these examples of specific implementations, a growing literature has developed on how reserve systems should be designed, all of which focus on spatially explicit mapping of the full scope of biological characteristics that are important to biological integrity, and the integration of these data to create a system of core areas, buffers, and zones of connectivity.[13]

Reserve Design Initiatives in the Northeast

No ecological reserve system has yet been developed in the northeastern United States that is as comprehensive as those mentioned above. However, some effort is being made to design and implement reserve systems, and some or all of these may provide the nucleus for such systems in the future.

Algonquin to Adirondack Connectivity Zone. Although technically not a reserve system, an ecological connector between Algonquin Provincial Park in Ontario, Canada, and Adirondack Park in New York has been designed.[14] The explicit purpose of the connector is to facilitate the movement of wolves from Algonquin Provincial Park, where they are reasonably abundant, to Adirondack Park, where they have been extirpated but could perhaps live again if they could colonize the area. Because the connector has been designed without an implementation strategy, it is possible that it could be developed as one single reserve stretching from Algonquin Park to Adirondack Park, but it seems much more likely that it will be implemented as a series of reserves buffered and connected in such a way as to achieve the overall goal of promoting wolf recolonization.

The approach to designing the Algonquin to Adirondack (A2A) Connectivity Zone is different than that taken by most other reserve design efforts. The A2A began with the explicit goal of providing for a single focal species, and assumed that other ecological benefits, such as protection of species other than the wolf, would derive from that. The portion of the connectivity zone in New York was designed by using the St. Lawrence River and the northern boundary of the Adirondack Park as "anchors" for the end points of the connectivity zone. The landscape in between the two was evaluated with respect to the following characteristics: road density, presence of major roads (i.e., highways), human population density, land use/land cover, and proximity to water. The entire region between the river and the park was divided into 90-meter by 90-meter areas, or cells, and evaluated with respect to these five parameters. Each of these cells was then ranked according to its "suitability" for wolves, based on an abundant scientific literature that indicates that wolves prefer areas with low road and human population densities, great distances to nearest roads, absence of major roads, and the presence of natural land-cover types. These areas were then mapped, first by displaying only the best 1 percent of the area, and then by successively including additional 1 percent increments (that is, best 2 percent, best 3 percent, and so on). A similar, but not completely identical approach was taken to identify the best connectivity zone in Ontario, using the St. Lawrence River and Algonquin Park as the anchors. As before, the best areas in 1 percent increments were displayed and matched against the analysis done in New York.

The region that visually provided the best connectivity between Algonquin and Adirondack Parks was the best 5 percent of the region (see map 5.1). Less land did not provide for complete connection between the two parks, or created bottlenecks through which passage by wolves would be difficult. More land did not substantially improve the apparent connectivity. A comparison of ecological conditions in this 5 percent corridor to other areas in the same general region indicated that the 5 percent corridor provides equal or overrepresentation for most natural aquatic ecosystems present in the area, but underrepresents many of the less-common terrestrial plant community types in the region. This indicates that to provide for complete ecological protection, the A2A Connectivity Zone would need to be augmented with other core areas.

Vermont Biodiversity Project. A group of agencies and organizations that are involved in the protection or management of land in Vermont to achieve conservation goals has organized the Vermont Biodiversity Project (VBP).[15] The purpose of the VBP is to identify lands in Vermont that, taken as a whole, are of importance for the protection and restoration of biological integrity within the state. The organizations that are associated with the VBP include the Nature Conservancy, Vermont Land

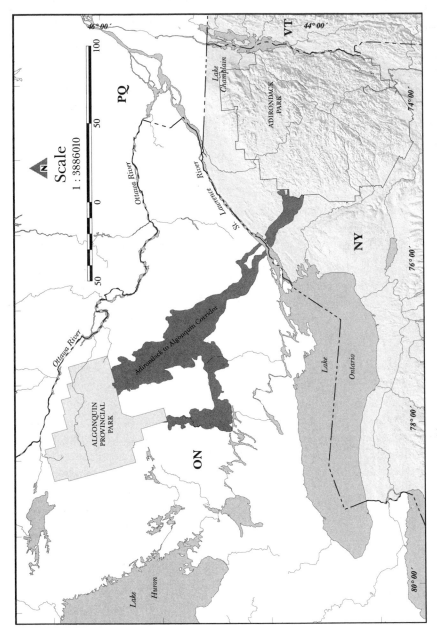

Map 5.1. Adirondack to Algonquin Corridor.

Trust, U.S. Forest Service, U.S. Fish and Wildlife Service, and various departments of the Vermont Agency of Natural Resources. The design work of the VBP is carried out by a group of about fifteen scientists, who receive their direction from the VBP Steering Committee, made up of representatives of each of the participating groups, and advice from a scientific advisory group, comprised of all conservation biologists in the state who are interested in being involved with the project. The work of the VBP is envisioned to include at least three phases. The first phase, which is still ongoing, involves the identification of areas that are priorities for conservation. The second and third phases, which have not yet begun, involve designing linkages among conservation areas and testing the proposed system to determine if it captures the full range of the state's biological diversity and provides the necessary conditions to support viable populations of wide-ranging species.

The first phase of the work involves several components. First, the Spatial Analysis Lab at the University of Vermont mapped the biophysical regions of the state. Despite its small size (about 6 million acres), Vermont is ecologically diverse. Seven separate regions were identified, each with distinct biological and physical characteristics.[16] Several scientists working on the project then compiled different data sets of ecological relevance from existing sources: soils, elevation, surficial and bedrock geology, distribution of species, distribution of natural communities, locations of biological elements of conservation concern (e.g., species, natural communities), roads, and existing conservation lands. Taken together, these parameters permitted a rough evaluation of physical, biological, and cultural features that might influence the location of areas that are priorities for conservation. The Spatial Analysis Lab then assessed these parameters within each biophysical region. The existing biological data sets were the weakest. Good statewide surveys previously had been done for few species groups, and of those for which the data were complete, few were done at a spatial scale smaller than that of a township. Further, statewide data on land cover had in the past only been classed into a few general types, such as deciduous forest and coniferous forest, which masked much of the diversity in plant community types found in the state, and did not permit the identification of rare community types. As a result, the physical parameters were given greater importance in selecting areas of importance for conservation, in the hope that diversity in physical parameters is correlated with diversity in biological parameters. (This is probably more true for some groups of organisms, such as soil microbes, than for others.) For all physical parameters (e.g., elevation, aspect, soil type), coverage was statewide and had comparatively greater resolution than did biological parameters. The VBP also facilitated the development of an aquatic communities classification system for the state, as well as the identification of exemplary representatives of each aquatic community type.[17]

The analysis carried out by the Spatial Analysis Lab involved combining the physical parameters—soil types, elevation classes, surficial geology types, and bedrock geology types—into landform classes. Within each biophysical region, the areas were identified that maximally captured the full range of landform types. The scientists involved with the VBP then created aggregates made up of these areas, exemplary aquatic community features, and hotspots of biological elements of conservation concern in order to identify the areas considered to be of primary importance for the statewide protection of biological diversity. These areas, called by the VBP "biological diversity resource areas" (BDRAs), now serve as the focus for the next phases of the work of the VBP, particularly assessment of whether the identified BDRAs alone are likely to protect viable populations of focal species.

New Hampshire Ecological Reserve System Project. As a direct outgrowth of one of the recommendations made by the Northern Forest Lands Council in 1994, a group of biologists, conservation advocates, state natural resource agencies, land managers, land owners, and representatives of the forest products industry began to address the conservation needs in New Hampshire and the design of an ecological reserve system for the state.[18] Working with the support of the New Hampshire Department of Fish and Game and the Division of Forests and Lands, a work group has so far compiled four important data sets from existing sources: forest cover, roads, public lands and private lands protected by conservation easements, and locations of biological elements of special conservation concern (e.g., species, communities). To date, this group has identified those biological elements that are not currently found on public lands and the locations of the largest blocks of unfragmented forests. Although no reserve design has been completed yet, the New Hampshire Ecological Reserve System Project plans to use this information to identify lands that are not currently protected but that contain either large forest blocks or biological elements of concern; and to identify public lands that should have their management plans strengthened in order to maximally protect large forest blocks or biological elements of concern. The project is advocating for the development of an integrated and comprehensive set of reserves that will protect globally rare species and communities, areas with high diversity of communities and physiographic features, large blocks of unfragmented forests, exemplary natural communities, and critical wildlife habitat.

Maine Wildlands Reserve Network. The Greater Laurentian Wildlands Project (GLWP), a regional effort of the Wildlands Project, has initiated the design of an ecological reserve system that will promote the biological integrity of Maine through the protection and restoration of large core areas, native carnivores, and landscape connectivity.[19] Beginning in 1997, a group of conservation advocates and scientists have sought to identify areas in Maine that should be incorporated into a reserve system by mapping locations of special elements of high conservation interest, and distributions of biophysical parameters. The special elements were defined as large roadless areas, public and conservation lands, stands of old-growth forests, wetlands, areas of potentially high species richness, areas of low human population, and lands in industrial timber ownership. The biophysical parameters assessed include biophysical regions, potential natural vegetation, watersheds, elevations, soil, and bedrock geology. Further the Maine Wildlands Reserve Network Initiative identified twenty-nine species of mammals, birds, reptiles, amphibians, and fish that were deemed by regional biologists to be good focal species, species whose ecological needs would help inform the size, shape, configuration, and management of the ecological reserve system.[20] Areas for inclusion in a reserve network were identified in a step-wise manner, sequentially adding land necessary to capture additional special elements and representative biophysical parameters not captured in previous steps.[21] This work is still in progress; the reserve network designed so far has only been assessed with respect to the optimal habitat for one focal species, the eastern timber wolf, and the GLWP intends to incorporate information about the other focal species in future iterations of the reserve design.

Maine Forest Biodiversity Project. Another effort to identify conservation lands in Maine, the Maine Forest Biodiversity Project was begun in 1994 following the recommendations of the Northern Forest Lands Council. This project group was quite large, and included representatives from state agencies, timber companies, conservation organizations, and academic institutions. Unlike the design efforts in Vermont and New Hampshire or of the Greater Laurentian Wildlands Project in Maine, however, its focus was strictly on designing a reserve system that would achieve representation of natural communities rather than biological integrity. Further, for political reasons, the Maine Forest Biodiversity Project looked only at the possibilities of establishing reserves on existing public lands, which comprise only about 4.5 percent of the state. Although the project disbanded in 1998, some of its reserve design work on the state's public lands is ongoing. It is doubtful, however, that a reserve system designed solely for representation will achieve all of the conservation goals identified at the start of this chapter.

Northern Forest Alliance Wildlands. In the mid-1990s, the Northern Forest Alliance, a coalition of conservation advocacy organizations, sought to develop a system of wild lands in Maine, New Hampshire, Vermont, and northern New York where efforts to limit development, protect critical ecological and recreational areas, and promote sound forestry could be targeted.[22] Using the technical expertise of the Appalachian Mountain Club, a member of the Alliance, areas with high concentrations of public values and undeveloped forests were identified from satellite imagery, aerial photography, and ground-based surveys. Further work to develop detailed proposals for a reserve system, such as how big specific reserves ought to be and how they ought to be integrated across the landscape, has not yet been done.

Comparisons to the West

Just as the concept of "wilderness" has different connotations depending on whether one's perspective derives from eastern or western U.S. landscapes, so too does the concept of an ecological reserve system. Two of the greatest differences between the Northeast and West today with respect to the biological integrity of the landscape are the extent to which natural habitats have been modified from their natural condition (e.g., by road building, clear-cutting, urban development), and the extent to which the full suite of native species, especially top-level carnivores, are still present. These distinctions are coupled with a difference in the amount of the landscape that is already in public ownership, and therefore more amenable to changes in management practices (see chapter 4). With the exception of the Adirondack Park in New York, the parcels of public land in the Northeast are very much smaller on average than those in the West. These differences have led to different approaches to designing ecological reserve systems in these regions. Western approaches to reserve system design have focused largely on identifying existing public lands that could, at least in theory, quickly be devoted to achieving conservation goals by simply revising existing management plans; identifying large roadless areas and working to ensure that they are protected and remain roadless; and evaluating whether a proposed reserve system could support viable populations of top-level carnivores, which are either still extant in the area or are present nearby. There is merit to this approach in western landscapes. The undeniable importance of bringing reserve systems into reality quickly argues for taking advantage of existing public lands to the greatest extent possible, and supplementing the system as necessary through the acquisition of new lands. The indisputable danger to ecological health posed by roads and the large cost involved in obliterating existing roads are arguments for the immediate protection of roadless areas, and their incorporation into reserve systems.[23] The ecological, economic, and aesthetic importance of top-level carnivores, as well as the likelihood that systems designed to promote their viability will also provide sufficient habitat and resources for other, less wide-ranging species, are arguments for a focus on their protection.

This approach is not possible in the Northeast, however. By and large, a much larger percentage of the land in the Northeast is in private ownership and much more of the land is roaded, both of which will dramatically increase the cost of implementing a reserve system, thereby increasing the importance of careful planning and site-by-site evaluation of the ecological characteristics of the landscape. Further, few top-level carnivores are still present, making evaluations of the proposed system with respect to its ability to support viable populations much more difficult. Indeed, in many cases the habitat requirements of extirpated carnivores are unknown, making their use as focal species more uncertain. For example, recent genetic work on eastern wolves has raised the possibility that the wolf that inhabited the northeastern United States through the early part of the 1900s was in fact the red wolf, and not the timber wolf as previously assumed.[24] Red and timber wolves exploit different prey — red wolves rely more on deer and small game than do timber wolves — and therefore reserve systems designed around their needs would look somewhat different.

Differences between eastern and western approaches are not about correct and incorrect approaches.[25] Nor are they about whether ecological reserve systems are appropriate or inappropriate in different parts of the continent. I believe that our ultimate goal as a people must be an integrated system of ecological reserves that spans the entire continent, linked through the Central American land bridge to a parallel reserve system in South America.[26] These differences between East and West merely highlight the tremendous importance of recognizing the character and ecological realities of the region for which a reserve system is being designed. Reserve systems in both the Northeast and the West will include core areas, some of which will be designated as wilderness under the Wilderness Act. Because of the differences in how these reserve systems will be designed, there will be differences in the size and degree of cultural modification of the landscape associated with the wilderness, and hence the aesthetics of the wilderness area. But they will both play central roles in the protection and restoration of their landscape's biological integrity.

Challenges to Achieving Reserve Design Goals in the Northeast

Clearly, none of the initiatives to develop ecological reserve systems in the Northeast have been completely designed, let alone implemented, at this point. Further, reserve design programs have not yet begun in most of the region. Several goals must be achieved before a regional system of ecological reserves is completed that will truly allow for ongoing conservation in the Northeast.

- **Continue to work on the current reserve design initiatives.** None of the reserve design initiatives described above are complete, and further work is required for them to have the greatest chance not only of being implemented but of achieving the ecological goals intended for them. For example, even the most well-developed of the designs, the A2A corridor, needs to be supplemented with additional ecological reserves to maximally protect communities and species that it does not capture in its area. The Vermont Biodiversity Project and the New Hampshire Ecological Reserve System Project need to complete their identification of the areas of conservation priority, and then engage in the processes of determining the best ways to link them together in a coherent system and to test whether this coherent system can support viable populations of wide-ranging species. The Maine Wildlands Reserve Network needs to be evaluated with respect to the full range of the focal species identified as important in the region. Sustaining such effort can be difficult, especially when funding for the work is hard to obtain, but it is very important that these initial efforts at reserve design are seen through to completion.
- **New initiatives need to be developed elsewhere.** Just as designs for reserve systems have begun in Maine, New Hampshire, Vermont, and northern New York, such systems need to be developed for the rest of the Northeast. Some states, such as Massachusetts, New Jersey, and Pennsylvania, already have significant areas of public land designated, in part, to achieve conservation goals, which can provide good starting

points for the development of a more expansive and inclusive system. Only Connecticut and Rhode Island do not already have the public land base on which to begin the development of a statewide reserve system. Regardless, such systems need to be developed in those states by bringing together the organizations and agencies responsible for the acquisition and/or management of conservation lands as well as the community of conservation biologists and naturalists who know the region and the science of reserve design.

- **Invest in the acquisition of data necessary to do adequate reserve design.** One of the greatest barriers to the development of the reserve system in Vermont has been the lack of good information on the geographic distribution of plants, animals, fungi, and bacteria. For most groups, the data were completely lacking. For others, knowledge of distributions was available only to the level of township (typically about 36 square miles), which was of very limited value in identifying precise locations of species "hotspots" or assessing the extent to which protection of one area would protect a given proportion of a particular taxonomic group. The experience in Vermont makes it clear that all efforts to design ecological reserve systems will benefit from good geographic information on at least some key taxa. I recommend that biodiversity inventories in the Northeast focus on taxa that collectively span the range of ecological and evolutionary types, including trees, groundcover herbs, aquatic plants, fungi, amphibians, fish, beetles, butterflies, and all types of pollinators. Further, these inventories need to be done on a spatial scale that is much smaller than a township. A procedure for locating random study plots within the range of natural community types within each township (or other appropriate unit) in a state would provide the data necessary to identify the community associations of species over broad areas and develop predictive models of species distributions, and to determine species turnover within natural communities. Other kinds of data are also important to obtain, such as the identification of biophysical regions and inventories of terrestrial and aquatic natural communities, and should also be given a high priority for biological surveys.

- **Use the reserve designs to guide land acquisition and/or protection.** A reserve design is of little value to conservation if it is not implemented. Agencies and organizations responsible for land acquisition, such as state conservation departments and the Nature Conservancy, should use the design to guide the establishment of their acquisition priorities. In this manner, a well-designed reserve system can be developed over time with funds that would go toward land acquisition anyway. Further, management plans for lands identified as important in a reserve system should come to reflect this need. Strategies for influencing management plans will differ on public and private lands (e.g., influence of agencies by public opinion versus purchase of conservation easements), but over time the primacy of conservation goals on reserve lands must be recognized and established.

- **Work with those involved in other initiatives within the region.** State boundaries are political constructs with little ecological relevance. At some point, reserve systems developed in one state need to connect to those in other states. This is particularly true in the northeastern United States, where the average size of states is smaller than anywhere else in the country. Core areas that border political boundaries must match up across the boundaries. Systems of reserves must include connectivity to other systems in neighboring states, such as along the Connecticut River as it flows southward between Vermont and New Hampshire, and then through Massachusetts and Connecticut.

- **Work with those involved in other initiatives outside the region.** The northeastern United States as a region is a collection of politically defined, not ecologically defined, units. The entire region connects ecologically in a seamless way with surrounding areas: the Maritime Provinces of Canada, the Mixed Laurentian Forest regions of southeastern Canada, the southern Appalachian Mountains, the mid-Atlantic coast, and the midwestern U.S. plains. As the system of ecological reserves is developed and connected within this region, careful attention must be given to their linkage with reserve systems in surrounding areas, just as the Algonquin to Adirondack Connectivity Zone has done between New York and Canada.

- **Plan acquisitions associated with current reserves.** Future acquisitions associated with existing conservation lands in the region, such as the Adirondack Park (New York), Baxter State Park (Maine), Green Mountain National Forest (Vermont), and Pinelands National Reserve (New Jersey), should be prioritized to achieve two important goals. First, future land acquisitions should aim toward allowing the reserve to better achieve its ecological goals. Acquiring inholdings, minimizing boundary perimeters, and protecting intact natural communities and watersheds will increase the conservation value of a reserve by maximizing its area and minimizing outside cultural disturbances of the landscape. Second, future land acquisitions should aim to promote linkages across the landscape with other areas, such as between the Adirondack Park and the Catskill Park in eastern New York.

In many ways, ecological reserves are not completely synonymous with wilderness. The goals of the two only partly overlap. Wilderness areas are usually envisioned to provide recreational and aesthetic escape from the influences of modern culture. Ecological reserves are envisioned as a central tool to promote and restore biological integrity in a region, especially for those communities, species, and ecological processes that do not fare well in the human sphere of influence. As such, one is generally intended for humans, and the other intended for wild nature. But a focus on the ecological contributions of our reserved lands, whether they are wild areas, or wilderness designated under the Wilderness Act, or whatever they may be called, will help to bridge the gap between northeastern and western perspectives on wild lands. If we can expand our view of wilderness beyond its historical interpretation and recognize the important role it can play in returning biological integrity to our continent—a role defined largely by its contribution to the protection and restoration of the full scope of diversity in the biological world—then differences between eastern and western views of wilderness become less a matter of relevancy and more a matter of opportunity. Relative to the West, the designation of wilderness in the Northeast will be constrained by human population density, habitat conversion, road building, and species extirpation. But the role that wilderness can play in allowing nature to operate in its own way in its own time and in allowing future generations of humans to experience and appreciate a world rich in biological form and function will be the same regardless of where on the continent the wilderness lies. A focus on the heavy footprint of human existence on the ecological health of our continent, and what we must do to lessen our impact, helps bridge this gap between Northeast and West.

CHAPTER 6

An Opportunity for Big Wilderness in the Northern Appalachians

JAMIE SAYEN

And what I have been preparing to say is that in wildness is the preservation of the world. Every tree sends its fibres forth in search of the wild. The cities import it at any price. Men plow and sail for it. From the forest and wilderness come the tonics and barks which brace mankind. Our ancestors were savages. The story of Romulus and Remus being suckled by a wolf is not a meaningless fable. The founders of every state which has risen to eminence have drawn their nourishment and vigor from a similar wild source. It was because the children of the Empire were not suckled by the wolf that they were conquered and displaced by the children of the Northern Forest who were.

—Henry David Thoreau, "Walking"

AS THE PRECEDING chapter makes clear, the restoration of ecological health and biological integrity to the region requires large tracts of wilderness. I believe the condition of our wild lands mirrors the condition of our culture, especially our democratic institutions. To restore vibrant local cultures and a tough, fair democracy, we'll need to restore big wilderness in the northeastern United States and throughout North America.

Early in 1988, followers of the timber industry in northern New England and the Adirondacks were stunned by the announcement that one million acres of timberland in New York, Vermont, New Hampshire, and Maine were for sale. Earlier in the decade, the English corporate raider Sir James Goldsmith had engineered a hostile takeover of Diamond International, the corporation that owned these timberlands. He quickly sold off the paper mills and equipment, and paid off almost all of the debt he had incurred in the takeover. He retained the timberlands until 1987, when he sold them to a French holding company, earning a huge profit for his successful dismantling of a large corporation.[1]

The Diamond land sale ushered into the region a new era, one that has seen blockbuster land sales occur with almost clockwork regularity over the past decade. From early 1988 until the summer of 1999, more than 5.5 million acres in northern New England were sold at least once. More than half of that land has been sold two or three times.

The frenzied pace of the land sales is accelerating. About three million acres of paper company lands in Maine were sold in the last two months of 1998. Half a million more acres were sold in the first half of 1999. What makes these sales especially noteworthy is that most major paper mills have also shut down paper machines, laying off thousands of paper workers, two mills have already shut down, and several more are tottering on the brink of closure. The Paper Century of northern New England is over.

Goldsmith understood that the parts of Diamond International were worth more when sold off separately than the value of the company's stock. So he took over the company and sold the pieces.

Ecology teaches us the opposite lesson: The whole—the ecosystem, the landscape—is greater than the fragmented pieces. Ecological restoration is much more than merely protecting native species and restoring the missing pieces—Atlantic salmon, caribou, and large carnivores such as wolf, cougar, lynx, and pine marten as well as lichens, mosses, and beetles—that depend upon mature and old-growth forests. We must ensure the eventual return of the whole, the old forest systems. We must protect and restore the relationships between and among species: predation, pollination, and decomposition. We must protect and restore assemblages of species: natural communities, ecosystems, and landscapes. We must assure the viable functioning of natural processes: hydrological, nutrient, disturbance cycles, and evolution. And our reserves must be able to withstand the most severe natural disturbances, such as hurricanes and ice storms, as well as human-caused stresses, such as atmospheric pollution and global climate change. These are the ecological reasons for establishing large wilderness reserves in undeveloped areas along with the smaller reserves in more-developed areas.

Goldsmith demonstrated the irreconcilable conflict between economic culture and ecology. In economics, the sum of the parts are greater than the whole. In the natural world, it is the other way around. Just as the Diamond land sale signaled the end of a century of paper company domination of the region, the realization that the ecological whole is greater that the sum of the parts signals the end of an economic approach to conservation that is fundamentally at odds with natural processes. We can no longer ignore the needs and limits and workings of the natural world, of which we humans are very much a part.

A decade after the sale of the Diamond lands, citizens of the Northern Appalachians, their politicians, the timber industry itself, and environmentalists remain divided over the region's destiny for the next century—and beyond. Most politicians, timber industry hardliners, and some old-school conservationists, remain in denial. They believe that a few more governmental subsidies, a fresh infusion of outside capital, and some clever public relations marketing of such outworn or irrelevant ideas such as "working forest," "sustainable industrial forestry," conservation easements, and green certification will prop up the failed status quo one more time.[2] They carry a heavy burden of proof.

This chapter offers a strategy for restoring wilderness and a land-based culture that reflects respect for and knowledge of the wild, natural qualities that make the Northern Appalachians so distinctive. Ending an era of exploitation offers us hope that the severely degraded forests, economy, and human culture of the region can begin to heal each other.

The large land sales offer us the opportunity to reverse four centuries of war against wild nature, wild critters, and, ultimately, against human welfare. The public can purchase most of these battered lands for between $200 and $300 an acre. The boldest proposals call for acquisition of 10 to 15 million acres in northern Maine, New Hampshire, Vermont, and the Adirondack Park. The cost for such purchases would be $2 billion to $4.5 billion. This is a very modest sum if we consider the waste of the Pentagon budget, the tax subsidies for wealthy corporations and individuals proposed by allegedly fiscally conservative politicians, and the fabulous wealth of certain individuals. The cost becomes even more modest if carried out over a ten- to twenty-year period.

Public opinion surveys taken in the region over the last decade of the twentieth century consistently demonstrate strong support for public acquisition to transform these battered timberlands into wilderness. The public supports the reintroduction of wolves to the Northern Appalachians. Public opposition to large industrial clearcuts and herbicide spraying are equally strong.[3]

And yet, the politicians continue to get away with maintaining that the public opposes wilderness by overwhelming margins. How do we explain this discrepancy? Is democracy any healthier than a clearcut forest?

Restoring big wilderness is a component of an integrated political ecology that addresses economic, social, cultural, and political problems of this troubled region at the same time. Healing the natural and human communities of the Northern Appalachians will require several conceptual and practical components.

- Big wild lands provide landscape-level protection of native species and natural communities and the interactions between them.
- Low impact forestry must be practiced on lands that are appropriate for timber management. This requires a regional economy that meets the needs of the region, rather than one that enriches absentee global investors and speculators while impoverishing the natural and human communities.
- Biological democracy ensures equal rights for all native species, natural communities, and future generations.
- Cultural restoration will involve development of a land-based culture whose economic, social, and political institutions respect the limits of the natural and physical world. Such a culture will teach us how to live here lightly with dignity and joy. Freeman House says that we need to restore human culture to natural succession.[4]

A Brief History of the Northern Forest

Americans tend to think of the western United States when they talk about wilderness. We hope that this book will serve as a corrective to the notion that the East has been forever tamed.

Visions of cowboys, the cavalry, and the western Native American tribes are the likely response to mention of the frontier. We forget that the first North American frontiers were along the Atlantic seaboard. The frontier was defined by the limits of European expansion into the wilderness. From the historian's perspective, most of the history of the frontier occurred east of the Mississippi. Less than one century elapsed from the date of the Louisiana Purchase in 1803 until the director of the U.S. Census declared—rather mistakenly—that the frontier had been closed in 1890.

It took two centuries for Europeans to stake out claims to all of Maine—and they were working on two fronts throughout the entire period! The headwaters of the Hudson River, a few hundred miles north of New York City, were located three decades after Lewis and Clark had located the headwaters of the Missouri and the Snake rivers and had reached the Pacific shore. Massachusetts was largely settled by 1676. It would be another eighty-five years before Vermont, New Hampshire (excluding the extreme southeast), and inland Maine were opened to successful settlement by Europeans. The wild, cold, harsh, mountainous lands were poorly suited to agriculture. The region was remote from settled areas. And the native peoples of northern New England presented such formidable barriers that the northern New England frontier lasted as long as it took to conquer the western two-thirds of the United States.[5]

The northeastern United States has an impressive wilderness tradition.

I speak in the present tense. In spite of the massive development of the Atlantic seaboard and northeastern United States, sizeable portions remain undeveloped—some are surprisingly wild. Millions of acres in northern Maine, New Hampshire, and Vermont, though degraded from nearly two centuries of logging, retain the potential to begin rewilding just as soon as we cease exploitative activities.

Two maps elegantly convey this message. One map shows the European settlement of the greater Laurentian region at various intervals from 1700 to 1815 (see map 6.1). Even in 1815, 195 years after the arrival of the Pilgrims and five years before Maine escaped colony status under Massachusetts, four-fifths of Maine remained unsettled. Settlement was confined to the coastal regions, the southernmost counties, and along the major rivers. New Hampshire north of the White Mountains was settled only sparsely and only along the Connecticut River.

A second map depicts the population densities of townships in northern New England and New York today (see map 6.2). Fully 8 million acres of northern Maine, New Hampshire, and northeastern Vermont remain uninhabited. Paper companies, large, absentee timberland corporations, and speculators own these lands. Over half of this acreage has been sold and resold over the past ten years. Almost certainly, several millions of acres will be sold in this region in the next decade. Table 6.1 documents those major land sales since 1988. More than half of the land in the proposed Headwaters Wilderness Reserve System and roughly two-thirds of the land in the proposed Maine Woods National Park has been sold one or more times since 1988 (see the discussion of the these two proposals below). This is a region in the midst of a profound transformation.

To the defenders of the failed status quo, it is a crisis. To those who believe we can fashion an ecologically responsive culture and economy out of the ruins of two centuries of unsustainable logging, it is an unprecedented opportunity.

The forest that sustained the Abenakis for thousands of years was very different from today's forest. Although our knowledge of the pre-European settlement forest of northeastern Vermont, northern New

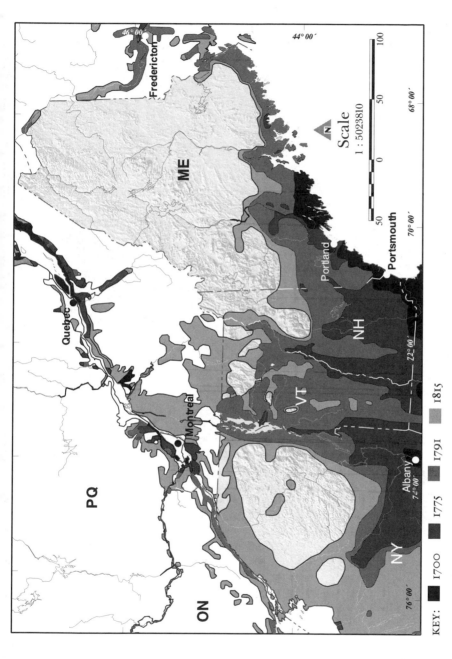

KEY: ▮ 1700 ▮ 1775 ▮ 1791 ▮ 1815

Map 6.1. European Settlement in the Greater Laurentian Region, through 1815.

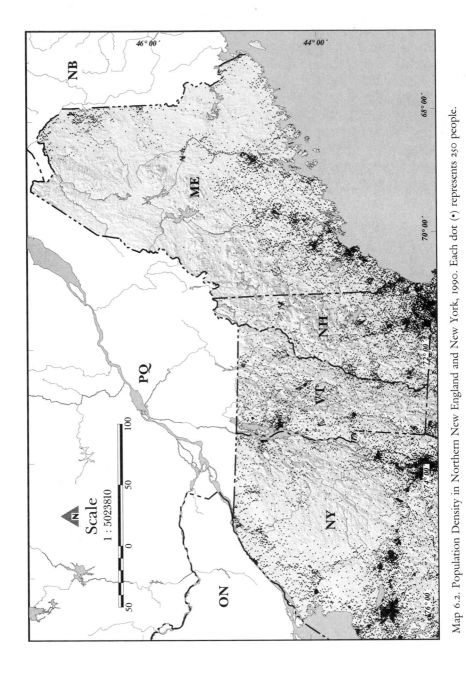

Map 6.2. Population Density in Northern New England and New York, 1990. Each dot (•) represents 250 people.

Table 6.1

Large Land Sales in Northern New England and New York, 1988–1999

Year	Seller	Buyer	Approximate acreage
1988	Diamond Occidental	Various: timber and speculators	970,000
1989	Great Northern	Georgia Pacific (hostile takeover)	2,100,000
1991	Georgia Pacific	Bowater	2,100,000
1994	Scott	SAPPI	905,000
1996	Boise-Cascade	Mead	667,000
1998	SAPPI	Plum Creek Timber Co.	905,000
1998	International Paper	Nature Conservancy	185,000
1998	Champion International	The Conservation Fund	300,000
1999	Bowater	McDonald Corp.	656,000
1999	Bowater	J. D. Irving, Ltd.	981,000
1999	United Timber Corp	New River Franklin, Ltd.; Buckfield Timber LLC	91,000
1999	Bowater	Inexcon	380,000
1999	Georgia Pacific	Yale U & McDonald Corp.	440,000

Note:

In addition to the large sales listed in the accompanying chart, there have been thousands of smaller transactions. By and large, these smaller sales should be viewed as "background noise," the inevitable result of efforts to consolidate holdings, to sell off nonstrategic assets, or to settle estates. What is unprecedented is the relentless succession of large land sales, turning forestland over at a rate far greater than the states disposed of these lands in the late eighteenth and nineteenth centuries.

Hampshire, and northern Maine is incomplete, some things are clear (see chapters 2 and 3):

- A higher proportion of late-successional tree species (beech, red spruce) dominated the pre-settlement forest, and a much lower percentage of early-successional species that dominate today's industrial forest (paper birch, aspen, red maple, balsam fir) were present.
- Researchers estimate that more than half of the forest canopy was dominated by trees older than 150 years of age. A quarter of the forest was dominated by trees older than 300 years. By 1980, researchers had found that 84 percent of the Maine forest was younger than 75 years.
- Natural disturbance regimes of the pre-settlement forest created small gap openings. Less than 1 percent of such openings were greater than one-quarter acre.
- Pre-settlement forests were unfragmented and were characterized by layered canopies. They had large amounts of standing and down dead

wood that was critical habitat to a variety of species. It probably requires 350 years or more for a clearcut to begin to recover this lost structural component.

- Substantial coarse woody debris and decayed matter lay on the forest floor and an abundance of epiphytes covered the trees and mosses on the forest floor.
- The forest floor of the pre-settlement forest had a high degree of local topographical diversity (pit and mound) due to root pulls and decayed stumps. This created microsites for a wide range of seedlings and herbaceous plants. Industrial forestry has flattened much of this diversity.
- Undisturbed forest floors were important sites for nutrient cycling and retention and provided critical protection against soil erosion. Industrial forestry has compacted these soils, caused significant soil erosion, depleted nutrients, and disrupted hydrological cycles and disturbance regimes. Naturally cool and moist soils have been baked following clear-cutting. These stressed soils are further assaulted by acid deposition from midwestern power plants, automobiles, and other industrial sources.
- Pre-settlement forests were home to large predators that have been extirpated by human activity.
- Recent research in Pennsylvania suggests that old-growth forests support associations of bird species that are not found in younger, managed forests.
- Loss of old growth in the Northern Appalachians has eliminated or severely reduced populations of old-growth–dependent species. Studies have identified lichens, mosses, and boreal beetles that are found only in old forest stands.[6]

Thoreau first visited northern Maine in 1846, just as the lumber industry was swinging into high gear. Only the great white pine had been heavily logged. The great spruce logging era was about to begin. He brought us a vivid and poetic appreciation of the essentially pre-settlement condition of the north Maine woods. "The primitive wood is always and everywhere damp and mossy," he wrote in *The Maine Woods*. Salmon, wolves, and cougars were still found there. On descending Mount Katahdin he encountered "primeval, untamed and forever untamable nature . . . exceedingly wild and desolate . . . something savage and awful, though beautiful." "There was clearly felt the presence of a force not bound to be kind to man," he concluded. "What is most striking in the Maine wilderness is the continuous of the forest, with fewer open intervals or glades than you had imagined . . . The forest is essentially uninterrupted.

It is even more grim and wild than you had anticipated, a damp and intricate wilderness, in the spring everywhere wet and miry." In contrast, he noted that the forest of Concord

> has lost its wild, damp, and shaggy look, the countless fallen and decaying trees are gone, and consequently that thick coat of moss which lived in them is gone too. The earth is comparatively bare and smooth and dry. The most primitive places left with us are the swamps, where the spruce still grows shaggy with usnea. The surface of the ground in the Maine woods is everywhere spongy and saturated with moisture. I noticed that the plants which cover the forest floor there are such as are commonly confined to swamps with us.[7]

Today, less than 0.2 percent of the pre-settlement forest remains in Maine.[8]

One reason northern New England remained inhospitable to Europeans throughout most of the eighteenth century is that the Abenakis allied themselves with the French in Quebec. English settlers were only able to penetrate the formidable pre-European-settlement northern forests after the British defeated the French in 1760. The French had been attracted to the St. Lawrence region a century and a half earlier because of the wonderful opportunities for fur trapping. Of all the species sought by the French, beaver was most popular. Fickle European fashions and an emerging global economy shaped European and Indian relations. The Indians were able to acquire European technology—knives, pots, beads, cloth, guns, and, unfortunately, whiskey—by trading furs they had trapped. Native subsistence trapping patterns that had been sustained for millennia were altered to feed the insatiable appetite of European fashion. Soon beaver were trapped out of districts near trading centers, and the trappers were forced to travel farther and farther afield to find pelts. Indian tribes found themselves in conflict over increasingly scarce beaver and other species. Territorial conflict became more deadly because of European guns. Although few French settlers arrived to displace Indian tribes, English and Dutch settlers arrived in increasing numbers. Conflict over land was inevitable and incessant. The superior European technology, its legacy of total war, and the biological accident that European-imported diseases killed Indians by the thousands doomed Native American cultures in southern New England.[9]

Where the Europeans displaced the Indians, they cut down, girdled, or burned the trees of the pre-settlement forest and introduced agricultural practices that profoundly altered the ecology of the native forests and aquatic systems. But, even where European settlement did not occur, for instance, in northern New England, the disappearance of beaver due to overtrapping caused cascading ecological consequences. Wolves lost an important source of protein. Beaver are important agents of natural disturbance in mixed-wood forests. Their dams transform low-gradient (small) streams into ponds, flooding adjacent low-lying areas. These ponds provide temporary habitat for a variety of plant and animal species. Frogs, turtles, great blue herons, swallows, otter, mink, and moose are some of the larger critters that exploit beaver ponds and openings. When the beaver have exhausted the nearby forest of their favored food sources, such as alders, aspen, and cottonwood, they abandon the pond for new sources of food, where they again alter the ecology of the stream with a new dam or rebuild a long-abandoned dam. Meanwhile, the newly abandoned pond begins to revert to marsh, meadow, and then forest, eventually reestablishing conditions favorable for recolonization by beaver. Removal of beaver halts this cyclic disturbance pattern, and deprives northern forests of a vital agent of diversity and disturbance.[10]

Early in the twentieth century, beaver were reintroduced to Vermont and New Hampshire. Their recovery has been astounding, but it is far from complete because beaver now exceed carrying capacity in many places, with the result that it is difficult to find undammed low-order streams.[11] What is the problem? It appears that beavers are easy prey for young wolves learning to hunt for themselves. But these predators were also exterminated in the eighteenth and nineteenth centuries. They have not been restored. Without wolves, beaver populations, like white-tailed deer populations in many suburban areas and most of the Northeast generally, have been unchecked by predation.

Our culture has taken an important step in the healing process by restoring beaver, but beaver restoration will remain incomplete until the top-level carnivore of the system has also returned to the region.

The story of beaver reminds us that ecology and culture are inextricably bound.

Following the French and Indian War, and especially following the American Revolution, the three states of northern New England worked aggressively to sell off or give away millions of acres of lands that were unsettled by Euro-Americans. Maine, in particular, unloaded millions of acres to timber barons and absentee land speculators. Initially, the Maine government thought that the timber men would clear the dense forest so yeoman farmers could transform northern Maine into a garden. Except for portions of Aroostook County, poor soils, a harsh climate, and re-

moteness doomed this fantasy. Instead, wealthy men acquired hundreds
of thousands, sometimes millions of acres in one transaction, usually for
pennies an acre. By the end of the Civil War, Maine (and Massachusetts,
which governed Maine as a colony prior to 1820) had disposed of about
15 million acres in central and northern Maine. New Hampshire had disposed of its unsettled lands in a similar manner by 1868.[12]

Early in the nineteenth century, the lumbermen began to liquidate the
great white pine of central and northern Maine, a grand tree that was
never found in abundance. By the 1840s, they were turning their attention
to red spruce, which surpassed pine as the number one tree cut by 1861.
From then until the end of the century, the mythic timber operations and
river log drives stripped away the ancient forests of Maine. Today, one
can locate scraps of the original forests tucked away in remote corners of
the state. This story was repeated in the other states of the region. By the
end of the nineteenth century, virtually all merchantable spruce timber
had been cut down. The loggers and timber barons were heading "over
the hump" to the Great Lakes states and the Far West to begin the liquidation of those forests. Shortly after the Civil War, scientists discovered that paper could be manufactured from wood pulp. Pulp mills, built
in Maine in the waning decades of the nineteenth century, did not require
large trees. Smaller-diameter softwood trees were ideal. Instead of abandoning the ravaged North Woods to benign neglect and natural restoration, the lumbermen sold out to the new pulp conglomerates, massive
capital-intensive corporations that were forming at the turn of the century.
International Paper was incorporated in 1898; Great Northern the following year.[13]

The period between the two World Wars saw a slackening of cutting
because of depredations of the spruce budworm between 1911 and 1919
and the Great Depression of the 1930s. Following World War II, technological advances and the mushrooming post-war economy set the stage
for the final assault on the Maine Woods and portions of northern New
Hampshire and Vermont.[14] Skidders, chainsaws, a massive road-building
program, and reckless expansion of paper mill capacity ushered in an era
of unprecedented overcutting in the 1970s. In the 1980s and early 1990s,
paper companies cut their spruce and fir, the softwoods most desired by
the mills, at twice the rate of regrowth. In some counties in Maine controlled by the large landowning corporations, the cut was five times the
rate of growth.[15]

By the time of the Diamond land sale in 1988, much of northern Maine
had been plundered. Logging operations often left behind only a thin

"beauty strip" along roadsides and rivers and lakes to hide the mayhem of industrial forestry.[16] No place was sacred. The fabled Allagash River, symbol of remote wilderness, had been "protected" in the mid-1960s. To stave off a more ambitious federal protection plan for this wild country, the large landowners agreed not to cut a 500-foot buffer strip along both shores of the Allagash. In the 1980s, the landowners stripped the forests bare right up to the Allagash beauty strip. Canoeists had the illusion of visiting a wild place. Birds and passengers in an airplane saw the devastated landscape beyond.[17]

The economic costs of two centuries of destructive logging have been high. The paper industry controlled the land, the politics, and the economy of the northern two-thirds of Maine for a century. Economic diversity had been thwarted. Paper was king, and few job opportunities were available outside the timber industry. Around 1980, the paper companies decided to invest in modern mills in the southeastern United States. Mills in Maine, among the oldest in the nation, could not compete without major new investment, which the paper companies refused to make. From 1985 to 1993, more than three thousand mill jobs disappeared in Maine. Since then, several more cutbacks have been made at Maine paper mills, machines have been closed, and locals constantly speculate about which major mill will be the first to shut down entirely.[18]

In northern Maine, the large landowners export most of their sawlogs to Canadian mills for processing. Raw log exports mean the export of job opportunities in lucrative value-added manufacturing enterprises. Even the loggers who cut the wood are often Canadians. Hiring Canadians has enabled the large landowners to suppress the wages they pay to loggers. Mechanization in the woods dramatically reduced jobs in the 1970s and 1980s. As the amount of wood cut increased each year, jobs declined. From 1984 to 1992, logging employment in Maine declined by 40 percent, and it is still dropping.[19]

With economic decline, members of the younger generation have been forced to leave the place of their birth. Northern Maine towns are dying. The population of the logging town of Allagash, at the confluence of the Allagash and St. John Rivers, has declined from 800 in the 1970s to 260 at the end of the century. When its school closed in 1997, it had thirteen students. About three-quarters of the town were older than sixty-five years.[20]

Ecological degradation, economic degradation, and cultural degradation are intertwined.

The destruction of North American wilderness, accompanied by the advance of European-American civilization along the frontier, is a story that has been played out all across the continent. In 1893, a young midwestern historian, Frederick Jackson Turner, suggested that the distinctive quality of American history and culture was explained by the influence of the frontier. As Europeans moved farther away from the influence of Europe, deeper into the North American wilderness, the American character was shaped in the struggle to subdue the wilderness. Turner believed that the democratic institutions that set America apart from eighteenth- and nineteenth-century Europe were forged on the frontier.[21]

Turner's "frontier thesis" with its focus on the role that the land played in shaping American history anticipated today's environmental historians by three-quarters of a century. He taught us to look at the landscape to understand ourselves and our culture. He appreciated the irony of the European conquest of North American wilderness: Even as Europeans struggled to transform the wild continent into an Europeanized agricultural landscape, the American wilderness transformed those Europeans.

In recent decades, however, the frontier thesis has been subjected to withering attacks and critiques.[22] Turner ignored the experiences of Indians, blacks, Mexican-Americans, women. He romanced the frontier. He overlooked economic and geographic influences, such as the abundant unexploited resources of North America that created the great material wealth of the nation. He ignored the fact that this great wealth was amassed by the destruction of nonrenewable natural capital, not by the sustainable utilization of the interest that accrues from that natural capital. He romanticized the heroic individualist on the frontier who supposedly conquered the wilderness. He ignored the truth that most of the conquest of the West had been underwritten by the government that had subsidized the railroads and sent out the cavalry to rid the land of Indians, so that Americans could settle the "free land." He overlooked the fact that most of the private land in the United States fell into the hands of a small number of corporations and wealthy individuals, not the common man. His thesis that democracy was forged on the frontier is no longer taken seriously.

However, Turner's observation that the frontier served as a "safety valve" for American culture and democracy helps explain our current environmental crisis. Whatever the problem, there was an instant solution: the disaffected could uproot, move west, and try again. Always, there was room for error. Always, there was "free land" somewhere else to bail us out of our profligate and ecologically ignorant ways. The safety valve deluded us into believing that there were no limits; that we could do anything we wished. When the timber barons had completed the liquidation of Maine's old-growth forests, they headed to the Great Lakes states and the Pacific Northwest. When farmers depleted the thin soils of northern New England, they set out for the richer soils of the Midwest or the Great Plains.

The safety-valve ethic has exerted a corrosive influence on evolving American democracy. A healthy democracy confronts problems, grapples with difficult social and political issues; it doesn't run away from them; it doesn't postpone addressing them until they are full-blown disasters.

The safety-valve experience rewarded waste and exploitation; it fostered a rootlessness that has always bedeviled American culture. It takes a long time living in one spot to learn how to live lightly on a landscape. Rootlessness condemns the wanderer to an alienated relationship to the land. Safety-valve thinking has shaped our economic system. Polluting industries learned that they need not clean up their toxic wastes; they could just dump them into the river or the air, and pass the costs on to society and the environment. By externalizing costs, profits are higher for private enterprise.

When we ran out of "free land" in the 1890s, we did not make a concerted effort to address all the problems we had deferred. Instead, we entered the world arena as an imperial power to seek new frontiers abroad to replace the seemingly vanished frontier at home. Today's global economy and our naive faith in unlimited economic growth are modern expressions of the safety-valve frontier mentality. As the twentieth century ends, the global economy is squeezing ecosystems and peoples. We still have not come to grips with the consequences of the ideology of unfettered growth in a finite system, an economy that rewards fragmentation and destruction of natural systems.

Past Conservation Strategies

There is an alternative tradition in American history, one that places limits on the behavior of humans, and values wild nature for noncommercial reasons. It offers us guidance in developing long-term strategies that will help sustain the natural and human communities of the region. Thoreau lamented the loss of so much of the forests of Concord. In the spring of 1856 he wrote in his journal:

> I listen to a concert in which so many parts are wanting . . . Many of those animal migrations and other phenomena by which the Indians marked the season are no longer to be observed. I seek acquaintance with Nature, — to know her moods and manners. Primitive nature is the most interesting to me. I take infinite pains to know all the phenomena of the spring, for instance, thinking that I have here the entire poem, and then, to my chagrin, I hear that it is but an imperfect copy that I possess and have read, that my ancestors have torn out many of the first leaves and grandest passages, and mutilated it in many places.[23]

By the 1890s, extensive tracts of forest, from the Adirondacks to Maine, had been liquidated. The early eastern conservationists responded to the perceived closing of the frontier by recognizing that there are physical and natural limits to human activity. Outraged by the deforestation, the silted streams and rivers, and the summer droughts that threatened the water supplies of New York City, Albany, and Manchester, New Hampshire, they organized to protect some of the ravaged forests from further logging damage. The results varied from state.

New York created the Adirondack and Catskill Forest Reserves in 1885, and by 1894 had decreed that state forest lands would be protected by the state's constitution as "forever wild." Today, more than 2.6 million acres of wilderness are protected in perpetuity in the Adirondack Park. New Hampshire conservationists led a twenty-year campaign to create eastern national forests. Finally, in 1911, Congress passed the Weeks Act authorizing the creation of eastern national forests. Success in this long struggle came after conservationists had forged alliances with forest advocates from the southern Appalachians and the textile mill operators of Manchester, New Hampshire, and Lowell, Massachusetts, who feared that summer droughts would rob them of needed water power.[24]

The White Mountain National Forest in New Hampshire and western Maine was the first northeastern national forest. About 15 percent of the National Forest is now designated wilderness, and perhaps another 30 percent is de facto wilderness. The remainder is exploited by logging, downhill skiing, snowmobiling—activities that are not compatible with wilderness.

Maine never seriously considered the public land protection strategy. Instead, control of the state's undeveloped North Woods was swiftly transferred from the timber barons to the paper companies at the turn of the century.

Today, wildlands lovers of northern New England cast an envious eye at the wilderness of the Adirondack Park. Sure, the Park has social and ecological problems, but wouldn't we dearly love to be so afflicted?

In Vermont and New Hampshire, less than 200,000 acres in the White and Green Mountain National Forests has been designated wilderness. Most of that is concentrated in the higher elevations, which have scant timber value. The Forest Service lands are too often managed for economic values that conflict with ecological values. Most of the natural communities of both states are on private lands and remain largely unprotected. Few examples remain of older forests and undisturbed ecosystems. Threats from development and unsustainable logging persist. The economy operates at the beck and call of the global economy—the ultimate instrument of death to local cultural and ecological integrity.

Then there is Maine. What scant wilderness Maine enjoys was a gift to the people of the state by Governor Percival Baxter, who bought 200,000 acres around Mount Katahdin in north-central Maine in the middle of the century. Baxter State Park is a great treasure, but it occupies only 1 percent of the land of Maine, and is hardly an adequate substitute for a comprehensive ecological reserve system. Baxter is, however, a promising nucleus for a much larger reserve system in northern Maine.

Why did the four neighboring states follow such different paths during that final decade of the nineteenth century? Why are Maine's forestlands so degraded while so much of the Adirondacks, and significant portions of the White and Green Mountains, are recovering? Economic diversity explains much of the difference.

In New York, lumbering dominated the post–Civil War economy in the Adirondacks, as it did throughout northern New England. Unlike the other three states, however, the New York state economy was quite diverse, and lumbering constituted a rather small percentage of the state's overall economy. The New York timber industry was not powerful enough to control the state legislature the way its counterpart has ruled Maine for two centuries. Competing economic and political interests, including concern for New York City's water supply, were able to override it. Recreation and tourism also flourished in the Adirondacks after the Civil War, assisted by the extension of railroad lines into the region.[25]

Maine had no great cities downstream of the North Woods, scant economic alternatives to timber, and no railroad lines hauling wealthy, politically well-connected tourists into the forest. In short, Maine had no powerful constituency to counter the timber barons. New Hampshire and Vermont enjoyed somewhat more economic diversity than Maine. New Hampshire, in particular, did have a powerful tourist industry in the White Mountains. Still, these states did not have the same degree of economic diversity as New York, and had no major metropolis like New York City or Albany along their major rivers. New Hampshire and Vermont protected less-productive lands from the timber barons, but the national forests remained within the timber base. Permanent wilderness protection for national forest lands had to await passage of the 1964 Wilderness Act.[26]

It has been nearly a century since the great gains in eastern conservation were made. The Adirondacks, the White and Green Mountain National Forests, and Baxter State Park are islands of maturing forests. They have not yet recovered their pre-European-settlement complexity and diversity. Many native species have not yet returned to them; some, like the once-abundant passenger pigeon, are gone forever. But these public lands are much more ecologically healthy than the wreckage the paper companies are leaving behind. Even if our public lands were placed into the public domain primarily for recreational and economic reasons, they have played a critical role in the recovery of ecological integrity in the region. They represent a great, but incomplete, legacy.

We are in the midst of a global extinction crisis, with extinction rates hundreds, perhaps thousands of times higher than in the pre-human past.[27] Ecologists are discovering that the resiliency to natural and anthropogenic stress of forests of the Northern Appalachians has declined for a variety of reasons, including atmospheric pollution, the introduction of forest pathogens such as chestnut blight, the gypsy moth, and Dutch elm disease, and unsustainable forestry. Researchers at Hubbard Brook in the White Mountain National Forest found in 1996 that the forest essentially stopped growing in 1987 due to the leaching of calcium and magnesium from the soil by acid deposition. Ecologist Tom Wessels wonders if, due to environmental stresses, native tree species are succumbing to pathogens they might once have resisted.[28]

Predictions for global warming caused by the greenhouse effect are ominous. Scientists project a temperature increase from 1950 to 2050 that is sixty times faster than the transition from the glacial to interglacial period twelve thousand years ago. How will tree species survive the warmer conditions when they can migrate only a fraction of a mile in a year? How will global warming affect natural communities? We cannot say. But, Wessels says, we can say with "certainty" that if these predictions come to pass there will be "noticeable reductions in biodiversity."[29] He is writing about central New England, but it is unlikely that northern New England will escape unscathed.

The Maine Natural Areas Program report, "Biodiversity in Maine," released in January 1996, included a number of disturbing findings:

- We know very little about the composition, structure, and function of Maine ecosystems. The "scarcity of inventory is particularly acute in northern Maine" [where the largest landowners have frequently been uncooperative with efforts to inventory their lands]. "The absence of consistent baseline data frustrates attempts to measure trends for almost all taxonomic groups; inference is the primary tool for assessing change."
- Early successional-dwelling species are "generally widespread and abundant." However, "species requiring undisturbed (or less disturbed) forest habitats have become less abundant."
- "Eight of twenty-five forest community types in Maine are rare; of the types that are not rare, good natural examples are rare." Currently there is inadequate protection of "natural forest diversity."
- "Older forests of all types are becoming uncommon in Maine."
- Aquatic ecosystems in Maine have been "profoundly and adversely" degraded by human activity.

The report pointed out that "most of the known sites for the rarest forest-community types remain without formal protection."[30]

Similar assessments of the status of biodiversity in New Hampshire and Vermont make it clear that past and current strategies have failed to arrest the decline in biodiversity.[31] The public land base is neither large enough, nor extensive enough to protect representative examples of all native communities and to protect habitat for viable populations for all species native to the region. Even though 48 percent of the Adirondack Park is forever wild forest, not all communities native to the park are adequately protected. Only about 4 percent of Maine enjoys any protection as public or private conservation lands, and most of Maine's public lands are still logged.

Studies from every continent have demonstrated that native biological diversity is only likely to persist for long periods of time in areas that are strictly protected. Assertions that biodiversity can be adequately protected in the so-called "working landscape" that permits forestry, herbicide spraying, agriculture, road building, and other human activities are wishful thinking unsubstantiated by objective research. True, a well-managed forestry operation will contribute more to biodiversity protection that a poorly managed operation. But, it is no substitute for reserves.

Earlier conservation strategies failed to preserve ecological and evolutionary integrity for a variety of reasons. They have generally been "ad hoc" instead of systematic. They have focused on scenery, recreation, rare species, and wildlife habitat, especially game species. As a result, today's conservation lands are small, isolated, incomplete ecosystems that only partially protect the full spectrum of native species and natural communities and the abiotic and biotic processes that sustain biological diversity.[32]

Small reserves are prone to produce isolated "museum pieces" of natural communities or relic populations of rare species that do not exist "in any meaningful way" because they require large investments of restoration and maintenance.[33] Small reserves lack wildness. Small reserves are very expensive to manage and monitor.

Large reserves are much more cost effective. They provide greater protection, thereby requiring less compensatory management. They usually have a much lower edge-to-interior ratio than corridors, buffer zones, and easement lands. We get much more protection for our money when we invest in large reserves.

Habitats for many small species of concern can be protected in small reserves. In the more developed parts of the Northern Appalachians—central and southern Maine, New Hampshire, and Vermont—small reserves are often our only option. However, if we desire the full concert, if we are to ensure long-term ecological and evolutionary integrity, we must establish many large reserves wherever we can. In the northern reaches of New England, we have the opportunity to establish large wilderness areas in the undeveloped, uninhabited timberlands that have been sold and resold over the past decade.

Much of the region's conservation community remains committed to old-style protection strategies that focus on small areas (and require relatively smaller amounts of money and political capital to acquire and manage the land). As the ecological and economic crisis in the region worsens, and as the shortcomings of traditional conservation strategies become more apparent, support is growing for restoring large tracts of wilderness that address landscape habitat fragmentation, loss of old-growth and mature forests, unprotected watersheds, airborne pollutants, catastrophic natural disturbance events, and extirpated large predators. Unfortunately, the political divisions within the conservation community provide cover for politicians to attack proposals for large wilderness reserves.

The timber industry has retained veto-power over regional forest policy initiatives, such as the Northern Forest Lands Study (1988–1990) and the Northern Forest Lands Council (1990–1994).[34] Public discussion of reforming industrial forestry, large-scale public acquisition of paper company lands, and the designation of large wilderness reserves was effectively suppressed. Unwilling to address core problems, these initiatives recommended expensive, ineffectual strategies that misdirect scarce conservation money into industry hands.

Today, in northern New England, two seductive alternatives exist to large wilderness reserve strategies that, while fashionable among most mainstream environmental groups, politicians, and the timber industry, are ultimately naive and dangerous. One approach seeks to protect "representative" examples of the natural communities. It was adopted by the Maine Forest Biodiversity Project, a collection of "stakeholders" in Maine that struggled in vain from 1994 to 1998 to develop consensus over some modest biodiversity protection strategies on state-owned lands, which cover about 4 percent of the state. Representatives of the large landowners vetoed discussion of more-ambitious strategies designed to preserve biological integrity, including reintroduction of large carnivores. Most mainstream environmental groups participating in this misguided exercise acquiesced to industry's outrageous demands.

A strategy of protecting representative examples of natural ecosystems, while a component of a larger regional strategy, is no substitute. It is unlikely, by itself, to protect the long-term viability of the protected sites; it is inadequate for assuring the integrity of protected areas subjected to catastrophic natural disturbances. Nutrient cycling and hydrological cycles are inadequately protected. And it offers faint hope of restoring large, wide-ranging species.

Industry supporters have promoted a second strategy—conservation easements—to prevent the establishment of large wilderness reserves. Conservation easements usually have been written to control development, but to permit forestry, usually including clear-cutting, pesticide spraying, and other unsustainable activities that are entirely incompatible with the preservation of biodiversity. Such easements usually cost from 40 to 90 percent of full fee acquisition, depending on the degree of threat posed by development. It makes no sense to expend scarce conservation funds for easements on lands that are under little or no threat of development. Lands with the greatest development potential commonly cost 75 to 90 percent of full fee acquisition. Why not buy them outright and manage for preservation?

Easements that include a "forever wild" clause, especially if partially or entirely donated to a reserve system, are a bargain (see chapter 8). Easements that permit some low-impact forestry, but proscribe logging activities that compromise long-term forest integrity, have value in buffer zones and in corridors connecting core areas. Such easements make sense in certain parts of the Adirondack Park that already have a large wilderness component in place, and in more fragmented and developed areas where the potential for large reserves is slight. But, easements as a substitute for large wilderness reserves undercut efforts to preserve ecological integrity. Alas, this has been happening with discouraging regularity in Maine, New Hampshire, and Vermont. Such easements are a misappropriation of scarce acquisition funds, and a misuse of a minor conservation tool. Once northern New England has a solid network of large wilderness reserves in place, then easements can, when the occasion warrants, play a useful role.

The Need for Large, Connected Wilderness Reserves

If small, isolated reserves fail to preserve the "variety and variability among living organisms and the ecological complexes in which they occur," we need to try a new strategy. Several large, connected reserves (in conjunction with smaller reserves) are necessary to preserve biodiversity on a landscape level over long periods of time.[35]

Large reserves are far more likely to preserve the long-term viability of wide-ranging species such as caribou, wolf, cougar, wolverine. They are much less susceptible to the consequences of large-scale disturbance events such as the 1938 Hurricane, the 1995 windstorms that affected approximately 700,000 acres of the Adirondack Park, and the January 1998 ice storm that affected hundreds of thousands of acres in northern New England and the Adirondacks. Large reserves are much more capable of sustaining hydrological and nutrient cycling on a landscape scale. They are much more resistant to the invasion of non-native species that can wreak havoc with native species and communities. They permit the eventual recovery of functional old-growth forest communities.

Large reserves serve as scientific controls to the experiment of industrial civilization. Conservation biologists assert that "management experiments with no controls are dangerous." Industrial forestry represents the final stage of a dangerous two hundred-year experiment. Establishment of large reserves at this juncture cannot fully compensate for our lost baseline information from the pre-settlement forest, but it can begin to rescue us from continued folly. Even if one subscribes to the value of managed forests and conservation easements for preserving biodiversity, we need scientific controls to test this unproven hypothesis.[36] Small reserves may serve as a sort of perverse control, as we monitor them to assess their ineffectiveness in preserving and restoring the landscape-scale qualities.

Today, several serious proposals for rewilding the region on different spatial scales are on the table.

The Wildlands Project. The Wildlands Project (TWP) proposes to establish a continent-wide system of connected ecological reserves to protect and restore the ecological richness and native biodiversity of North America. The recovery of entire ecosystems and landscapes throughout every region of the continent is necessary to halt the disappearance of wildlife and wildness. TWP proposes the creation of wilderness reserves that connect Panama and the Caribbean to Alaska; the Pacific shores with the Atlantic coasts. Proponents of the goals of the Wildlands Project articulate a strategy designed to ensure that all native species are capable of flourishing within the "ebb and flow of ecological processes, rather than within the constraints of what industrial civilization is content to leave alone."[37] In less than a decade, TWP has already stimulated profound rethinking about the subject of reserve design and the need for vast tracts of wilderness. Critics initially dismissed the Wildlands Project as hopelessly utopian and politically naïve; today growing numbers of conservation biologists and the mainstream environmentalists are inspired by its bold and ecologically responsible message.[38]

Maine Woods National Park. The Maine Woods National Park proposal, offered by Restore: The North Woods, would preserve 3.2 million acres in the heart of the northern Maine woods from Baxter State Park in the southeast, to Moosehead Lake in the southwest, and the headwaters of the Allagash and St. John rivers to the north (see map 6.3). It contains the watersheds of the East Branch and West Branch of the Penobscot River, over 700 miles of rivers on the American Rivers *Outstanding Rivers List*, including the first fifty miles of the Allagash Wilderness Waterway, the headwaters of the Aroostook, Kennebec, and St. John rivers, and most of Moosehead Lake, the largest lake in New England. The proposed park provides habitat for endangered and sensitive species such as the Canada lynx, bald eagle, pine marten, northern bog lemming, spruce grouse, blueback trout, pale-green orchid, and small whorled pogonia, as well as critical spawning habitat for the endangered Atlantic salmon. Extirpated species such as the wolf, whether the eastern timber wolf or the red wolf, cougar, wolverine, and woodland caribou will find abundant habitat.[39]

Public acquisition of the SAPPI and Bowater lands that were sold in 1998 would have brought more than half of the proposed national park

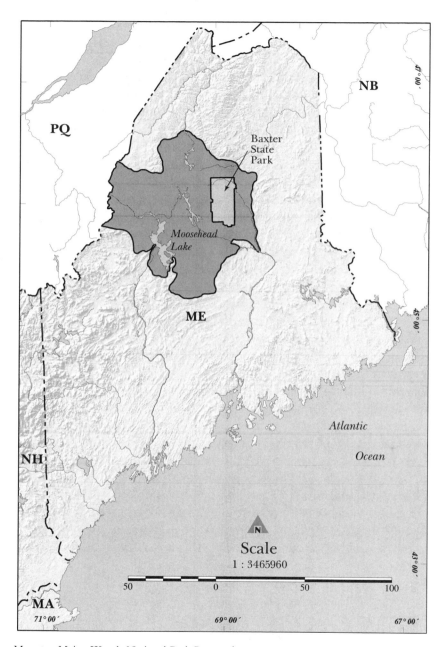

Map 6.3. Maine Woods National Park Proposal.

into public ownership at bargain basement prices. Unfortunately, even though these land sales have been occurring with regularity, Maine has not bothered to develop a strategy (in conjunction with the federal government) to acquire these lands. While political demagogues disparage "wilderness romantics," public support for the park is growing inside and outside Maine. An opinion poll taken in the autumn of 1999 showed greater than 70 percent of Maine citizens favor the national park; only 5 percent opposed it.

In the summer of 1999, I interviewed a logger in northern Maine who cannot get work because the large landowners prefer to hire bonded Canadian loggers at lower wages than Maine loggers can survive on. He told me that he and all the loggers he knows support the national park proposal to save the forests of northern Maine from further industrial logging.[40] As the region's paper industry continues to collapse, support for the national park among former loggers, mill workers, and citizens throughout Maine will grow. Indeed, the Maine Woods National Park is likely to be one of the next great success stories in American conservation history. It will make an important contribution to the restoration of our region's battered economy and culture as well.[41]

Headwaters Wilderness Reserve System. The Northern Appalachian Restoration Project (NARP) has proposed an 8-million acre Headwaters Wilderness Reserve system for northern and western Maine, northern New Hampshire, and northeastern Vermont (see map 6.4).[42] This plan to establish a network of sixteen publicly owned wilderness reserves will take longer to achieve than the national park. However, with each new blockbuster land sale, we can begin to protect elements of the Headwaters reserve system. The Headwaters proposal includes all of the proposed Maine Woods National Park, as well as the entire Allagash River watershed and the St. John River watershed as far as the town of Allagash, Maine. It also extends into northern New Hampshire and Vermont, moving us closer to the day when we can connect ecological reserves in Maine with the Green Mountains, the Adirondacks, and the Berkshires and Taconics.

The following considerations guided the development of the Headwaters proposal:

- **Location of undeveloped areas.** As noted, all the lands included in the Headwaters proposal presently are owned by absentee corporations and speculators. *No year-round human settlements exist within the boundaries of any of the proposed sixteen Headwaters reserves.* No residents of

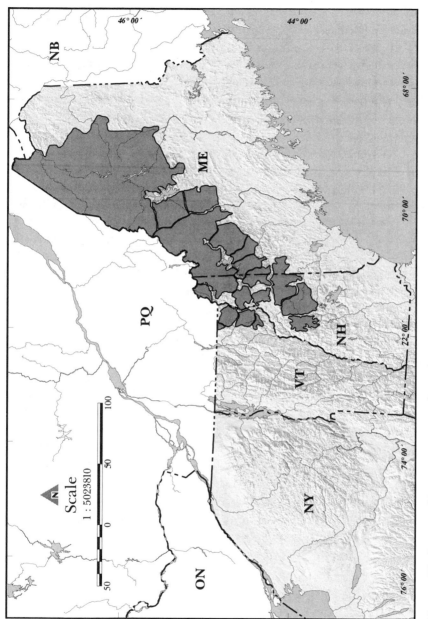

Map 6.4. Headwaters Wilderness Reserve System Proposal.

the area will be displaced. Except for an extensive network of logging roads, there is essentially no development.

- **Watersheds of high value, as intact as possible.** The Headwaters proposal contains the headwaters of all the major rivers of northern New England east of the Connecticut River. It encompasses the entire watershed of the fabled Allagash River and almost all of the headwaters of the St. John, the most remote and wild river in New England.

- **Existing public lands.** Existing public lands cover only about 5 percent of northern New England. Although currently all are not managed primarily for the protection of ecological integrity, they enjoy varying degrees of protection and are the anchors of the Headwaters proposal. The largest public tracts within the Headwaters are Baxter State Park, Bigelow Preserve, Namakanta Public Reserve, the Allagash Wilderness Waterway in Maine, the Appalachian Trail corridor in all three states, the White Mountain National Forest in Maine and New Hampshire, the Nash Stream Forest in New Hampshire, the Conte National Wildlife Refuge in Vermont and New Hampshire, and Victory Bog State Forest and Wildlife Management Area in Vermont.

- **Extirpated species.** The large native carnivores that have been extirpated, or, in the case of the lynx in Maine, driven to the brink, require large reserves. While it is true that wolves and lynx can secure sufficient prey in disturbed forests, it is not so certain that they can survive the two-legged poachers and their four-wheeled vehicles. Only large roadless areas provide assurance that wolves, lynx, cougars, caribou, and, eventually, wolverines can recover in the Northern Appalachians. There is evidence that large predators are not entirely extinct in the region. A lynx successfully bred in western Maine in 1999. DNA testing has confirmed that two canids killed in Maine since 1993 are wolves. Cougar scat was found in Craftsbury, Vermont, in 1994. Still, we have a long way to go before viable populations of these species can survive in the Northeast. Anadromous fish such as Atlantic salmon were formerly abundant in the rivers of the region. They transport large quantities of biomass and protein from high productivity systems in the ocean into lower productivity environments in the headwaters of rivers.[43] In colonial times, a law stated that a master could not serve salmon to the servants more than three times a week. Today, thanks primarily to dams, but also to pollution, fertilizer and pesticide runoff and soil erosion from agriculture, forest mismanagement, and development, Atlantic salmon are on the brink of extinction, despite expensive, but poorly designed recovery programs. In 1998, fewer than two thousand Atlantic salmon returned to rivers in New England.[44]

The Headwaters proposal outlined above only considers the undeveloped region of northern Maine, New Hampshire, and Vermont, where the creation of truly large wilderness reserves is possible. In the rest of these states, development and human settlement generally preclude establishment of large core areas. Not surprisingly, most of the rare, threatened, and endangered species and natural communities are found in these more-developed areas. A regional biodiversity conservation strategy cannot ignore areas that lack the potential for large wilderness areas.

Small core reserve areas are essential to protect rare species and communities in more-developed areas (see chapter 5). Successful establishment of small reserves will require more restoration work, more monitoring and buffering, and will cost more per acre. Linkage with other smaller reserves and the large reserves to the north may often be difficult, but it is essential. Here is where thoughtfully designed conservation easements can be helpful supplements to fully protected core areas.

Efforts are underway at the state level in Maine, New Hampshire, and Vermont to design reserves employing a rigorous scientifically informed approach alongside more traditional conservation approaches (see chapter 5). Wilderness proponents need to work with these initiatives to provide support for the creation of a network of larger wilderness reserves in the more undeveloped areas of the respective states.

Two other interesting wilderness proposals would provide linkage from the Northern Appalachians and Adirondacks to wilderness reserves in other regions.

A2A. A2A—Adirondacks to Algonquin—links the Northern Appalachian region with wild lands of Ontario (see chapter 5). A2A will facilitate the return of wolves and lynx to the Adirondacks along the Frontenac Axis, a geologically and geographically distinct zone stretching between the Adirondack Park and Ontario's Algonquin Provincial Park. The Frontenac Axis is the most extensive, least degraded north-south corridor across the St. Lawrence Valley. It connects the boreal forests of Canada with the forests of the northeastern United States, and also contains hemlock-pine-northern hardwoods forests. Wide-ranging species such as wolf, lynx, and moose could use this protected corridor to migrate back to the United States.

Appalachian Trail Corridor. The 2,000-mile Appalachian Trail (AT) corridor could link wilderness areas in the Northern Appalachians to those of the central and southern Appalachians. The AT corridor would have to be at least five miles wide, and corridors must be designed to connect wilderness reserves throughout the Appalachians to the AT wilderness backbone so that a wilderness network could join Maine and the Maritimes with Georgia and Florida.[45] Some conservation biologists recognize that an AT wilderness corridor, running north-south, could play a valuable role in helping plant and tree species migrate north in the event of global warming.[46]

Critics allege that large wilderness proposals are naive and utopian. Leading conservation biologists certainly do not think so. Soulé and Terborgh state that "every strand of the scientific argument suggests that if we wish to maintain a viable landscape that allows 100 percent of the native species to persist, then the primary goals of reconnecting the landscape make excellent sense ecologically."[47] Bold proposals are always greeted with scorn initially. History is replete with examples such as the American independence movement and the abolition of slavery.

Obligatory skepticism is an especially pernicious disease in conservation work. I have often been told: "I agree with you, however, I would lose my credibility if I said so publicly." At the root of this problem is a confusion of ecological and political realities. Politics is a game of negotiation and compromise. Ecology is the study of physical and biological laws and limits that are beyond the power of humans to override. Applying the art of political compromise to the biodiversity crisis yields half-measures or worse. Until we, as citizens of the biotic community, insist that our culture respect physical and ecological limits, biological degradation and extinction will only worsen. If a thing is scientifically defensible, then we must insist upon a politics that is mature enough to implement it. It is folly to continue to acquiesce to a prevailing philosophy of unlimited economic growth on a finite planet.

We have many reasons for optimism that the next generation will have the courage to protect vast tracts of wilderness in the Northern Appalachians and throughout North America. Public opinion is already very sympathetic to biodiversity and wilderness protection strategies. A new generation that is ecologically literate is coming of age, replacing a generation that never heard of ecology until middle age.

But proponents of big wilderness in the Northern Appalachians must articulate a clear vision. They must not seek to appease politically and economically motivated opponents to wilderness. They must persist, and they must insist that protection of wild nature is fundamentally an ethical issue, not more politics as usual. If they nurture a discussion of the value and importance of wilderness to a healthy local culture, they will discover allies in impoverished rural communities.

As Thoreau wrote in *Walden*: "In the long run men hit only what they aim at. Therefore, though they should fail immediately, they had better aim at something high."[48]

A Golden Opportunity for Big Wilderness

The option to save the status quo in the Northeast is not available. The woods have been too degraded to sustain current cutting levels; the mill infrastructure is obsolete. Today the public has an unprecedented opportunity to acquire most of these lands and establish wilderness reserves. Many residents object that we need to retain these overcut lands in the timber base to sustain the local economy; but it is too late. They should have intervened twenty or thirty years ago to stop the industrial foresters before they launched the final assault. The management options for northern Maine and parts of northern New Hampshire and Vermont for the next fifty to one hundred years are identical: These lands must be managed more or less as wilderness whether the goal is recovery of managed forests or recovery of wild lands. These lands are not in fit condition to make a significant contribution to the timber-dependent economy in our lifetimes. The paper industry unilaterally decided to remove millions of acres of Northern Appalachian forests from the timber base. We have no choice but to develop an alternative economy for at least the next half-century. Why not extend this economy indefinitely? What would such an economy look like?

A regional economy must meet the needs of its citizens, not those of far-off corporations. Today, we export most of our raw logs and raw milk instead of processing them locally. We need to develop a much more diversified timber and agricultural value-added economy. We need to stop importing most of our food and manufactured goods. We need to scale back—better yet, withdraw from—the consumer economy. We must avoid non-essential energy uses. Human population must decline. We need to recognize the value of wild lands in our lives, to view them as a positive good instead of a locked-up resource. As we face the growing global climate crisis, we will recognize the value of wild lands for locking up carbon in live and dead biomass.

Significant economic benefits can be derived from establishing large wilderness cores, such as protecting soil from erosion, protecting watersheds, maintaining water and air quality, regulating local climate, and buffering against anticipated global climate changes. Wilderness offers an improved quality of life that attracts responsible economic investment.

A transformation of our economy will not be easy. Old habits are hard to break. The start-up and transition costs to a lower-impact economy are significant, especially in view of the current condition of the industrial forest. We'll need help from the government. But after all, the government has subsidized the destruction of the woods and our economy by promoting the interests of the absentee corporations; perhaps it can help to heal the damage.

The Adirondack Park—a "second-chance wilderness"—demonstrates that people and wilderness can coexist.[49] But the Adirondacks are too small; we need to conduct the experiment on a much larger scale. Adding another 10 to 15 million acres of wilderness in northern Vermont, New Hampshire, and Maine would be a great step forward in the rewilding of North America and North American culture.

Wilderness is necessary in shaping our low-impact economy. We need to surrender the safety-valve economic ethic that seemingly forgave our errors and exploitations because more free land was always available "over the hump." We need to cash in that delusional insurance policy for a real insurance policy—a healthy life support system. We need to operate in a system that is forgiving, but not excessively forgiving. Ecosystems are resilient. They can bounce back. They can recover from anthropogenic disturbances, provided we do not degrade them so severely that they require centuries to heal.

Wilderness protection is right for ecological, ethical, cultural, and economic reasons. It is necessary to protect the integrity of our life support system. It is a prerequisite for establishing a healthy, beneficial, and sustainable relationship with the wild and natural landscape of North America. It is the foundation upon which a healthy, enduring, low-impact culture can be built.

We are calling for a reversal of that mythical frontier line that marched so inexorably "forward" into the wilderness, wreaking havoc on native ecosystems, cultures, and economies. What was progress for the European despoilers and invaders was regress for native cultures that had lived here for millennia. The agri-culture and silvi-culture imposed on the native ecosystems did not nurture a terra-culture, a land ethic that respected land and its limits. How can we know and understand natural limits if we have no natural laboratories in which to observe, and even measure, limits at work?

Wilderness represents a voluntary renunciation of our options. It opens us to the possibility of discovering new worlds. Who among us is old enough to remember the climate of the pre-settlement forest? Who has fished for Atlantic salmon in the headwaters of the region's great rivers?

It will be generations before the industrial forest recovers its natural resilience. But, as soon as the healing begins, conditions all around will begin to improve. This is what happened in the Adirondacks and the White Mountains. This is the magic of wilderness and natural systems: that irrepressible urge to heal, to recover, to succeed to the next stage. Wilderness healing can drive the healing we need in our nature-estranged culture.

We will have to pitch in. While ecosystems naturally heal themselves, we humans have much work to do to facilitate that natural process. Freeman House, a pioneer in the grassroots ecological restoration movement, writes:

> A primary benefit of any attempt at environmental restoration is that it creates a situation that allows us to begin to learn from the patterns of the wild around us and within us, the patterns which shaped our mental capacities in the first place, shaped the automatic processes that maintain our daily functioning unbidden.[50]

The huge paper company land sales in the Northern Appalachians afford us an opportunity to reopen the wild frontier—to rewild a large segment of the northeastern United States. Instead of a false dichotomy between wilderness and civilization, between wild and managed lands, we need to merge these seeming irreconcilables on the new frontier.

One of the paradoxes of Turner's pioneers was that in "abandoning settled society for wilderness," they replaced the wilderness with the civilization they had abandoned. Today, we must again abandon settled society for wilderness by withdrawing our exploitative activities from lands so they can begin to rewild. Some day we will become a wilderness-loving civilization.

Wilderness is the key to revitalized democracy. Democracy was not forged on the anvil of wilderness destruction as Turner believed; wilderness destruction stunted the development of democratic institutions. Absentee ownership of land stifled democracy. We need a fundamental land reform—no absentee ownership. Caring landowners must live on the land they "own." The lands now undemocratically controlled by absentee corporations must be restored to public ownership to restore democracy, as well as wilderness. If we wish to revive and restore democracy, we must necessarily restore wilderness all across the continent. The reharmonization of human culture with wild nature requires the restoration of huge, wild, functional ecosystems and large carnivores. So long as there is wilderness, there is the possibility of democracy.

CHAPTER 7

Restoring the Wild

Species Recovery and Reintroduction

STEPHEN C. TROMBULAK AND KIMBERLY ROYAR

🐝 NORTHEAST OR WEST, wilderness should be more than simply an expanse of land and water declared to be wild. The concepts of wilderness and wildness are inherently linked to the presence of biological conditions that resemble those that would be present in a landscape if it were unmodified by the development of human culture. These conditions are diverse in character; they include the types and frequencies of disturbances like fire, the range of age classes of the dominant plant species, and the spectrum of communities in close proximity to each other. To the vast majority of people, however, the most noticeable condition of a seemingly natural place is the suite of species that inhabit the landscape. Indeed, when lamenting the transformation of the woods of Massachusetts, Henry David Thoreau, writing in 1856, made specific note of the species—particularly game species such as bear, moose, deer, beaver, and turkey—that had been lost since earlier times.[1]

The close connection that we make between the species composition of a region and our sense of the region's wildness means that the designation of wilderness requires more than simply drawing lines on a map and developing management plans to limit any further biological degradation. The loss of species through anthropogenic causes (e.g., over-harvesting, habitat destruction) in times past means that the development of wilderness requires the reintroduction of species that were once a part of the region's biological communities.

Due to the historical patterns of European settlement in North America, the need to consider species reintroductions as part of the reestablishment of wilderness is greater in the Northeast than in the West. In the Northeast, many more species were extirpated during the four hundred-plus years of European settlement in the region. Further, more of the region is ecologically fragmented today, so that individuals from other populations of species once native here find it more difficult to disperse into the region and aid in recolonization. Therefore, species reintroductions necessarily will play a more central role in our thinking about an eastern concept of wilderness than in the West, where more of the discussion has been driven by considerations of preservation of current conditions.

With respect to the establishment, or reestablishment, of wilderness in the Northeast, those discussing reintroduction immediately face at least two important philosophical issues. The first is the need to distinguish between introductions and reintroductions. The term "introduction" is reserved for the establishment in an area of a species that is not native to that area, such as zebra mussels (originally from the Caspian Sea and Ural River in southeastern Europe) or ginkgo trees (from China) into North America. The introduction of non-native, or exotic, species is widely regarded as one of the most dangerous forms of biological manipulation occurring in the world today. The introduction of exotics that are invasive or pathogenic is responsible for the decline and loss of native species, for modification of habitats and ecosystem processes, and for billions of dollars worth of damage to agricultural crops and forests.[2]

Species can be introduced either directly (by specific transportation of a species to an area by humans, either accidentally or on purpose) or indirectly (by human modification of physical conditions that improves the chances for the successful colonization by a new species); either way, the consequences can be unpredictable and unfortunate, and the temptation to introduce species that may appear to be harmless or that might have economic benefits should be resisted.

"Reintroduction," on the other hand, refers to the reestablishment by human action in an area of a species that was once native but had, for whatever reason, been eliminated or lost. Because the reintroduced species was once a natural part of the landscape, not only is it much less likely to cause the kinds of negative effects an exotic species might cause, but the biological community to which it is returned might actually benefit if that species is one that performed an important ecological function. Extirpated species can, of course, become reestablished in an area under their own power without human assistance, and although this is an important contributor to ecological restoration, it is usually thought of as recolonization rather than reintroduction.

Acknowledging the distinction between introduction and reintroduction immediately raises practical questions when we think about the steps necessary to reestablish a sense of wildness in a place. Should it make a difference how long an extirpated species has been absent from a community or why it disappeared when we decide whether it would be an exotic or native species? This question has practical importance in determining whether a species should be removed from an area as an exotic or allowed to remain as a reintroduced native. For example, horses roamed the western United States, until about twelve thousand years ago, when they, along with numerous other species of large mammals, went extinct. Their extinction is thought by many paleontologists to have been caused by overhunting by Paleo-Indians newly arrived in North America.[3] Horses remained absent from North America until feral herds became established from those that escaped from the Spanish explorers in the early 1500s. Are horses an introduced species because those here today were established from stocks brought from Europe, and the species had been absent from North America for more than ten thousand years? Or are they reintroduced because the species was once native to the region? There are no clear answers to these questions; it depends on how one chooses to define native and exotic.

The other important issue that confronts the goal of ecological restoration is that species are themselves not genetically uniform entities in either space or time. Individuals are not identical and, therefore, largely interchangeable across their range. Rather, individuals from populations in one part of the species' range may vary genetically—and therefore perhaps morphologically and behaviorally—from those from populations elsewhere. Similarly, species continually evolve, so that the genetic identity of a single population at one time may differ from that of the same population at another time. From a philosophical perspective, then, exact restoration of a species simply may not be possible.[4] This is both because the unique genetic identity of the population that was extirpated may no longer be present elsewhere, and because the genetic identity that would have evolved in the population over time had the extirpation not occurred cannot be known.

Species reintroduction also involves at least one serious practical limitation: Some species no longer present in an area are, in fact, globally extinct, and therefore cannot be reintroduced regardless of any value of doing so. The passenger pigeon, for example, was once so numerous in the eastern United States that, as late as the mid-1800s, individual flocks of birds numbered in the billions. By the late 1800s, however, market hunting and land conversion had dramatically reduced their numbers, and the last passenger pigeon in the world died in captivity in 1914.[5] Other recently extinct species once native to the Northeast are the Carolina parakeet, great auk, and Labrador duck. Additionally, fossil evidence indicates that many species of large mammals roamed throughout the Northeast until ten to twelve thousand years ago, including mammoth, mastodon, dire wolf, giant short-faced bear, stag moose, American lion and cheetah, and giant beaver.[6] Unlike the horse, however, these species did not survive elsewhere in the world, and therefore cannot be reintroduced.

Despite the philosophical and practical challenges associated with species reintroduction, there are many reasons to reintroduce species to an area, and therefore to target species reintroductions as an important component in the restoration of wilderness. First, a given species may perform an important role in determining community structure, and its reintroduction may perhaps improve the ecological health of the region. Carnivores, for example, have long been recognized as important for controlling numbers of herbivores; without predators, herbivore populations may grow too large, degrade communities through overexploitation of food supplies, and then suffer from starvation.[7] Other types of "keystone species" may play roles in creating disturbances, altering physical conditions, or serving as critical resources for other species.[8] Second, a species may provide a specific resource to the human communities in a region. A species may have been an important game animal, for example, and its reintroduction would allow it to be so once again. Third, a species may contribute to the essential wild character of a landscape, enhancing the aesthetic, spiritual, and recreational value of a region. The howl of a wolf, the sight of a bull moose wading through a swamp, or the imprint of mountain lion tracks in the snow dramatically transform the feeling of a landscape in ways that transcend the ecological or utilitarian value of the species.

History of Reintroductions of Species in the Northeastern United States

Numerous species have been extirpated from portions of the Northeast at different times over the past four hundred years. Some of these have been the targets of reintroduction efforts, although the list is highly biased toward the charismatic birds and mammals. This list focuses on reintroductions of species that were extirpated, or reduced to such low numbers that they were effectively extirpated, from an entire state.[9] Numerous translocations of species from one location within a state to another have occurred, often for the purpose of mitigating the destruction of a population elsewhere, but these are not documented here. The difference between a reintroduction and translocation is purely arbitrary. The difference in based solely on the location of politically defined boundaries, which rarely have any ecological meaning. Our focus on reintroductions of extirpated species is not meant to devalue the ecological importance of translocations, but is rather intended solely to highlight in a limited amount of space one extreme class of tools to augment a species.

White-tailed deer (*Odocoileus virginianus*). Deer were widespread and perhaps locally abundant throughout the northeastern United States prior to European colonization, but they were extirpated or drastically reduced from most states in the region by overhunting and habitat loss throughout the 1800s. They were so important as a source of meat for people in the region, that they were reintroduced in many states in the nineteenth or early twentieth centuries. As examples, seventeen deer were reintroduced to southwestern Vermont from New York in 1878 (and they are now present statewide), and deer stocking began in Pennsylvania around 1906. Deer reintroductions have been so successful and habitat change favoring deer survival is so widespread that their population sizes are now greater than they were prior to European colonization.

Caribou (*Rangifer tarandus*). Once native to Maine, New York, New Hampshire, and Vermont, caribou were eliminated by hunting during the 1800s. Two reintroduction efforts were made in Maine. In the 1960s, the Maine Fish and Wildlife Department released some number of animals into the Mount Katahdin area. They scattered soon after and apparently died. A second effort was instigated by a private organization in 1988–1989; approximately thirty animals were brought to Maine from Newfoundland, but they became infected with brainworm and died.

Elk (*Cervus elaphus*). Elk once were distributed widely throughout the northeastern United States, but were extirpated throughout this range by the mid-to late 1800s. They were successfully reintroduced into Pennsylvania through a series of releases from 1913 to 1926. Elk taken from Wyoming and private captive herds in Pennsylvania were released widely throughout the state, and currently a single herd of over 450 is flourishing in the Allegheny Plateau region. Efforts to reintroduce elk to Massachusetts from 1910 to 1926 failed.

Beaver (*Castor canadensis*). Beaver were once abundant throughout the region, but are generally believed to have been eliminated from most of the northeastern United States between the eighteenth and nineteenth century as a result of loss of habitat and unregulated trapping for an export trade to Europe. For example, beaver are believed to have been extirpated from Massachusetts by the time of the Revolution, and the last known beaver in Vermont prior to recent times was trapped in 1841. They were protected by state law in 1910, and began to reestablish themselves in the northeastern part of the state, presumably from unknown remnant populations or populations to the north. Beaver were successfully reintroduced to southern Vermont in 1921 from six individuals trapped in New York, and other reintroductions occurred elsewhere in the state during the next ten to fifteen years. By 1941, they had expanded their range to encompass the entire state. Similarly, they were extirpated from Pennsylvania by the late 1800s, and successfully reintroduced in 1917 from a single pair imported from Wisconsin.

Allegheny wood rat (*Neotoma magister*). The New York Department of Environmental Conservation released twenty-nine wood rats in 1991 at two sites near New Paltz that they had historically occupied. This effort is described as being less of a reintroduction effort and more of an experiment to determine why they disappeared from the state; the reintroduced individuals were never expected to survive. Although the released population successfully reproduced, all individuals were dead after twenty months. At least eleven of twelve animals that could be examined died of the raccoon roundworm (*Balyisascaris procyonis*) in their brains, suggesting that wood rats cannot survive where raccoons and their parasites are abundant. This indicates a serious barrier to future reintroduction efforts.

Fisher (*Martes pennanti*). Unregulated trapping and habitat degradation dramatically reduced fisher populations throughout much of the northeastern United States (except for Maine, New Hampshire, and New York) by the mid-1800s; fisher were extirpated in southern New England, Pennsylvania, and New Jersey. They were successfully reintroduced into Vermont in the mid-1960s (from populations in Maine; described in more detail below), into Connecticut in 1990 (thirty animals from New Hampshire and four from Vermont), and into Pennsylvania in an ongoing effort beginning in 1994 (from populations in New York and New Hampshire).

Pine marten (*Martes americana*). Again, habitat loss and unregulated harvest led to the extirpation of pine martens from much of the Northeast by the mid-1940s. An effort to reintroduce them into the White Mountains in New Hampshire was made in 1975 (twenty-five animals from Maine), but there is no evidence that this was successful. An effort to reintroduce them in Vermont began in the late 1980s, but it too has so far not been successful (described in more detail below).

Lynx (*Lynx lynx*). Lynx were widespread at low population densities throughout the northeastern United States during pre-colonial times, but were eliminated throughout much of their range through trapping and loss of habitat. They are known to have been extirpated in Massachusetts, New York, and Pennsylvania, and are present in very low numbers, if at all, in Vermont and New Hampshire. A small population is still present in Maine, and shows evidence of successful breeding. The first effort to reintroduce lynx anywhere in North America took place in the Adirondack Mountains of New York in the late 1980s. Eighty-three cats captured in the Yukon Territory were translocated to the Adirondacks, where they were released. Over the next several years, the population declined, primarily due to roadkill mortality, and few, if any, lynx are believed to be present there today.[10]

Wild turkey (*Meleagris gallopavo*). Once common throughout the Northeast, turkey were eliminated throughout the region (except for Pennsylvania) by the mid-1800s through a combination of forest clearing and overhunting. As forests became reestablished and hunting regulations were developed, conditions for turkeys improved. In 1969 and 1970, Vermont relocated thirty-one turkeys from western New York (from stock that originally derived from Pennsylvania) to the Taconic Mountains in the southwestern part of the state. This initial release was successful, and turkeys have since been translocated from the Taconic Mountains to other parts of that state. In 1975, New Hampshire successfully reintroduced twenty-five turkeys in the Connecticut River Valley, from populations in New York and Vermont. Successful reintroductions were also made in Massachusetts (1972), New Jersey (1977), Connecticut (1978), Maine (1977–1978), and Rhode Island (1980), all from various northeastern stocks. Not all reintroduction efforts of turkey have been successful, however. Attempts to reintroduce turkey to Rhode Island beginning as early as the late 1950s apparently failed because forest cover was not yet sufficient to support birds in the wild, and because the released birds were from domestic stock that apparently could not survive in the wild. Fifteen different attempts to reintroduce turkey in Massachusetts from 1912 to 1967 all failed.

Peregrine falcon (*Falco peregrinus*). Peregrine falcons were one of the most publicly recognized victims of the increased use of the insecticide DDT through the 1960s. DDT worked its way up the food chain and into the bodies of peregrine falcons, top-level avian carnivores, where it caused the thinning of eggshells and widespread reproductive failure. Peregrine falcons were extirpated throughout the eastern United States, and by 1970 were placed on the endangered species list. In 1972, DDT was banned, and successful reintroduction efforts began in the northeastern

United States in the early 1980s. For example, 168 captive-bred peregrines were hacked in New York from 1974 to 1988 at a variety of sites—both cliffs and buildings—from New York City to the Adirondack Park. Peregrines first returned as breeding birds to New York in 1983 at two bridges in New York City. Four breeding pairs of peregrines were released from the cliffs of Owls Head in Glen, New Hampshire. In Massachusetts, thirty-six chicks from varying ancestry were hacked at several sites from 1975 to 1988, and successful breeding began in 1987. Ninety-three chicks were hacked in Vermont, and chicks were even hacked in downtown Philadelphia (1981). Peregrine falcons have become reestablished throughout the Northeast and elsewhere to the point that the U.S. Fish and Wildlife Service announced in 1999 that it would remove the species from the endangered species list by the end of that year.[11]

Osprey (*Pandion haliaetus*). Like the peregrine falcon, osprey declined from DDT-induced reproductive failure. In the late 1970s, a successful effort to reintroduce them into Pennsylvania was begun.

Bald Eagle (*Haliaeetus leucocephalus*). The bald eagle was also virtually extirpated due to DDT-induced reproductive failure in Pennsylvania (reduced to two nesting pairs), New Jersey (one nesting pair), and New York. All three states have successfully reintroduced the species. In New York, restoration began in 1976 and ended in 1988. In total, 198 eaglets were released at four sites around New York. Almost all of the nestlings were collected in southeast Alaska. By 1999, there were forty-five breeding pairs with sixty-four young fledged. Similarly, young adult and juvenile bald eagles captured in Saskatchewan were released at a number of sites in Pennsylvania from 1979 to 1989. Historically, bald eagles were uncommon breeders in Massachusetts, but were extirpated as breeders in 1905 (and thus not as a result of DDT poisoning). Forty-one eaglets from Michigan, Manitoba, and Nova Scotia were hacked in central Massachusetts from 1982 to 1988, and successful breeding first occurred again in 1989.

Atlantic salmon (*Salmo salar*). This anadromous species was eliminated in the Connecticut River watershed and in many other watersheds in New England as the development of many dams along that river's length blocked spawning adults from access to their upstream breeding grounds. Populations were reestablished in the 1970s in the Connecticut River watershed and Merrimac River watershed from hatchery-reared stock taken from Maine and southern Canada. As of 1993, the stocking rate in the Connecticut River watershed as a whole was four to five million fry per year.

Shad (*Alosa sapidissima*). Shad were extirpated from many watersheds in New England, presumably due to dams that blocked their movements. Shad were successfully reintroduced from the lower Connecticut River in Massachusetts into the upper Connecticut River of Vermont (late 1970s), Pawcatuc River of Rhode Island (early 1980s), and Merrimac River in New Hampshire (early 1980s). At least part of the success of these reintroductions can be credited to the building of fish passageways around the dams on these rivers.

Northeastern beach tiger beetle (*Cicindela dorsalis dorsalis*). Once found widely on Atlantic and Chesapeake Bay coastal beaches from Maryland to Cape Cod, this predatory insect was extirpated throughout much of its range by the 1950s. At present, it is only found in the Chesapeake Bay region and in two small populations in southeastern Massachusetts. The decline is thought to have been caused by heavy off-road vehicle use, pedestrian traffic, beach stabilization structures, and erosion. An effort by the U.S. National Park Service and the Massachusetts Division of Fisheries and Wildlife to reintroduce this species to the Cape Cod National Seashore in 1992 failed, primarily because the adults dispersed from the reintroduction site. Another experimental population was recently reintroduced to the Gateway National Seashore in Sandy Hook, New Jersey. Rather than adults, late-stage larvae were reintroduced, and the effort so far appears to be successful.[12]

American burying beetle (*Nicrophorus americanus*). This species was extirpated throughout its eastern range, except for one population on Block Island in Rhode Island, by the 1950s. The cause of its extirpation is not known for sure, but is thought to be caused primarily by a decline in the carrion it uses as a site to lay its eggs. Reintroductions were carried out at two sites in Massachusetts: Penikese Island (212 individuals from 1990–1993) and Nantucket Island (569 from 1994–1999). Both populations are extant, but these reintroduction efforts are still quite recent, and uncertainties about the food supply and competition with congeners on these islands raise concerns about the long-term potential for their success.[13]

Some species that were extirpated from all or part of the Northeast have become reestablished in the region under their own power, demonstrating that under some conditions, reestablishment of species can take place without human influence. A good example of this is the moose in Vermont. Moose sightings were rare in that state up through the mid-1900s; populations had declined due to overhunting, habitat conversion from forest to agriculture, and the elimination of the beaver, which played

Figure 7.1. Northeastern beach tiger beetle. *Photo by Tim Simmons.*

a crucial role in creating wetland habitat important for the moose. Moose were protected by law in Vermont in 1986, which, coupled with the return of both the forests and the beaver in the early 1900s, allowed moose to recolonize the state from populations to the north in Quebec. Sightings remained low until the late 1970s, when moose populations began to expand southward. They are now present statewide.[14] This power for re-colonization can be quite considerable, especially for wide-ranging species that are known to disperse over long distances. Possible evidence of one or a few individual mountain lions in northeastern Vermont in 1993, for example, suggests that carnivores might reestablish themselves in this region from more northern populations if barriers to dispersal are not severe and habitats recover to the point that their populations can once again support themselves.

Case Studies: Fisher and Pine Marten Reintroduction in Vermont

The pitfalls and potential for species reintroductions are best shown by the details of two reintroductions in Vermont: the fisher and the pine marten. These species are closely related, live in roughly comparable hab-itat, and were extirpated at roughly the same time by the same causes. Yet one reintroduction effort succeeded while the other failed.

The Reintroduction of the Fisher

Fisher (*Martes pennanti*), once common inhabitants of Vermont's forests, were perhaps never completely extirpated in Vermont but were at the least considered extremely rare to the point of being ecologically extirpated, by the early to mid-1900s.[15] Long trapping seasons (over one hundred days from 1900 to 1929) and widespread loss of forests in Vermont as a result of logging, farming, and fire limited low numbers of fishers to small isolated pockets in remote habitats. Similar declines occurred in other states in the Northeast; however, because the habitat destruction was more widespread in Vermont, fisher population declines came earlier and were more extreme than those that occurred in other states. By 1929, the state legislature closed the fisher season in Vermont. Other northeastern states followed suit; New Hampshire closed its season in 1935, New York in 1936, and Maine in 1937. By the 1950s, much of Vermont's farmland had reverted back to forest. The widespread recovery of the fisher's habitat, coupled with the ban on trapping, set the stage for the return of fisher.

While fisher populations were in a precipitous decline throughout the late 1800s and early 1900s, populations of porcupines, a major prey item of fisher, were flourishing. Porcupine feed on the vascular tissue of living trees, and the increase in porcupines led to a decrease in healthy trees. A bounty on porcupines was put into effect from 1903 to 1953, ranging from 15 to 50 cents for each porcupine taken to a town clerk. By 1953, the state of Vermont had paid out $162,336 on porcupine bounties, with what appeared to be little to no effect on the population. The Vermont Legislature passed Act 216 in 1953, which provided the Department of Forests and Parks with $2,000 dollars to study "porcupine damage and pest control." An additional $5,000 dollars was allocated in fiscal years 1958 and 1959 for porcupine control. In 1959, porcupine control was designated to be one of the regular responsibilities of the Pest Control Division of the Department of Forests and Parks, and the legislature appropriated funds to support that work.

In 1958, the Pest Control Division considered a proposal to reestablish fisher in Vermont. According to Edward Walker, who was at that time the assistant in charge of pest control, the project was "an attempt to return the balance of nature to the normal status it enjoyed before man interfered with nature's way." He went on to say: "We are convinced that this is the soundest, safest, and most sensible approach to pest control, for most of our pest problems seem to arise from man-made disturbances."[16]

Figure 7.2. Fisher. *Photo © Susan C. Morse.*

The Forest and Parks Department conducted considerable research prior to initiating the fisher reintroduction effort. Several experts in other northeastern states and southeastern Canadian provinces were contacted for information on the habits of fisher in their regions. In addition, the department worked closely with the Vermont Department of Fish and Game and the U.S. Fish and Wildlife Service. The goal of the program, although not clearly defined in the records, appeared to be, "To reestablish fisher to a normal level and thereby restore a balance which since broken has permitted abnormal development of porcupine populations."[17]

Formal recovery plans were not part of reintroduction efforts in the 1950s. Documentation of the number and general location of released animals is surprisingly good, although formal documentation regarding the specifics of the methodology is somewhat limited. According to Walker, a habitat assessment of the state was conducted by aerial reconnaissance prior to the initiation of the reintroduction effort.[18] An attempt was made to identify areas of dense, unbroken conifer forests, which constitute the fisher's preferred habitat. Areas in which the department had records of high densities of porcupines were also targeted as release sites.

Forests and Parks hired a trapper in Maine to live-trap fisher. The trapper conducted the trapping in northern Maine in the spring of the year, because he had sufficient amounts of beaver meat to use as bait and he assumed that the fisher would be most vulnerable to the trap during the late winter period. After capturing the animals, the trapper transferred them into unlined wooden boxes, threw in a handful of hamburger, and loaded the animals into the baggage compartment of a commercial airline out of Dover-Foxcroft, Maine. The plane landed in Montpelier, Vermont, at 10:00 or 11:00 p.m. after a one hour flight. Personnel from Forests and Parks picked up the animals at the airport, drove to a predetermined release site, and, in most cases, released the animals within hours after their arrival in Vermont. Attempts were made to transport animals from Maine by both car and railroad express, but neither method was as cost effective as the commercial flight. From 1959 through 1967, 124 fisher were released in thirty-seven towns in Vermont. Most of the releases occurred in the northeastern part of the state and along the spine of the Green Mountains.

Animals were not ear-tagged or marked prior to their release, so monitoring was difficult. Population analysis was based on sightings and an assessment of porcupine densities in locations central and adjacent to release areas. The University of Vermont initiated a study in 1973 to collect information on the status of the fisher population.[19] From January 1973 through December 1974, fisher were positively identified either by tracks or sightings in ninety-six towns throughout the state. Populations were well established in the northern and eastern parts of the state and densities were somewhat lower along the western slopes and foothills of the Green Mountains. Fisher were still rare or nonexistent in the Champlain Valley and along the western border of the state. In 1974, the first trapping season for fisher in nearly half a century was established in the part of the state with the highest fisher densities. Two hundred forty fisher were legally taken and reported during the sixteen-day trapping season. Trappers submitted carcasses to the University of Vermont for further analysis of their age, reproductive status, and disease.

Today, fisher are well distributed throughout the entire state, and their population in Vermont is likely the highest it has been since the early to mid-1800s.

The Reintroduction of the Pine Marten

Similar to the fisher, the pine marten (*Martes americana*) was historically part of the native fauna of Vermont. Prior to European settlement, the species ranged from the Canadian border to Massachusetts, and according to Zadoch Thompson was plentiful throughout most of the state.[20] Mar-

Figure 7.3. Pine marten. *Photo © Susan C. Morse.*

ten populations declined in the late 1800s due to widespread habitat conversion and overharvest. Records of pine marten in Vermont since the turn of the century are scarce.[21] The most recent record is from Hogback Mountain, Windham County, in 1954.[22] In Vermont, marten are legally classified as an endangered species and therefore are protected against taking.

In 1986, the U.S. Congress initiated the United States Forest Service Challenge Cost-Share Program, designed to promote partnerships between the Forest Service and other organizations. The allocation of federal funds was contingent upon receiving matching contributions from those other organizations.[23] The U.S. Forest Service approached the Vermont Fish and Wildlife Department's Furbearer and Nongame and Natural Heritage programs in June 1986 to explore the possibility of implementing a marten reintroduction effort that would focus on the Green Mountain National Forest (GMNF).

The recovery team in the Vermont Fish and Wildlife Department conducted an initial literature search to review all relevant information regarding reintroductions of mustelids (the family of mammalian carnivores to which the marten belongs). Many other states and provinces, including Wisconsin, Michigan, Ontario, South Dakota, and New Hampshire, had attempted marten reintroduction efforts with varying degrees of success.[24]

The design of Vermont's reintroduction effort was based on an analysis of programs that appeared to be successful, although it later became apparent that specific pitfalls and problems often are not described in summary publications and therefore may be difficult to anticipate. Studies attributed failures most commonly to poor quality habitat in the potential release area, low numbers of release animals, a sex ratio that included more males than females, injury to animals during relocation, release into areas with potential competitors, and poor planning.[25]

The recovery team then drafted a recovery plan to determine the viability of a marten reintroduction and to formalize a process within which the recovery team would operate. The following goal was established:

> To restore a viable population of martens to suitable habitats within Vermont. Should the plan succeed, martens will become eligible for a change in legal status from endangered to protected furbearers. Upon recovery martens should be retained and encouraged for their intrinsic and ecological value, as well as for scientific, educational, and recreational purposes for the people of Vermont.[26]

The recovery plan included the following objectives:
1. To relocate wild-trapped martens from other states to two primary sites in Vermont. (The original recovery plan included an additional, state-funded effort, to release martens onto state-owned land in the Northeast Kingdom. The idea was abandoned due to pressure from timber companies worried about a potential "spotted owl" controversy.)
2. To establish a minimum of two self-sustaining populations of martens in Vermont by 1995.
3. To reconsider the legal classification of martens from endangered to protected furbearers when a minimum of three hundred adult animals is estimated to exist within any population in the state.

Concurrent with the writing of the recovery plan was an effort to evaluate the release site to determine the suitability of the area for marten. Habitat assessments of the release area were performed in two ways. A University of Vermont student conducted an evaluation of the habitat on the southern portion of the GMNF as part of a senior thesis project.[27] Sharman Buechner tested the GMNF stand-inventory data against slightly revised versions of the Allen and Ritter Habitat Suitability Models (HSI) to determine whether the release area could potentially support martens.[28] In addition, the recovery team conducted fieldwork to collect information on several variables, including percent of the stand in softwoods, tree size class, and an assessment of dead and downed woody material. The results of the habitat assessment indicated that the overall HSI for marten on the southern GMNF was good to excellent. The models suggested that the limiting factor, if there were one, would be the low percentage of softwood canopy closure. Inventory data indicated that 80 percent of the forest composition was hardwood while only 10 to 12 percent was softwood. The release area in Vermont compared favorably, however, to those sites in New York and Maine that supported viable marten populations.

An effort was also made to solicit comments from the public. The Fish and Wildlife Department distributed the recovery plan to Vermont conservation organizations and resource agencies. Further, it issued press releases announcing the possibility of a marten recovery effort and offering opportunities to comment, and held two public meetings in the vicinity of the release area. In general, the public supported the reintroduction of marten into Vermont. However, significant opposition came from the timber industry to a release in the northeastern portion of the state.

The Vermont Fish and Wildlife Department contacted northeastern states and southeastern provinces as potential providers of source animals. Initially, the intention was to purchase animals from Chapleau Game Preserve in Ontario, Canada, and conduct the release in the winter. However, due to stringent (and for marten somewhat unrealistic) transporting criteria as stipulated by the then-recently adopted United States Federal Animal Welfare regulations, as well as the difficult logistics associated with midwinter transport and release, Ontario was abandoned as a source. A new focus for source animals shifted to Maine and New York. Some thought was given to the genetics of the reintroduced population. The recovery team hypothesized that genetic variability would be enhanced if individuals came from two geographically distinct populations; therefore, a reintroduction involving two source populations was thought to be the best approach. Recent studies suggest, however, that such situations can result in outbreeding depression and should be carried out with caution.[29]

The Fish and Wildlife Department purchased two hundred cage-type live-traps in two different sizes and distributed them to participating trappers (two in Maine, three in New York). Many of the traps had to be retrofitted by the trappers to eliminate escapes between the trap door and the wall of the trap. Trappers also received holding/transportation cages and marten food (strawberry jam and cat food). Due to the extremely long commute from northern Maine to the holding area in Vermont (three to four days), trappers often had to hold animals in cages for up to five days. Marten are voracious chewers and can chew out of a wire cage made of anything but welded wire. They are also capable of chewing out of wooden boxes made of one-half-inch plywood or one-inch pine. Other marten recovery projects recommended metal lined cages for holding and transport.[30] However, in this situation the long holding period was unavoidable and precluded the use of metal-lined cages. It is possible that tooth wear resulting from cage chewing negatively influenced the success of the project.

All of the animals were released within or adjacent to the White Rocks National Recreation Area (NRA) or the Lye Brook Wilderness on the southern unit of the GMNF. White Rocks NRA includes a total of 36,400 acres, of which 13,640 acres are federally designated wilderness (the Big Branch and Peru Peak wilderness areas). Vegetative management in the NRA (excluding the wilderness) is limited to management for recreational purposes or the improvement of wildlife habitat for "deepwoods" species. All clear-cutting is restricted to 5-acre patches or less.[31] No vegetative manipulation is allowed in the Lye Brook Wilderness Area, but a variety of vegetative management goals can be applied to the remainder of the forest. Although trapping is allowed on the forest, much of the release area is inaccessible to humans in the winter during the fisher-trapping season. In addition, the Vermont Trappers Association notified trappers to avoid trapping in the release area and to contact the Department of Fish and Wildlife if they inadvertently trapped a marten. One marten was trapped and reported in 1990, approximately 10 miles north of the GMNF in Shrewsbury, Vermont, one year after its release.

In 1989, contract trappers in both Maine and New York began trapping during the normal marten season (New York: October 29 to December 4; Maine: October 24 to December 4). Although trappers checked the traps at least once and sometimes twice a day, some mortality of trapped females occurred during the first year in Maine. Trappers generally used a type of set called a "cubby," which often required covering the traps with softwood branches. Weather conditions were such that snow would pile up on the branches, melt, and drip water on the animal held inside the trap. Females appeared to be prone to mortality from exposure under these conditions. After this, the trappers wrapped the traps in tarpaper, which prevented moisture from getting into the trap and eliminated any additional mortality.

The trap and release effort ran from 1989 through 1991. The initial attempt in the fall of 1989 yielded forty marten, six from New York and thirty-four from Maine. Following capture, the animals were transported to Vermont by truck and held for processing and release. Generally, the recovery team anesthetized the animals with ketamine hydrochloride, checked them for tooth wear, ear tagged, and, when applicable, equipped them with radio collars within two to three days of arrival. The recovery team kept a record on each individual, including its source, the release site, date of release, ear tag numbers, general health, and sex. During the first year, twelve of the forty animals were "slow" released and twenty-eight were "quick" released. The literature regarding the benefits of quick versus slow release is conflicting. However, based on the possibility that slow release might encourage more fidelity to the release area, the recovery team made an effort each year to slow release a portion of the animals.

The target of the trapping effort was to acquire sixty animals, thirty males and thirty females, for release in each of the two locations originally proposed (the GMNF and Northeast Kingdom). Trappers were paid $100 for each animal regardless of sex. Initially, a fifty-fifty sex ratio was to be imposed; however, males tended to be much more vulnerable to trapping and the sex ratio of released animals was uneven and skewed toward males every year. In the second and third years, the recovery team asked trappers to make a judgement regarding the sex of the animals based on size and to release marten that appeared to be male. This proved to be impractical and was not supported by the trappers, who were extremely reluctant to release animals that they had spent significant amounts of time and effort to trap. Because females were so difficult to trap, participants also felt that in order to justify their time and expense, they would have to ask $300 per female if a fifty-fifty sex ratio was imposed. After discussing several options to ameliorate the problem, the recovery team eventually concluded that the most cost-effective and perhaps even biologically appropriate action would be to continue to purchase males and females at the same monetary rate until the number of females released came close to the original recovery plan target of thirty. However, in hopes of enhancing the opportunities for trapping more females, the Department of Fish and Wildlife negotiated a one-time exception for the two Maine trappers and received permission from the Maine Department of Inland Fisheries and Wildlife to begin trapping on October 14, approximately two weeks prior to the opening of the regular season. The recovery team speculated that early-season trapping might increase the vulnerability of females to the trap and therefore increase the female take. In addition, better weather would make transportation much easier, so transport time would be shorter. Finally, releases could occur during periods of warmer weather, moderating the stress that below-zero temperatures can have on newly released animals.

Prior to releasing the marten, the recovery team enhanced the sites by distributing deer and beaver carcasses donated by Vermont trappers and game wardens. Several other recovery efforts suggested that food in the form of carcasses during the "period of adjustment" could result in a higher percentage of martens establishing territories within the release area and could ultimately increase the success of the recovery effort.[32]

The reintroduction effort ended in 1991 after three consecutive fall releases. The program translocated 115 marten to the southern portion of the GMNF. Of the total, 11 were from New York and 104 were from Maine. Twenty-seven of the released animals were female and eighty-nine were male; seventy-six were "quick released," thirty-nine "slow released." The cooperation received from the biological staff in the two source states was extremely important to the recovery effort. Both the trappers and the state biologists put in many days of personal time to support the program and, except for the $100 paid to the trappers for each animal, these participants charged no additional fee for the feeding, cleaning, and transporting of marten, or for the many other logistical tasks associated with a recovery effort of this magnitude.

In order to document the success or failure of the recovery effort, the recovery team monitored the reintroduced marten using radio telemetry, track count surveys, track-plate boxes, direct observations, and two different remote camera-based systems.[33] The objectives of the monitoring efforts were to evaluate mortality, dispersal, distribution, population trends, and reproductive success of the marten population during, and one to five years following, the reintroduction effort; and to monitor marten population trends over an eight- to twelve-year period through the identification of occupied home ranges over time.[34] Track count surveys, direct observations, telemetry, and more recently camera-based techniques have been used by several other states to monitor mustelid populations.[35]

The recovery team fitted thirteen animals with radio-collars in the 1989 and 1990 releases. The New York Department of Environmental Conservation designed the collars to fall off approximately four months following release. The main objective of the telemetry effort was to determine whether the released animals maintained any fidelity to the release site or whether animals immediately moved out of the vicinity of the release area and off the GMNF.

Establishing and maintaining radio contact proved to be difficult. The collars were small and the signal relatively weak. In addition, weather conditions, scheduling problems, and an underestimation of manpower and equipment hampered monitoring efforts.[36] The study area is relatively inaccessible in the winter except on foot or by snowmachine, and small topographic changes in the terrain often blocked radio signals. As a result, locating radio-collared animals from the ground proved to be extremely time consuming and at times impossible. In 1990–1991, monitoring efforts with aerial telemetry were more successful.

Of the thirteen collared animals, five were female. The recovery team monitored most of the females over a period of several months, and contact was often made more than once. Four of the five appeared to establish home ranges on the GMNF. The fifth animal was triangulated only once, ten miles east of the GMNF. The recovery team collared eight males, three of which were never found again. Three appeared to establish home ranges on the GMNF, and two either had collars that malfunctioned, or they left the area. Most of the home ranges were in habitats of softwood or mixed forests in or near forested wetlands or streams.

The recovery team conducted track count surveys on snowshoes or skis (although access was often facilitated by snowmachines), through the winters of 1989–1990 and 1992–1993. The routes were dispersed throughout the study area in an attempt to assess marten distribution. In order to compare track counts over time, it was important that survey routes be standardized and conducted when the likelihood of seeing tracks was the highest. Due to scheduling constraints, however, transects had to be conducted at the convenience of the observers and therefore often were executed during marginal snow conditions. Identification of tracks was often difficult, negatively influencing the validity of the surveys. The results of the track count surveys suggested the presence of at least four to six marten. Because of the marginal cost-effectiveness of the track surveys, the recovery team investigated other monitoring techniques. Several baited track-plate boxes were installed on the GMNF in the winter of 1992, but snow drifting and use of the boxes by rodents negatively influenced the usefulness of the track-plates. These boxes detected no marten tracks.

The recovery team compared two camera-based systems for their use in monitoring marten in 1994–1995.[37] The infrared Trailmaster camera system paired with track-plate boxes retrofitted with automatic 35-mm cameras was installed in five to six of the release sites and in preferred conifer habitat. Three pictures of marten were taken at two different locations. Both animals appeared to have ear-tags. Fisher and flying squirrels were the other species most frequently photographed.

In the winter of 1997–1998, the recovery team installed forty-eight camera boxes (retrofitted track-plate boxes) in release areas and in preferred conifer habitats in the southern GMNF.[38] Some of the boxes were placed at high elevation sites, which up until then had not been surveyed for marten. No pictures of marten were taken; however, 79 percent of the boxes had pictures of fisher.

By 1999, the Department of Fish and Wildlife in Vermont had received almost twenty reports of marten. One animal was trapped in Shrewsbury in 1990. Three other marten were hit by cars and recovered; one from Candia, New Hampshire, in 1990, one on Route 84 in Connecticut, and one on Route 11 in Winhall, Vermont, in 1991. One animal released in East Wallingford, Vermont, in 1989 was trapped eight years later in Rangely, Maine. Interestingly, this animal was one of the eleven that had been reintroduced from New York state. A marten was trapped in Barton, Vermont, during the 1997 fisher season. This animal had no ear tags, however, and may have been an immigrant from New Hampshire rather than one of the reintroduced individuals.

The results of the reintroduction are inconclusive and somewhat discouraging. No evidence has been found of marten reproduction on the GMNF, and if any animals remain from the original release, it is likely that they exist only in very low numbers. There has been some speculation that high fisher densities limit marten populations.[39] Fisher pelt prices and corresponding trapper effort dropped drastically in 1989. Since that time, Vermont's fisher population has increased dramatically, particularly in the more heavily forested areas of the state, such as the GMNF. It is possible that the increasing fisher densities that coincidentally and unpredictably began just prior to the release of the marten negatively influenced the success of the marten recovery effort.

The Lessons of Successful Reintroductions

The lessons of the fisher and pine martin reintroduction programs in Vermont can be coupled with those from the many other attempts to reintroduce species throughout the world over the past several years to derive rules of thumb about the factors that increase the chances that a reintroduction will be successful. No single factor seems to guarantee success; for animals, only about two-thirds of reported reintroduction or translocation efforts are considered successful, and for plants fewer than one-third are considered successful.[40] Yet some factors appear to be more influential than others in helping populations to become reestablished.

- **Habitat quality of the release area.** The better the quality of the habitat into which the population is being reintroduced, the better the chances that the reintroduction will be successful. This relates to the resource needs of the species (e.g., food, substrate, breeding sites, hibernation sites, protection from predators), mitigation of the factors that led to the disappearance of the species in the first place (e.g., habitat modification, hunting, harvesting, pesticide loads), and mitigation of new factors that might prevent successful reestablishment (e.g., roads, habitat destruction). For example, the reintroduction of lynx in New York has been unsuccessful, largely because of roadkill mortality to released animals. The failure of the pine marten reintroduction in Vermont may well have been due to the selection for political and social reasons of suboptimal habitat as the release site. The success of the fisher reintroduction, however, is likely due to the widespread return of dense forest cover, the fisher's preferred habitat. This rule of thumb will be important to consider in future discussions about the potential for the reintroduction into the Northeast of the timber wolf. Timber wolves primarily eat large mammals, and their absence would certainly doom any reintroduction effort to failure.[41] Also, wolves are sensitive to road density, and a reintroduction of wolves into an area with a road density greater than a region-specific critical threshold would dramatically reduce the chances of success.

- **Range of the release site relative to the historical distribution of the translocated species.** The reintroduction of a species into the core of its historical range is better than reintroduction on its periphery. This is probably because the limits of a species' geographic range are usually controlled by the limits of tolerance to physical conditions. The core of a range represents the area of least stress. Therefore, individuals are able to devote more energy to reproduction and less to survival and maintenance of homeostasis in the core areas, increasing the chances that the population can grow.

- **Number of individuals released.** The more individuals released in a reintroduction program, the better. This is probably true for two reasons. First, the more individuals, the more likely it is that some will survive the random events that kill individuals, such as mortality from roadkill and severe weather events. Second, the more individuals, the more likely that reproduction can occur successfully. Among animals, males and females must be able to find each other to form mating pairs or social groups to successfully rear young. Among plants, especially obligate out-crossers, pollen from one individual must successfully find another individual.

- **Diet**. Among animals, there is evidence that omnivores tend to have a higher success rate than do species with more narrow diets, such as strict herbivores or strict carnivores. This seems intuitive; the more potential food items in the area of the reintroduction, the more likely it is that reintroduced individuals will find food.

- **Genetic similarity**. Because populations are, at least in theory, genetically adapted to local or regional environmental conditions, a reintroduced population is more likely to be successful the more similar it is genetically to that of the extirpated population. Ideally, reintroduced individuals should come from the same genetic stock as the extirpated population; if that is not possible, then they should come from the same subspecies. Only in the case of complete extirpation of a subspecies should a different subspecies be used for the reintroduction effort. In the absence of information on genetics, individuals for reintroduction should come from areas as near to the site for the reintroduction program as possible.

- **Perceived local support**. Reintroductions are more successful when there is local support for the program. Where local support for a program is strong, regulations intended to promote the species' reestablishment are more likely to be effective, and the impacts of illegal hunting or collecting on the reintroduced population are likely to be lower. Interestingly, the establishment of education programs intended to increase local support tends not to be correlated with program success, leaving open the question of what factors promote local support.

- **Long-term monitoring**. Reintroduction programs tend to be more successful if the population is monitored to assess how well individuals are coping with their new environment. This seems to be especially true for plants, since they have less of an ability to adjust their location to better meet their needs compared to animals. The lack of program monitoring to correct problems faced by a reintroduced population may be the single most-important cause for failure of plant reintroductions.

The role of many other factors in increasing success is ambiguous, being both supported and rejected by different studies. These include reproductive potential (particularly age of first reproduction and number of offspring), taxonomic class (birds versus mammals), status (game versus threatened, endangered, or sensitive), and length of the reintroduction program. Not all factors thought by many to influence the success of a reintroduction program appear to be important. For example, the source of translocated animals—wild-captured versus captive-bred—seems not to be important as a general rule, although it may be influential in certain cases (e.g., wild turkey in Rhode Island).

Potential Reintroductions in the Future

Although many species of birds and mammals that have been extirpated in the Northeast have already been the subject of reintroduction programs, most of which were successful, a number of species have not yet been attempted. Among the charismatic megafauna, potential reintroductions could be considered for the wolf, mountain lion, and wolverine. Indeed, the U.S. Fish and Wildlife Service and regional conservation advocacy groups have already assessed the potential for wolf recovery in the Northeast, particularly in northern Maine and the Adirondacks of New York, and such an effort may occur in the not-too-distant future. The species whose reintroductions have not so far succeeded, such as the marten and lynx (as well as species like the elk that have been successfully reintroduced into only a part of its former range), are also obvious candidates for further efforts, but only after the causes that led to their decline and to the failure of earlier reintroduction efforts have been eliminated. Experience shows that reintroductions can succeed even after previous unsuccessful attempts, especially if efforts to correct the causes of the failures are made. The general success of reintroduction efforts for birds and mammals in the northeastern United States bodes well for the success of future reintroduction programs. Perhaps one day, the species whose losses were lamented by Thoreau in 1856 will all have been returned to the landscape. If so, a significant portion of our region's wild character will have been restored, demonstrating that a northeastern approach to the restoration of wilderness can be successful.

Perhaps the greatest challenge, however, lies not in the return of the charismatic vertebrates, but in the restoration of smaller, less-noticeable species whose loss is little noted or lamented. Efforts to restore the northeastern beach tiger beetle and the American burying beetle are noteworthy, in large part because they occur as rare examples of efforts to reintroduce species with little public profile. More attention ought to be paid to the need for reintroduction of such species of all types, including reptiles, amphibians, freshwater mussels, butterflies, beetles, and plants. These species may play just as critical of a role in ecosystem processes as do large, terrestrial vertebrates—as pollinators, nutrient recyclers, micropredators, and water purifiers—and arguments for their reintroduction are just as sound. The challenges in rewilding the northeastern landscape with these groups are large, especially since we generally have little baseline information on the status and habitat needs of most of these species, and the causes of their declines are often uncertain or difficult to correct. But the knowledge gained from past reintroduction efforts, both those that have succeeded and those that have failed, gives us some hope that species reintroductions can increasingly play a role in the reestablishment of the full spectrum of the region's former biological diversity and the achievement of the general goal of rewilding in the northeastern U.S.

CHAPTER 8

Making It Happen

Protecting Wilderness on the Ground

EMILY BATESON AND NANCY SMITH

We can save the significant parts of the American wilderness—if we don't waste time doing it.
— Howard Zahniser[1]

🌿 EARLY SETTLERS ARRIVED in New England with a clear vision—to tame the wilderness, turning savage wilds into plowed fields, new settlements, and personal wealth. This vision was methodically carried out by determined individuals and through legal and economic systems that encouraged development and exploitation of the country's land and natural resources. Today, we face an even more daunting task than our forebears: to reverse this trend, protecting and restoring a portion of those tamed wilds. But do we have the vision and determination to accomplish this goal? How exactly will we build on the foundations of regional wilderness visionaries such as Henry David Thoreau, Bob Marshall, Percival Baxter, and Edward O. Wilson? And do we still have that ultimate luxury: time?

These questions are urgent ones. Today, northern New England has unparalleled opportunities for land acquisition and wilderness protection as the timber industry continues to sell off large blocks of land, hundreds of thousands of acres at a time. In the last quarter of 1998, almost 3 million acres in Maine, or roughly 12 percent of the state, changed hands due to massive timberland sales. Large blocks of watershed lands are becoming available because of the deregulation of the electric utility industry. The large-scale opportunities we have today for wilderness protection and restoration will not last forever.

Although we have seen some recent promising trends in land protection, overall market and political forces continue to encourage unrestrained land development and unsustainable resource extraction. Only a small fraction of the possible wilderness acres have been protected during the past ten years of major Northern Forest land sales. With changes in land ownership have come the proven risks of subdivision, fragmentation, and expanded settlement into unpopulated areas.[2] No one has yet been able to turn the tide of sprawl that consumes shorelines, forests, and farms alike. Industrial timbering methods have continued to degrade and impoverish ecosystems.

We have not leveraged this era of opportunity into major wilderness gains. We have lost ground. As the Queen observed in Lewis Carroll's *Through the Looking Glass*: "Now here, you see, it takes all the running you can do to keep in the same place. If you want to get somewhere else, you must run at least twice as fast as that."

So we must run at least twice as fast. New England habitat will never be cheaper, more available, or more intact than it is today. The acre that Percival Baxter bought for $2 is now worth hundreds, while waterfront and coastal lands are worth exponentially more. The current era of large-scale land sales is caused by a confluence of global economic factors and related cost-cutting measures by the forest products industry, including widespread sale of "nonstrategic assets" and departure from the Northeast for areas with better growing conditions and lower costs. This ownership transition is underway but will not last forever. Recent promising trends towards land acquisition and protection must be accelerated. One day soon wilderness will not be available for purchase at any reasonable scale or price.

We have before us a remarkable but fleeting opportunity, and it is up to us not to squander it. This chapter addresses the nuts and bolts of getting to work on the critical task of putting the vision of wilderness on the ground, through building a stronger, science-based wilderness ethic, finding the funds and buying more wild lands, and protecting those lands with forever wild conservation easements, so that what we achieve today will endure for the many generations of all species that follow.

How Much Protected Land *Do* We Have?

Some day—maybe in your day—there won't be any really wild areas left.

— Percival Baxter[3]

Before we move forward with a new resolve to put wilderness on the ground, we need to look at what has been done before us, and why. To assess conservation, it is important to understand that many "protected land" and "conservation" maps do not distinguish between lands protected as commercial farms, timberland, or ecological preserves—even though the levels of conservation vary dramatically. Often, maps demarcate all municipal and state land as "open space" even when the site is a landfill, golf course, or apt to be sold by the town for revenue. Most give no indication of the ecological attributes of the land or whether native habitat protection is a management goal.

In 1998, Sweet Water Trust asked the Nature Conservancy to analyze extensive existing data in order to create a map of the Northern Forest region showing not only what lands have been conserved but also how such conserved lands are being managed. The first draft depicted four different management status categories:

Status 1. An area protected from conversion of natural landcover, with a mandated management plan in operation to maintain a natural state, within which disturbance events (of natural type, frequency, and legacy) are allowed to proceed without interference, or are mimicked through management (e.g., wilderness areas on national forests; the Adirondack Park).[4]

Status 2. An area protected from conversion of natural landcover, with a mandated management plan in operation to maintain a primarily natural state, but which may receive uses or management practices that degrade the quality of existing natural communities, including suppression of natural disturbance (e.g., heavily recreated lands, forested lands that include selected areas of light, experimental forestry).

Status 3 (not shown on map). An area protected from conversion of natural land cover for the majority of the area, but subject to extractive uses of either a broad, low-intensity type (e.g., logging) or localized intense type (e.g., mining). It also confers protection to federally listed endangered and threatened species throughout the area (e.g., most land protected by the Society for the Protection of New Hampshire Forests; most state agency lands throughout northern New England).

Status 4 (not shown on map). An area with no known public or private institutional mandates or legally recognized easements or deed restrictions held by the managing entity to prevent conversion of natural habitat types to anthropogenic habitat types. The area generally allows conversion to unnatural land cover throughout (e.g., schools, prisons, golf courses, commercial farms).

Map 8.1 highlights lands protected primarily for habitat values (status 1 and 2 lands). As always, a picture is worth a thousand words. What leaps out from this map is how blank it is, particularly in the state of Maine. Maine, with the lowest percentage of public land in the Northeast at 5 percent, has less than 1 percent protected wilderness lands.[5] It is at once the wildest and least-protected state in the Northeast.

Examination of this map shows that the landscape-level wild lands successes of Northern Forest conservation so far are all on public lands. The Green Mountains and especially the White Mountains afford some high-quality protection, while the Adirondack Mountains are protected by the foresight of its citizens who voted to put a "forever wild" provision in their state constitution in 1894 to stop logging abuses in the state park. Baxter State Park, discussed further below, was protected solely through the determination and generosity of one man: Percival Baxter. Every day, activists defend these areas from efforts to change land management in ways that would degrade wilderness qualities.

It is worth noting that most of these protected public lands were purchased after intensive logging. Today, they still lack some of the ecological characteristics of old-growth forests, but they are areas of great beauty, healed or healing from earlier abuses, a testament to the resilience of our lands, waters, and wildlife. The map also shows clearly the ecological importance of ongoing campaigns focused on expanding and better protecting these pivotal public lands.

The outlined areas on the Northern Forest map represent two recent acquisitions by conservation groups. In December 1998, the Nature Conservancy acquired full and partial interest in 220,000 acres along the St. John River in northern Maine and has launched a scientific process to determine the ultimate management scheme for these lands. In 1999, the Conservation Fund purchased nearly 300,000 acres of Champion International land in New Hampshire, Vermont, and New York, and has re-sold all but 18,000 acres in New Hampshire to achieve a mix of protected habitat and timbered lands.[6] Only time will tell how much shading will be added to the map as a result of these major acquisitions (see below for more detail on the two sales).

The Northern Forest map also illustrates the extent to which conservation is located in mountainous terrain. Although protecting mountain-tops traditionally allowed an uneasy truce between recreation and logging, this strategy has left many natural community types and species unprotected. Conservation science tells us we need to protect a full complement of community types and species along an elevational gradient, in areas

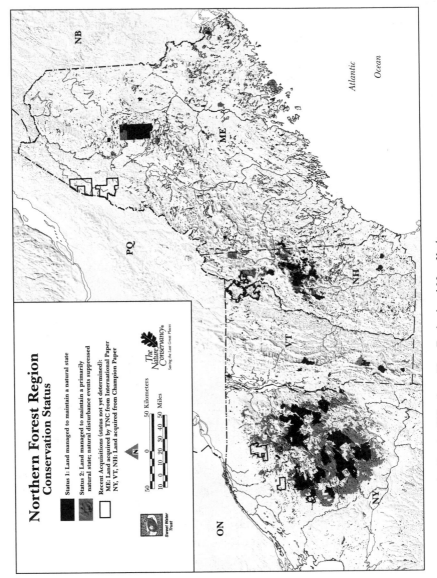

Northern Forest Region
Conservation Status

■ Status 1: Land managed to maintain a natural state

▨ Status 2: Land managed to maintain a primarily natural state; natural disturbance events suppressed

☐ Recent Acquisitions (status not yet determined):
ME: Land acquired by TNC from International Paper
NY, VT, NH: Land acquired from Champion Paper

The Nature Conservancy®
Saving the Last Great Places

Sweet Water Trust

50   0   10 20 30 40 50 Kilometers
50   0   10   20   30   40   50 Miles

N

PQ

ON

NB

ME

NH

VT

NY

Atlantic

Ocean

Map 8.1. Conservation Lands of Northern New England and New York.

large enough to be ecologically meaningful given migration, natural disturbance, climate change, and other factors.

In many mountainous places that have been studied for how species richness varies according to elevation, a biased pattern of habitat protection has been clearly established. The pattern of conservation in high elevations, resource extraction in mid-elevations, and high-density human development and habitat fragmentation in low elevations is particularly well documented in the western United States.[7]

Graph 8.1 illustrates the pattern of conservation and the range of biodiversity by elevation in Vermont and New Hampshire combined. The diagram shows that the percentage of protected land decreases dramatically with a drop in elevation, while the number of rare species increases. Each tree symbol represents three hundred element occurrences (EO). An EO is a documented record of a rare plant or rare animal, a rare natural community, or an exemplary natural community (that is, the best known example of a common natural community).

Clearly, there is an inverse relationship between our most vulnerable species and our protected habitat. From this we can infer that other species will also eventually decline if we do not increase the amount of conservation land in lower elevations.

Conservation has been predicated on economic expediency. Fertile valleys are good for growing crops, trees, highways, and houses. However, lower elevations have the greatest concentrations of biological diversity that remain unprotected. We need to increase our protection efforts in these lower elevation lands, focusing on significant and unfragmented habitats first.

Ecological information and mapping can and must inform land protection strategy. It is time to move beyond outdated and flawed strategies for conservation. Conservation science must play a far more dominant role as we work to put more shading on the map, protecting biodiversity and restoring real, tangible wilderness on the ground.

The Previous Act: Traditional Conservation in the Northern Forest

There are more things in heaven and earth, Horatio, than are dreamt of in your philosophy.
—William Shakespeare, *Hamlet*

Although northern New England is vitally important to the Northeast as its wildest region, it is among the regions in the country with the least

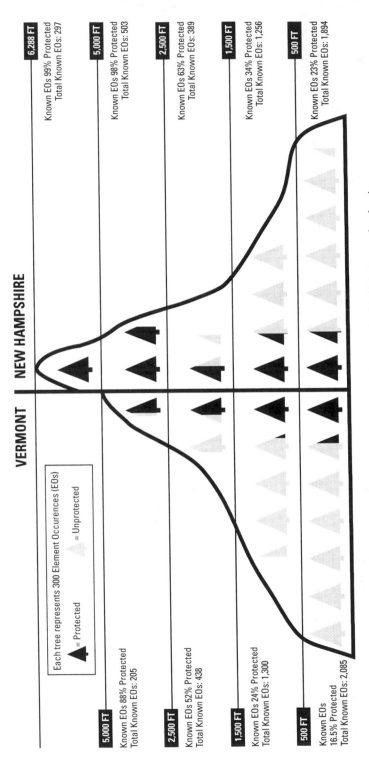

VERMONT   NEW HAMPSHIRE

6,288 FT
Known EOs 99% Protected
Total Known EOs: 297

5,000 FT
Known EOs 98% Protected
Total Known EOs: 503

2,500 FT
Known EOs 63% Protected
Total Known EOs: 389

1,500 FT
Known EOs 34% Protected
Total Known EOs: 1,256

500 FT
Known EOs 23% Protected
Total Known EOs: 1,894

Each tree represents 300 Element Ocurrences (EOs)
▲ = Protected   ▲ = Unprotected

5,000 FT
Known EOs 88% Protected
Total Known EOs: 205

2,500 FT
Known EOs 52% Protected
Total Known EOs: 438

1,500 FT
Known EOs 24% Protected
Total Known EOs: 1,300

500 FT
Known EOs
16.5% Protected
Total Known EOs: 2,085

Most protected land is located at high elevations, resulting in little protection for the rare species, natural communities and most wildlife which live in lower elevations.

Graph 8.1. Protected Open Space in New Hampshire and Vermont by Elevation.

amount of protected land. Only large timberland ownerships with public access have lulled people into thinking otherwise. Because of the former stability of those private timberlands, many major conservation organizations traditionally focused primarily on protecting and improving that status quo. Over time, such groups became philosophically rooted in a vocabulary that describes forests as "working" or "productive" only if they are managed for timber, and trees as "overmature" when they are ready for the sawmill but not yet ecologically mature. Wilderness campaigns have been limited and sporadic compared to the great wilderness battles of the West. The regional wilderness ethic has grown weak from disuse.

Today, we have wilderness opportunities in the Northeast that were inconceivable only ten years ago, and conservation science that virtually didn't exist ten years before that. We have a population brought up to believe that "wilderness" exists out West, or on a nature calendar, separate from the communities of New England. Can we change our conservation philosophy fast enough to take advantage of the truly breathtaking opportunities we have before us today?

Sometimes the results of New England ecological protection resemble nothing less than an unwelcome guest at a party: protected areas are isolated up on mountain tops, or squeezed into thin strips along river banks and lake shores—as if no one wanted to invite them in the first place. Such efforts are more an aesthetic illusion of wildness than the real thing. Anchored in a tradition of timbering their own lands, some conservation-forestry groups and state agencies depend on the revenue stream from timber harvesting. Others have developed a comfortable pattern of conserving farms and timberland because of the chronic shortage of funds to buy wild land. Too many are not up to date on the principles of conservation biology.

Of course, protecting farms and timberland from development conversion is an important strategy for the land use and cultural future of the region.[8] However, too often conservation in New England is dominated by short-term economics at the expense of long-term ecological health. State and federal funding is funneled to timberlands, farms, and recreational lands, and much less often to habitat and wilderness protection. Farm and forest protection programs, such as the federal Forest Legacy Program, often provide funding without requiring reasonable or even minimal standards for management. Agencies hesitate to acquire ecological lands because of lack of timber revenue or management funds. Meanwhile, a growing and more mechanized population puts increasing recreational pressure on the scant "protected" lands we have. Towns use conservation lands as a piggybank for development, building schools and water treatment facilities as need arises. In multiple ways, our natural world is shrinking.

Agricultural and forestry protection must focus more on improving management, and be implemented *in concert* with the primary strategy of large-scale and linked habitat protection rather than *in competition* with it. The principles of conservation biology must play a dominant role no matter how land will be managed. How much habitat do we need to protect for biological integrity, and where? How do different land management actions affect native species, natural communities, and water and air quality? Fortunately, the Northeast has witnessed some promising trends toward "green" forestry and farming (see chapters 9 and 10). But too often these hard questions are not asked. People are making land use choices that they think have no ecological consequences.

Conservationists and the media too often fail to distinguish the difference in quality of land protection projects. A recent *Boston Globe* headline emblazoned: "$76 Million Purchase Lets States Preserve 300,000 Forest Acres."[9] In fact, none of the Champion lands purchased by the Conservation Fund across three states has been preserved as status 1 land to date. A specific goal of the acquisition was to retain 70 percent of the land in active timber management.[10]

In New York, 29,000 acres have been purchased by the state for the Adirondack Park and will be designated status 1 or 2 by the New York Department of Environmental Conservation. (This acreage is approximately 10 percent of the total sale.) The remaining 103,000 acres in New York have been sold to a private timber investment group, and will be actively timbered, but open to the public for the first time in a century and restricted from other development. The New Hampshire Champion lands have not yet been resold by the Conservation Fund and their future remains uncertain.

The Vermont Champion lands have been resold, and none has been protected as status 1. The 133,000 acres of Champion land in Vermont was the largest contiguous piece of private property anywhere in the state, and potentially represented Vermont's last chance for big wilderness. Conservationists had long eyed for protection the property's centerpiece, the ecologically rich Nulhegan Basin and River.[11] Wilderness advocates read the early headlines and were enthused. When the dust settled, here's how the 133,000 acres of potential Vermont wilderness were categorized:

Status 1 Lands. None of the land has been preserved as status 1.

Status 2 Lands. Less than 50,000 acres, or 36.6 percent, has been preserved as status 2. Although the management plan for the status 2 lands in Vermont may include additional habitat protection, such administrative protection (similar to Forest Service "management area" designations) is not guaranteed or permanent and is not reflected in status category determinations. Status 2 lands were placed under the following management:

- **Silvio Conte National Wildlife Refuge.** Some 26,500 acres has been added to the refuge, managed primarily for natural resources with some recreational development and timber management to enhance game species.
- **Agency of Natural Resources state land.** An additional 22,150 acres will be managed by the Agency of Natural Resources for natural resources and extensive recreation, including bear baiting and other hunting, snowmobiling, and ATV use in certain areas.

Status 3 Lands. About 63.4 percent, or 84,100 acres has been resold to the Essex Timber Company. The timber easement will protect lands from housing development while allowing development of sawmills and associated structures, subdivision of land into four parcels, and construction of three small seasonal camps. The easement includes environmental safeguards along streams and other identified sensitive areas, and provisions requiring the owner to timber the land at "net annual growth" after the property is fully stocked. This economic provision, highly unusual in an easement, appears to preclude additional ecological protection on the property over time regardless of future findings. An additional easement guarantees public access.[12]

While protection of all kinds is valuable depending on the situation, blurring the distinction lowers the bar for future conservation. When such mixed use projects focus on "sustainable logging," for example, it is important to understand that definitions of that term vary widely. To some, "sustainable forestry" means trying to sustain a constant supply of timber. To conservation scientists and others who care about biodiversity, it means attempting to sustain the overall ecosystem. More importantly, the fact remains that "sustainable logging" today is a goal rather than a proven concept. As conservation biologist Thomas Struhsaker notes: "Are any harvests of natural resources sustainable? Long-term and critical evaluations of attempts at sustainable harvest are painfully scarce and generally do not support the concept."[13]

Fragmentation of habitat through logging, roadbuilding, development, farming, and other economic activities is a leading cause of biodiversity decline. "[Sustainable use] will almost always lower biological diversity," writes Reed Noss, "whether one considers individual species or entire biological communities, and if sustainable use is our only goal, our world will be the poorer for it."[14] We cannot rely solely on timbered lands to protect our region's biodiversity in the long term, since, as E. O. Wilson so bluntly puts it, we have "only the vaguest idea of how ecosystems work."[15] If sustainable timbering of a few tree species is insufficiently understood, how could we possibly understand how to "sustain" the intricacies of thousands of forest species and complex ecological processes?

To protect ecosystems, we must employ the "precautionary principle," taking responsibility to protect our natural world in the face of scientific uncertainty, rather than developing and exploiting resources until it can be definitively proven (too late) that harm will be caused.[16] While it is crucial for the Northeast to have more ecologically sensitive farming and forestry, we must not take the extraordinary ecological gamble of diminishing the primary goal of protecting and linking large, undisturbed natural areas.

In the prevailing conservation atmosphere, organizations that have stuck their necks out for wilderness have been labeled radical or unreasonable, and have sometimes been politically marginalized. How sad. Nothing is more reasonable than protecting the wild in which we evolved for over two million years and on which our health and welfare depends. As a body politic, we must start to make decisions based on biodiversity and ecological health. As Theodore Roosevelt said: "What good is a house without a healthy planet to put it on?"[17] More people must begin to think of wilderness protection in terms of such sound common sense. We need to build bridges between wilderness advocates, private landowners, and all people who love nature, and collectively "turn [our] philosophy to the central questions of human origins in the wild environment."[18]

The Next Act: Strengthening the Wilderness Movement

To withhold yourself from where you are is to be cut off from communion with the source. It has taken me half a lifetime of searching to realize that the likeliest path to the ultimate ground leads through my local ground. I mean the land itself, with its creeks and rivers, its weather, seasons, stone outcroppings, and all the plants and animals that share it. I cannot have a spiritual center without having a geographical one: I cannot live a grounded life without being grounded in a place.

— Scott Russell Sanders[19]

We all love nature. According to a recent article in *Orion*, "It's why Ronald Reagan lived on a ranch, why NRA members hunt, and why rich capitalists live in shady suburbs and on rural estates."[20] Most Americans, however, don't think of themselves as "environmentalists."

Even so, polls and referenda questions reflect a startling fact: Citizens consistently outpace mainstream environmental organizations in their desire for better environmental protection, including more wilderness, less pesticide use, and restrictions on clear-cutting. For example, recent Forest Service polls reflect a strong public desire to protect public land in New England for wilderness recreation.[21] Wildlife viewing is now the number one outdoor activity in the United States.[22] Interest in "green" forestry and farming is on the rise.

We need to reconnect the environmental movement to those people, and build on that natural urge to protect one's own community, family, and the health and splendor of the natural world. Rather than put wilderness on a distant pedestal, somewhere out West, we must expand out from our own backyards, embracing and building upon what people already know in their hearts.

Since the birth of land trusts in Massachusetts over one hundred years ago, their subsequent proliferation in New England and throughout the Northeast has derived its vigor from the same tradition as the town hall meeting: the sovereignty of an empowered people who care about their community and their land. The movement in the Northeast today is vibrant, with 417 land trusts in New England alone, and another 177 in Pennsylvania, New York, and New Jersey: almost half of all the land trusts in the nation.[23]

Land trusts are nonprofit organizations that, among other activities, work to protect land through the purchase or acceptance of gifts of land or conservation easements. As of 1998, 1,213 local and regional land trusts nationwide had helped protect approximately 4.7 million acres of land, an area larger than the states of Connecticut and Rhode Island combined. Of that number, about 1 million acres have been conserved as park land, wildlife refuges, and green spaces as a result of partnerships between land trusts and public agencies. About one million individuals are supporters. More than 40 percent of land trusts are staffed solely by volunteers.[24]

Many communities also have effective local watershed groups that date from the time of activism around the systematic pollution of many of the region's water sources and the passage of the Clean Water Act of 1972. This act has had a profound effect on remedying point-source pollution. Watershed groups have taken the step into landscape thinking by stepping over political boundaries to care for ecological units that shed water into the same stream or river. Most groups are presently focusing on water testing, stream flow (volume and dam impediments), point and nonpoint

Working with Land Trusts to Put Wilderness on the Ground

- If no land trust exists in your region, team up with like-minded people and form one.
- No matter what the other missions of the land trust are, help the Board of Directors and staff consider land's ecological value as home to legions of soil microorganisms, insects, and plants, as nesting places for birds and animals, as paths of migration, and as the body through which water flows that supports aquatic and terrestrial life.
- Advocate that strategies for land protection and land management always be informed by good conservation science, no matter what the primary management of the land will be.
- Promote ecological assessments and biological inventories and cross-political boundary reserve design. Through such science-based planning, land trusts can avoid reactive, last-minute projects responding unsystematically to sudden development threats. Protect the best examples of biological communities to serve as reference sites for restoration work on degraded lands.
- In farmland conservation, encourage the trust to focus on small organic farms; promote ways that the community can support the farmer. Through conservation easements, map out ecological zones inappropriate for tilling or removal of natural vegetation, such as riparian and shoreline zones along streams, rivers, wetlands, and ponds.
- In forestry easements, encourage ecologically friendly silviculture; create zones in which no commercial harvesting is allowed nor removal of natural vegetation in sensitive places, and in shoreline zones along streams, rivers, wetlands, vernal pools, and ponds.
- Provide technical and scientific research whenever possible to guide public and private decision-making, such as zoning, open space plans, public acquisitions, and the creation of tax incentives for preservation.
- Learn how to lobby. Land trusts, watershed groups, and other nonprofit entities cannot engage in partisan elections. But federal regulations expressly allow 501(c)(3) nonprofit groups to lobby as a fraction of their budgets. Wilderness funding and good land use policies depend absolutely on effective lobbying.
- Work with state agency managers and administrators.
- Land trusts and wilderness advocates must develop relationships with public officials and the press from the local to the federal levels. It takes time to build the connections, bring officials and reporters on site visits, and prepare materials conveying the principles of conservation biology. Without this effort, conservation of the wild will continue to be inadequately funded, and much public policy will have adverse effects on wild nature.

- Become familiar with land protection techniques. Keep your ear to the ground for potential sources of acquisition funding, and lobby to ensure that conservation funds can and will be used for wilderness and biological conservation (see below).
- Learn how to draft good ecological language for forever wild easements. Use some of this language to write any kind of limited development, agricultural, or forestry easements to make biodiversity protection a feature of them all.
- Educate land trust staff and volunteers at the annual Land Trust Rally hosted by the Land Trust Alliance and at other such educational events, and encourage hosts to focus more on conservation science training.

pollution, and exotic species control. Lake and pond associations tend to be localized in their efforts and focused on water quality issues. All of these land trust and watershed groups need to work together to protect those places where land and water meet—the riparian zones, the wetlands and estuaries, and their uplands where so much biodiversity is cradled.[25]

Unfortunately, these groups collectively have not made a splash on our Northern Forest map. Only blown up to mural size would map 8.1 show where smaller parcels have been protected as forever wild. Although these local efforts do not add up to regional biodiversity protection, these small reserves and constituencies are important, connecting people to nature, and represent a rock-solid foundation on which to build. They are the vanguard of a very exciting regional trend. To more fully protect the places where we live and upon which we draw solace, we need to link arms with neighbors throughout our region.

Knowing that in a democracy, our strength is in numbers, many groups have also formed land-protection partnerships. The Shawangunk Ridge Biodiversity Partnership in New York is comprised of many public agencies, land trusts, and other nonprofit entities. Their Ecosystem Research Program is creating an information base on a landscape scale to assist in ecological management of the 90,000-acre northern Shawangunks. The Northern Forest Alliance, professionally staffed and comprising about forty organizations, is examining a host of regional cultural and conservation issues. The Massachusetts Environmental Collaborative, over thirty land trusts and grassroots organizations linked together by a sophisticated communications network, works to strengthen land use policies and water resource protection statewide. Throughout the region, partnerships are beginning to form across political borders.

However, multiple issue coalitions tend to stray toward a comfortable middle ground that supports the status quo. People who love nature must work with such groups to tell them that wild lands conservation is not receiving the attention or money needed for wild nature to endure. People should also embrace the science-based land protection of groups such as the Wildlands Project and the Nature Conservancy, and encourage them not to dilute that important mission. We all need to keep abreast of conservation biology and help translate it into conservation on the ground.

Grassroots wilderness groups are also working hard, mostly on shoestring budgets, to save and expand the special places of our region. Increasing signs show that these groups are starting to work more closely together, melding their common agendas and increasing their overall effectiveness. They must work to form broader-based coalitions, joining with local land trusts, conservation agencies, watershed groups, building bridges to constituencies such as schools, scouts, community leaders, hunters, the medical establishment, cancer victims, anglers, parents, cultural preservationists, religious groups, native peoples, and urban activists.

Until a coalition of many groups and diverse constituencies come together with the will and the expertise to put wilderness on the ground, efforts will continue to be ecologically piecemeal, underfunded, and politically undermined. Only together, as a chorus of united voices, will we find the funding to accomplish our wilderness goals.

Just Buy It: Funding the Wilderness Vision

Private Wild Lands Philanthropy

Some folks pay $10,000 for a painting and hang it on the wall where their friends can see it while I buy a whole mountain for that much money and it is hung by nature where everybody can see it and it is infinitely more handsome than any picture ever painted.

—Joseph Battell[26]

Much of the vast woods of the Northern Forest is cheap, unpeopled, essential for restoring wilderness, and for sale. Why hasn't it been simple to acquire and protect this land? The major stumbling block to land preservation in the region boils down to one issue: money. Conservationists and philanthropists today have an unprecedented opportunity to buy Northern Forest habitat, and forever protect the natural legacy of this region. And there is unprecedented wealth and economic prosperity in the country. Yet conservationists—with few exceptions—have not been players at the negotiating table. Major public and private capital is necessary if we are to start competing with timber investors to take advantage of this historic but finite wilderness opportunity.[27]

Why private philanthropy? Because private dollars can vault over the short-term politics and economics that represent the major stumbling blocks to land acquisition. For more than a century, individuals have led the way in buying and protecting critical lands threatened by resource exploitation and development, and these lands today represent a breathtaking national legacy. Private gifts can break political logjams and lead to an outpouring of public dollars for additional acquisition. For example, Acadia National Park, Grand Teton National Park, Virgin Islands National Park, and others were created largely through the vision and generosity of the Rockefeller family, most notably John D. Rockefeller, Jr, and his son, Laurence Rockefeller.

The most legendary example in the region is Baxter State Park in Maine, currently the largest wilderness area in all of New England. Percival Baxter had a vision that Mount Katahdin and the surrounding lands should be public. But when Baxter was governor, the legislature twice voted against purchasing the lands, influenced primarily by the local timber lobby. To realize his dream, Baxter patiently and persistently purchased chunks of the land for years after he left office. Few remember his record as governor, but no one will ever forget Percival Baxter and his extraordinary 200,000-acre gift to the people of Maine.[28] Other historic examples of wild lands philanthropy include:

- In 1974, Mine Crane gave the Crane Wildlife Refuge in Essex Bay, Massachusetts, to the Trustees of Reservations, forever protecting 2,000 acres of islands, barrier beaches, salt marshes, and tidal creeks.
- Arthur D. Norcross, Sr, spent twenty-five years assembling a 3,000-acre reserve in Monson and Wales, Massachusetts, and established the Norcross Wildlife Foundation, which continues to expand the reserve and provide funding for other land acquisition.
- In western Maine, Bessie Phillips gave more than 5,000 forever wild acres to protect Rangely Lake and Kennebago River, launching a land protection effort by the Rangely Lakes Heritage Trust on a scale that few other land trusts nationwide have equaled.
- Betty Babcock's gift of 3,000 acres to the Society for the Protection of New Hampshire Forests (which she modestly named for a friend, Charles Pierce), has led to concerted land protection efforts under-

scored by extensive conservation science supported by the Forest Society and Sweet Water Trust.

- Vermont's Helen Buckner Memorial Preserve at Bald Mountain was created through a family gift to the Nature Conservancy.
- In eastern New York, the Smiley brothers sold 5,300 acres at very reduced cost to the Mohonk Preserve, which has become the keystone piece for a 23,000-acre mosaic of lands protected by the Shawangunk Ridge Biodiversity Partnership. The Reserve also has a research center that holds an extremely valuable body of natural science data spanning more than 125 years.
- The Lila Wallace/Reader's Digest Fund has quietly helped the Open Space Institute and other organizations spend more than $200 million on land acquisition in the Hudson River Valley region over the past twenty years.

Because there has been a chronic shortage of funds for land protection overall, land trusts and agencies are used to buying small pieces retail, rather than taking advantage of the wholesale marketing of large tracts. They have long focused on the stuff that no one else wanted, such as mountaintops and wetlands. Organizations have stretched dollars as best they could, but over and over have been forced to make considerable compromises on land better conserved as wild.

There are promising signs of change. Because of increased ecological understanding and the sheer magnitude of land available, some big steps have been taken in the right direction. Foundations not traditionally involved in land acquisition have become engaged in the Northern Forest and elsewhere.[29] New philanthropists are entering the fray. The largest intergenerational transfer of wealth ever seen in this country is currently underway. Also, many people with substantial new wealth, particularly because of technology-related ventures, are in pursuit of smart philanthropic investments, characterized by the kind of innovation and effectiveness that made their businesses successful. Experts characterize these new philanthropists as smart givers. In 1998, donations to nonprofit organizations in the United States rose more than 10 percent.[30] We have every reason to hope that increasing amounts of money will be directed toward the preservation of global ecosystems. Finally, land acquisition organizations, inspired by the several organizations that have dared to think big in the past year, are anticipating how they too might become players in the larger land sales (see box on the St. John River acquisition). It is a good start for the new era of conservation.

While public funding and support of wilderness acquisition are of

St. John River Acquisition

In December 1998, the Nature Conservancy purchased full and partial interests in 220,000 acres of land (185,000 acres of "full fee equivalent") in the St. John River watershed of northern Maine, achieving a major conservation purchase along a river long-heralded as the last undammed wilderness river east of the Mississippi and in an area long-identified as a top ecological priority for the state. However, the purchase put the organization into $35 million of debt, and accountable for roughly $8,000 per day in interest costs. The land cost twice as much as any previous acquisition by the organization anywhere in the world. The Nature Conservancy is now undertaking an ecological assessment of the lands, and formulating a strategic protection plan for the entire watershed. No project more ambitious or ecologically exciting has been undertaken in the region. However, the fact remains that the organization has not raised all the money needed to pay for the land, let alone additional watershed lands, and cannot as of this writing rule out partial resale or major timbering in the long-term. Today, pre-existing timber contracts are covering the TNC's interest payments. Only an outpouring of wild lands support on this and other projects will tell organizations loudly and clearly that they can—and must—dare to reach for wilderness.

course essential long-term goals, public funds have not caught up to the acquisition opportunities in the Northern Forest, even after ten years. As Vice President Al Gore noted about politics and the environment in 1993: "The maximum that is politically feasible, even the maximum that is politically imaginable right now, still falls far short of the minimum that is scientifically and ecologically necessary."[31]

Securing public dollars at the state or federal level is difficult and time-consuming in the best of times. When they do appear, few of these dollars are generally slated for wilderness protection. Well-organized special interests tend to demand that such funds be used for land to accommodate recreational uses incompatible with wilderness values. For these and other reasons, private wild lands philanthropy has a critical supplemental role to play.

We need capital to get the job done: major acquisition funds, bridge loans, outright gifts of land and easements, and science, mapping, and stewardship funds. New players are taking advantage of the major land sales in northern New England, particularly timberland investment groups (representing institutions and pension funds) and the subsidized Canadian pulp and lumber industry. Wilderness conservationists need to be creative players in this important game. A major infusion of capital from private wild lands philanthropists for projects big and small would fundamentally change the political as well as the ecological landscape, encouraging and leveraging more funds and commitment from governmental agencies, conservation groups, and local communities to protect our natural heritage.

In an era of doom and gloom environmental news, saving land is a celebratory act. It ensures protection of beautiful, critical habitat—forever. Donors and their families can walk or canoe the land and appreciate its splendor. Decades and even centuries later, future generations will marvel at the foresight, as we marvel today at the vision of John D. Rockefeller and Percival Baxter. Today, we have unprecedented wealth in America. People only need to realize that they, too, can help leave an enduring legacy of natural beauty and wild nature for the generations that follow.

Public Funding Sources

Something will have gone out of us as a people if we ever let the remaining wilderness be destroyed; if we permit the last . . . forests to be turned into comic books and plastic cigarette cases . . . and push our paved roads through the last of the silence.

—Wallace Stegner[32]

To put the wilderness vision on the ground will also require public money and widespread public support over the long term. Advocates need to become more sophisticated about finding and creating funding mechanisms for land acquisition. Potential sources of public funds are out there, but will take substantial work to bring home to this region. And as public land funds seldom focus on wilderness and biodiversity protection, wilderness advocates will also have to work hard to strengthen such existing programs. The following list of funding categories and programs is a sampling of important current and potential opportunities.[33] But buyer beware. Work with the funding source to see if accommodation of wilderness goals can be achieved. Make sure not to pursue monies that conflict with preservation goals because of incompatible management requirements.

Taxes. Some forms of taxation have been used for land conservation programs, including real estate transfer taxes, sales taxes, hotel and tourism taxes, and severance taxes. A promising discussion is beginning on taxation that supports sustainability; such tax revenues could get double mileage by funding land conservation. Examples include taxes on carbon, motor vehicle emissions, industrial pollution discharges, fertilizers, pesticides, and cut timber.[34] Severance taxes are levied by many states as well as by the federal government on natural resources when they are extracted. Sometimes this money is earmarked for conservation. The logic of this funding source for land and easement acquisition is that those who make a profit exploiting resources should help protect resources elsewhere. The most notable example in this category is the Land and Water Conservation Fund (LWCF).

Since Congress created the LWCF in 1964, it has been the nation's most significant funding source for federal acquisition of park and recreational lands, and for matching grants to state and local governments for acquisition and development of outdoor recreation areas and facilities. LWCF receives the bulk of its revenues from federal offshore oil and gas leasing revenues. It is the big pot of money that *could* provide the financing for major land preservation in the Northern Forest and elsewhere in the Northeast. However, there are a number of hurdles. First and foremost, Congress has failed to authorize LWCF funding at the $900-million level available from oil and gas leasing revenues. Instead, Congress has funneled those funds into other programs.

During the thirty-year history of LWCF, 7 million acres of natural areas have been protected. Federal land acquisition monies are appropriated through a formula that gives precedence to areas adjoining existing federal lands. The Northeast does poorly under the formula, and has received considerably fewer funds than states with vast federal land holdings.[35]

A second part of the LWCF land acquisition program (the "stateside program") is geared toward local and state needs. About 37,000 parks and recreational projects have been funded under the stateside formula. These monies are appropriated in part through a population-based formula. Again, the Northern Forest does not fare well using this funding screen. Moreover, this program has received little funding from Congress for years.

As of this writing, bipartisan support is growing to pass legislation for a more fully and permanently funded LWCF. Many obstacles remain. The present compromise legislation neither permanently funds LWCF nor provides funds for the acquisition of significant, once in a lifetime opportunities such as those in the Northern Forest. Undoubtedly a strenuous role must be played by wilderness advocates to get LWCF money channeled to projects that protect wild lands and nongame species.[36] Federal money could not be better spent.

Mitigation Funds. Some public agencies require that a developer proposing a project that would degrade sensitive land must provide funds for acquisition of land with a similar resource value. Settlements in a lawsuit by an agency over pollution violations can also involve mitigation funding for land protection or settlements involving land given as compensation. Often land trusts can benefit from these settlements because land trusts are generally seen as nonlitigious. For example, EPA Region One in New England has a Supplemental Environmental Projects (SEP) policy, under which a defendant in an environmental enforcement action can agree to put money into an environmentally beneficial project. Land and water protection are considered potential SEPs.[37] Potential also exists for land restoration and protection as part of mitigation banking in each state. The Nature Conservancy and some states have successfully set up banks to efficiently fulfill mitigation requirements by selling credits to a developer for state of the art mitigation projects.

The potential of carbon sequestration mitigation has the conservation community beginning to buzz. Forests are significant reservoirs of both carbon and biological diversity. The alarming buildup of CO_2 in the atmosphere is linked primarily to the burning of fossil fuels, and also to global deforestation. The 1997 Kyoto Protocol established emission reduction goals for a number of developed nations including the United States. Regardless of how quickly Congress acts on this global warming treaty, corporations and conservationists are beginning to calculate forests into carbon accounting.

A forest-friendly interpretation of the Kyoto agreement and the global climate change problem could promote the sequestering of carbon through permanent forest protection. A vast amount of money would become available through carbon mitigation funds (for example, through forest-based carbon credits), perhaps becoming the major source of revenue for the establishment of forest preserves. The task for forest advocates and scientists is to ensure that the forest activities permitted under the Protocol and by congressional statute do not create short-sighted, perverse incentives that would harm forest ecosystems by encouraging the clear-cutting of mature forests and the establishment of short-rotation plantations.

Public Bonds. For capital expenditures, governments will often issue bonds on the open market. Frequently this is how land acquisition is paid for on a town, state, or regional level. The promising news is that state and local government bond act monies for land acquisition are on the rise across the country. Fueled by community concern about sprawl, disappearing natural areas, and water quality, people across the nation have flocked to the voting booths to vote for bonds to pay for significant land acquisition.

The Green Acres Program in New Jersey is regarded as one of the most successful state land preservation programs in the country's history. Financed by an unbroken record of nine bond approvals totaling $1.4 billion, the program has protected over 350,000 acres. This year the voters stepped up their land protection efforts by passing a $1 billion constitutional amendment that will protect half the state's remaining 2 million acres of open space over the next ten years. One-quarter of one cent of the state sales tax is designated for that purpose. In 1996, New York passed a $1.75 billion bond act for clean water and air initiatives that has already fueled some important acquisitions in the Adirondack Park. In Florida, voters stepped up to the plate in 1998, approving Forever Florida, a bonding program that will raise $3 billion for conservation over the next ten years. This builds on Florida's Preservation 2000, under which one million acres were protected since 1990.[38]

In the face of these impressive numbers, it is clear that northern New England lags far behind. New Hampshire spent almost $50 million on land acquisition from 1987 to 1993 through its New Hampshire Land Conservation Investment Program, but no money has been available since that time. Little further action is expected until the state reforms its education funding through implementation of a new state tax structure. Although the people of Maine approved a $50 million bond act in November 1999, there will be considerable competition for these funds. For example, a state land acquisition priorities committee has recommended that it be spent predominantly in southern and coastal Maine where sprawl pressures are great and land prices high.[39]

If Maine and other Northern Forest states wait too long to put serious money into land acquisition, they will be in the same position that more-urban states are in today, spending billions of dollars and scrambling to save the last remnants of available land. If they act now, they can save the larger landscape, based on conservation science, at a fraction of the cost. No other states in the country have such an extraordinary opportunity to map and implement an ecologically based conservation future.

State funds can be as problematic as federal funds for wilderness acquisition. State agencies traditionally spend money for lands with high recreational value; state politics often demand intensive recreational and extractive management that conflicts with wilderness values and biodiversity protection. Many states have a tradition of logging most state lands, and have been lukewarm about the need to create ecological reserves on current or future state lands. Nonetheless, the explosion of state bond acts for land acquisition is an important trend, and with concerted effort more of this money could be steered toward wilderness preservation.

Loans. Bridge financing is often necessary to complete the transaction of an important acquisition before full funding is in place. Short-term financing can be provided by the seller or by another party. Innumerable creative opportunities can be invented for working out seller financing that meets the seller's needs and buys time for the buyer. To help in bridge financing, some foundations will make program-related investments (PRIs) in keeping with the mission of the foundation. Some nonprofit groups have revolving funds that can lend money at a reasonable rate. A private individual or a business may advance a loan because of a belief in the conservation project, for public relations benefit, or other reasons. Borrowing from an institutional lender is sometimes ill-advised because of a land trust's need for flexibility, speed, and lower costs and interest rates than conventional financing usually provides. However, local institutions with strong community ties can be excellent land trust partners on local projects.

Some towns have established installment-purchase agreements. This borrowing agreement would be structured to pay interest only for a period of up to thirty years, and then to pay a specified balloon principal amount at the end of the period. The market value of the land should have appreciated considerably by time of the principal payment at the end, making the original purchase price insignificant compared to land values and budgets of the future.[40]

Noting concern across the region about the vanishing natural landscape, the Clinton administration has proposed a "Build a Better America" Bond Act that would funnel $1.9 billion into zero interest bond funding for state and municipal land acquisition over the next five years. Such a program could help provide much-needed access to financial capital. The prognosis for this new initiative remains uncertain, but low or zero interest funds could help the conservation community bridge the enormous gap between seizing a great opportunity and raising sufficient capital.

This sampling of a range of public funding possibilities for wilderness acquisition needs to be accompanied by the vigilance of advocates who work on state and federal land management policy. In the public and nonprofit sectors alike, it is important to acquire wilderness areas *and* protect them as wilderness into the future. Both are critical to the persistence of wild nature.

Forever Is a Long Time: Protecting Wild Land in Perpetuity

It being the principal object of this devise to preserve intact said wildlands . . . and . . . Considerable tracts of mountain forests . . . in their original and primeval condition.
—Last Will and Testament of Joseph Battell[41]

Joseph Battell was a wilderness visionary on the scale of Percival Baxter, who wanted to "preserve intact wild lands . . . as a specimen of the original Vermont forest."[42] Battell began his legacy of wild lands philanthropy with a gift to Vermont of 1,200 critical acres on and around the summit of Camel's Hump Mountain, creating the state's first natural area strictly protected for wilderness values. For many years thereafter, Battell collected additional wild lands "much as a school boy collects postage stamps."[43] Upon his death, Battell bequeathed well over 30,000 acres of additional forestlands to Middlebury College in Vermont.

Over time, however, much of that 30,000 acres was sold to the U.S. Forest Service, which has used the lands for timber cutting and ski area development. The Forest Service and the college believe that Battell's intentions were mixed, and that the title was cleared of any restrictions when the federal agency acquired the land. The Vermont activist group, Forest Watch, disagrees, and has launched a campaign to restore Battell's forever wild vision.[44]

Whatever the ultimate resolution of the Battell land debate, the story is far from unique. Scores of habitat donations given to public agencies, academic institutions, nonprofit organizations, or family members have been sold without restriction, and timbered, developed, or otherwise altered from the original purpose of the gift. Over time, institutional memories fade, priorities shift.

Once lands are in public hands, they tend to be increasingly developed to placate the agencies' loudest constituents. ATVs, snowmobiles, jetskis, developed campgrounds, camper hook-ups, logging, mechanized hunting, and boat ramps proliferate. Environmentalists spend valuable time fighting defensive battles to protect these "protected" lands. A quick scan of Maine headlines in the past year documents the inexorable march of mechanized recreation across the public landscape: "Allagash Plan Favors Sportsman and Access"; "Motorized Access Gaining Ground in Public Lands Debate"; and "Forever Wild Meets Politics of the Day."[45]

Unfortunately, wild nature fares poorly when stacked up against pressures such as logging, skiing, and mechanized recreational interests. As E. O. Wilson explains: "every country has three forms of wealth: material, cultural, and biological . . . The essence of the biodiversity problem is that biological wealth is taken much less seriously."[46]

In central Massachusetts, for example, the 2,000-acre Wachusett Mountain State Park safeguards over 100 acres of old-growth forest, a rare find in a state that has lost all but .03 percent of its original forests (see chapter 3). In addition to northern red oaks and yellow birch over 300 years old, many other diverse community types and species unique to old-growth habitat are found in the park. Discovered in 1994, this remarkable find has not stopped the state from tentatively approving an expansion of the Wachusett Ski area, on a 20-acre site buffering the old-growth area and including trees over 120 years old.[47]

The pressures on our protected land base, as well as on unprotected private lands, will only continue to grow over time. How do we safeguard more of these lands, buffering them from the politics, economics, fading memories, and changing priorities of the future? Conservation easements are an important part of the answer.

Protecting the Protected through Conservation Easement

In the Northeast, where most land is privately owned, conservation easements are one of the best tools in the toolbox for land protection. A conservation easement is a voluntary legal agreement between a landowner and a land trust or public agency that permanently restricts certain development or extractive uses of the land and delineates allowable uses. This agreement can be given or sold by a landowner. The conservation easement is recorded in the Registry of Deeds, and runs with the land through all future ownerships. It is an actual conveyance of property rights to the easement holder, thereby functionally extinguishing those rights. It is a solid property transaction, with antecedents in common law and broad statutory basis.[48]

Because they are extremely flexible, conservation easements can fit all sorts of public and private situations, and adapt to every sort of terrain. In many cases, significant property and estate tax benefits accrue to owners who use them. Easements are perhaps best known as a way to permanently protect farmland or timbered land from incompatible development.[49] However, landowners can also place "forever wild" easements on all or part of their land, securing its wild qualities in perpetuity. More needs to be done to tell landowners throughout the region about this powerful option.

Conservation easements are also a pivotal tool for guaranteeing permanent protection of conservation land owned by a public agency or nonprofit conservation group. In this scenario, the land is owned in fee by one entity. The easement is held and enforced by another agency or a nonprofit conservation group. This ensures a double layer of protection. Because public or private management goals may fall prey to future economic or political pressures, the extra protection afforded by an easement helps steady the course for management of biological conservation and wilderness values. Perhaps only federally designated wilderness matches the protection afforded by a well-crafted forever wild easement. Even the "forever wild" lands of the Adirondack Park are under increasing pressure to be designated "wild forest" instead of "wilderness," an administrative designation that would allow intensive mechanized recreation.[50]

Through conservation easements, we can effectively protect large natural areas from the twitchy human hand that wants to "improve" everything over time. Multiple layers of protection also give many parties a vested ownership interest in a conservation property. When the local land trust holds the easement, the community has an actual property interest in what may be public land.[51]

A forever wild easement is an essential wilderness protection tool. However, it is not to be undertaken lightly. It needs to be held by a conservation organization committed to protecting natural areas on the principles of conservation biology. Rag-tag remnants of land might be inappropriate for such an easement, unless the possibility exists to expand the area into a scale that has biological meaning.

Sweet Water Trust provides roughly $1 million in grant money each year for the acquisition of New England wild lands, and requires forever wild easements on the majority of those tracts. Properties that might have fallen under the vagaries of state or nonprofit management have thus been secured with permanent wild lands protection instead. For example, in 1995, a number of state, federal, and private entities gathered to try to acquire a critical 2,780-acre tract of land adjoining Camel's Hump State Park in Vermont. Sweet Water Trust attended a number of meetings to discuss a possible grant commitment and its "forever wild" requirement. A number of parties argued against forever wild protection for the usual reasons: It was too soon; people weren't ready for it; it would be redundant with good state management. Ultimately, the parties agreed to place a forever wild easement on the 2,100 truly wild acres of the property. Joseph Battell would be pleased that his vision for Camel's Hump has been further realized by future generations.

What's in a Name: The Specifics of Forever Wild Easements

"Wild," of course, defies strict definition. Because ongoing disagreements about habitat and species management persist among fish and game managers, foresters, and conservation biologists, it is easier to define what is *not* natural. In a forever wild easement, activities that degrade nature are written into a "prohibited uses" section, which is the heart of the document. When writing forever wild easements, these are the issues that can make agreement between parties a delicate negotiation. Government agencies as well as most nonprofit groups and their legal counsel do not relish relinquishing the market value and management options on their lands. The right to build condo units is easy to give away. Other rights are tougher.

Road closure is a particularly hard sell. Public officials and hosts of conservationists have for years "improved" land through road-building for emergency access to put out fires and rescue recreationists, and for timber harvesting. The biological imperative of road-closing, unless eloquently articulated by scientists, may not be compelling next to the arguments raised by strong voices who want them. The decision to leave open or close roads and trails needs to strongly consider the biological consequences of such actions. Other important prohibitions include no commercial timber management, no biocides or other chemicals, no erection of permanent or temporary structures of any kind, no purposeful introduction of non-native or genetically engineered species, no disruption of soils and water courses, and no motorized access.

A forever wild easement should protect wild lands, but not micromanage the future. Sweet Water Trust and the Massachusetts Nature Conservancy have drafted a generic forever wild easement that contains a management section allowing flexibility to override some of these prohibited uses if necessary for future ecological restoration actions. It is essential to write easements that sufficiently restrict harmful activities, but are flexible enough for management of rare species and significant natural communities, exotic species, infestations, and the like according to the dictates of good conservation science.

Land conservationists are increasingly responsive to conservation science, and often show openness to drafting such provisions into their management plans. The management section should require consensus of recognized experts in the field of conservation biology, proper permitting, and agreement between owner and easement holder for any significant override of prohibited uses.

The Northeast has been very receptive to the use of easements, particularly since a number of state and federal statutes were passed in the 1960s and 1970s that provided statutory authority and clarification concerning their permanence and availability, as well as their deductibility if donated. Today, the region boasts the four states with the most easements in the country: Pennsylvania (743), Massachusetts (700), New Hampshire (622), and New York (610). Now it is time to dramatically increase the use of *forever wild* easements. Had Joseph Battell had the opportunity to place a forever wild easement on the 30,000 acres he so generously bequeathed as wild land only eighty-five years ago, his priceless legacy would still be intact today.

Conclusion

And let us go beyond mere salvage to begin the restoration of natural environments, in order to enlarge wild populations and stanch the hemorrhaging of biological wealth. There can be no purpose more enspiriting than to begin the age of restoration, reweaving the wondrous diversity of life that still surrounds us.

—E. O. Wilson[52]

The Northeast is in the midst of land ownership change so enormous it is almost impossible to fathom. The last time such a confluence of ecological concern, economic prosperity, and acquisition opportunity occurred was roughly at the turn of the last century, when badly degraded timberlands were acquired to create the Adirondack Park, the White Mountain National Forest, the Green Mountain National Forest, and Baxter State Park. Now we must determine our own legacy to the future.

Today, as we only begin to understand how our humanity is inseparable from the natural world, we stand at the brink of irreversible destruction of wild nature as we never have before. Yes, we must devise ways to control sprawl. Yes, we must make resource extraction and agriculture more sustainable. And yes, we must seize the current opportunity to save and restore the wild lands of our region, protecting the rich mosaic of plants, animals, and ecological functions that have evolved over the course of evolution on Earth.

It will take all of us to achieve these goals, a blend of passionate philosophy and hard-headed practicality. And we must begin today. The threats are far greater and the stakes far higher than they were at the turn of the last century. Fortunately, for a brief moment in time, we have a wondrous second chance.

Part III

NORTHEASTERN WILD
LANDS IN CONTEXT

CHAPTER 9

Stewardship and Sustainability

Lessons from the "Middle Landscape" of Vermont

NORA MITCHELL AND ROLF DIAMANT

> By perceiving ourselves as part of the river, we take responsibility for the river as a whole.
> — Vaclav Havel[1]

IN THE QUIET twilight, a lone series of hoots echoes through the Mount Tom forest. On silent wings, a young barred owl flies low over a carriage road that winds through the forest stands planted in the nineteenth century and the second-growth woodlands of abandoned farm fields. This owl, a species that inhabits the forest interior, has returned with the woodlands. As in many other areas of Vermont, by the mid-nineteenth century, Woodstock's Mount Tom was cleared of most of its tree cover. When nineteenth-century conservationist George Perkins Marsh explored this mountainside as a child, he probably did not hear the barred owl calling. During Marsh's childhood in the early 1800s, the forest was fast disappearing, first cleared for agriculture and later for live-stock grazing. Marsh was later to reflect in his landmark book, *Man and Nature*, on the wasteful agricultural and deforestation practices that he had observed in Vermont and on his first-hand experience with similar environmental destruction in the Middle East and Europe.[2] First published in 1864, *Man and Nature* warned of the threats posed not only to the environment, but also to the foundations of civilization itself. In Marsh's view, good land management and husbandry were the corner-stones for a productive and civil society. He called for improved steward-ship of land — stewardship with the future in mind, what today we call sustainable land management.

One of the earliest and most energetic responses to Marsh's call for action came from fellow Vermonter Frederick Billings, who purchased the Marsh homestead in 1869. Through Billings's reforestation efforts, the forest returned to Mount Tom in the late nineteenth century almost as dramatically as it had disappeared. Planting thousands of trees throughout his 1,500-acre estate, Billings created a forest that today represents one of the earliest planned and continuously managed woodlands in America. Billings's heirs continued management of this forest over two succeeding generations, including the last fifty years during the tenure of Billings's granddaughter, Mary French, and her husband Laurance Rockefeller. In 1998, the Rockefeller family donated these woodlands as part of Marsh-Billings-Rockefeller National Historical Park. The park, which interprets conservation history and the evolving nature of land stewardship in America, continues the tradition of sustainable forestry on 550 acres of the original Billings forest.[3]

The rewilding that has taken place on Mount Tom, and in much of Vermont in concert with traditional agriculture and forestry, has resulted in a richly woven landscape tapestry of ecology and history.[4] This long-settled "middle landscape" challenges the dichotomy that has dominated our perceptions of the relationship between nature and culture and many of the tenets of our conservation philosophy and practice. John Elder has pointed out the power of "the stories of this long-settled landscape," and how these

> may help us to imagine a more inclusive paradigm for American conservation. In the syntax of these mountains, "loss" and "recovery," "wilderness" and "stewardship" may all be spoken, and connected . . . [I do] not see such reevaluation as rejection of the wilderness ethic, but hope instead that we will now find new ways to integrate our vision of wilderness into a more socially inclusive perspective on the environment.[5]

In this chapter, we explore this concept of a "middle landscape" and probe its value for cultivating stewardship and learning sustainability. Our perspective is shaped and informed by the history of land stewardship in places such as Mount Tom and by the conservation efforts of many organizations and communities today. The lessons of land management, described by Marsh in the nineteenth century, today are written on the rewilded forest landscape of Vermont and many places in the Northeast. Past land management efforts tell stories of sustainability—some through failure and others through continuity. These stories can be used as guides and as encouragement to seek sustainability alongside rewilding. Viewed in this light, our northeastern landscape can be our compass for new directions in environmental thought and development of a broader, more inclusive conservation ethic.

Figure 9.1. Historic carriage road through Mount Tom Forest, reforested by Frederick Billings in the late nineteenth century. *Photo: Property of the Woodstock Historical Society, Inc.*

Figure 9.2. Overlooking Marsh-Billings-Rockefeller National Historical Park, the Billings Farm and Museum, and the village of Woodstock in the Ottauquechee Valley, Vermont. *Photo by Barbara Slaiby.*

Rewilding and Reconnecting on the Middle Landscape

Defining the "Middle Landscape"

The long-settled landscape of Mount Tom has been described as the humanized landscape—the ecotone where civilization and wilderness meet. These are lands that have long had a human imprint, areas traditionally used for agriculture and forestry or developed as towns and cities. These areas have been given various names—nonwildlands, cultural landscapes, working landscapes, or protected landscapes.[6] In this chapter, we will use the term "middle landscape." This middle landscape traditionally has not received great attention from the conservation community. Yet the middle landscape provides a vital connection between remote areas of wilderness and the places where most people live and work. In the middle landscape, we have an opportunity to sustain and cultivate knowledge of wildness close to home and to explore the relationship with more remote wilderness. This ecotone landscape is also the place where we can learn to live on the land in a sustainable way.

Rewilding and the Middle Landscape

Recent literature is rich in celebration of the rewilding of Vermont and other areas of the Northeast. Bill McKibben has described this reforestation as "an explosion of green" and noted that eastern wilderness offers an opportunity to integrate culture and wild lands.[7] John Terborgh and Michael Soulé have described a vision of "large-scale networks and megareserves" employing a strategy of linking core areas with corridors as an exciting new approach to conservation biology with a focus on keystone species that range over large geographic areas.[8] The Wildlands Project, closely allied with *Wild Earth*, a quarterly journal on conservation biology and wild lands activism, is "drafting a blueprint for an interconnected continental-scale system of protected wildlands linked by habitat corridors."[9]

This vision of large-scale reserves creates a future for wild lands dependent upon and interconnected with the cultivated middle landscape. In this vision, the humanized landscape is a critical component in the strategy and is recognized for its important role as corridor and buffer for the wild lands of the core.

Reconnecting on the Middle Landscape

In addition to playing a critical role in maintaining a viable network of ecological buffers and corridors, the middle landscape can promote a respect for and understanding of place, nurture a land ethic, and enhance democratic values and civil society.

These are the lands where people can build a strong association to place and a connection to nature. These are also places where people know the land and learn to respect the landscape through work, particularly agriculture and forestry. William Vitek has written that in rural communities there "is an opportunity for the land's rhythms to become part of everyday life, an immediate linkage between the land's fertility and the community's prosperity. Those who work directly on the land know it in ways that are simply unavailable to those who wish to keep their hands clean and their preconceptions unchallenged."[10] This does not imply, as Wendell Berry wrote in *Orion*, "that everyone ought to be a farmer or forester." However, Berry observed, "people now are living on the far side of a broken connection, and that this is potentially catastrophic."[11] Vitek and Berry are noting that the type of relationship developed through work or other direct experiences with land is fundamental to knowledge and understanding of place, and to the respect that follows. The connection to nature for most Americans has become increasingly conceptual, experienced through books, magazines, and television. "There is no significant urban constituency," Berry warns, "no formidable consumer lobby, no noticeable political leadership, for good land use practices, for good farming and forestry, for restoration of abused land, or for halting the destruction of land by so-called 'development.' "[12] More than ever, we need places to reinforce the tangible over the conceptual, to bring people in contact with land in a way that enhances understanding and that ultimately nurtures a constituency for the better stewardship of both wild and nonwild middle landscape.

This need for new constituencies identified by Berry is particularly relevant to how we approach education. As we seek an ever-increasing emphasis on place-based learning, the importance of these middle landscapes is growing. Incorporating farming and forestry and other real life experiences connected to sustainable land use in school curricula in conjunction with internships and field projects can help in reestablishing a fundamental connection to the land and a respect for work associated with land. This can be viewed as a long-term investment in creating a land ethic that students carry with them throughout life. Such an ethic encourages a constructive role in civic life and creates a multi-generation constituency necessary for making important decisions on the future of all lands—wild lands and the middle landscape.

In the quest for stewardship and sustainable practices on the middle landscape we, as a society, are challenged to resolve conflicts and contradictions on many different levels. We are engaged in a difficult and complex dialogue about how we care for both public and private land. The success of this dialogue will be measured by our ability to develop new ways of working together, new models of sustainable economic enterprise, and effective methods for conflict resolution and democratic decision making. An informed public discussion on the role, importance, and necessary scale of wild lands can only be accomplished in the context of this more inclusive discourse. "Truly protected wilderness," argues Brian Donahue in his book *Reclaiming the Commons*, "will follow from a society that has at last worked out a healthy relation with its everyday landscape, with its productive forests and farmlands."[13] If we are successful in creating the necessary understanding and political will for change, it will benefit all our landscapes, including wild lands, and we will have come a long way in building and maintaining a civil society that is defined by its commitment to equity, tolerance, sustainability, and environmental health.

Defining Stewardship and Sustainability

We are unlikely to achieve anything close to sustainability in any area unless we work for the broader goal of becoming native in the modern world, and that means becoming native to our places in a coherent community that is in turn embedded in the ecological realities of its surrounding landscape.

—Wes Jackson[14]

The term "stewardship" itself is derived from an old Norse word *sti-vardr,* meaning "keeper of the house."[15] The word's origin incorporates a sense of responsibility for one's personal house as well as the collective home, and suggests continuity with the past as well as a commitment to the future. "Keeper of the house" also implies a respect for both nature and culture, all things associated with the feeling of home and belonging. It is interesting to note that the term "ecology" has a similar root word of "eco" from the Greek "oiko" for house.

Environmental historian William Cronon has noted the importance of connecting our relationship with nature to our sense of home in his essay in *Uncommon Ground: Toward Reinventing Nature,* where he speaks of discovering a "middle ground, in which all of these things, from the city to the wilderness, can somehow be encompassed in the word 'home.' Home, after all, is the place where finally we make our living. It is the place for which we take responsibility, the place we try to sustain so we can pass on what is best in it (and in ourselves) to our children."[16] Gary Snyder, Pulitzer Prize–winning author, also includes both remote areas and domicile in his definition of home: "Nature is not a place to visit, it is *home*—and within that home territory there are more familiar and less familiar places."[17] The idea that home encompasses a spectrum of landscapes from wilderness to intensively managed areas also expands the notion of familiarity, attachment, and responsibility for an equally wide array of places.

In an article in *Orion,* John Elder highlighted the intergeneration nature of the concept of stewardship when he wrote "we must conceive of stewardship not simply as one individual's practice, but rather as the mutual and intimate relationship, extending across the generations, between a human community and its place on earth."[18] Defining stewardship in this way embraces everything people personally value and wish to see passed on to the next generation—or in terms being used for sustainability, to the seventh generation.

The word "sustainable" has its origins in the eighteenth- and nineteenth-century European forests. At that time, deforestation caused concerns among the foresters and, in response, they developed scientific or sustainable forestry, primarily in Germany. Their working principle was to plant enough trees to replace those harvested every year and to monitor closely rates of growth and change to ensure that the harvest was sustainable over time.[19]

There is no one definition of sustainability. The one most often cited is from *Our Common Future*, the report of the 1987 United Nations World Commission on Environment and Development (frequently referred to as the Brundtland Commission after its chair, Gro Harlam Brundtland). Sustainable development "meets the needs of the present without compromising the ability of future generations to meet their own needs."[20] The Brundtland report initiated a global conversation on sustainability. This concept was further developed at the United Nations Conference on Environment and Development in 1992 in Rio de Janeiro, Brazil (frequently referred to as the Earth Summit), when the Rio Declaration was adopted. The Declaration's twenty-seven principles establish a global commitment to further create a sustainable society.[21]

This definition and these principles of sustainability have been further refined. For example, the goals of the Sustainable Agriculture Research and Education Program, Northeast Region, state that "Sustainable agriculture and forestry systems will: promote good stewardship of the land . . . rely on—and encourage—greater diversity among farms and on individual farms . . . [and] contribute to the quality of life for producers, communities, and society as a whole."[22] It has also been argued that "the best way to communicate the meaning of sustainable agriculture is through the real-life stories of farmers who are developing sustainable farming systems on their own farms."[23] In the Northeast, a number of sustainable agriculture initiatives have been undertaken, including "marketing coops, value-added enterprises, CSAs [community supported agriculture], urban gardens, farmers markets, [and] food coops" as well as sustainable forestry initiatives such as community-based forestry and "green certified" lumber (see chapter 10).[24]

In today's context, the terms stewardship and sustainability can be used to extend the meaning of conservation, which in the past has often had an exclusive focus such as biodiversity or recreation, to embrace the complexity of the wide range of connections between people and the places they live and care about. Artist and conservationist Alan Gussow has used the term "place" to describe a holistic perception of the environment.

> A place is a piece of the whole environment that has been claimed by feeling
> . . . Viewed as a resource that sustains our humanity, the earth is a collection
> of places. We never speak, for example, of an environment we have known;
> it is always places we have known—and recall. We are homesick for places,
> we are reminded of places, it is the sounds and smells and sights of places
> which haunt us and against which we often measure our present.[25]

A more inclusive definition of conservation is shaped by our association with places—including wild lands, townscapes, cityscapes, and the middle landscape. Our attachment to these places is fertile ground for cultivating a stewardship ethic and a commitment to living sustainably.

Stewardship and Sustainability on the Ground in Vermont

In reexamining wilderness from an eastern perspective, we have the opportunity to reintegrate concepts of wildness, human history, and stewardship. This new approach to conservation is being tested and honed in Vermont, in the rest of the Northeast, in other places with complex environmental histories, and where individuals and communities are investing in stewardship. We next examine the stewardship efforts of three organizations that are beginning to tap the vast potential for reconnecting the wild and human communities, balancing ecology and economy, and valuing cultural connections of people to the land.[26] Their work provides an example of the innovation and creativity that characterizes conservation work in the Northeast today.

Discovering and Stewarding the Wild in Our Neighborhoods and Communities

"Tracking is teaching me that landscapes where nothing seems to be going on are full of business, if you learn to read the memos and reports written in the mud."[27] This testimony from a graduate of one of Keeping Track's six-day outdoor training sessions illustrates the insights that are at the heart of this organization's mission. Keeping Track has been working in

Figure 9.3. Keeping Track volunteers inspect sign of moose—a species expanding its range in Vermont. *Photo © Susan C. Morse.*

Vermont since 1994, when Susan Morse created a nonprofit organization to train and educate citizens about the presence of wildlife in their communities and to cultivate a concern for protecting their habitats. The focus is on tracking wide-ranging mammals—such as black bear, fisher, river otter, mink, and bobcat—that need extensive tracts of undeveloped land to survive. According to Morse, "these species are particularly vulnerable to habitat loss because they require relatively large home ranges and have low population densities and reproductive rates . . . Protecting habitat for these species ensures that habitat will be protected for other species, too."[28] As their habitat becomes increasingly fragmented, these mammal populations decrease, providing an indicator of the health of the wild lands on which they depend.

Wildlife observations recorded by Keeping Track's trained citizen volunteers are entered into town databases. Keeping Track assists participating towns with the maintenance and analysis of this information. These data can then be incorporated into local and regional land use planning and conservation initiatives. In the future, Keeping Track plans to establish a network of volunteers from different communities and to establish a central database that will identify core habitats and corridors that link them. This regional level of information opens the possibility of working with a broader sphere of people, towns, agencies, and organizations. Recently, Keeping Track co-initiated a countywide collaborative project with the Winooski Valley Park District and all the towns in Chittenden County.[29] This work will be coordinated with the Geographic Information System (GIS) mapping resources of the Chittenden County Regional Planning Commission.

Today, Keeping Track is working with over sixty communities, including forty-two in Vermont, sixteen in New Hampshire, and several in New York, and two organizations in California.[30] By bringing locally gathered knowledge of wildlife to the table in the local planning process, landowners, citizens, and planners can make better informed decisions.[31] In addition to the community program, Keeping Track offers field trips and classroom presentations on wildlife tracking and the importance of habitat protection within their community to schoolchildren of all ages and their teachers. Keeping Track also works with organizations such as the Vermont Institute of Natural Science, Northern Woodlands, Vermont Leadership Center, the Greater Laurentian Wildlands Project, and Vermont Coverts to encourage cooperation among their efforts on wildlife and to encourage conservation planning for larger geographic areas.

Vermont Coverts is a complementary program that works with landowners to manage their forests with wildlife habitat in mind and to consider cooperating with their neighbors in this effort. This organization, which began fifteen years ago, also places an emphasis on citizen education and offers a three day program on wildlife and forest management for private landowners. This is an important audience, since the Vermont Agency of Natural Resources estimates that of the 4.6 million acres of forested land in Vermont (78 percent of the state's acreage), roughly three-quarters is privately owned by individuals; some of whom are actively managing their forestland, some of whom are not.[32]

Figure 9.4. Forestland owners work with consulting forester as part of Vermont Coverts "Woodlands for Wildlife Cooperator Training Workshop." *Photo by Gary W. Moore.*

Individuals who complete Covert's training return to their neighborhoods and communities and find various ways to share what they have learned. Some of these graduates offer programs in the local schools, others serve as peer counselors to other landowners and talk with their neighbors about managing their adjacent land through collaboration. David Clarkson, a graduate of Coverts training from Newfane, Vermont, has worked with his neighbors for the last thirteen years, building collaboration among forty landowners. Through informal neighbor-to-neighbor arrangements, Clarkson and other landowners have affected the management of almost 6,000 acres within three towns, a project they call "Wildlife Habitat Improvement Group" (W.H.I.G.). The landowners are a diverse group, including "locals and summer people, loggers and doctors, farmers and philosophy professors," who, according to Clarkson, found they all shared "a deep affection for the land."[33] These neighbors have hired a professional forester to work with them to develop a management plan, and the landowners cooperate on implementation. They work together on projects such as leaving brush cover for grouse and woodcock and retaining sections of mature forest for large mammals such as bears and secretive species such as thrush and winter wrens. Although the goal of W.H.I.G. was to preserve wildlife habitat, the collaborative project has also been successful in cultivating a sense of place and responsibility for stewardship.[34]

Vermont Coverts currently has six other projects in the state in various stages of implementation, involving between 12,000 and 15,000 acres.[35] Vermont Coverts represents a wider trend of cooperation among private landowners across boundaries to protect wildlife habitat on a regional scale. Clarkson calls his effort a "neighborhood cooperative"; others refer to this as "community-based forestry."[36] This program "fosters land stewardship through a sense of community," according to Farley Brown, program coordinator for Vermont Coverts. David Dobbs, co-author of *The Northern Forest*, has pointed out that "cross-boundary management is in part a return to social connections that over the centuries have been fragmented along with landscape and culture." This is echoed by his co-author, Richard Ober, a senior director at the Society for the Protection of New Hampshire Forests, who noted that "when our first towns were established here in New England, neighbors had to work together very, very closely. This is merely a renewed recognition that we share vital community interests that cross private boundaries."[37]

George Perkins Marsh and Henry David Thoreau—both astute observers of their world—wrote about the power of discovery and the insight that comes from careful observation. Thoreau also spent time tracking wildlife, as his journal entry for 30 January 1841 attests. He wrote, "Here is the distinct trail of a fox stretching a quarter of a mile across the pond. I know which way a mind wended this morning, what horizon it faced, by the setting of these tracks; whether it moved slowly or rapidly, by the greater or less intervals . . . for the swiftest step leaves yet a lasting trace."[38] Marsh's observation skills were honed under the tutelage of his father, and throughout his life Marsh kept detailed environmental records. In writing *Man and Nature*, his goal was "to stimulate, not to satisfy curiosity." "[T]he power most important to cultivate," he says, "and, at the same time, hardest to acquire, is that of seeing what is before him. Sight is a faculty; seeing an art."[39]

John Elder has written about cultivating an "attentiveness to place." He argues that "focusing on the specific, local connections of geology, soil, and climate, flora and fauna, indigenous cultures, immigrant cultures, and contemporary literature and art is a habit . . . It is a practice of mindfulness and personal commitment that can enhance a person's relationship to a new home."[40] Elder also points out the potential for the educational system to cultivate this "attentiveness" and that "locally grounded, interdisciplinary teaching" can initiate a "process of helping people cultivate and extend their inherent perceptiveness. . . . tuning people in to their place and giving them a sense of strength."[41] David Orr has described this as education that "equips people to 'become native to a place.' "[42]

The programs of Keeping Track and Vermont Coverts demonstrate how personal observation and experience can enhance a person's knowledge of place and connection to their community. While the objective of both organizations is to identify and protect wildlife habitat, they carry out their work in a way that builds knowledge of place, develops individual and collective responsibility, and contributes to the stewardship of wild lands and the middle landscape.

The Work Ethic and the Land Ethic

This farm is in our blood. I can't visualize ever leaving here. I want to make sure my children will be able to make a good living here, too. We hope at least one of them will be the seventh generation on the farm.

—Tim Leach[43]

Tim Leach and his wife, Dot, own a 428-acre dairy farm along the Mettowee River in southwestern Vermont. They are the sixth generation of the Leach family to operate Woodlawn Farm, which today milks 350 Holsteins and sells its registered stock around the world. Tim and Dot, along with many of their neighbors, have voluntarily sold the development rights on their land to the Vermont Land Trust in order to enhance the farm's financial stability and preserve the agricultural heritage and rural character of the Mettowee Valley. With this decision, the Leach family has joined with thirty-four other landowners in the towns of Rupert, Pawlet, and Dorset, and with the Vermont Land Trust to conserve a total of 5,700 acres in the Mettowee Valley. In addition to retaining the agricultural landscape, a buffer area has been established along the entire length of the river to protect areas of floodplain forest and maintain water quality and good habitat for fish and other aquatic life.[44]

Since its founding in 1977, the Vermont Land Trust (VLT) has conserved more than 330,000 acres of farmland and forestland, including over 240 farms, protecting approximately 6.5 percent of Vermont's privately owned land.[45] The success of VLT has made it a model for many other smaller land trusts in the Northeast and across the country. VLT's mission is "to conserve land for the future of Vermont." This statewide achievement was recognized with the presentation of the 1999 Vermonter of the

Figure 9.5. Tim and Dot Leach and family, Woodlawn Farm, Pawlet, Vermont. *Photo by Jeffrey P. Roberts.*

Year award to VLT's president Darby Bradley. The award praised VLT and noted that its work

> has prevented sprawl from consuming key productive soils. It has assured Vermonters of recreational access to some of the state's finest lands. It has preserved natural beauty. It has provided an example for building consensus among disparate interests. It has assured a future for land-based industries that are central to Vermont's character and values. It has fostered a greater sense of community in this state.[46]

In 1997, the VLT joined the Nature Conservancy of Vermont in creating the Atlas Timberlands Partnership (ATP) to purchase 26,000 acres of forest in the Green Mountains of northern Vermont. Bob Klein, director of the Vermont chapter of the Nature Conservancy (TNC), explains how the Atlas Timberlands Partnership draws on the strength of both organizations.

> This project protects those portions of the forested landscape where the missions of the Vermont Land Trust and TNC overlap. TNC focused historically on the protection of biological resources without a great deal of

Figure 9.6. Mettowee Valley, looking south from Woodlawn Farm, Pawlet, Vermont. *Photo by Jeffrey P. Roberts.*

thought to timber production, while VLT emphasized the conservation of productive agricultural land and forestland through conservation easements. We realize these are not separate directions if we are to maintain the integrity of Vermont's ecosystems and forests in the future. Vermont's history showed a balance between ecology and economics long before the term sustainability was in vogue. ATP will help us understand how to maintain this balance in the future, so that the natural world Vermonters enjoy will thrive.[47]

Darby Bradley, also chair of Vermont's Forest Resources Advisory Council, notes that the forest products industry is Vermont's largest employer in the manufacturing sector and is critical to the economy of rural Vermont. "This industry provides over eight thousand jobs to Vermonters, including six thousand jobs in furniture-making and other finished wood products. With the ownership of so much of Vermont's woodlands in a state of flux, we must find ways to maintain large blocks of woodland to provide the raw material for the industry, protect our environment, and preserve a way of life for Vermonters."[48] For both organizations, this project represents a vision for a new direction in forest stewardship, bal-

Figure 9.7. David McMath marking trees for Atlas Timberlands Project, Richford, Vermont. *Photo by Jeffrey P. Roberts.*

ancing timber production with the protection of biological resources and the continuation of traditional recreational access.

The Atlas project was followed a year later by an even larger undertaking, the Champion Lands Project. The Conservation Fund, a national conservation organization based in Arlington, Virginia, purchased 294,000 acres of forested land from Champion International Paper Company for $72.25 million — 132,000 acres in the Northeast Kingdom of Vermont, 144,000 acres in New York, and 18,000 acres in New Hampshire.[49] As the Vermont partner to the Conservation Fund, VLT had three principal goals in the acquisition and planning for the acres in Vermont:

- protecting the important wildlife habitat and natural areas that occur on the property;
- maintaining a large component of the Champion lands as a working forest, where timber and other wood products will be harvested to support the forest products industry and the local economy; and
- preserving traditional public access to the property for hunting, fishing, trapping, snowmobiling, hiking, and other forms of recreation.[50]

The Conservation Fund and VLT worked closely with the Nature Conservancy of Vermont, the Vermont Agency of Natural Resources (ANR), and others to identify which lands were the most ecologically significant

Figure 9.8. The Yellow Bogs, former Champion International Paper property, Lewis, Vermont. *Photo by Jeffrey P. Roberts.*

and which could continue to be managed as a working forest and provide recreational opportunities. Based upon a scientific evaluation, the Conservation Fund and VLT concluded that approximately 48,000 acres in Vermont should be protected as wildlife habitat and would best be placed in public ownership. The 26,000 acres in the Nulhegan Basin, which contains many rare species, Vermont's largest deer wintering areas, other important wildlife habitat, and recreational areas, was conveyed to the U.S. Fish and Wildlife Service as part of the Silvio O. Conte National Wildlife Refuge. The ANR will acquire 22,000 acres of land in the Nulhegan and Paul's Stream watersheds, a property that contains numerous lakes, wetlands, and natural areas.

The Conservation Fund and VLT agreed to sell the remaining 84,000 acres in Vermont to a group of investors headed by Wil Merck of Hamilton, Massachusetts and Peacham, Vermont, called the Essex Timber Company. The property is subject to permanent easements stipulating a sustainable harvest for the working forest; protecting "Special Treatment Areas" of old growth, riparian corridors, wetlands, and other sensitive ecological areas (totaling approximately 5,000 acres); and providing public access for hunting, fishing, snowmobiling, and other traditional recreational pursuits. The working forest easement is held by the Vermont Land Trust and the Vermont Housing and Conservation Board, and

ANR administers the public access easement. The forest easement requires that the owner prepare a forest management plan consistent with the conditions of the easement prior to conducting a commercial timber harvest. The goal is to encourage sustainable harvest of high-quality timber that can benefit the economy of the region through value-added processing and products such as furniture making.[51]

John Roe, director of conservation programs at the Nature Conservancy's Vermont chapter, reflected on the importance and complexity of establishing a goal of sustainable forestry for this project: "The protection of the Champion lands is an exciting example of ecological sustainability at the landscape scale . . . it is still an exceedingly complex melding of the region's ecology, the economic use of the forest, and the longstanding cultural uses of the land." Nancy Bell, the Vermont representative for the Conservation Fund, looked back on the last two years of work and how this project, in many ways, represents the future of conservation. "This project heralds the challenges conservationists must face as we enter into the next millennium." According to Bell, "The diverse uses and interests both dovetail and compete with each other. The effort to strike an equilibrium between timber production, traditional recreation and ecological protection has been demanding. It is my hope that as the forests come back, the rivers clarify and the wildlife flourishes, future generations will deem that we have done right by the land and the people who use it."[52]

Conclusion: Lessons from the Middle Landscape of Vermont

We need to reweave the threads of wildness, wilderness, biological diversity, agriculture, rivers, forests, roads, human settlements, and economy into a new view of the landscape. We need visions that stretch our notions of ecological possibilities.

—David Orr[53]

Earlier in this chapter and elsewhere in this book, we have argued that the middle landscape is an important complement to conservation of wild lands, providing viable networks of ecological corridors for habitat and movement of key species as well as buffers for protected wild lands. The middle landscape, as demonstrated through a series of Vermont narratives, has another equally important role to play in conservation. Vermont is rich with stories from the middle landscape, illustrating a new and still-evolving approach to stewardship. Whether seen from the perspective of neighbors working together on community-based forestry, a novice tracker on the trail of a bobcat, or a forester working on the Champion lands in the Northern Forest, the face of conservation today is constantly changing. People are finding connections between wild lands and the working landscape and developing a more inclusive definition of conservation, one that integrates the concepts of stewardship and sustainability. This more-inclusive vision restores the vital connections among culture, nature, and community. As William Vitek has observed,

> Rediscovering the landscape and our place in it requires new ways of thinking about the relationship between humans and the natural world, and offers new challenges as well. Slowing down, staying put, opening our senses, practicing humility and restraint, knowing and caring for those around us, and finding our place in the natural world are simple yet significant steps in the rediscovery of place and the sense of community it holds.[54]

To fully explore new ideas about conservation, we will need new language, a new vocabulary that makes these concepts accessible to the majority of people. We need to move beyond terminology that limits our vision. For example, William Cronon suggests that the dichotomy we have created to conceptualize nature and culture hinders the development of integrated models. He writes that "we need to embrace the full continuum of a natural landscape that is also cultural, in which the city, the suburb, the pastoral and the wild each has its proper place, which we permit ourselves to celebrate without needlessly denigrating the others."[55] Breaking the dichotomy and reconnecting the wild and humanized landscape offers the conservation movement an opportunity to significantly expand its base, include a broader and more diverse public, and maintain relevance in a changing world. New language also contributes to our ability to communicate, to listen, to cultivate tolerance and civility, and to seek common ground. As John Elder has observed, "we must pursue stewardship not simply as the maintenance of valuable resources but also as a way of fostering a broader experience of democracy and community."[56]

Following in the footsteps of George Perkins Marsh—literally and figuratively—on the slopes of Mount Tom, we are raising our field of vision beyond the often fragmented preservation of individual areas and critical habitats, to focus on the connecting fabric of larger landscapes and ecosystems, and the complex interdependent relationship that exists between people and their sense of place. Vermont and the Northeast can make a fundamental contribution to a new paradigm for conservation. This new vision is described by Will Rogers, president of the Trust for Public Land: "Land conservation, like the soil under our feet, must be the bridge between home, good work, meaningful lives, and a hopeful future."[57] This approach suggests that there really are no refuges in the literal sense of the term. Even the largest and most remote wild areas are dependent on the responsible stewardship of the communities and productive lands that influence the greater ecosystems that surround them. In Vermont and elsewhere, the success of conservation will ultimately be measured by the integrity and vitality of wild lands, the sustainability of the middle landscape, and the health and stability of communities.

CHAPTER 10

Vermont Family Forests

Building a Sustainable Relationship
with Local Forests

DAVID BRYNN

The two great ruiners of private lands are ignorance and economic constraint.

—Wendell Berry

ON 4 JULY 1609, Samuel de Champlain paddled down the lake that now bears his name with a band of French explorers. Looking to the east at what is now Vermont, Champlain saw a landscape that was blanketed by a diverse, healthy, primeval forest. The forest was the result of eleven thousand years of "intimate balance between Native Americans and their environments."[1] The minimal demands placed on the forest community by humans allowed the ecological functions and processes by which forests sustain themselves over time to continue unabated.

Historians point to Champlain's brief visit in 1609 as the point at which the era of intimate balance ended and the era of exploitation began. Over the next two centuries following Champlain's exploratory paddle, Vermont was carved up and cleared for subsistence farming and timber mining. By 1850, most of Vermont's accessible forests had vanished. Stripped bare by exploitive logging and agriculture, large areas of Vermont's green hillsides had become gullied and impoverished. "The Green Mountains of Vermont, in short, had become a biological wasteland, offering little for people to live upon—a dramatic change from the bounty of a century earlier."[2] By 1900, many of Vermont's hill farms had been abandoned by "the lure of the farmland to the west, the draw of the cities, and the decreasing attractiveness of the hill farms."[3] Between 1910 and 1920, the human population of Vermont actually declined.[4]

As the human pressures upon the landscape subsided, the balance tipped back in favor of the ecological functions and processes of the forest.

234

Natural communities began the long, slow task of ecological restoration. Pioneer species invaded the severely degraded sites by sending down roots to stabilize eroding soils and by tightening leaky nutrient budgets. The pioneer species also paved the way for the reintroduction of other species of flora and fauna by improving soil productivity and diversifying habitats. As the forests matured, a protective organic mantle developed over the forest floor, increasing infiltration capacity and reducing overland flow, soil erosion, and stream sedimentation. Streams became cooler and their oxygen carrying capacity increased. As large dead trees fell, habitats improved for many species, from reptiles and amphibians to mayflies and brook trout.

Today—due in large measure to the benign neglect that resulted from the lure of natural resources available for exploitation elsewhere—over three-quarters of Vermont is once again blanketed by forests. Though still relatively young and simple when compared to the old-growth forests Champlain encountered, the return of Vermont's forest is a remarkable example of the ecological, economic, and social recovery that is possible when humans place realistic demands upon natural systems. To perpetuate the recovery and to prevent the mistakes of the past from undoing it once again, many "sustainable" solutions have been recommended. To be sustainable, commentators have pointed out that the solutions must be at once ecologically viable, economically feasible, and socially equitable.[5] Vermont Family Forests—a young, grassroots forest conservation effort in west central Vermont—is one attempt at forging a more sustainable relationship with our forests.

Family Forests in the Vermont Context

About 78 percent of Vermont's nearly 6 million acres is now forested, and this percentage is increasing.[6] As recently as 1948, only about 63 percent of Vermont was forested. Over 97 percent of the forestland is capable of and available for growing crops of wood on a commercial basis (see table 10.1). In 1996, the equivalent of 1,237,700 cords of sawlogs, pulpwood, and chipwood were harvested from Vermont's forests.[7] These raw materials provide the foundation for an industry that contributes over $1.2 billion to the Vermont economy through value-adding and that employs over 17 percent of Vermont's manufacturing workforce. In addition, these forests must contribute many nontimber values, including wildlife habitat, high-quality water supplies, scenic beauty, and recreational opportunities.

Table 10.1
Vermont's Forestland and Timberland, 1998
(acres and percentage)

Total land	Forestland	Timberland
5,919,000	4,609,000	4,461,000
(100)	(78)	(75)

Note:
   Timberland is forestland producing or capable of producing crops of wood (more than twenty cubic feet per acre per year) and not withdrawn from timber utilization by statute.

Forging a sustainable relationship with these forests is critical to the Vermont "way of life."

Over 77 percent of Vermont's forests are privately owned, non-industrial, "family forests" (see table 10.2).[8] Encouraging the practice of sustainable forestry on these family forests is definitely in Vermont's long-term best interests. Most family forests are owned primarily for reasons other than timber production. When asked what benefits they anticipated from owning forestland over the next ten years, over 95 percent of Vermont's family forest owners cited land value increases, recreational and domestic uses, aesthetic enjoyment and firewood as the ownership reasons that were most important to them.[9] However, even though timber harvesting was not a primary reason for owning their woodlands, over 90 percent of these same family forest owners stated that they intended to harvest timber at some time in the future.

In 1994, the Northern Forest Land Council (NFLC) outlined nine principles of sustainability for forest management:

- maintenance of soil productivity;
- conservation of water quality, wetlands, and riparian zones;
- maintenance or creation of a healthy balance of forest age classes;
- continuous flow of timber, pulpwood, and other forest products;
- improvement of the overall quality of the timber resource;
- scenic quality;
- habitats that support a full range of native flora and fauna;
- protection of unique or fragile natural areas; and
- continuation of opportunities for traditional recreation.

These principles cover the full range of functions and values of forested ecosystems. Malcolm Hunter and Robert Seymour recognized that every acre could not be expected to fulfill all purposes. They suggested that—

Table 10.2

Vermont Forestland Ownership, 1997
(acres and percentage)

Ownership class	Area	
Private	3,906,354	(84.9)
Non-industrial private forest	~3,540,700	(77.0)
Forest industry	~367,850	(8.0)
Public		
U.S. Forest Service	366,509	(8.0)
Other federal	8,600	(0.2)
State	284,997	(6.2)
Municipal	31,886	(0.7)

within the larger context—some forestlands should function as ecological reserves while others should be intensively managed for commodities. Still other areas should function as buffers between the ecological reserves and intensively managed areas. In these areas, "new forestry" or "light-on-the-land" forestry would be practiced. This type of forestry would appear to have great appeal to many family forest owners.[10]

Several approaches have been used in Vermont to encourage sustainable forestry on family forests. The Use Value Assessment Program (UVA) allows land that is managed according to an approved timber management plan to be assessed at its use value rather than its fair market value. In 1999, the use value of "productive" forestland in Vermont was $97 and the annual property tax was about $2.50 per acre. Under UVA, productive forestland is capable of growing over 20 cubic feet per acre per year and is actively managed. Wetlands, vernal pools, talus slopes, and other areas that are low in biomass production or reserved from timber harvesting are regarded as "nonproductive." Vermont has also encouraged sustainable forestry by minimizing overly restrictive regulations that unduly limit the management of forestlands. The regulations that do exist pertain primarily to the protection of water quality and high elevation areas, and the proper implementation of regeneration cuts on areas over 40 acres in size.

Woodland stewardship is also encouraged on family forests in Vermont through federally funded cost-share practices for timber production, wildlife habit improvement, access enhancement and water resources protection. Technical and educational assistance is available through county foresters, while private consulting foresters provide a wide range of forest management planning and commercial harvesting and administration services. Landowner associations and programs such as the Vermont Tree Farm Program and Vermont Coverts have also encouraged stewardship.

Despite the broad range of initiatives designed to foster stewardship on family forestlands, sustainable management of these forests over long periods of time has been limited. When asked what keeps them from being careful woodland stewards, surveys of family forest owners nation-wide have repeatedly obtained the same answers: inadequate information, lack of financial incentives, and fear. Wendell Berry summarized this when he wrote "that the two great ruiners of private lands are ignorance and economic constraint."[11]

The sale of standing timber or "stumpage" represents one of the most common methods for obtaining economic returns from family forest ownership. Timber is one of the few commodities family forest owners can sell periodically in order to pay property taxes and upkeep and to obtain some returns on their investments. Growing timber is a long-term proposition that is subject to great risks from damaging elements such as ice storms, hurricanes, insects, disease, drought, and fire. In addition, the "stumpage value"—which is the value of timber standing in the forest—can be fairly low compared to the real costs of production. For example, an intensively managed, even-aged hardwood stand growing on a mod-erately good site can be expected to produce about 10,000 board feet of timber in eighty-three years.[12] The gross financial returns from this inten-sive hardwood management would be about $40 per acre per year over the course of the rotation (see table 10.3). However, due to high-grade logging and poor management practices, the gross return from forest management on an average acre in southern Vermont is closer to $15 per acre per year.[13] When debt service and stewardship costs are factored in, this represents a loss of over $15 per acre per year from the sale of stump-age!

Family forest owners are frequently at a competitive disadvantage in the marketplace. Timber harvesting on small family forests often involves limited volumes and a wide mixture of species, sizes, and quality. Long periods can elapse between harvests, and family forest owners are often out of touch with the best market opportunities and operators. Timber harvested from carefully tended family forests must also compete in the marketplace with timber from unsustainable operations. In unsustainable forestry operations, many costs—such as those associated with water pol-lution, stream sedimentation, site degradation, and habitat destruction—are externalized, that is, the operator does not incur them.

Still other factors put many carefully managed family forests at a severe

Table 10.3

Stumpage Values on an Intensively Managed Northern Hardwood
Stand

Log quality (% of volume)	White ash (3%)	Sugar maple (36%)	Yellow birch (34%)	Paper birch (11%)	Other (16%)
Veneer (10%)	29 BF[a] ($.25/BF) $7	362 BF ($.69/BF) $249	337 BF ($.38/BF) $129	116 BF ($.20/BF) $23	162 BF ($.20/BF) $32
High (55%)	157 BF ($.25/BF) $39	1,992 BF ($.69/BF) $1374	1,855 BF ($.38/BF) $714	637 BF ($.20/BF) $127	889 BF ($.20/BF) $177
Medium (20%)	58 BF ($.15/BF) $8	724 BF ($.27/BF) $199	674 BF ($.15/BF) $101	232 BF ($.10/BF) $23	323 BF ($.10/BF) $32
Low (15%)	42 BF ($.10/BF) $4	544 BF ($.10/BF) $54	506 BF ($.08/BF) $40	174 BF ($.04/BF) $6	242 BF ($.04/BF) $9
TOTAL	286 BF $58	3,622 BF $1876	3,372 BF $984	1,159 BF $179	1,616 BF $250

Total volume = 10,005 BF = 120 BF/acre/year

Total gross value = $3347 = $40.00/acre/year

Table presents a very rough calculation of stumpage on a very good day in Vermont (Site Index 60, 83-Year Rotation Age). Stumpage values are based on stumpage prices for 1 January 1998 through 31 March 1998, and assume that medium and low stumpage prices correspond to medium and low timber quality.

[a]BF = board feet.

economic disadvantage in the timber marketplace. In a typical "mill scale" sale, landowners—and the loggers who work for them—must rely on the purchasing sawmill to scale and grade their timber. Although scaling and grading systems are supposed to be objective, they fluctuate widely depending upon market conditions, the seller, the log scaler and grader, the trucker, and a host of other variables. To further confuse matters, no two sawmills in Vermont use the same combination of grading and scaling methods.

Many family forest owners depend upon their private consulting foresters to help them with their forest management and commercial timber harvesting operations. The services of consulting foresters appear to have led to a substantial improvement in the quality of the forest management and landowner power in the marketplace. However, family forest stewards continue to face severe economic constraints.

In summary, many family forest owners in Vermont are very interested in managing their forests sustainably. Timber harvesting is acceptable to most of them to some degree and at some point as long as the nontimber functions and values of their forests are protected through careful woodland stewardship. To enable family forest owners—and the loggers and foresters who work for them—to become better forest stewards, educational efforts must be broadened to include the full range of forest stewardship functions from high quality timber production to successful marketing. In addition, options for more favorable economic returns to cover the increased costs associated with careful woodland stewardship must be identified and made readily available.

The "Birth" of Vermont Family Forests

In 1995, the Addison County Forester of the Vermont Department of Forests, Parks, and Recreation—me—and the Lewis Creek Association teamed up to sponsor a series of workshops on sustainable forestry for family forest owners. These workshops covered a wide range of forest-related subjects, from amphibians to riparian zones and from portable sawmills to wood identification. The teaming of the Lewis Creek Association and the county forester was a mutually beneficial arrangement. The role of the county forester is to provide family forest owners with technical information on careful woodland stewardship. The Lewis Creek Association—a nonprofit organization with several hundred members—is dedicated to sustaining healthy communities within the 53,000-acre, mainly forested watershed of the Lewis Creek.

The intent of the workshops was to provide landowners with the information they needed to make sound decisions when managing their forests. It was hoped that they would then be empowered to identify and achieve their ownership objectives while practicing ecologically sustainable forestry. Ecologically sustainable forestry is a type of forest management that seeks first to understand and maintain the health of forest ecosystems as indicated by the functions and values of aquatic communities and water resources, site productivity, and the biological integrity of those systems. In ecologically sustainable forestry, sustained commodity extraction is of secondary importance to sustaining forest ecosystem health.

In 1996, two other nonprofit conservation organizations—the Otter Creek Audubon Society and the Watershed Center—joined in the sponsorship of the sustainable forestry workshops. The educational effort became known as "Vermont Family Forests" (VFF) and adopted as its mission: "to cultivate local family forests for economic and social benefits while protecting the ecological integrity of the forest community as a whole." VFF developed the following set of principles to guide the educational effort:

- All members of the forest community have inherent value.
- As members of the forest community, people have legitimate needs for the economic, ecological, and social values of forests.
- The needs of people—like those of all other earthly beings—must not exceed ecological carrying capacities.
- Recycling, substitution, and durable uses of forest products should be promoted.
- Working landscapes should include interconnected forest reserves and sustainably managed forests.
- Sustainable forestry should conserve biodiversity, water quality, and site productivity; use biological pest control; and mimic natural processes.
- Economically-secure, well-informed family forest stewards—including landowners and the loggers and foresters who assist them—are most capable of practicing sustainable forestry.
- Local forest products—from sustainable forestry operations—should be promoted over non-native products.
- Public forests should complement family forests.
- Local value-adding networks—including empowered family forest stewards, wood-using business, and loyal forest product customers— are essential to the well-being of the forest community.

VFF also published a "Voluntary Timber Management Checklist" for family forest owners to consider when practicing forestry on their lands.

Timber management in the family forest should follow these practices:

- The single-tree and small-group (up to 1 acre) selection methods should be used for shade-tolerant species and the irregular shelterwood method should be used for shade-intolerant species. Clear-cutting should be avoided.
- Retain a minimum of six cavity and/or snag trees per acre with one exceeding 18 inches diameter at breast height (DBH) and three exceeding 16 inches DBH.
- Retain a minimum of two large down trees per acre.
- Grow the largest trees and use the longest rotations possible within site- and log-quality limitations. (Example: For high-quality red and

sugar maple, yellow birch, beech, and white ash, the DBH objective should be 18 inches or greater. Culmination of mean annual board foot growth for these species occurs at 100 to 120 years.)

- Any forest management in natural communities that are ranked as "very rare" (S1) and "rare" (S2) or in natural communities ranked as "uncommon" (S3), "common" (S4), and "very common" (S5) but with little or no evidence of past human disturbance should be reviewed by the Vermont Fish and Wildlife Natural Heritage Biologists.
- When planting, use only local sources of native species, plant three or more species, and include deciduous species.
- When thinning or regenerating stands, favor native species over non-native species.
- Use natural regeneration to the maximum practical extent.
- Biological legacies of the forest community—including coarse dead wood, logs, and snags; trees that are large, living, and old; buried seeds; soil organic matter; invertebrates; sprouting plants; and mycorrhizal fungi—should be retained to aid in post-harvest recovery and to keep the forest from becoming "oversimplified."
- Promote the seed-bearing capacities of poorly represented members of the stand.
- Tree felling should be avoided on slopes exceeding 60 percent.
- Leave on the site all materials that are less than 5 inches in diameter.
- Promote a vertical stand structure that includes overstory, midstory, shrub, and herbaceous vegetation layers.
- The use of pesticides—including insecticides, fungicides, and herbicides—should be extremely limited, and only those pesticides accepted by the Northeast Organic Farming Association should be used.
- Residual stand damage—including basal wounds, broken and/or scraped tops, and exposed roots—should be confined to 10 percent or fewer of the dominant or co-dominant trees.
- All trees to be removed should be marked prior to the inception of harvest.
- Average annual harvest volumes should not exceed 70 percent of the average annual growth.
- Avoid grazing by domestic animals.

Skid trails, truck roads, and log landings for accessing the family forest should be designed according to these guidelines:

- Avoid spring harvests and/or rutting that extends beyond the A soil horizon.

- All skid trails, truck roads, and log landings should be flagged or otherwise marked prior to the inception of harvesting.
- Use equipment that is as small as possible and that exerts the lowest possible ground pressure.
- The timber harvesting access network—including truck roads, skid trails, and log landings—should be carefully designed and constructed and should not expose mineral soil on more than 10 percent of the treated area.
- Truck roads should be built at grades from 3 percent to 10 percent and skid trails should be built at grades from 3 percent to 15 percent.
- Skid trails, truck roads, and log landings located on easily compacted soils should only be used when adequately dry or frozen.
- Minimize the number and extent of truck roads and skid trails, particularly in or near sensitive areas such as stream crossings, protective strips, and steep slopes.
- Truck roads and skid trails should be properly drained during and after use according to Table 1 in the Vermont AMPs.
- Log landings should be located on nearly-level, stable ground, be kept away from protective strips, have water diversions installed, and be graded to prevent erosion and sedimentation.
  Protective strips and buffer strips should be maintained as follows:
- Protective strips—characterized by minimal soil disturbance, nearly complete canopy closure, and many large, mature trees—should be maintained between the access network and surface waters according to Table 4 in the Vermont AMPs.
- Areas of exposed soil that occur within the protective strip should be seeded and mulched according to Table 3 in the AMPs.
- Stream buffer strips should be kept free of logging vehicles, have only little or no tree cutting, and be at least 25 feet in width.
  Stream crossings, particularly fragile areas, need special attention:
- Stream crossings should be restored and nonpermanent structures should be removed as soon as possible.
- Streams should be crossed with bridges or culverts that are properly sized according to Table 2 in the Vermont AMPs and installed at right angles.
- Sediment should be prevented from reaching streams by using turn-ups or broad-based dips on truck roads and skid trails prior to all stream crossings.
- Drainage ditches should not feed directly into streams or other surface waters.

Closeout requires the following:

- Postharvest use of the access network should be restricted in order to prevent erosion, compaction, and site disruption.

In the event that a family forest includes sensitive and Special Habitat Areas, VFF recommends:

- Harvesting and road building in areas with wetlands, raptor nests, upturned tree roots, seeps, vernal pools, hard/soft mast species, and other unique or fragile natural or cultural sites require additional and specific precautions.
- Construction of new roads or expansion of the width of existing roads by more than 20 percent in wetlands will require a permit or review by the Wetlands Office of the Water Quality Division.

Later in 1996, I asked an informal group of local advisors to help guide the development of the VFF project. In addition, the VFF target area was expanded to include the New Haven River, Little Otter Creek, and Lewis Creek watersheds, totaling 170,000 acres (see map 10.1).

By the end of 1997, VFF had held many hands-on, educational workshops, which had all been well received and attended. Workshop attendees indicated that their understanding of sustainable forestry practices had improved. However, many family forest owners expressed concerns over the lack of financial incentives to help them accomplish the careful woodland stewardship outlined in the workshops. It became very apparent that a special focus was required to address the economic constraints facing family forest owners.

Vermont Family Forests "Green" Certification Project

In 1997, Vermont Family Forests launched its "Green" Certification Project to address the economic constraints of family forest owners interested in practicing sustainable forestry. The Vermont Sustainable Jobs Fund provided financial assistance for the project. The objectives of the three-phase project were:

- to promote the use of sustainable forestry practices on family forests;
- to improve the financial returns of family forests;
- to increase the availability of sustainably produced, locally grown forest products to local wood-product manufacturers; and
- to develop an affordable model for independent "green" certification.

Sustainable forestry is by definition ecologically viable, economically feasible, and socially equitable. To be ecologically viable, the forestry must

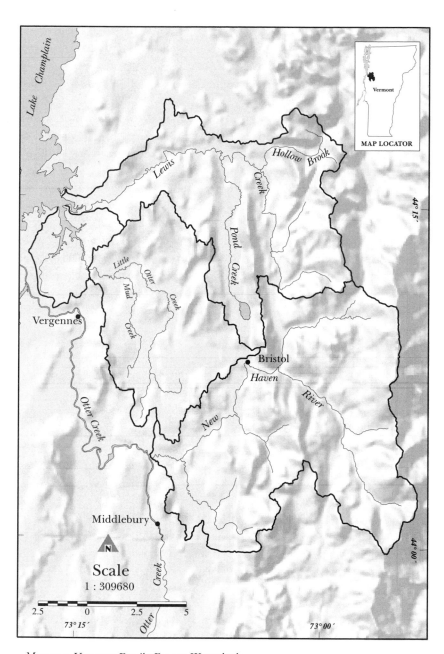

Map 10.1. Vermont Family Forests Watersheds.

protect water quality, site productivity, and biological diversity and integrity on a landscape basis. To be economically feasible, sustainable forestry must fully account for costs while providing favorable financial returns. To be socially equitable, all participants in the value-adding process must be treated fairly.

As described above and in some detail, family forest stewards have not been well situated in the marketplace to participate from a position of power. The stumpage paid to landowners in Vermont represents only 3 to 4 percent of the ultimate economic contribution of the raw materials to the state's economy and it is often exceedingly difficult to obtain favorable economic returns from the sale of standing timber.

Green certification is a nonregulatory, voluntary method that recognizes, rewards, and encourages sustainable forestry practices. It provides a mechanism for wood-product customers to differentiate between forest products that come from woodlands managed with sustainable forestry practices. It allows purchasers of wood products to differentiate in much the same way that the organic label allows differentiation of agricultural products. In some cases green-certified wood can attract a premium price as well as expanded marketing opportunities. Green certification may also serve two other important functions. It could provide the "glue" to hold forest landowners together for marketing benefits and educational opportunities. It could also serve to regulate the flow of forest products at sustainable levels in the event that substantially improved marketing opportunities should be developed. To date, green certification has not been widely available to small family forest owners.

Another emerging opportunity for family forest owners is the marketing of forest products more directly to users such as local, secondary wood-product manufacturers. Although many family forest owners suffer from low financial returns from their managed forestlands, local secondary wood-product manufacturers must pay very high prices for their raw materials. It would appear that by marketing wood more directly, a mutually beneficial arrangement could exist between wood producers and users. This arrangement could give local wood-using enterprises better control over product quality, diversity, and supply while providing family forest owners with closer-to-retail markets for their wood products. Secondary wood-product manufacturers in Vermont have started looking for ways to access locally grown, sustainably harvested wood products. Furniture-maker Beeken-Parsons of Shelburne, for example, has installed a kiln and has begun to purchase logs—of mixed quality and species—directly from family forest owners.

Table 10.4

Vermont Maple Sugaring Economics

Rent taps	Sell sap	Sell syrup
60 taps × $.50/tap	60 taps × 10 gallons sap × $.35/gallon sap	60 taps × .25 gallons syrup × $30/gallon syrup
Yields		
$30/acre/year minus costs	$210/acre/year minus costs	$450/acre/year minus costs

A "typical" Vermont sugarbush has about 60 taps per acre. Each tap will typically produce 10 gallons of sap that will boil down to 1 quart of syrup on a typical year.

The active participation of woodland stewards in the value-adding processes is not without precedent in Vermont. One need not look any further than the maple sugaring industry. Although some sugarbush owners opt to rent their trees for $.50 per tap and $30 per acre per year, others remain involved through at least a portion of the value-adding process (see table 10.4). Some sugarbush owners elect to sell their sap with gross returns of roughly $210 per acre per year. Other sugarbush operators produce syrup, cultivate a reputation for high quality, and sell as close to retail as possible with gross returns of $450 per acre per year. When sap production is aided by vacuum collection systems and when more advanced marketing techniques are employed, gross returns of over $2,000 per acre per year are theoretically possible.

By combining green certification and improved local markets for sustainably harvested wood, significant ecological, economic, and social benefits may be achieved for family forest owners, secondary wood-product manufacturers, and the community as a whole. Vermont Family Forests is one attempt to encourage woodland stewards to practice sustainable forestry by helping them switch from the rental of low-value "taps" (i.e., low-value standing trees) to the sale of high-value "syrup" (i.e., value-added forest products)!

VFF "Green" Certification Project: Phase One

VFF conducted phase one of the "Green" Certification Project to develop an affordable model for independent green certification of family forests and to identify local markets and value-adding opportunities with secondary wood-product manufacturers located in the vicinity of the New Haven River, Lewis Creek, and Little Otter Creek watersheds. VFF asked owners of forty family forests if they were interested in participating in the VFF "Green" Certification Project. All candidates had a history of careful forest management. Recognizing that the VFF standards were not for everyone, all candidates were asked to review the VFF "Mission and Principles" and "A Voluntary Timber Management Checklist" to see that they meshed well with their ownership objectives. Thirty-one (77 percent) of the candidates agreed to participate in the project. About 4,718 acres of forestland were enrolled, with individual parcels ranging from 32 to 1,783 acres.

The SmartWood Program of Richmond, Vermont, conducted an independent assessment of these thirty-one parcels. The purpose of the assessment, as described in the "SmartWood Resource Manager Certification Assessment Report," was "to evaluate the ecological, economic, and social sustainability of Vermont Family Forests (VFF) forest management." Pre-assessment planning began in June 1997, and the field assessment was conducted in November 1997. The assessment team consisted of Alan Calfee, forestry specialist; Ross Morgan, consulting forester; and Charles Cogbill, forest ecologist. The team used a stratified sampling methodology to compare VFF forest management practices with criteria contained in the "Northeast SmartWood Guidelines for Assessing Natural Forest Management."[14]

The results of the SmartWood Assessment are detailed in a report entitled "SmartWood Resource Manager Certification Assessment Report," portions of which are available upon request from Vermont Family Forests. According to the report, "based on the findings and conditions described in this report the assessment team recommends that SmartWood approve the certification of Vermont Family Forests." This certification was finalized in July 1998. The conditions of the certification included an annual audit, expanded use of the VFF management plan template, development of a standardized monitoring program and field inventory, preparation of timber sale harvesting plans, and the establishment of a VFF constitution.

Although all of the thirty-one VFF parcels have been well managed in recent years, many of them still suffer the effects of decades of high-grade logging, which has removed the best-quality logs and left behind the low-quality material. Practices such as these have led to a depleted forest inventory made up of low-grade logs and less-desirable species. Log grade is based on a number of characteristics that influence the ultimate yield and value of lumber derived from them. These characteristics include log diameter, the number of clear faces, and the extent of sweep and crook. Based upon the periodic forest inventory conducted by the U.S. Forest Service, it is estimated that about 64 percent of the VFF hardwood lumber inventory is comprised of #2 common quality or lower (see table 10.5). The profit margins generated from the sale of low-quality lumber such as these have historically been very low.

VFF began assessing the opportunities for family forest participation in local value-adding by sending survey forms to fifty secondary wood-product manufacturers located in Addison County and southern Chittenden County, Vermont. VFF also contacted a canoe manufacturer located in western Washington County and a furniture manufacturer in New York state. Thirty-eight completed surveys were returned. Over half of the businesses responding to the survey were located in Addison County and all were located within fifty miles of Bristol, Vermont, the approximate center of the three-watershed target area of Vermont Family Forests. VFF created a directory listing company name, address, phone number, contact person, products sold, processing equipment, wood materials purchased, species used, and work force.

VFF summarized information about the businesses and analyzed the potential for improving local networks between and among family forests and local secondary wood-product manufacturers. The firms sell a wide range of wood products. The most commonly reported wood products were custom furniture (43 percent), custom cabinets (40 percent), architectural millwork (38 percent), doors (30 percent), moldings (27 percent), and millwork (24 percent). The businesses reported having a wide range of wood processing tools and equipment. Many operations have planers (70 percent), shapers (60 percent), and lathes (43 percent). Four firms own their own sawmills for processing raw logs. In general, the capacity to add value to locally produced wood is well developed in the target area.

The one element of existing infrastructure that had limited capacity or access for family forest owners was wood-drying kilns. Only two firms (5 percent) in the survey had their own wood kilns, and many reported inadequate access to local wood kiln-drying facilities or services. Significant kiln capacity exists and is available, for example, in St. Johnsbury at the Caledonia Kiln Corporation. This generally requires quantities of 8 thousand board feet (MBF) or more. It also requires trucking costs of

Table 10.5

Estimated Hardwood Lumber Grades in the Vermont Family Forests'
Certified Pool

Grade	Minimum size of clear cuttings	Proportion of length in clear	% of total annual production
FAS	4 in. × 5 ft.	10/12	12
#1 Common	4 in. × 2 ft.	8/12	24
#2 Common or less	3 in. × 2 ft.	6/12	64

about $130 to $170 per MBF and all of the associated costs of burning
fossil fuels to get the wood to and from the kiln. It would appear that
development of high-quality, energy-efficient kiln facilities would greatly
enhance local value-adding opportunities.

The local secondary wood-product manufacturers purchase a wide
range of wood products, including plywood (57 percent), rough and kiln-
dry lumber (54 percent), dressed and kiln-dry lumber (51 percent), and
rough air-dry lumber (46 percent). Only 22 percent of the respondents
purchase rough and green lumber and less than 14 percent purchase sawlogs. In summary, the largest market appears to be rough sawn, kiln-dried,
and graded lumber.

Local manufacturers use many species of locally grown wood. The
most commonly used species are black cherry (59 percent), sugar maple
(59 percent), white pine (57 percent), white ash (57 percent), red oak (54
percent), white oak (51 percent), yellow birch (48 percent), red maple (43
percent), and butternut (40 percent). It is unknown to what degree species selection is a function of wood properties, consumer demand, cost,
or local availability.

Retail outlets (57 percent) and Vermont sawmills (51 percent) were the
most commonly cited sources of wood for the local secondary wood-
product manufacturers. A few firms reported purchasing their wood directly from landowners (16 percent) and loggers (11 percent). Just under
two-thirds of the firms reported that they were satisfied with their suppliers. The remainder said they were either not satisfied or only partially
satisfied with their suppliers. The most commonly cited reasons for dissatisfaction were high prices (25 percent), lack of "unique wood" (22 percent), lack of selection (19 percent), and low wood quality (16 percent).
A few firms cited dissatisfaction with drying and conditioning (9 percent)
and grading (6 percent). Several firms suggested a need for more green

certified wood, reduced lead time for special orders, and wood that was grown less rapidly. It would appear that local family forests could be in an ideal situation to provide wood products that meet some or all of these very specific, local needs.

About half of the firms sell all of their products on a custom basis. Of the firms that reported selling on a custom basis, 73 percent sell all of their products that way. This indicates a close relationship between the customer and the producer. Only 7 percent of the firms export their wares out of the country. About 57 percent of the firms sell their products retail.

Over three-quarters of the firms said that they were interested in purchasing more wood from Vermont forests. The most commonly cited reasons for this were improvement of the local economy (57 percent), lower prices (40 percent), improved species selection (36 percent), better wood quality (36 percent), improved access to unique wood (36 percent), and access to a stable supply (21 percent). Respondents also mentioned better drying (18 percent) and better grading (9 percent).

At the completion of phase one, VFF successfully demonstrated an affordable model for independent certification of family forests. The per acre cost for each of the thirty-one parcels that participated in the pilot project was less than $1.50 per acre. Additional acreage can be added annually, further reducing this per-acre cost. VFF estimates that the annual audit will cost about $700 or $.15 per acre per year. The VFF "Green" Certification Project should serve as an excellent model for other organizations that are interested in independent certification. In addition, secondary wood-product manufacturers expressed a strong interest in using sustainably produced Vermont forest products in their operations. It was clear that much of the necessary value-adding infrastructure is in place and readily available to organized family forest owners, with the notable exception of energy-efficient wood-drying kilns.

Middlebury College's Bicentennial Hall: A Partial and Preliminary Test

In 1998, VFF became aware that Middlebury College—located about twelve miles from Bristol—was constructing facilities that would require the use of approximately 125,000 board feet of hardwood sawlogs. Middlebury College was committed to obtaining these materials from certified sources and was also interested in obtaining local materials if at all possible.

Middlebury College entered into an agreement with Richard Miller of Natural Forest Products in Burlington, Vermont, to supply the lumber for the project. Miller in turn asked Vermont Family Forests to supply some or all of these materials. Four parcels that were part of VFF's certified pool eventually provided about 70,000 board feet of logs from nine species of hardwoods. Coincidentally, many of the VFF logs came from trees that were heavily damaged by the January 1998 ice storm. All harvesting complied with approved forest management plans and practices and all trees to be removed were marked prior to harvest.

The final payment price was determined at the landing based on the actual volume and grade of the logs as measured on the landing. This gave the landowners and the loggers a decided advantage over conventional practices of scaling and grading. The purchaser and sellers agreed upon an explicit log specification sheet and price list and this was made part of the contract. This ensured that the landowner and purchaser obtained the proper values, volumes, and quality of logs sold or purchased. Full payment for all logs was made when the logs had been graded on the landing. The landowners received substantially higher prices (50 to 100 percent more) for their sawlogs. The loggers were paid about 60 percent more than normal.

In addition to substantially higher payments to the landowners and loggers, additional economic benefits resulted from local value-adding. The project helped keep money in Vermont by involving over thirty Vermont firms. As part of the agreement with Middlebury College, only sawmilling that could not be completed in Vermont due to time, price, or equipment limitations could be processed outside of the state. Much of the material was dried in Vermont. Middlebury College obtained its materials for the project at about 5 percent above average market prices. This was the result of direct marketing from stump to end user. The cost savings of this "network approach" were passed back to each of the participants in the process: family forest owner, forester, logger, trucker, mill operator, and dry-kiln operator.

Finally, and perhaps most importantly, were the ecological and social benefits of careful woodland stewardship made possible by paying landowners and logging operators more. Ecological and social benefits from forestry that meets certification standards are very difficult to calculate. However, the benefits resulting from the careful woodland stewardship included the conservation of water quality, site productivity, and biological integrity.

VFF "Green" Certification Project: Phase Two

In 1999, VFF initiated a business planning process to transform VFF into a viable forest conservation organization capable of changing the centuries-old practice of "forest mining" into a new model of "forest cultivation." One of the first steps was to establish Vermont Family Forests as a nonprofit corporation. The planning process also clarified the purposes of VFF. These are:

- to educate landowners, foresters, loggers, and the public at large about the values of practicing ecologically sound, community-based forestry on family forests within the larger Vermont landscape;
- to encourage the development and use of sustainable forest management practices that are economically feasible and socially responsible and that conserve the ecological capacity of family forests for self-renewal;
- to promote family forest stewardship by providing affordable access to green certification and by increasing the acreage of certified family forests;
- to demonstrate the benefits of properly scaled, resource-efficient, and local value-adding equipment, facilities, and services—such as "eco-logging," log aggregation and sorting, saw milling, and resource-efficient wood-drying kilns—in promoting healthy family forests and strong local economies and communities; and
- to educate family forest owners about the full range of forest product sales and marketing strategies and opportunities.

VFF now provides education, information, and affordable access to certification. VFF is also in the process of aggregating the timber inventory from a certified family forest land base that includes nearly 5,000 forested acres. Efforts are underway to expand this certified pool to 20,000 acres or more. Once an aggregated and secure inventory of certified wood is available, commercial firms can be engaged that are capable of adding substantial value to this resource *and* returning more of that value to the family forests.

A board of directors currently operates VFF, with substantial assistance from the Addison County Forester. Efforts are underway to hire a full-time executive director who will report to the VFF board of directors and be responsible for the day-to-day activities of the foundation. In the short term, VFF's revenues will continue to be generated through grants as well as in-kind contributions, workshop fees, and the sale of publications.

Looking to the Future

It is anticipated that the Vermont Family Forests will soon become a self-sustaining organization capable of providing family forest owners with improved access to education, sustainable forestry, green certification, local value-adding, and markets. Future activities will likely include workshops; a VFF newsletter; a familyforests.com Web site; forest demonstration areas; access to a central geographic information system (GIS) data base; a continuous forest inventory system; a "chain of custody" tracking system for certified forest products; a demonstration area for portable sawmills, solar wood-drying kilns, and other resource-efficient steps in the value-adding process; and development of log aggregation and sorting capacity.

VFF examined the potential of activating a professionally managed subsidiary with the resources and freedom needed to compete in the marketplace. This commercial entity will earn profits for the Vermont Family Forests Foundation through management and licensing of the Family Forests brand. VFF has determined that the best strategy for the long-term sustainability of VFF's commercial entity will be to invest in the market rather than in the infrastructure. At some time, it may make sense for the VFF commercial entity to have more control over the infrastructure, but in the immediate future, with excess capacity already in place, it appears to make more sense to build a market for VFF's products rather than to build a plant to produce them. The hardwood flooring market is rapidly expanding and holds great potential for products with the Family Forest brand.

The key operating objective will be to organize a flexible, competent chain of custody and the systems to coordinate and manage those elements on lands in VFF's certified pool. At start-up volumes, the only missing link in the chain is the capacity to kiln-dry and condition the lumber. The VFF commercial entity will have to invest in resource-efficient wood-drying kilns and storage facilities during start-up and build incrementally to match volume growth. During the start-up phase, the goal will be to build the network within the original three-watershed area. As the brand grows, and the land under management grows, the network can be expanded geographically to meet those needs. VFF will encourage and support the formation of additional entities that can contribute finished goods to VFF's Family Forest brand program.

Conclusion

Vermont Family Forests has an ambitious mission. It is a mission that requires fundamental change in the ways people view forests and forestry. It is a mission that requires major changes in the current marketplace. VFF believes that these changes are possible, for several compelling reasons. Most family forest owners love their forests and are thirsty for the information that will allow them to do right by them. Many of these same family forest owners are not satisfied with their lack of power in the current marketplace and are looking for something better. As timber supplies become more and more limited, family forest stewards who work collaboratively with other like-minded stewards should be in an excellent position to change the marketplace. By providing high-quality educational opportunities to forest stewards and by helping to empower those same forest stewards in the marketplace, Vermont Family Forests hopes to win the battle against "the two great ruiners" of family forests.

CHAPTER 11

A Conversation at the Edge of Wilderness

JOHN ELDER

🐜 OUR SIX WILDERNESS areas within the Green Mountain National Forest range from fewer than 4,000 acres in Bristol Cliffs to almost 22,000 at Bread Loaf. Gates of the Arctic they're not. Stone walls break through the ferns and jewelweed of these slopes, broken choker cables lie half-buried beside trails that were logging roads not so long ago, and cellar holes collect and compost leaves in the thick woods far from any trail. These tracts of third-growth forest were not included under the original 1964 Wilderness Act, being neither "primeval" nor "untrammeled." Only after passage of the 1975 Eastern Wilderness Act, which Vermont's George Aiken helped move through the Senate, were the lands protected because of their beauty and their biological significance. They were allowed, in effect, as afterthoughts — honorary wildernesses.

Such Vermont woodlands may have seemed marginal when they were added to the National Wilderness Preservation System in 1975 and in 1984. I believe, however, that they and the other wilderness areas of the Northeast are now emerging as central to our national conversation about nature and culture. I don't mean this in a spirit of regional competitiveness. The great wildernesses of the West and Alaska are incomparably magnificent. I will always be grateful for the protection those holy sites have received and for the opportunity to travel to them on pilgrimage. But we do seem to have arrived at a moment in our nation's ongoing dialogue about how human society will accommodate wildness when a place like Vermont might have a helpful word to say. Our modest wilderness areas here offer an ecological edge, or ecotone, between both landscapes and perspectives that might earlier have seemed to be distinct, or even opposed. Wildernesses like those in Vermont are, to put it another way, centrally marginal. They define a boundary zone where the wilderness ethic may engage with recent developments in the field of environmental history, and where the ideal of preservation transcending a narrow utilitarianism may engage with the tradition of stewardship. We need to move beyond polemic in our discussion of these important matters. Vermont's wilderness offers one promising landscape within which to reframe the conversation.[1]

Like much of northern New England, as well as the Adirondack region of New York, Vermont is a landscape in recovery. The first half of the nineteenth century saw deforestation in our region that was as rapid and relentless as anywhere in America. Trees were cleared not only to open fields for crops but also to raise cash for the farmers and other early entrepreneurs of the region. Throughout the Green Mountains, logs were stacked up to form enormous, pyramidal kilns that smouldered day and night, producing charcoal and potash for the forges, mills, and factories along the nearby rivers. Between the deforestation and the scantiness of our heavily glaciated topsoil, Vermont went from being the fastest-growing state in the Union after the Revolution to being the slowest-growing one for most of the time between the Civil War and World War II. Since the middle of the last century, however, this wet land so good at growing trees has also gone from being 60 to 70 percent deforested to being almost 80 percent reforested. Bill McKibben has described our region's natural resurgence as "an explosion of green."

The irony of eastern wilderness is that, while it may have seemed to receive that title as a courtesy, the vector of wildness may actually be more remarkable here than anywhere in the West. Not just the trees but also the animals have returned to a dramatic extent. When Zadock Thompson wrote his *Natural History of Vermont* in 1854, he described an ecological wasteland in which most of the larger wild mammals, including deer and beavers, were effectively extinct. Today, not only do we have those two particular species in bewildering abundance, but we also have rapidly increasing populations of moose and substantial numbers of such animals as bobcats, fishers, and black bears. Sightings of catamounts too are reported with increasing frequency. And current proposals to reintroduce wolves into the Adirondacks and Maine hold out the possibility that we may some day see those predators in at least the northern portions of Vermont, as well.

"Recovering wilderness" would perhaps have seemed an oxymoron just a few years ago. But that concept reflects an intriguing convergence between the environmental history of Vermont and the current emphasis upon "rewilding" within the Wildlands Project. Corridors, or "connectivity," between relatively undisturbed areas of wild habitat are one main emphasis of the project. The striking resurgence of wildlife in Vermont, even in the absence of large "core reserves," suggests that special possibilities for connectivity already exist within our state's distinctive natural and human situation. I don't just mean corridors connecting and extending protected habitat. I am also referring here to the connections between human culture and the wild, as well as to the potential for a more diverse and ecologically inclusive approach to conservation thought in America.

A good place to reflect on the promising ironies of eastern wilderness is in the meadow across from the Bread Loaf Inn, in Ripton. State Highway 125 crosses the Green Mountains here, and the beautiful old buildings where the Bread Loaf School of English and Writers' Conference are held each summer run along the highway for a couple of hundred yards. But this spot is also in the middle of the northern block of the Green Mountain National Forest. The Bread Loaf Wilderness begins right at the edge of the campus, not too far behind the Inn. To the south, in the towns of Hancock, Goshen, and Rochester, lies a part of the National Forest that is in many ways equally wild. A group of Vermont conservationists has recently begun discussing ways to expand the system of protected wilderness in our state; any future proposal might well include wild lands in the stretch of the forest just below Bread Loaf. On the level of corridors and rewilding, such designation would certainly make sense. This area already fosters robust populations of moose and bear. Credible reports have been made of catamounts near the Bread Loaf building known as the Printer's Cabin—less than one hundred paces west of this meadow. Those big cats were tracking along in a band of rugged, heavily forested land—one that reaches down this ridge to connect the southern part of our state with the much less interrupted habitat of northeastern Vermont and Canada.

Discussions of rewilding in *Wild Earth* describe the need for certain forms of human agency, including careful scientific analyses and vigorous policies to protect or establish wildlife corridors. This is an exciting prospect. It's also worth noting, though, that another kind of rewilding has already been accomplished in Vermont, more or less while people weren't looking. By the time the National Forest was established in 1932, the hill-farms, sheep pastures, and forges had long since been abandoned. The forests had returned without sponsorship. Ours is a providential wilderness and, accordingly, a messy one. The forested heights define a wild corridor running north and south between the towns planted along Route 7 and those following Route 100. But the east-west traffic on Route 125, with its Victorian resort turned writers' conference, also establishes a human presence in the midst of wilderness. Such a convergence makes this a good place to ponder the ways in which nature and culture have each other surrounded.

Wilderness in Vermont is a fruitful confusion, inseparable from the history of human enterprise and excess, failure and insight, associated with this place. Such a landscape of reversals may help us move beyond the current polarization between advocates of wilderness and their critics among environmental historians. When I follow the sometimes contentious exchanges between representatives of these groups, I am often struck, in fact, by how important the insights are on both sides. On the one hand, I identify strongly with the wilderness movement's testimony about the inherent value, and the sanctity, of wild places. One of the greatest contributions of environmentalism in the tradition of Muir has been its resolute challenge to narrow economic assumptions about the uses and value of land. At the same time, it is important to acknowledge that the wilderness movement itself is a historical phenomenon, inextricable from the social history, religious values, and economic situation of its proponents. Such a recognition does not mean defeat or repudiation of the wilderness ideal. It's simply a reminder that the transcendent values people espouse are always informed by and complicated by their immediate human contexts. I am convinced that the best way to consolidate and extend the wilderness ethic today—and to protect wild habitat—will be to integrate it with a more inclusive social perspective and a more ironic self-awareness.

William Cronon's essay "The Trouble with Wilderness" has caused particular consternation among activists, with its description of "a dualism at the heart of wilderness." I believe there is truth in this assertion, if not the whole truth. From John Muir to the present, there has been a religious dimension to the wilderness movement. Not surprisingly, sectarian language has sometimes been the result. One example would be Bill Devall and George Sessions's influential 1985 book *Deep Ecology*, which provided a valuable service in pulling together many of the sources informing spiritual and ethical aspects of the wilderness movement. But it sometimes slid into an approach of separating the sheep from the goats—to the extent of downgrading a constructive environmental thinker like Rene Dubos for his "narrow Christian stewardship" or declaring that a writer of Wendell Berry's stature "falls short of deep ecological awareness." The point I want to make, though, is that our thinking about wilderness continues to evolve. This holds true for subsequent writing by wilderness thinkers, including Sessions and Devall, and is even more dramatically evident in the ambitious innovations of the Wildlands Project. My main reservation about Cronon's essay is finally that it wields too broad a brush, painting the wilderness movement as both more monolithic and more static than it really is. Still, his analysis remains a useful spur forward.[2]

The part of Cronon's essay that I find most useful is his discussion of "wildness." He points out that Thoreau preferred this word, with its more qualitative connotations. Muir, by contrast, emphasized the expansiveness of "God's wilderness." From my Vermont vantage point, I find both words useful—"wildness" for evoking the exhilarating recovery of our cutover landscape, and "wilderness" for defining the new protectiveness and ambitiousness with which we are beginning to regard our forests. There need be no war between these alternative terms, any more than celebration of Vermont's third-growth implies a lessening of support for Oregon's old growth. Whatever the differences in their language, the fact remains that Muir claimed Thoreau as one of his chief inspirations, propping his Concord ancestor's picture on the mantel of his Martinez ranch. The most important task is not to defend a particular vocabulary, but rather to protect the land, and the human and nonhuman communities that it supports. This distinction might emerge even more clearly from the Cronon essay if its title were slightly altered to read "The Trouble with 'Wilderness'." Though "wilderness" is an exciting and resonant word, the mysterious web of life to which it points is not captured by any language. Our plans and our vocabulary are fine as far as they go, but the world always offers vistas beyond our expression.[3]

We need not only to understand ecology as a biological dynamic, but also to enact it as a more encompassing, less hierarchical approach in our thinking about conservation and culture. The science of ecology describes a circuit of energy that includes and sustains the full range of biological diversity. As Aldo Leopold evoked in "Thinking Like a Mountain," wolves have always been much more than the "natural enemy" of deer. By controlling the size of a herd, they protect an entire mountain against overgrazing and allow it, in turn, to continue supporting healthy populations of deer and other animals. In our environmental thinking no less than in our approach to wildlife, we need to focus less on apparent antagonisms and more on a broader ecology of relationships. While never ceasing to affirm the value of wolves and wilderness, we must also pursue a respectful dialogue with those whose livelihood is on the land and with advocates of healthier cities. Many efforts of this sort are already under way.[4]

One reason to avoid defensiveness is to keep from getting stuck at an earlier stage of our own thinking. I have already referred to a shift in wilderness thought over the past decade and a half. One aspect of this, as my colleague Chris McGrory Klyza has pointed out to me, has been a move from valuing wilderness primarily in relation to human solitude to focusing on its importance for the protection of endangered species. Similarly, as the Wildlands Project moves from the conceptual phase to that of implementation, it places greater emphasis on such concepts as stewardship. An illustration of this evolution comes in a recent Sky Island Alliance document co-authored by Dave Foreman. "Stewardship Zones," both at low-use and moderate-use levels, are affirmed as supporting the health and connectivity of core reserves. Such a discussion is pertinent to "linkages" or "corridors" at the biological level. But it also reflects an enhanced sense of connectivity within the ecology of our environmental thought.[5]

It may be helpful to place the recent arguments of environmental historians within a larger context. Native American writers, for example, pose their own trenchant challenges to the wilderness ethic when they argue for the importance of human experience and stories to the character and value of sublime western landscapes. Leslie Marmon Silko has written in this connection about her own Pueblo ancestors' reliance on storytelling to sustain their bond with the landscape, not simply in a narrow utilitarian way but rather at the deepest level of personal and spiritual identification. These stories, which often have a specific topographic reference, have been passed down from the ancestors but constantly revised in light of individuals' own experience. Silko writes that her people "perceived the world and themselves within the world as part of an ancient continuous story composed of innumerable bundles of other stories." "Bundles," like "ecology," is a helpfully inclusive image for our ongoing conversation about wilderness. New perspectives add to, and sometimes help to correct, our previous insights. There's always room for one more story if it's rooted in attentiveness to the land, or for a new take on one of the beloved old tales.[6]

The wilderness of Vermont adds its own story to the bundle. It offers an antic, and an encouraging, tale in which the wilds surge across and between the roads of history. Such apparent incongruity can be disconcerting, but it can also be an opportunity to tune our ears to new harmonies. When the great New England composer Charles Ives was growing up, his father George was a town bandmaster who loved to have two bands march past each other on the town green playing different tunes. Ives' compositions, such as "The Fourth of July" and "Putnam Camp," lovingly recreate such effects. Harmonies grow thicker, discords more jagged, as the bands march closer and closer. It's hard work listening to such massive and playful novelty, just as it is trying to negotiate a vocabulary in which "wilderness" and "stewardship" can enter into nonantagonistic dialogue with one another. But it's also exciting to begin discerning new harmony where we earlier found only conflict. As the different tunes and vocabularies converge, moments also come when the familiar songs soar up with a new glisten. Then the bands march on, though with new ears, and the music and controversy fade into the quiet of this dusky corridor in the Green Mountains. Now comes evening, and the darkness of a Vermont unrestricted by the history or politics of "Vermont." Now begins the nightly conversation of a wilderness more wary and improvisatory than any lexicon.

CHAPTER 12

Some Lessons from Wilderness, East and West

JOHN DAVIS

🔆 THE PROBLEM WITH wilderness in the West is that it is too small. The problem with wilderness in the East is that it is way too small.

Wilderness—as concept and as place—has fallen on hard times lately. Physical wilderness in North America remains under attack from transnational timber and mining companies, livestock producers, motorized "recreationists," developers, and all of us who consume the products of these exploiters.

Meanwhile, at this worst of all possible times, various academics have been challenging the concept of wilderness and parks. Most of these critics (including William Cronon, Baird Callicott, Ramachandra Guha, Robert Gottlieb) undoubtedly mean well, and indeed have correctly pointed out weaknesses in the traditional conservation camp (an overemphasis on saving the remote and the spectacular remnants of pristine nature while paying too little attention to local or ordinary places, by a community of activists who by and large do not know how to enlist people from other walks of life, and at times may seem insensitive to the interests of other peoples, et cetera). These critics' net effect, though, I would argue, has been negative, for they have helped coax conservation groups away from wilderness advocacy and into the "working landscape" fold.

In my estimation, the trends among conservationists toward "working forests," "working landscapes," "consensus-based processes," "community-based conservation," and "win-win solutions," are as dangerous as anything we face from our opponents in the "wise use" camp and remarkably similar. Not that these notions are necessarily bad, but that they are displacing advocacy of true protected areas in many parts of the East and the West.

Even as conservation biologists are finding that huge portions of every landscape must be preserved if the full range of native biodiversity is to be accommodated, mainstream conservationists seem content to "conserve the working forest" in the East, where less than 5 percent of the land enjoys full protection, and to support working ranches in the West, where the vast bulk of public as well as private land is grazed and trampled by livestock. As part of a larger strategy that included vast core wilderness areas buffered by stewardship zones and connected by wildways—with the "work" done lightly and sustainably within the stewardship zones— working landscapes could serve the needs of many species, besides just *Homo sapiens* (see chapter 5). Absent strictly protected ecological reserves, however, the working landscape model almost certainly dooms the most sensitive and wide-ranging of our native species to diminution, extirpation, or even extinction. Indeed, the "working forest" basically means the status quo in the East, where we lost many of these species long ago and must restore big wilderness if we are to see them return (see chapter 6). In the West, perpetuating welfare ranching—livestock producers who run their cows or sheep on public lands, with federal or state subsidies— means ever-growing lists of endangered species, the spread of exotic species, disrupted water and fire regimes, and essentially a gradual domestication of the landscape.

I hasten to acknowledge the important—beautiful, even—kernel of truth in the working landscape concept. Drawn with great care, including prohibitions on heavy machinery, road-building, and planting of exotic species, the working landscape model could help us do just what Aldo Leopold presciently and poetically told us five decades ago we must do: become just plain members of the biotic community.

Trouble is, most purveyors of the "working landscape" ("worked over" landscape, *Wild Earth* editor Tom Butler suggests) do not appreciate the need for large areas completely protected from human manipulation and exploitation and do not recognize that so long as humans use chainsaws, skidders, bulldozers, trucks, and other motorized machines, we cannot possibly restore harmony with the natural world. Moreover, working landscapers often serve as unwitting apologists for the very industries and practices that are chiefly responsible for the biological impoverishment of North America.

Again, then, in both East and West, the problem with wilderness is that we have preserved far too little of it, and that in desperately struggling to save what few wilderness remnants we could, we conservationists have sometimes forgotten that the rest of the land needs our attention too. Every scrap of wild nature, no matter how small and beleaguered, deserves our concern and veneration. Every productive area—whether it be growing trees or crops—deserves the benefit of the highest ecological ethics and science and common sense that our species can muster.

With some common ground established, I hope, between wilderness advocates (preservationists, the biocentric subset of conservationists) and well-meaning critics, I wish to reiterate and amplify the points made by the authors in this volume. There is indeed something special about the integration of human into natural communities in New England and northern New York, though the alliance is partial, imperfect, and at constant risk of being destroyed by absentee corporate landowners and developers. New England and New York enjoy a rich history of close work with the land that has fostered a land ethic—still inchoate and rejected by the most heavily armed of local citizens—favoring protection of wild places, appreciation of nature for its own sake, and humility before the awesome elemental forces of the natural world. To their (our) credit, citizens of the northeastern United States have allowed recovery to begin across much of our forestland, have cheered the return of the moose and beaver, and now in growing numbers support future recovery of the gray wolf and eastern cougar in the northeastern forest. For reasons cultural, historical, and geographical, the boundaries between natural and human communities are softer, more porous in the East than they generally are in the West.

From my perspective, then, as a wilderness advocate who has worked in New York and Vermont in the East and Arizona and California in the West, and has worked with conservation groups throughout North America, both West and East have important lessons to teach conservationists, even though in neither half of the country are we anywhere near achieving viable preservation goals (see table 12.1). Again, the unifying message we hear from both East and West is that we need much more wilderness and better-connected wilderness, as well as much gentler, ecologically sound use of lands outside reserve systems; but the particular lessons of East and West deserve more consideration, too.

From the East, we learn:

- In conservation, anything less than complete honesty, the full ecological truth, can be dangerous. In their efforts to win more supporters and defuse opposition, many mainstream conservationists have embraced the "working forest" model and some have even equated continued logging with conservation. Yes, subdivision is usually worse than logging, but logging is a greater threat to most of the northeastern forest than is subdivision. Conservationists who equate conservation easements that allow continued logging with ecological protection are

Table 12.1
Largest Federal Wilderness Areas, Northeast and West
(in acres)

Northeast
Pemigewasset (N.H.)—45,000
Presidential Range–Dry River (N.H.)—27,380
Sandwich Range (N.H.)—25,000
Bread Loaf (Vt.)—21,480
Lye Brook (Vt.)—15,503

West (outside of Alaska)
Death Valley NP (Calif.)—3,158,038
Frank Church–River of No Return (Idaho/Mont.)—2,365,821
Selway-Bitterroot (Idaho/Mont.)—1,089,017
Bob Marshall (Mont.)—1,009,356
Absaroka-Beartooth (Mont./Wyo.)—920,327

Alaska
Wrangell–St. Elias NP—9,078,675
Arctic NWR—8,000,000
Gates of the Arctic NP—7,167,192
Noatak NP—5,765,427
Katmai NP—3,384,358

being disingenuous and setting precedents that could undermine land protection long into the future. The two biggest conservation deals in the Northeast in recent years—the Conservation Fund's purchase (with regional partners) of Champion International's 300,000 acres in New England and New York and the Nature Conservancy's purchase of 180,000 acres of International Paper's land in northwestern Maine—may save little more than riparian buffers, unless money restricted to Forever Wild protection is soon raised. At this writing (July 1999) prospects for the Conservation Fund's new lands look grim (except in the Adirondacks, where New York state's Forever Wild constitutional clause ensures protection for the 29,000 acres the New York Department of Environmental Conservation purchased in full fee); but the Nature Conservancy seems willing to fully protect the portion of its huge purchase that wild lands funders pay for—the rest may go back to the timber industry. *Resource conservation* (especially consumption reduction) is a crucial part of an overall conservation strategy, but it is not the same as *nature preservation*.

• Invoking the purity principle in wilderness advocacy is a mistake. Land can recover, especially in the well-watered East, and ought not to be denied permanent protection on account of having been abused in the past. The Adirondacks offer perhaps this country's greatest examples of land severely damaged by nineteenth-century logging but now restored to wilderness condition (see map 12.1). Full recovery takes centuries, if not millennia and if possible at all; but if we let it be, land will heal remarkably quickly and can be awarded the status of wilderness recovery area until it clearly meets the definition of wilderness. Of course, the land's capacity to recover should never be used as an excuse to damage an area in the first place.

- Every natural area deserves protection, no matter how small or isolated. Yes, highest priority should be given to protecting those remnants of nature identified by conservation biologists as critical to the maintenance of biological diversity and ecological processes; but every wild acre merits preservation and veneration, and people should be encouraged to work for the protection of whatever place they love, even if it be the outskirts, of say, Hackensack, New Jersey, or Annohuac, Texas. Indeed, knitting back together our remaining fragments of wild nature — the practice of restoration ecology — must become a work project shared by all citizens, if we are to preserve our natural heritage.

- We owe many, perhaps most, of our protected areas in America at least in part to wild lands philanthropists. Over the last century, numerous generous families, foundations, individuals, and land trusts have employed the tried and true tactic of land acquisition to save wild places. Wild lands philanthropy success stories include Acadia National Park, land bought and saved by George Dor and friends; Baxter State Park, bought and saved by Percival Baxter, after his unsuccessful effort to save the land while he was governor of Maine; Hawk Mountain, bought and saved through private donations in an effort led by Rosalie Edge; and many national and state parks, including Grand Teton, Great Smoky Mountains, and Redwood, saved largely through the benefaction of the Rockefeller family. Historian Robin Winks writes in the wild lands philanthropy theme issue of *Wild Earth* that almost all U.S. national parks benefited from the generosity of conservationists with the means to buy and save the land or endow the park.[1]

- Told the truth, or at least a sizable portion thereof, the public supports wild lands acquisition and protection, wilderness recovery, the return of large carnivores and ungulates, and other ecological desiderata. Despite its booming population, Florida — having a relatively well-

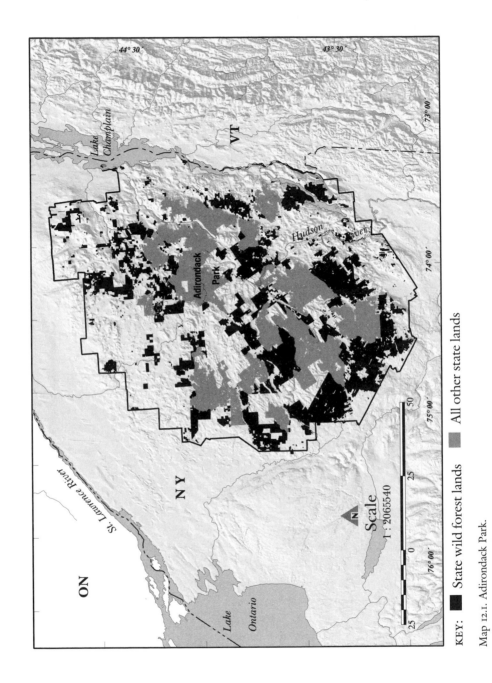

KEY: ■ State wild forest lands   ▨ All other state lands

Map 12.1. Adirondack Park.

educated population—approved the expenditure of $3 billion over ten years for the purchase and protection of critical wild lands on the market in 1990 (Florida Preservation 2000). Floridians were so pleased with the program that they extended it for another decade, and another $3 billion, as Florida Forever. Several other eastern states have also passed bond measures for habitat acquisition and protection, second-most notable being New York (and third, New Jersey). Aside from the 1992 election, when anti-environmentalists all rallied and voted, whereas many open-minded people failed to notice the environmental bond measure on the ballot, and notwithstanding a few malicious property rights extremists in northern New York, the citizens of that state have generally supported state conservation acquisitions. New York now has a fully protected wilderness system and a mostly protected—no logging, but motor vehicles still allowed on designated roads and some trails—wild forest system that adds up to more protected forest in the East's most populous state than is protected in all of New England. Moreover, polls show that most people throughout the region favor the reintroduction or natural recovery of extirpated species, including large carnivores, particularly the gray wolf. Undoubtedly, support for wilderness, large carnivores, conservation acquisitions and the like rises with ecological literacy—another argument for better education, emphasizing the natural sciences, environmental ethics, and time out in the wilds. Indeed, a big part of our job as conservationists is to offer people information and education on why wilderness, large carnivores, preservation acquisitions, and other ecological goals are good and needed.[2]

From the West we learn:

- Even the largest existing national parks and wilderness areas are too small to ensure the long-term viability of all native species. William Newmark's landmark study of fragmentation and extirpation in western parks found that even these protected areas have lost some native species, with losses inversely proportional to their size. Only the huge Banff/Jasper/Kootenay Park complex retained its full biota. Conversely, small parks, such as Zion in Utah, have lost many species. If logging and mining and other development continue to destroy more and more of the habitat around existing parks, wide-ranging and sensitive species will be lost from all except perhaps the largest Alaskan and Canadian Arctic parks.[3]

- From this it follows that protected areas must be greatly enlarged and reconnected if we are to save our natural heritage—a lesson that is repeated all over the world, but particularly clearly in the American West. Many science-informed preservation groups engaged in reserve design and implementation (led by the Wildlands Project, short for the North American Wilderness Recovery Strategy) are striving to accomplish such large-scale wild lands recovery.

- Culture cannot be safely ignored. Those of us who want to see wolves and bears and big cats and other large predators back in their rightful places will not likely succeed unless we learn to talk to and work with local people. Not necessarily all local people—unrepentant reactionaries will always oppose wild nature, no matter what we do—but all reasonable local people. Until we find common ground, chambers of commerce, farm bureaus, town and county government officials, and people who get their news from the local paper will probably generally oppose preservationists' efforts to restore the full range of native biodiversity. The starkest, most enraging reminder of this lesson recently has been the willful killing—yes, murder—of most of the Mexican wolves released in eastern Arizona, stalling the recovery effort for *Canis lupus baleyii* in the Southwest. Conservation officials had not succeeded in raising local support, so the wolves were gunned down, easy prey for motorized thugs cruising the back roads around this not-yet-wild-enough region. Wolf recovery, then, demands not only road closures but also conversations with local, vocal critics and fence-sitters.

- Public lands work. Although the U.S. Forest Service and the Bureau of Land Management, and to a lesser extent the Fish and Wildlife and National Park Services, are in the thrall of extractive industries and developers, public lands include most of this country's remaining wilderness, old-growth forests, and other original ecosystems. The public land agencies need to be drastically reformed—if not abolished and replaced with a federal Wild Lands and Wildlife Protection Agency—but concerned citizens do at least have some say over what is and what is not allowed on our public lands. The best protected areas are often those secured by wild lands philanthropy individuals or groups, but most wild lands philanthropists turn their lands over to public agencies for permanent protection. Moreover, conservationists have won passage of laws to stem the worst abuses of federally managed public lands. Prospects are growing that logging, mining, and livestock grazing will be phased out of public lands, as the economics turn against the extractive industries and as more and more Americans learn that their taxes are subsidizing commercial exploitation of their own public lands. If all public lands were fully protected for their highest and best uses—as wildlife habitat and places of rejuvenation for the human spirit—we could see nearly 800 million acres of wilderness and wilderness recovery areas in the United States (eight times the present amount) established with just a few strokes of administrative or legislative pens.

- Lowest-common-denominator conservation, or resource conservation without a strong complement of nature preservation, serves well only the extractive industries and their allies from the "wise use" movement. The "cows not condos" refrain may occasionally forestall a subdivision, but it perpetuates a practice that is responsible for the imperilment of more species than any other single industry in the West. (Yes, ranching even surpasses logging as a cause of biological impoverishment in the West, as studies by George Wuerthner, Tom Fleischner, Joy Belsky, and others have shown.)[4]

This final lesson unites East and West, for in both halves of the continent, the threat of subdivision and development is being used as a bludgeon to force concerned citizens to accept continued logging and livestock grazing, under the assumption—which we conservationists must disprove—that our two choices are the status quo or the suburbs. Conservationists must show that we don't always have to choose between the lesser of two evils; good solutions do exist. Instead of a West of clearcuts and overgrazed rangelands punctuated by circumscribed subdivisions, we could have a West of comfortable yet carefully contained towns and cities in a matrix of wild natural (or recovering) forests, deserts, and grasslands.

Likewise, in the East, we could have large, interconnected wild forests, free from motors and commercial exploitation, around most of our towns and cities. Wilderness recovery is the work of centuries, surely; but if we have the vision, passion, and courage that the conservation movement's greatest evangelist, Dave Foreman, has been calling for in the last two decades, our children may live to see the day that North America is mostly, expandingly wild and healthy and whole once again.

Part IV

FINAL THOUGHTS

Epilogue

BILL McKIBBEN

SOMETIME EARLY IN his tenure as Interior Secretary, Bruce Babbitt paid a visit to Albany on some political errand. After his speech, a couple of us sat with him drinking beer and telling him about the Adirondacks. We spread out the Blue Line map, with Lake Champlain on one side and Lake Ontario on the other, the St. Lawrence at the top and the Mohawk at the bottom, and we spent some time describing some controversy or another. He listened for a while, asked some intelligent questions, and then, as I was folding the map, he swept across northern New York with his hand and said, "so this is what—about twenty miles across?"

Twenty miles! I can walk twenty miles out my back door and still be in the Wilcox Lake Wild Forest. Why, I started to tell him, the Adirondack Park alone is larger than Glacier, Grand Canyon, Yellowstone, and Yosemite combined. And then there's the rest of the Northern Forest, the 10 million acres of the Maine woods, the . . .

But then I stopped. I remembered that it was only a few years before that I had begun to sense the real scale of the North Woods, its real possibilities. I'd grown up in the suburbs of Boston, gone to work in New York City; to me the Northeast seemed crowded. I read Ed Abbey when I wanted to think about the wild. And then, by a sort of fluke, I found myself living in the Adirondacks. At about the same time, I was reading through the *Earth First! Journal* and, in amongst the accounts of stirring battles in the Siskiyous or the Gila Wilderness, I came across a piece that Jamie Sayen had written offering a vision for a rewilded East, stretching up the spine of the Appalachians, "which in time would enable the return of unique plants and large animals—panthers, bears, wolves, and moose—that have been exterminated throughout all or part of the mountain chain."

In the fifteen years since Sayen wrote that first piece, much has happened, good and bad: The moose has returned to New York, the paper companies have sold and resold their lands across New England, national parks have been proposed, Vermont game officials have confirmed the return of at least a panther or two to the state, the *Earth First! Journal* metamorphosed into *Wild Earth* and moved to Vermont, Bruce Babbitt returned to knock out the Edwards Dam. But by far the biggest change is this: The notion of a rewilded East has moved from the category of hazy hallucination to the category of clear and prophetic vision. As the superb essays in this book make clear, both on the ground across these states and in the minds of more and more of their citizens, a new North Woods is taking shape. No longer the half-forgotten remnant of some past glory long since turned over to the paper companies for liquidation, the north country is now the foundation of a possible future glory, a place where human beings and the rest of creation could manage to make their separate, and sometimes intertwined, livings in reasonable proximity. It is, in conservation terms, all of a sudden the most rousing spot on the planet.

That new vision is not in completely clear focus, of course. Reading this volume, you might think there were two separate schools of thought on how to proceed. One focuses on big wilderness, and the other on gentler human habitation of the land; one focuses on new national parks, and the other on woodlots; one focuses on large-scale federal or state acquisition of local lands, and the other on conservation easements, land trusts, and the like; one focuses on helping nature make a living, the other on helping people fit into that landscape. These are both important ideas, but it seems to me that they are less in contrast than they first appear; or rather, that the differences begin to disappear when you look at a map and a calendar.

On the map, some areas make such obvious sense as big wilderness that we all should simply agree and get to work. Huge chunks of Maine's North Woods are cut over and abused; to insist that they be a "working forest" is absurd. The work they need to do is rest, relax, regrow, rebound—the same work that has been going on in the Adirondacks for a century, since the time when much of the vast land bordering the Hudson looked like the land that borders the Allagash today. Big chunks of wildland exist in Vermont and New Hampshire as well; in particular, every poll tells us that the managers of the national forests would serve the desires of their owners by preserving them as wild places. Other lands in those states, too, could serve as critical cores of wildness, connected by spokes and corridors to the vaster reserves east and west.

By the same token, any glance at the map will show millions of other acres that won't be set aside as wilderness any time soon—the sugar-bushes, woodlots, and timberlands that need both to be saved *from* second-home development, and saved *for* what one might call first-home development. David Brynn, with his Vermont Family Forests, is doing the work of conservation as much as David Brower; real networks of ecologically and economically sustainable small forestry projects will help cement in place a new culture of people who really *live* here, who draw their livelihoods, their recreation, and their dreams of what might some-day be from these woods and hills and streams.

Few of us can do our best work on a truly regional basis—we've learned to concentrate our efforts on our particular valleys or ranges, where we know the neighbors and the terrain. But if you're working on land trusts in Vermont, you should also tithe some effort toward the Maine Woods National Park, and you should take the occasional trip across Champlain and into the big, peopled woods of the Adirondacks. And vice versa. Sense the scope and scale of this project, sense how it fits together, sense the continuing devastation that drives the anger, sense what it might someday become. This synthesis is already beginning—you can hear in the tone of the essays in this book the growing sense of shared purpose, even among the disagreements. (And for this we have much reason to thank that troika of Middlebury thinkers, Elder, Klyza, and Trombulak.) But the best way for this spirit to grow is for more of us to wear down the soles on our boots, visiting woodlots, visiting mountain-tops, visiting neighbors human and not. None of this land will be saved in theory; it will only be saved in practice.

"Saved" is probably the wrong word anyway—the planet on which we live is suddenly so dangerously dynamic that the thought of saving some-thing for any long term is preposterous. To use the most obvious ex-ample, climate change is no longer some possible future scare; it is a very real presence in a region whose winters become shorter and milder each year. That heat has already begun to alter the economy and character of land both wild and tame, affecting everything from sugar production to species composition to skier visits, and the pace of that change will ac-celerate in the next few decades. Some computer projections already show that the hemlock, say, won't exist south of the Canadian border by the end of the century due to higher temperatures (if the wooly adelgid doesn't do it in first).

So the best that we can do is to see that this land is as successfully inhabited as is possible in a tenuous time. In a lot of places, that means inhabited by beaver, birch, and bog, not by people; in other spots, it

means small farms and orchards that return a decent living to their cus-
todians, small woodlots that support families instead of being sold for
taxes; and in other spots it means compact, working cities that fit neatly
into the landscape—imagine Burlington, say, as a gravitational regional
center, drawing in folk instead of spitting them out in an ever-sadder
sprawl.

Were we able to inhabit this land successfully, we would provide a
useful model for a world in dire need of models. Already this is starting
to happen. Researchers and development planners flood into the Adirondacks, realizing that here they have a century-old working model of a
biosphere reserve. Tibetans come, and Russians, Chinese, Bolivians, all
wanting to understand a place that looks at least a little like their places.
But its power as an example will only grow as the scale of the effort
expands. And the world stands in desperate need of examples. Increasingly
we realize that we're hitting a dead end as we pursue endless economic
growth, but we find it desperately hard to imagine something else—for
most of the past century, "more" has been the only dream.

Here, in a place of relative affluence (and relatively stable population
size), it's time to figure out a different dream, as a gift to both ourselves
and the planet. If we can conjure it up here, in the same part of the world
that birthed suburb and megalopolis, that hourly sends out the Madison
Avenue enchantment across the planet, then it will matter. Sometimes I
think we are being led toward this different dream, led by a landscape
that never really vanished. Through four centuries of hard use, the phan-
tom reality of this place was submerged, but it was not destroyed, and
when we step back for very long that ghost map reasserts itself—the fields
give way to pine and then to forest; the beaver and the bear crowd back
in; the corner maples grow right around the strands of rusting barbed
wire. It is our job to interpret that: as decline or as delight, as chaos or
as a second chance to get this place right. And our job too to try to find
our rightful place amidst it.

Sources for Graphs, Maps, and Tables

Graphs

Graph 5.1. Reed F. Noss, "The Wildlands Project: Land Conservation Strategy," *Wild Earth* (Special Issue 1992): 15.

Graph 8.1. Data for element occurrences and conservation by elevation furnished by the Vermont Chapter of the Nature Conservancy and the Spatial Analysis Lab at the University of Vermont as part of the Vermont Biodiversity Project, and by the New Hampshire Chapter of the Nature Conservancy, the New Hampshire Natural Heritage Inventory (New Hampshire Department of Resources and Economic Development), and New Hampshire GRANiT (University of New Hampshire). Although the analysis of such data is not new, the idea for the mountain diagram came from Henry Barbour, Tim Simmons, Patricia Swain, and Henry Woolsey, *Our Irreplaceable Heritage: Protecting Biodiversity in Massachusetts* (Boston and Westborough: Massachusetts Division of Fisheries and Wildlife and Massachusetts Nature Conservancy, 1998). Frank Lowenstein, Geoffrey Hughes Berkshire Program Director of the Nature Conservancy, interpreted the data through graphs and diagrams.

Maps

Map 1.1. Northern Cartographic, South Burlington, Vermont.

Map 2.1. Albert W. Franzmann and Charles C. Schwartz, eds., *Ecology and Management of the North American Moose* (Washington, D.C.: Smithsonian Institution Press, 1997), 5, 132, 135; Cedric Alexander, Vermont Department of Fish and Wildlife, personal communication, April 2000; John McDonald, Massachusetts Division of Fisheries and Wildlife, personal communication, April 2000.

Map 3.1. Locations supplied by Robert T. Leverett, Holyoke, Massachusetts.

Map 4.1. Connecticut Department of Environmental Protection, PropDEP and PropFed GIS Coverages, 1994; Maine Office of GIS, MEPub100 GIS Coverage, 1993; MassGIS, OPS (all towns: 1–355) GIS Coverages, 1999; New Hampshire GRANIT Net, CONS (all towns: 1–213) GIS Coverages, 1994; New Jersey Department of Environmental Protection, NJOpenSpace GIS Coverage, 1999; New York GIS Coverage from the GIS Office, Eastern Conservation Science, Northeastern Chapter of the Nature Conservancy, Boston, Massachusetts, May 2000; Pennsylvania Spatial Data Access, MGDLand GIS

Coverage, 1998; RIGIS, S4400590 GIS Coverage, 1990; Vermont Center for Geographic Information, ConsPub GIS Coverage, 1999.

Map 5.1. Peter Quinby, Steve Trombulak, Thomas Lee, Jeff Lane, Michael Henry, Robert Long, and Paula MacKay, "Opportunities for Wildlife Habitat Connectivity Between Algonquin Park, Ontario and the Adirondack Park, New York," report by the Greater Laurentian Wildlands Project, South Burlington, Vermont, 1999.

Map 6.1. Marcus L. Hansen, *The Mingling of the Canadian and American Peoples*, vol. 1 (New Haven: Yale University Press, 1940), 90.

Map 6.2. U.S. Department of Commerce, Bureau of Census, *1990 Census of Population*, CD-ROM (Washington, D.C.: Government Printing Office, 1992).

Map 6.3. "Maine Woods Proposed National Park & Preserve," pamphlet (Concord, Mass.: Restore, 1994).

Map 6.4. Jamie Sayen, "A Second Chance for the Northern Forests," *Wild Earth* (Winter 1995/96): 38.

Map 8.1. GIS data from throughout the region was collected, analyzed, and mapped by Frank Biasi and Dan Morse of the GIS Office, Eastern Conservation Science, Northeastern Chapter of the Nature Conservancy, Boston, Massachusetts. The Status codes were modified from Patrick J. Crist, *Mapping and Categorizing Land Stewardship: A Handbook for Conducting Gap Analysis* (Moscow: Idaho Cooperative Fish and Wildlife Research Unit, University of Idaho, 1998). Data sources: the Vermont Chapter of the Nature Conservancy, the Spatial Analysis Lab at the University of Vermont, the New Hampshire Chapter of the Nature Conservancy, the New Hampshire Natural Heritage Inventory (New Hampshire Department of Resources and Economic Development), New Hampshire GRANiT (University of New Hampshire), Adirondack Park Agency, New York Chapter of the Nature Conservancy, New York Department of Conservation, and New York State Parks Department.

Map 10.1. Vermont Center for Geographic Information, LKCH_VTBASINS GIS Coverage, 1994.

Map 12.1. Adirondack Park Agency, Adirondack Park Geographic Information CD-ROM, vol. 1.4, 1998.

Tables

Table 1.1. R. S. Kellogg, *The Timber Supply of the United States*, USDA Forest Service, Circular 166 (Washington, D.C.: Government Printing Office, 1909), 7; U.S. Census Office, *Twelfth Census of the United States: Manufactures: Part III* (Washington, D.C.: Government Printing Office, 1902), 833–36; U.S. Forest Service, "Northeastern Forest Inventory and Analysis Project," http://www.fs.fed.us/ne/fia/acre.html, visited 23 June 1999. Data for circa 1990 based on Forest Service inventories conducted between 1983 and 1995.

Table 4.1. *Federal Conservation Lands*: These figures are the sum of acreage owned by the Army Corps of Engineers, the National Park Service, the U.S. Fish and Wildlife Service, and the U.S. Forest Service. The figures are from 30 September 1998. General Services Administration, Office of Governmentwide Policy, Office of Real Property, Worldwide Inventory, personal communication, August 1999. *Federal Wilderness Acreage*: U.S. Fish and Wildlife Service, "Wilderness Areas in National Wildlife Refuges and National Fish Hatcheries," http://www.fws.gov/r9realty/table10.html, 1997, visited 23 April 1999; U.S. Forest Service, "Forest Service—National Wilderness Areas Summary," http://www.fedstats.gov/index20.html, 1997, visited 22 April 1999; U.S. National Park Service, "Wilderness in the NPS," http://www.nps.gov/partner/nwpsnps.html, 1994, visited 23 April 1999; "Wilderness Areas of the United States," *Wilderness* (Fall 1994): 3–9. *State Conservation and Wilderness Lands*: Connecticut Department of Environmental Protection, Land Acquisition and Management Division, personal communication, July 1999; Maine Baxter State Park Authority, personal communication, August 1999; Maine Bureau of Parks and Lands, personal communication, August 1999; Maine Bureau of Parks and Lands, "State Parks, Public Reserved Lands, Historic Sites," http://state.me.us/doc/prkslnds/chart.htm#lands, visited 30 July 1999; Maine Department of Inland Fisheries and Wildlife, "Locate Wildlife Management Areas by Region," http://janus.state.me.us/ifw/wma/index.htm, 1998, visited 6 August 1999; Massachusetts Executive Office of Environmental Affairs, personal communication, August 1999; New Hampshire Department of Fish and Game, personal communication, August 1999; New Hampshire Department of Resources and Economic Development, Division of Forests and Lands, personal communication, August 1999; New Jersey Department of Environmental Protection, Division of Parks and Recreation and Green Acres, personal communication, July 1999; New Jersey Department of Environmental Protection, Division of Fish, Game and Wildlife, "Wildlife Management Areas," http://www.state.nj.us/dep/wma-land.htm, 1999, visited 29 July 1999; New York Department of Environmental Conservation, Bureau of Public Lands, personal communication, August 1999; New York State Office of Parks, Recreation and Historic Preservation, personal communication, August 1999; Pennsylvania Department of Conservation and Natural Resources, "Pennsylvania State Parks and Forests," 1998; Pennsylvania Department of Conservation and Natural Resources, Bureau of Forestry, personal communication, August 1999; Pennsylvania Game Commission, personal communication, August 1999; Rhode Island Department of Environmental Management, personal communication, August 1999; Vermont Agency of Natural Resources, "Vermont State Lands," http://www.state.vt.us/anr/fpr/lands/landinfo/land_sum.htm, 1999, visited 27 July 1999.

Table 6.1. Compiled by Jamie Sayen, Groveton, New Hampshire.

Table 10.1. Vermont Agency of Natural Resources, *Environment 1999: An Assessment of the Quality of Vermont's Environment* (Waterbury: Vermont Agency of Natural Resources, 1999), 2.

Table 10.2. Vermont Agency of Natural Resources, *Environment 1999: An Assessment of the Quality of Vermont's Environment* (Waterbury: Vermont Agency of Natural Resources, 1999), 4.

Table 10.3. Vermont Family Forests, Bristol, Vermont.

Table 10.4. Vermont Family Forests, Bristol, Vermont.

Table 10.5. Vermont Family Forests, Bristol, Vermont.

Table 12.1. "American Wilderness," *Wild Earth* (Winter 1998/99): 35; "Wilderness Areas of the United States," *Wilderness* (Fall 1994): 3–9.

Notes

1. An Eastern Term for Wilderness (pages 3–26)

I thank Tom Butler, Leanne Klyza Linck, Bob Linck, Sheila McGrory-Klyza, Jamie Sayen, and Steve Trombulak for their helpful comments on an earlier draft of this chapter.

1. Henry David Thoreau, "Walking," in *Nature, Ralph Waldo Emerson and Walking* (1862; reprint, Boston: Beacon Press, 1991), 95.

2. We limit our attention in this book to the Northeast, defined as New England, New Jersey, New York, and Pennsylvania, in order to focus our discussion. We believe that the upper Midwest and the Southeast also have contributions to make to the wilderness discussion, often along lines similar to ours.

3. Among the major works making the case for Native American manipulation of the landscape, see William Cronon, *Changes in the Land: Indians, Colonists, and the Ecology of New England* (New York: Hill and Wang, 1983); William M. Denevan, "The Pristine Myth: The Landscape of the Americas in 1492," *Annals of the Association of American Geographers* 82 (1992): 369–85; Stephen J. Pyne, *Fire in America: A Cultural History of Wildland and Rural Fire* (Seattle: University of Washington Press, 1997) (see pp. 45–65 on the Northeast). Both Pyne's and Cronon's discussions of Native American use of fire in New England center almost exclusively on southern New England, more densely populated and more reliant on agriculture than northern New England. Indeed, Cronon himself is far more careful in making this distinction than many who cite his work. He writes, for instance, that "Northern Indians do not appear to have engaged in such burning. Because they did not practice agriculture and so were less tied to particular sites, they had less incentive to alter the environment of a given spot" (50); and that in terms of native effects on animals, "In the north, where Indian populations were much smaller in relation to their land base and fewer colonists came to settle, pressure on animal populations resulted almost wholly from trade rather than competition over land" (104). Indeed, even in his discussion of Native American fires in southern New England he writes they were "limited . . . to the local vicinity of village sites" (181).

Significant empirical studies focusing on the role of Native Americans, offering a more nuanced reading of the role of natives on the landscape, include Emily W. B. Russell, *People and the Land through Time: Linking Ecology and History* (New Haven: Yale University Press, 1997); Thomas R. Vale, "The Myth of the Humanized Landscape: An Example from Yosemite National Park," *Natural Areas Journal* 18 (1998): 231–36; Gordon G. Whitney, *From Coastal Wilderness to Fruited Plain: A History of Environmental Change in Temperate North America from 1500 to the Present* (New York: Cambridge University Press, 1994), 98–120. Whitney, for instance, writes, "The cumulative impact of the Indian's activities was substantial.

. . . The effects, however, were still localized. Large segments of the interior, i.e., northern New England, the Allegheny Plateau region of Pennsylvania and New York, and the High Plains region of Michigan, were almost devoid of Indian activity" (120).

4. William Cronon, "The Trouble with Wilderness; or, Getting Back to the Wrong Nature," in *Uncommon Ground: Toward Reinventing Nature*, ed. by William Cronon (New York: Norton, 1995), 69, 89. See also J. Baird Callicott and Michael P. Nelson, eds., *The Great New Wilderness Debate: An Expansive Collection of Writings Defining Wilderness from John Muir to Gary Snyder* (Athens: University of Georgia Press, 1998).

5. Cronon, *Changes in the Land*, 48–51; William A. Haviland and Marjory W. Power, *The Original Vermonters: Native Inhabitants, Past and Present*, rev. ed. (Hanover, N.H.: University Press of New England, 1994), 159; R. S. Kellogg, *The Timber Supply of the United States*, USDA Forest Service, Circular 166 (Washington, D.C.: Government Printing Office, 1909), 7; Pyne, *Five in America*, 46–51, 63; Whitney, *From Coastal Wilderness*, 120.

6. Christopher McGrory Klyza and Stephen C. Trombulak, *The Story of Vermont: A Natural and Cultural History* (Hanover, N.H.: University Press of New England, 1999); Whitney, *From Coastal Wilderness*; Harold F. Wilson, *The Hill Country of Northern New England: Its Social and Economic History, 1790–1930* (1936; reprint New York: AMS Press, 1967).

7. Craig W. Allin, *The Politics of Wilderness Preservation* (Westport, Conn.: Greenwood Press, 1982), 186–92.

8. Public lands acreage: U.S. Bureau of Land Management, *Public Land Statistics 1997* (Washington, D.C.: Government Printing Office, 1998), 7–11; U.S. Fish and Wildlife Service, "Query the National Wildlife Refuge System Lands Database," http://www.fws.gov.r9realty/nwrs.htm#statesum, 1997, visited 22 April 1999; U.S. Forest Service, "Forest Service Lands by State," http://www.fedstats.gov/index20.html, 1997, visited 22 April 1999; U.S. National Park Service, "The National Park Service-Listing of Acreage by Park," http://www.nature.nps.gov/stats/acreagebypark.htm, 1998, visited 22 April 1999. Wilderness acreage: U.S. Fish and Wildlife Service, "Wilderness Areas in National Wildlife Refuges and National Fish Hatcheries," http://www.fws.gov/r9realty/table10.html, 1997, visited 23 April 1999; U.S. Forest Service, "Forest Service—National Wilderness Areas Summary," http://www.fedstats.gov/index20.html, 1997, visited April 22, 1999; U.S. National Park Service, "Wilderness in the NPS," http://www.nps.gov/partner/nwpsnps.html, 1994, visited 23 April 1999; "Wilderness Areas of the United States," *Wilderness* (Fall 1994): 3–9.

9. Chad P. Dawson and Ed Zahniser, "The Influence of the Adirondacks on the Wilderness Preservation Contributions of Robert Marshall and Howard Zahniser," in *Proceedings: Wilderness Science in a Time of Change*, ed. David N. Cole and Stephen F. McCool (Ogden, Utah: USDA, Forest Service, Rocky Mountain Research Station, forthcoming); Dave Foreman and Howie Wolke, *The Big Outside: A Descriptive Inventory of the Big Wilderness Areas in the U.S.* (Tucson: Ned Ludd Books, 1989), 385–93; Philip G. Terrie, *Forever Wild: A Cultural History of Wilderness in the Adirondacks* (Syracuse: Syracuse University Press, 1994).

10. On the justifications of wilderness, see Roderick F. Nash, *Wilderness and the American Mind*, 3d ed. (New Haven: Yale University Press, 1982), 238–71.

11. Richard Tobin, *The Expendable Future: U.S. Politics and the Protection of Biological Diversity* (Durham, N.C.: Duke University Press, 1990).

12. Reed F. Noss, "The Wildlands Project: Land Conservation Strategy," *Wild*

Earth, Special Issue, (1992): 10–25; Reed F. Noss and Allen Y. Cooperrider, *Saving Nature's Legacy: Protecting and Restoring Biodiversity* (Washington: Island Press, 1994); Michael E. Soulé and John Terborgh, eds., *Continental Conservation: Scientific Foundations of Regional Reserve Networks* (Washington, D.C.: Island Press, 1999).

13. Natural disturbance in much of the Northeast, though, was and is on a small scale. As Whitney writes in *From Coastal Wilderness to Fruited Plain*:

> Fires apparently dominated much of the birch, aspen, pine, and oak forests of the upper Midwest and isolated areas in the Northeast, while hurricanes, occurring at a frequency of one every 100 to 150 years, kept much of southern New England in a state of flux. Over the remainder of the area, however, it was probably the death of an occasional tree in the canopy that determined the dynamics of the stand. [George Perkins] Marsh was apparently correct, at least for northern New England, when he states that 'trees fall singly, not by square roods.' If the primeval forest 'did not consist of stagnant stands of immense trees stretching with little change over vast areas,' neither was it an amalgamation of pioneer species recovering from one form of disturbance or another." (76)

14. Florida Department of Environmental Protection, "Preservation 2000," http://p2000.dep.state.fl.us/, visited May 4, 1999.

15. As used in this chapter, "rewilding" refers to action at the landscape level with a goal of reducing human control and allowing ecological and evolutionary processes to reassert themselves. "Restoration" refers to work on a specific parcel of land where active management is used to return ecological functions.

For a useful discussion of issues regarding restoration in the western United States, see Dan Flores, "Making the West Whole Again: A Historical Perspective on Restoration," in *Reclaiming the Native Home of Hope: Community, Ecology and the American West*, ed. Robert B. Keiter (Salt Lake City: University of Utah Press, 1998); Daniel B. Botkin, *Discordant Harmonies: A New Ecology for the Twenty-First Century* (New York: Oxford University Press, 1990); and Russell, *People and the Land*, 18.

16. Russell, *People and the Land*, 236; Whitney, *From Coastal Wilderness*, 202–204, 279.

17. The source for extinct species in the Northeast is the Nature Conservancy and the Association for Biodiversity Information, Natural Heritage Central Databases, Arlington, Virginia, 1999. The sources for extirpated species of the Northeast are lists supplied by state natural heritage programs: Connecticut Department of Environmental Protection, "Natural Diversity Data Base," http://dep.state.ct.us/cgnhs/nddb/nddb2.htm, 1998, visited 13 May 1999; Maine Natural Heritage Program, personal communication, May 1999; Massachusetts Natural Heritage Program, personal communication, July 1999; New Hampshire Natural Heritage Program, personal communication, May 1999; New Jersey Natural Heritage Program, personal communication, June 1999: New Jersey Natural Heritage Program, "Special Plants of New Jersey," http://www.heritage.tnc.org/nhp/us/nj/njplant1.htm, 1998, visited 15 June 1999; New York Natural Heritage Program, personal communication, May 1999; Pennsylvania Natural Heritage Program, personal communication, June 1999; Rhode Island Natural Heritage Program, personal communication, May 1999; Vermont Natural Heritage Program, personal communication, June 1999. More generally, see J. A. Allen, "The Former Range of Some New England Carnivorous Mammals," *The American Naturalist*, 10 (1876): 708–15; Alfred J. Godin, *Wild Mammals of New England*, field guide ed. (Chester, Conn.: Globe Pequot Press, 1981), 200–205; Stephen C. Trombulak,

"Ecological Health and the Northern Forest," *Vermont Law Review* 19(1995): 301–302; Whitney, *From Coastal Wilderness*, 284, 286, 305–12.

18. Russell, *People and the Land*, 118, 230, 243.

19. Henry David Thoreau, *The Writings of Henry David Thoreau: Journal*, vol. 8, ed. Bradford Torrey (1856; reprint Boston and New York: Houghton Mifflin, 1906), 220; Bill McKibben, *Hope, Human and Wild* (Boston: Little, Brown, 1995), 36, and more generally. See also John Elder, *Reading the Mountains of Home* (Cambridge: Harvard University Press, 1998).

20. Klyza and Trombulak, *The Story of Vermont*, 187–88, 190.

21. It must be noted that the word "sustainable" is becoming increasingly problematic. The word is overused to the point of becoming meaningless. It also suggests that humans know what is or is not sustainable over long periods of time, something we don't yet know in industrial society. A more accurate phrase might be "ecological" or "low-impact" forestry or agriculture. However, the phrase "sustainability" is in such widespread use that for the purposes of this chapter it makes sense to continue its use in order to make the relevant points about changing current agricultural and forestry practices.

22. Wendell Berry, *Another Turn of the Crank* (Washington, D.C.: Counterpoint, 1995), 71–72, 59; Wes Jackson, *Becoming Native to this Place* (Washington, D.C.: Counterpoint, 1994), 67.

23. See Jackson, *Becoming Native* generally on this point.

24. Richard W. Judd, *Common Lands, Common People: The Origins of Conservation in Northern New England* (Cambridge: Harvard University Press, 1997), 203, 102–11; Northern Forest Alliance, *Forestry for the Future* (Montpelier, Vt.: Northern Forest Alliance, 1999), 20; Jym St. Pierre, "Doing Deals in Maine," *Northern Forest Forum* (Mid-Spring, 1999): 23–26; Steve Trombulak, "Wild Forests Are Working Forests: Some Thoughts on the Language of Despoilment," *Wild Earth* (Fall 1998): 73–76. Judd points out an interesting potential parallel in his book: Turn of the century forestland speculation in the White Mountains served as a major catalyst to the creation of the White Mountain National Forest.

25. Other efforts at sustainable forestry, such as the Atlas Timberlands Project between the Vermont Land Trust and the Vermont Nature Conservancy, have yet to demonstrate a significant enough commitment to ecological forestry.

26. On the return of the wolf to the Northeast, see John Elder, ed., *The Return of the Wolf: Reflections on the Future of Wolves in the Northeast* (Hanover, N.H.: University Press of New England, 2000); Nancy Bazilchuk, "State, Conservationists to Acquire 130,000 Acres," *Burlington Free Press*, 9 December 1998, A1; "Canada: Ontario Creates 378 Parks, Protects 6M Acres," *Greenwire*, 30 March 1999; "Conservation: ME Family Announces Largest US Easement," *Greenwire*, 3 March 1999; "Dams: Demolition Signals New Era in River Restoration," *Greenwire*, 2 July 1999; "Forests: New Forestry Helps MA Economy, Env't—Study," *Greenwire*, 14 August 1998; "Public Lands: For Whom and For What?," *Forest Watch Newsbrief*, June 1999, 1; Greg Fullerton, "Protected Areas in N. B.," *Northern Forest Forum* (Mid-Spring 1999): 5; David Lindsay, "Nova Scotia Reserves 700,000 Acres," *Northern Forest Forum* (Mid-Spring, 1999): 4; "Maine: Gov King Proposes $75M Land Purchase Plan," *Greenwire*, 9 February 1999; "NE Forests: $35M Deal Preserves 185,000 Acres in Maine," *Greenwire*, 15 December 1998; "New Englanders Working to Protect Unroaded Forest Lands," *Wilderness Society Quarterly Newsletter* (Fall 1999): 3; "New Jersey: Whitman Signs $1B Open-Space Measure," *Greenwire*, 1 July 1999; David E. Sanger, "Clinton Proposes Wider Protection for U.S. Forests," *New York Times*, 14 October 1999, A1.

2. "Remote, Rocky, Barren, Bushy Wild-Woody Widerness" (pages 27–46)

The authors gratefully acknowledge insights and edits from David Barrington, Elizabeth Thompson, Paul Bierman, and Steve Trombulak. The quotation in the title is from William Cronon, *Changes in the Land: Indians, Colonists, and the Ecology of New England*, (New York: Hill and Wang, 1983), 5.

1. "Millennium Moments: Biodiversity: New Term, Old NGS Concern," *National Geographic* (February 1999): xiv.

2. Wilson Flagg, *A Year Among the Trees, or The Woods and By-ways of New England* (Boston: Estes and Lauriat Press, 1881), 5.

3. Helenette Silver, *A History of New Hampshire Game and Furbearers*, Survey Report No. 6 (Concord, N.H.: New Hampshire Fish and Game Department, 1957), 21.

4. Cronon, *Changes in the Land*, 23.

5. Ibid., 22–23.

6. Ibid., 34–35.

7. Gordon G. Whitney, *From Coastal Wilderness to Fruited Plain: A History of Environmental Change in Temperate North America from 1500 to the Present* (New York: Cambridge University Press, 1994), 48.

8. Whitney, *From Coastal Wilderness*, 49.

9. Christopher McGrory Klyza and Stephen C. Trombulak, *The Story of Vermont: A Natural and Cultural History* (Hanover, N.H.: University Press of New England, 1999), 7–18.

10. Cronon, *Changes in the Land*, 38.

11. Silver, *A History of New Hampshire Game*, 2.

12. Whitney, *From Coastal Wilderness*, 120.

13. Stanley W. Bromley, "The Original Forest Types of Southern New England," *Ecological Monographs*, 5 (1935): 74.

14. Flagg, *A Year Among the Trees*, 226.

15. Bromley, "Original Forest Types," 65; Whitney, *From Coastal Wilderness*, 213.

16. George Perkins Marsh, "Address Delivered Before the Agricultural Society of Rutland County," *Rutland Herald* (Vermont, 1848), 18.

17. Henry David Thoreau, *The Journal of Henry D. Thoreau*, ed. Bradford Torrey and Francis H. Allen (Boston: Houghton Mifflin, 1906), 220–21; Henry David Thoreau, *Faith in a Seed: The Dispersion of Seeds and Other Late Natural History Writings* (Washington, D.C.: Island Press, 1993), 169.

18. Mary Byrd Davis, *Old Growth in the East: A Survey* (Richmond, Vt.: Cenozoic Society, 1993), 10.

19. Thomas G. Siccama, "Presettlement and Present Forest Vegetation in Northern Vermont, with Special Reference to Chittenden County," *American Midland Naturalist* 85 (1971): 160.

20. Whitney, *From Coastal Wilderness*, 56–59.

21. John R. Stilgoe, *Common Landscape of America, 1580–1845* (New Haven, Conn.: Yale University Press, 1982), 46; Whitney, *From Coastal Wilderness*, 135–38.

22. Stilgoe *Common Landscape*, 43–45.

23. Ibid., 77–80.

24. Whitney, *From Coastal Wilderness*, 132.

25. John Canup, *The Emergence of an American Identity in Colonial New England* (Middletown, Conn.: Wesleyan University Press, 1990), 22.

26. Whitney, *From Coastal Wilderness*, 325.

27. Ibid., 151–54.

28. Cronon, *Changes in the Land*, 139–40.

29. Charles W. Johnson, *The Nature of Vermont* (Hanover, N.H.: University Press of New England, 1980), 53.

30. Ibid.; Whitney, *From Coastal Wilderness*, 147–48.

31. Cronon, *Changes in the Land*, 118.

32. Tom Wessels, *Reading the Forested Landscape: A Natural History of New England* (Woodstock, Vt.: The Countryman Press, 1997), 72; Whitney, *From Coastal Wilderness*, 82; Bromley, "Original Forest Types," 66.

33. Whitney, *From Coastal Wilderness*, 190.

34. Ibid., 285–86.

35. Timothy Dwight, *Travels in New England and New York*, vol. 1 (Cambridge: Harvard University Press, 1821), 222.

36. Whitney, *From Coastal Wilderness*, 224–26.

37. Ibid., 226.

38. Ibid., 193.

39. Flagg, *A Year Among the Trees*, 5.

40. Whitney, *From Coastal Wilderness*, 286–87.

41. Ibid., 242–45. A study of pond sediments and alluvial fans in Vermont linked European settlement with the highest rates of hillslope erosion since the retreat of the Laurentide Ice Sheet, 12,000 years b.p. See Paul Bierman, Andrea Lini, Paul Zehfuss, Amy Church, P. Thompson Davis, John Southon, and Lyn Baldwin, "Postglacial Ponds and Alluvial Fans: Recorders of Holocene Landscape History," *GSA Today*, 7, no. 10 (1997): 1–8.

42. Cronon, *Changes in the Land*, 148.

43. Marsh, "Address," 18.

44. Greg Streveler, Gustavus, Alaskan naturalist, personal communication, July 1993.

45. Whitney, *From Coastal Wilderness*, 305–12.

46. Zadock Thompson, *Natural History of Vermont* (Rutland, Vt.: Charles E. Tuttle Company, 1853), 51.

47. Aldo Leopold, *A Sand County Almanac* (New York: Oxford University Press, 1949), 132.

48. Bill McKibben, "An Explosion of Green," *The Atlantic Monthly* (April 1995), 67.

49. Alfred J. Godin, *Wild Mammals of New England* (Baltimore: John Hopkins University Press, 1977), 271.

50. Ibid., 291.

51. Ernest Thompson Seton, *Lives of Game Animals*, vol. 1, (Garden City, N.Y.: Doubleday, Doran & Company, 1929), 64–65.

52. McKibben, "An Explosion of Green," 83.

53. Ibid.

54. Peter Matthiessen, *Wildlife in America* (New York: Viking, 1987), 79.

55. Whitney, *From Coastal Wilderness*, 301.

56. Dwight, *Travels in New England*, vol. 2, 72.

57. Bill McKibben, *Hope, Human and Wild: True Stories of Living Lightly on the Earth* (Boston: Little, Brown, 1995), 13.

58. Johnson, *Nature of Vermont*, 52–58.

59. Wessels, *Reading the Forested Landscape*, 61.

60. Thanks to Chris McGrory Klyza for supplying this data. His sources are cited in chapter 1.

61. Cronon, *Changes in the Land*, 42; Whitney, *From Coastal Wilderness*, 99–101.

62. Whitney, *From Coastal Widerness*, 183.

63. Ibid., 290.

64. Clayton D. A. Rubec and Gerry O. Lee, eds., *Conserving Vitality and Diversity: Proceedings of the World Conservation Congress Workshop on Alien Invasive Species* (Ottawa, Canada: North American Wetlands Conservation Council, 1996), 1–5.

65. European species spread rapidly through the New World. Native Americans called the common plantain "Englishman's Foot" since it seemed to spring up wherever the colonists walked (Cronon, *Changes in the Land*, 142).

66. McKibben, *Hope, Human and Wild*, 36; Chris Bright, *Life Out of Bounds: Bioinvasion in a Borderless World* (New York: Norton, 1998), 78.

67. John Pastor and W. M. Post, "Response of Northern Forests to CO_2-induced Climate Change," *Nature* 334 (1988): 55.

68. Ibid., 55–58.

69. McKibben, *Hope, Human and Wild*, 51.

3. Old-Growth Forests of the Northeast (pages 47–74)

1. Simon Schama, *Landscape and Memory* (New York: Knopf, 1995).

2. John Grena, Charles Cogbill, Lissa Widoff, and Hank Tyler, "Natural Old-Growth Forest Stands in Maine and their Relevance to the Critical Areas Program" (Augusta, Maine: State Planning Office, 1983).

3. Stephen Kulik, Pete Salmansohn, Matthew Schmidt, and Heidi Welch, *The Audubon Society Field Guide to the Natural Places of the Northeast Inland* (New York: Pantheon Books, 1984), 75–76.

4. Howard S. Russell, *Indian New England before the Mayflower* (Hanover, N.H.: University Press of New England, 1980), 8.

5. Gifford Pinchot, *Breaking New Ground* (1947; reprint, Washington, D.C.: Island Press, 1987), 325.

6. Mary Byrd Davis, *Old Growth in the East: A Survey* (Richmond, Vt.: Cenozoic Society, 1993).

7. Mary Byrd Davis, ed., *Eastern Old-Growth Forests: Prospects for Rediscovery and Recovery* (Washington, D.C.: Island Press, 1996), 113–24.

8. Dr. Lee Frelich, University of Minnesota, personal communication, August 1999.

9. Lucy Tyrrell, Geogory J. Nowacki, Thomas R. Crow, David S. Buckley, Elizabeth A. Naeuetz, Jeffrey N. Niese, Jeanette L. Rollinger, and John C. Zasada, *Information about Old Growth for Selected Forest Type Groups in the Eastern United States* (St. Paul, Minn.: U.S. Forest Service, North Central Forest Experiment Station, 1998).

4. Public Lands and Wild Lands in the Northeast (pages 75–103)

I thank Tim Allen, Larry Davis, Chad Dawson, Paula Martin, Sheila McGrory-Klyza, Carol Morris, David Vail, Harold Ward, and Ian Worley for their helpful comments on an earlier draft of this chapter.

1. In addition, the Army Corps of Engineers owns over 100,000 acres in the Northeast connected to its water projects. Throughout this chapter, information on acreage of federal conservation lands, federal wilderness, state conservation lands, and state wilderness is from the sources identified for table 4.1. These figures are constantly changing—usually increasing. In order to maintain some consistency, the federal figures are from 1998, the most current data available for all federal conservation agencies on a state-by-state basis (supplied by the General Services Administration). Figures for state lands were obtained from relevant state agencies, and are as up to date as possible. In some instances, more recent figures for particular federal and state units are used. When this is done, the source is indicated.

2. William E. Shands, "The Lands Nobody Wanted: The Legacy of the Eastern National Forests," in *The Origins of the National Forests*, ed. Harold K. Steen (Durham, N.C.: Forest History Society, 1992), 19–44.

3. Ibid., 21–29.

4. Craig W. Allin, *The Politics of Wilderness Preservation* (Westport, Conn.: Greenwood Press, 1982), 158–61, 186–92; Dave Foreman and Howie Wolke, *The Big Outside: A Descriptive Inventory of the Big Wilderness Areas of the U.S.* (Tucson: Ned Ludd Books, 1989), 363–66; "Roadless Forests Topic of National Meeting," *Addison Independent* (Vermont), 16 December 1999, 10A; David E. Sanger, "Clinton Proposes Wider Protection for U.S. Forests," *New York Times*, 14 October 1999, A1.

5. Many histories of the Adirondacks have been published. Among the most useful are: Frank Graham, *The Adirondack Park: A Political History* (1978; reprint, Syracuse: Syracuse University Press, 1984); Philip G. Terrie, *Forever Wild: A Cultural History of Wilderness in the Adirondacks* (1985; reprint, Syracuse: Syracuse University Press, 1994); Philip G. Terrie, *Contested Terrain: A New History of Nature and People in the Adirondacks* (Syracuse: Syracuse University Press, 1997).

6. Department of Environmental Conservation, *State of New York Adirondack Park State Land Master Plan* (Albany: State of New York, 1997); Elaine Moss, ed., *Land Use Controls in New York State: A Handbook on the Legal Rights of Citizens* (New York: Dial Press, 1975), 106–31. All acreage figures for the Adirondack Park are state-supplied estimates. Much of the land has not been surveyed since state acquisition. Of the total park acreage, roughly 335,000 acres is water. Hence, private lands constitute about 52 percent of the park land; state lands about 48 percent of the park land.

7. The Commission of the Adirondacks in the Twenty-First Century, *The Adirondack Park in the Twenty-First Century* (Albany: State of New York, 1990); New York Department of Environmental Conservation, Bureau of Public Lands, personal communication, August 1999.

8. New York Department of Environmental Conservation, Bureau of Public Lands, personal communication, August 1999. These figures total nearly 300,000 acres less than the total given for state-owned lands in the Adirondack Park. The discrepancy is accounted for by lands awaiting classification and by the previously mentioned point that New York has not surveyed many of these lands since their acquisition.

9. New York Department of Environmental Conservation, Bureau of Public Lands, personal communication, August 1999; Moss, *Land Use Controls*, 132–44. The land categories in the Catskill Park have the same meaning as those in the Adirondack Park.

10. Department of Environmental Conservation, Bureau of Public Lands, personal communication, August–September 1999; Alvin T. M. Lee and Hugh H.

Wooten, "The Management of State Lands," in *Land, USDA Yearbook of Agriculture, 1958* (Washington, D.C.: Government Printing Office, 1958), 77–79; New York State Office of Parks, Recreation and Historic Preservation, personal communication, August 1999.

11. Shands, "The Lands Nobody Wanted," 32, 34; U.S. Fish and Wildlife Service, "Query the National Wildlife Refuge System Lands Database," http://www.fws.gov.r9realty/nwrs.htm#unitsum, 1997, visited 26 August 1999; U.S. National Park Service, "The National Park Service—Listing of Acreage by Park," http://www.nature.nps.gov/stats/acreagebypark.htm, 1998, visited 22 April 1999.

12. Pennsylvania Department of Conservation and Natural Resources, Bureau of Forestry, personal communication, August 1999; Gordon G. Whitney, *From Coastal Wilderness to Fruited Plain: A History of Environmental Change in Temperate North America from 1500 to the Present* (New York: Cambridge University Press, 1994), 331.

13. Pennsylvania Department of Conservation and Natural Resources, Bureau of Forestry, "Pennsylvania State Forest Natural Areas and Wild Areas," no date.

14. Pennsylvania Department of Conservation and Natural Resources, "Pennsylvania State Parks and Forests," no date; Pennsylvania Department of Conservation and Natural Resources, Pennsylvania State Parks, "Natural Areas," http://www.dcnr.state.pa.us/stateparks/natural/naturalareas.htm, visited 17 August 1999.

15. Pennsylvania Game Commission, personal communication, August 1999; Pennsylvania Game Commission, "What You Should Know about the Pennsylvania Game Commission," http://www.state.pa.us/PA_Exec/PGC/shouldkn.htm, 1999, visited 19 August 1999.

16. Allegheny National Forest, "Allegheny National Forest," http://www.fs.fed.us/r9/allegheny/ANF_statistics_070699.html, 1999, visited 20 August 1999; Appalachian National Scenic Trail, personal communication, August 1999; Delaware Water Gap National Recreation Area, personal communication, August 1999; U.S. Forest Service, "Land Areas by State," http://www.fs.fed.us/land/staff/LAR98/table4_areas_by_state, 1998, visited 20 August 1999.

17. Appalachian National Scenic Trail, personal communication, August 1999; U.S. Fish and Wildlife Service, "Query the National Wildlife Refuge System Lands Database," http://www.fws.gov.r9realty/nwrs.htm#unitsum, 1997, visited 26 August, 1999; U.S. National Park Service, "Listing of Acreage by Park"; David Vail and Lars Hultkrantz, "Property Rights and Sustainable Nature Tourism: Adaptation and Mal-Adaptation in Dalarna (Sweden) and Maine (USA),"*Ecological Economics* (forthcoming).

18. Percival Baxter is quoted in John W. Hakola, *Legacy of a Lifetime: The Story of Baxter State Park* (Woolrich, Maine: TBW Books, 1981), 101; also see pages 101–23 and generally; Lloyd C. Irland, *Wildlands and Woodlots: The Story of New England's Forests* (Hanover, N.H.: University Press of New England, 1982), 99–100.

19. Irland, *Wildlands and Woodlots*, 104–105; Maine Bureau of Parks and Lands, "State Parks, Public Reserved Lands, Historic Sites," http://state.me.us/doc/prkslnds/chart.htm#lands, visited 30, July 1999; John Perry and Jane Greverus Perry, *The Sierra Club Guide to the Natural Areas of New England*, rev. ed. (San Francisco: Sierra Club Books, 1997), I–III.

20. Maine Bureau of Parks and Lands, "State Parks, Public Reserved Lands, Historic Sites," http://state.me.us/doc/prkslnds/chart.htm#lands, visited 30 July, 1999.

21. Maine Bureau of Parks and Lands, personal communication, August 1999.

22. Foreman and Wolke, *The Big Outside*, 387–402; "NE Forests: $35M Deal Preserves 185,000 Acres in Maine," *Greenwire*, 15 December 1998; Northern Forest

Alliance, "Wildlands: A Conservation Strategy for the Northern Forest" (Mont-pelier, Vt.: Northern Forest Alliance, 1997); "Eight Million Acre Headwaters Wilderness Reserve System Proposed," *Northern Forest Forum*, Headwaters Restoration Issue, 1995. The *Northern Forest Forum* provides excellent coverage of land sales in Maine, New Hampshire, Vermont, and the Adirondacks.

23. Irland, *Wildlands and Woodlots*, 101–103; Richard W. Judd, *Common Lands, Common People: The Origins of Conservation in Northern New England* (Cambridge: Harvard University Press, 1997), 99–111; William E. Shands and Robert G. Healy, *The Lands Nobody Wanted: Policy for National Forests in the Eastern United States*, (Washington, D.C.: Conservation Foundation, 1977), 237–44; U.S. Forest Service, "Land Areas In Multiple States," http://www.fs.fed.us/land/staff/LAR98/tables_areas_in_multiple_states, 1998, visited 12 August 1999.

24. New Hampshire Department of Resources and Economic Development, personal communication, August 1999; New Hampshire Department of Resources and Economic Development, "Public Lands of the Department of Resources and Economic Development" (Concord, N.H., 1996); Perry and Perry, *Natural Areas of New England*, 168–231.

25. Foreman and Wolke, *The Big Outside*, 400–405; The Wilderness Society, Appalachian Mountain Club, and Conservation Law Foundation, "Mountain Treasures: Roadless Areas in the White Mountain National Forest" (Boston: The Wilderness Society, Appalachian Mountain Club, and Conservation Law Foundation, 1999).

26. Christopher McGrory Klyza and Stephen C. Trombulak, *The Story of Vermont: A Natural and Cultural History* (Hanover, N.H.: University Press of New England, 1999), 133.

27. Appalachian National Scenic Trail, personal communication, August 1999; Klyza and Trombulak, *The Story of Vermont*, 98–100, 136; U.S. Fish and Wildlife Service, "Query the National Wildlife Refuge System Lands Database," http://www.fws.gov.r9realty/nwrs.htm#unitsum, 1997, visited 26 August 1999.

28. Klyza and Trombulak, *The Story of Vermont*, 98, 109, 125, 132–35; Vermont Agency of Natural Resources, "WMA Maps," http://www.anr.state.vt.us/wma-maps/index.html, 1999, visited 27 July 1999; Vermont Agency of Natural Resources, "State Lands Listing," http://www.state.vt.us/anr/fpr/lands/lands.htm, visited 27 July 1999.

29. Vermont Agency of Natural Resources, "State Lands Listing"; Vermont Agency of Natural Resources, "State Natural Areas," http://state.vt.us/anr/fpr/lands/landinfo/nat_area.htm, visited 30 July 1999.

30. Foreman and Wolke, *The Big Outside*, 401; Vermont Land Trust, "An Update on the Vermont Champion Lands Project," http://www.vlt.org/CIupdate.html, 1999, visited 3 August 1999.

31. Henry Barbour, Tim Simmons, Patricia Swain, and Henry Woolsey, *Our Irreplaceable Heritage: Protecting Biodiversity in Massachusetts* (Boston and Westborough: Massachusetts Division of Fisheries and Wildlife and Massachusetts Nature Conservancy, 1998), 68.

32. Massachusetts Natural Heritage and Endangered Species Program, personal communication, August 1999; Massachusetts Department of Forests and Parks, personal communication, August 1999; Massachusetts Department of Forests and Parks, "Massachusetts Forests and Parks: A Guide to Recreation" (Boston: Department of Environmental Management, 1999); Massachusetts Department of Forests and Parks, "One Hundred Years of Massachusetts State Forests and Parks," http://www.state.ma.us/dem/forparks.htm, 1998, visited 29 July 1999; Metropolitan District Commission, Quabbin Reservoir, personal communication,

July 1999; Perry and Perry, *Natural Areas of New England*, 232–339; U.S. National Park Service, "Listing of Acreage by Park."

33. Barbour et al., *Our Irreplaceable Heritage*, 66–80; Thomas Conuel, *Quabbin: The Accidental Wilderness* (Amherst: University of Massachusetts Press, 1990); Jan E. Dizard, *Going Wild: Hunting, Animal Rights, and the Contested Meaning of Nature* (Amherst: University of Massachusetts Press, 1994), 5–14, 25–33.

34. Robert J. Mason, *Contested Lands: Conflict and Compromise in New Jersey's Pine Barrens* (Philadelphia: Temple University Press, 1992), 2, 73–105; New Jersey Pinelands Commission, personal communication, July 1999; New Jersey Pinelands Commission, New Jersey Pinelands Commission Homepage, http://www.state.nj.us/pinelands/, visited 29 July 1999; Kevin J. Rielley, Wendy U. Larsen, and Clifford L. Weaver, "Partnership in the Pinelands," in *Land Reform, American Style*, ed. Charles C. Geisler and Frank J. Popper (Totowa, N.J.: Rowman and Allanheld, 1984), 131.

35. Mason, *Contested Lands*, 50–59.

36. Michael P. Brown, *New Jersey Parks, Forests, and Natural Areas: A Guide*, rev. ed. (New Brunswick, N.J.: Rutgers University Press, 1997); Mason, *Contested Lands*, 73–74, 121–22; New Jersey Division of Parks and Forestry, "New Jersey State Parks, Forests, Recreation Areas and Marinas," http://www.state.nj.us/dep/forestry/parks/parkindx.htm, visited 29 July 1999; New Jersey Division of Fish, Game and Wildlife, "Wildlife Management Areas," http://www.state.nj.us/dep/fgw/wmaland.htm, 1999, visited 29 July 1999; U.S. Fish and Wildlife Service, "Query the National Wildlife Refuge System Lands Database."

37. Delaware Water Gap National Recreation Area, personal communication, August 1999; New Jersey Division of Parks and Forestry, "New Jersey State Parks, Forests, Recreation Areas and Marinas."

38. Brown, *New Jersey Parks*; New Jersey Division of Fish, Game and Wildlife, "Wildlife Management Areas"; New Jersey Division of Parks and Forestry, "Natural Resources," http://www.state.nj.us/dep/forestry/natural.htm, visited 29 July 1999; New Jersey Division of Parks and Forestry, personal communication, July 1999.

39. Connecticut Department of Environmental Protection, "State Forests," http://dep.state.ct.us/rec/parks.htm#Forests, 1998, visited 27 July 1999; Connecticut Department of Environmental Protection, personal communication, August 1999; Connecticut Department of Environmental Protection, Land Acquisition and Management Division, personal communication, July 1999; Perry and Perry, *Natural Areas of New England*, 376–436.

40. Perry and Perry, *Natural Areas of New England*, 340–75; Rhode Island Department of Environmental Management, personal communication, August 1999.

41. Northern Forest Alliance, "Wildlands."

42. Barbour et al., *Our Irreplaceable Heritage*, 71.

43. Mark R. Peterson, "Wilderness by State Mandate: A Survey of State-Designated Wilderness Areas," *Natural Areas Journal* 16 (1996): 192–97. The other states with such programs are Alaska, California, Maryland, Michigan, Minnesota, Missouri, and Wisconsin.

5. Ecological Reserve Design in the Northeast (page 107–123)

1. Reed F. Noss, "The Wildlands Project: Land Conservation Strategy," *Wild Earth*, Special Issue, (1992): 10–25.

2. James R. Karr and D. R. Dudley, "Ecological Perspectives on Water Quality Goals," *Environmental Management*, 5 (1981): 55–68.

3. Discussed in more detail in Reed F. Noss, Eric Dinerstein, Barry Gilbert, Michael Gilpin, Brian J. Miller, John Terborgh, and Steve Trombulak, "Core Areas: Where Nature Reigns," in *Continental Conservation: Scientific Foundations of Regional Reserve Networks*, ed. Michael E. Soulé and John Terborgh (Washington: Island Press, 1999), 99–128.

4. Martha Groom, Deborah B. Jensen, Richard L. Knight, Steve Gatewood, Lisa Mills, Diane Boyd-Heger, L. Scott Mills, and Michael Soulé, "Buffer Zones: Benefits and Dangers of Compatible Stewardship," in *Continental Conservation*, 171–97.

5. Andy Dobson, Katherine Ralls, Mercedes Foster, Michael Soulé, Daniel Simberloff, Dan Doak, James A. Estes, L. Scott Mills, David Mattson, Rodolfo Dirzo, Hector Arita, Sadie Ryan, Elliot A. Norse, Reed F. Noss, and David Johns, "Connectivity: Maintaining Flows in Fragmented Landscapes," in *Continental Conservation*, 129–70.

6. Noss et al., "Core Areas."

7. Groom et al., "Buffer Zanes."

8. Craig W. Allin, *The Politics of Wilderness Preservation* (Westport, Conn.: Greenwood Press, 1982), 278.

9. Reed F. Noss, "Protecting Natural Areas in Fragmented Landscapes," *Natural Areas Journal* 7 (1987): 2–13; UNESCO, "Task Force on Criteria and Guidelines for the Choice and Establishment of Biosphere Reserves," Man and the Biosphere Report No. 22 (Bonn, Germany: UNESCO, 1974).

10. Reed F. Noss, "Wilderness Recovery and Ecological Restoration: An Example for Florida," *Earth First! Journal* (22 September 1985): 18–19; Noss, "Protecting Natural Areas."

11. Reed F. Noss, "Conserving Oregon's Coast Range Biodiversity: A Conservation and Restoration Plan" (Newport, Oreg.: Coast Range Association, 1992); Reed F. Noss, "A Conservation Plan for the Oregon Coast Range: Some Preliminary Suggestions," *Natural Areas Journal* 13 (1993): 276–90.

12. Sky Island Alliance, "Home Page of the Sky Island Alliance," www.lobo.net/skisland/siaopen1.htm, 1977, visited on 16 August 1999; James R. Strittholt, Reed F. Noss, Pam A. Frost, Ken Vance-Borland, Carlos Carroll, and G. Heilman, Jr., "A Conservation Assessment and Science-based Plan for the Klamath-Siskiyou Ecoregion," report to the Siskiyou Regional Education Project, 1999; Reed F. Noss, James R. Strittholt, Ken Vance-Borland, Carlos Carroll, and Pam Frost, "A Conservation Plan for the Klamath-Siskiyou Ecoregion," *Natural Areas Journal* (forthcoming); "The Yellowstone to Yukon Conservation Initiative," www.rockies.ca/y2y/, 1999, visited on 16 August 1999; Theodore Weber and John Wolf, "Maryland's Green Infrastructure: Using Landscape Assessment Tools to Identify a Regional Conservation Strategy," presented at the annual meeting of the Society for Conservation Biology, College Park, Maryland, June 1999.

13. Noss, "The Wildlands Project"; Steve Trombulak, "How to Design an Ecological Reserve System," *Wild Earth Special Report* 1 (1996): 1–20; Reed F. Noss and Alan Y. Cooperrider, *Saving Nature's Legacy: Protecting and Restoring Biodiversity* (Washington, D.C.: Island Press, 1994).

14. Peter Quinby, Steve Trombulak, Thomas Lee, Jeff Lane, Michael Henry, Robert Long, and Paula MacKay, "Opportunities for Wildlife Habitat Connectivity between Algonquin Park, Ontario, and the Adirondack Park, New York," report by The Greater Laurentian Wildlands Project, South Burlington, Vermont, 1999.

15. Because its work is not yet complete, the VBP has not published any details of its work. The following description is based on my own involvement with the project's technical work group and on conversations with other members of the technical workgroup.

16. Phil E. Girton and David E. Capen, "A Report on Biophysical Regions in Vermont," unpublished report (Waterbury, Vt.: Vermont Department of Forests, Parks, and Recreation, 1997).

17. Aquatics Classification Workgroup, *A Classification of the Aquatic Communities of Vermont*, private printing, prepared for the Vermont Nature Conservancy and the Vermont Biodiversity Project, 1998.

18. Northern Forest Lands Council, *Finding Common Ground* (Concord, N.H.: Northern Forest Lands Council, 1994); Jamie Sayen, personal communication, July 1999; Mike Stevens, personal communication, August 1999.

19. Robert Long and Paula MacKay, personal communication, August 1999, based on an unpublished draft report of the Maine Wildlands Reserve Network. The final report, when completed, will be available from the Greater Laurentian Wildlands Project, 4 Laurel Hill Drive, South Burlington, VT 05403.

20. Brian Miller, Richard Reading, James Strittholt, Carlos Carroll, Reed Noss, Michael Soulé, Oscar Sánchez, John Terborgh, Donald Brightsmith, Ted Cheeseman, and Dave Foreman, "Focal Species in the Design of Nature Reserve Networks," *Wild Earth* (Winter 1998/99): 81–92.

21. Trombulak, "How to Design an Ecological Reserve Sustem."

22. David Publicover, personal communication, August 1999.

23. Stephen C. Trombulak and Chris Frissell, "Review of the Ecological Effects of Roads on Terrestrial and Aquatic Communities," *Conservation Biology* (forthcoming).

24. Paul Paquet, personal communication, August 1999.

25. Michael E. Soulé and Reed F. Noss, "Rewilding and Biodiversity: Complementary Goals for Continental Conservation," *Wild Earth* (Fall 1998): 18–28.

26. John Terborgh and Michael E. Soulé, "Why We Need Mega-Reserves — and How to Design Them," in *Continental Conservation*, 199–209.

6. An Opportunity for Big Wilderness in the Northern Appalachians (pages 124–156)

1. On the Diamond International lands, see Norman Boucher, "Whose Woods These Are," *Wilderness* (Fall 1989): 18–41.

2. Stephen C. Harper, Laura L. Falk, and Edward W. Rankin, *The Northern Forest Lands Study of New England and New York* (Rutland, Vt: U.S. Department of Agriculture, Forest Service, 1990); Northern Forest Lands Council, *Finding Common Ground: Conserving the Northern Forest* (Concord, N.H.: Northern Forest Lands Council, 1994); Northern Forest Alliance, "Wildlands: A Conservation Strategy for the Northern Forest" (Montpelier, Vt.: Northern Forest Alliance, 1997).

3. Center for Rural Studies, "Attitudes and Resource Use: A Study of North Country Citizens" (Burlington: University of Vermont, Center for Rural Studies, 1990; also cited in Harper, Falk, and Rankin, *The Northern Forest Lands Study*, 49); Robert Manning, Jennifer Treadwell, Ben Minteer, William Valliere, "Forest Values, Environmental Ethics, and Attitudes toward National Forest Management" (Burlington: University of Vermont, School of Natural Resources, 1998), 25); "Public Opinion on and Attitudes toward the Reintroduction of the Eastern

Timber Wolf to Adirondack Park," Responsive Management under contract to Defenders of Wildlife, 1996. Public opinion surveys conducted in the dozen years since the announcement of the Diamond land sale consistently reveal that between 70 and 85 percent of the residents of the region support the reforms necessary to achieve an ecologically healthy culture. In 1990, residents of the northernmost Connecticut River Valley in Vermont and New Hampshire overwhelmingly supported public acquisition of timberlands for wilderness and wildlife protection. Eighty-five percent supported acquisition for wilderness protection. More recently, surveys of users of the White Mountain National Forest and the Green Mountain National Forest found overwhelming support for more wilderness designations and strong opposition to clearcutting on national forests. The results were such a slap in the face of longstanding Forest Service management practices that the agency suppressed the studies until they were leaked to the public. Early in 1996 the Maine timber industry conducted a survey of Maine voters and discovered that over 70 percent intended to vote to ban clearcutting in a referendum ballot initiative scheduled for the fall. The referendum was subsequently defeated by the expenditure of about $6 million in political advertising. Another survey found strong support for wolf reintroduction in the Adirondacks.

4. Jamie Sayen, "On Wilderness and Cultural Restoration in the Northern Appalachians," *Wild Earth* (Winter 1998/99): 24.

5. Christopher McGrory Klyza and Stephen C. Trombulak, *The Story of Vermont: A Natural and Cultural History* (Hanover, N.H.: University Press of New England, 1999), 55; Colin G. Calloway, *The Western Abenakis of Vermont, 1600–1800: War, Migration, and the Survival of an Indian People* (Norman: University of Oklahoma Press, 1990).

6. Maine Natural Areas Program, "Biological Diversity in Maine: An Assessment of Status and Trends in the Terrestrial and Freshwater Landscape" (Augusta, Maine, 1996); Craig G. Lorimer, "The Presettlement Forest and Natural Disturbance Cycle of Northeastern Maine," *Ecology* 58 (1977): 139–48; David Publicover, "The Current Condition of New Hampshire's Forests Is Considerably Different than that Found in Pre-settlement Times," in *New Hampshire Forest Resources Plan: Assessment Report* (Concord, N.H.: New Hampshire Department of Resources and Economic Development, Division of Forests and Lands, 1995); Gordon G. Whitney, *From Coastal Wilderness to Fruited Plain: A History of Environmental Change in Temperate North America 1500 to the Present* (New York: Cambridge University Press, 1994); James R. Runkle, "Patterns of Disturbance in Some Old-Growth Mesic Forests of Eastern North America," *Ecology* 63 (1982): 1533–46; Steven B. Selva, "Using Lichens to Assess Ecological Continuity in Northeastern Forests," in *Eastern Old-Growth Forests: Prospects for Rediscovery and Recovery*, ed. Mary Byrd Davis (Washington, D.C.: Island Press, 1996); Robert S. Seymour and Ronald Lemin, "Timber Supply Projections for Maine 1980–2080," University of Maine Cooperative Forestry Research Unit, Bulletin 7, Misc. Reprint 337 (Orono: University of Maine, Agricultural Forestry Experiment Station, 1989).

7. Henry David Thoreau, *The Maine Woods* (1864; reprint, New York: Penguin, 1988), 377, 37, 189, 93, 107, 206.

8. Mary Byrd Davis, ed., *Eastern Old-Growth Forests*, 20–21.

9. Calloway, *Western Akenakis*; Gregory H. Nobles, *American Frontiers: Cultural Encounters and Continental Conquest* (New York: Hill and Wang, 1997), 52.

10. Tom Wessels, *Reading the Forested Landscape: A Natural History of New England* (Woodstock, Vt: Countryman Press, 1997), 99–111.

11. Ibid., 111; Klyza and Trombulak, *The Story of Vermont*, 47–50.

12. Martha Carlson and Richard Ober, 1998 "The Weeks Act," *Forest Notes* (Summer, 1998): 3–7; Philip T. Coolidge, *History of the Maine Woods* (Bangor, Maine: Furbish-Roberts Printing Company, 1963); Richard W. Judd, *Aroostook: A Century of Logging in Northern Maine* (Orono: University of Maine Press, 1989); David C. Smith, *A History of Lumbering in Maine, 1861–1960* (Orono: University of Maine Press, 1972); Richard G. Wood, *A History of Lumbering in Maine, 1820–1861* (Orono: University of Maine Press, 1971).

13. Wood, *Lumbering in Maine, 1820–1861*; Smith, *Lumbering in Maine, 1861–1960*.

14. Smith, *Lumbering in Maine, 1861–1960*.

15. Mitch Lansky, "The 1995 U.S. Forest Service Inventory of the Maine Woods: What Does it Show?" (Lancaster, N.H.: Northern Appalachian Restoration Project, 1998), 9.

16. Mitch Lansky, *Beyond the Beauty Strip: Saving What's Left of Our Forests*, (Gardiner, Maine: Tilbury House, 1992). Lansky's book is the definitive critique of the paper industry in Maine. After nearly a decade, it remains timely. The author's foresight has been verified by dozens of strange developments in the Maine paper industry since its publication.

17. Lloyd C. Irland, *Wildlands and Woodlots: The Story of New England's Forests* (Hanover, N.H.: University Press of New England, 1982), 104–105.

18. Mitch Lansky, "Maine Paper Industry Changes by Year 1985–1993," *The Northern Forest Forum* (Spring Equinox 1994): 12–13.

19. Ibid., 12; Mitch Lansky, "The Northern Forest Forum Index," *The Northern Forest Forum* (Mid-Autumn, 1994): 21.

20. "Challenging the Paper Plantation: An Interview with Hilton Hafford, July 13, 1999, Allagash, Maine," *The Northern Forest Forum* (Autumn Equinox 1999): 7–13.

21. Frederick Jackson Turner, "The Significance of the Frontier in American History," in *The Frontier in American History*, (1899; reprint New York: Dover, 1996), 1–38.

22. For a discussion of the many different critiques in recent years, see John Mack Faragher, "The Significance of the Frontier in American Historiography," in *Rereading Frederick Jackson Turner* (New York: Henry Holt, 1994), 225–41.

23. Henry David Thoreau, *The Writings of Henry David Thoreau: Journal*, vol. 8, ed. Bradford Torrey (1856; reprint Boston and New York: Houghton Mifflin, 1906), 221.

24. Philip G. Terrie, *Contested Terrain: A New History of Nature and People in the Adirondacks* (Syracuse: Syracuse University Press, 1997); Carlson and Ober, "The Weeks Act."

25. Terrie, *Contested Terrain*.

26. Richard W. Judd, *Common Lands, Common People: The Origins of Conservation in Northern New England* (Cambridge: Harvard University Press, 1997); Klyza and Trombulak, *The Story of Vermont*.

27. Michael Soulé and John Terborgh, eds., *Continental Conservation: Scientific Foundations of Regional Reserve Networks* (Washington, D.C.: Island Press, 1999), 39.

28. Wessels, *Reading the Forested Landscape*, 96, 156, 158.

29. Ibid., 164.

30. Maine Natural Areas Program, "Biological Diversity in Maine," 56, 71.

31. Scientific Advisory Group, "An Assessment of the Biodiversity of New Hampshire with Recommendations for Conservation Action" (Concord, N.H.: New Hampshire Ecological Reserve System Project, 1998). See chapter 5 for Steve Trombulak's comments on the Vermont initiative.

32. Soulé and Terborgh, *Continental Conservation*, 1–2.

33. Ibid., 71.

34. Carl Reidel, "The Political Process of the Northern Forest Lands Study," in *The Future of the Northern Forest*, ed. Christopher McGrory Klyza and Stephen C. Trombulak (Hanover, N.H.: University of New England Press, 1994).

35. This definition of biodiversity comes from a 1987 report by the U.S. Office of Technology Assessment.

36. Soulé and Terborgh, *Continental Conservation*, 101–104.

37. The Wildlands Project Mission Statement, from *Wild Earth* (Winter 1995/96): inside cover, 1.

38. The following conservation biologists contributed to *Continental Conservation*, which grew out of a workshop sponsored by the Wildlands Project: Hector Arita, Diane Boyd-Heger, Eric Dinerstein, Rodolfo Dirzo, Don Doak, Andy Dobson, James A. Estes, Mercedes Foster, Barrie Gilbert, Michael Gilpin, Martha Groom, Deborah B. Jenson, Richard Knight, Carlos Martinez del Rio, David Mattson, Brian J. Miller, L. Scott Mills, Lisa Mills, Elliott A. Norse, Reed F. Noss, Paul Paquet, Katherine Ralls, J. Michael Scott, Daniel Simberloff, Michael Soulé, John Terborgh, and Steve Trombulak. For information on the Wildlands Project, contact: TWP, 1955 W. Grant Rd, Suite 148A, Tucson, AZ 85745; telephone: 520-884-0875.

39. Michael Kellett, "Maine Woods National Park: A Proposal," *The Northern Forest Forum* (Mid-summer 1994): 10–11.

40. "Challenging the Paper Plantation: An Interview with Hilton Hafford, July 13, 1999, Allagash, Maine," *The Northern Forest Forum* (Autumn Equinox 1999): 7–13.

41. For information on how to help make the Maine Woods National Park vision a reality, contact Restore: The North Woods, 9 Union St., Hallowell, ME 04347; telephone: 207-626-5635.

42. "Eight Million Acre Headwaters Wilderness Reserve System Proposed," *The Northern Forest Forum*, Headwaters Restoration Issue, 1996.

43. Soulé and Terborgh, *Continental Conservation*, 31.

44. David Carle, "Wild Atlantic Salmon: Dammed Near Extinct," *The Northern Forest Forum* (Summer 1999): 4.

45. Jamie Sayen, "The Appalachian Mountains: Vision and Wilderness," *Earth First!* (1 May 1987): 26–29, 30.

46. Malcolm L. Hunter, George L. Jacobson, and Thompson Webb, "Paleoecology and the Coarse-filter Approach to Maintaining Biological Diversity," *Conservation Biology* 2 (1988): 375–85.

47. Soulé and Terborgh, *Continental Conservation*, 158.

48. Henry David Thoreau, *Walden* (1854; reprint Boston: Beacon Press, 1997), 24.

49. See Bill McKibben, *Hope, Human and Wild: True Stories of Living Lightly on the Earth* (Boston: Little Brown, 1995).

50. Freeman House, *Totem Salmon: Life Lessons from Another Species* (Boston: Beacon Press, 1999), 198.

7. Restoring the Wild (pages 157–181)

1. Henry David Thoreau, *The Writings of Henry David Thoreau: Journal*, vol. 8, ed. Bradford Torry (1856; reprint Boston and New York: Houghton Mifflin, 1906), 220–22.

2. U.S. Congress, Office of Technology Assessment, *Harmful Non-Indigenous Species in the United States*, OTA-F-565 (Washington, D.C.: Government Printing Office, 1993).

3. E. Chris Pielou, *After the Ice Age: The Return of Life to Glaciated North America* (Chicago: University of Chicago Press, 1991).

4. Alastair S. Gunn, "The Restoration of Species and Natural Environments," *Environmental Ethics* 13 (1991): 291–310.

5. Arlie W. Schorger, *The Passenger Pigeon: Its Natural History and Extinction* (Norman: University of Oklahoma Press, 1973).

6. Pielou, *After the Ice Age*.

7. John Terborgh, James A. Estes, Paul Paquet, Katherine Ralls, Diane Boyd-Heger, Brian J. Miller, and Reed F. Noss, "The Role of Top Carnivores in Regulating Terrestrial Ecosystems," in *Continental Conservation: Scientific Foundations of Regional Reserve Networks*, ed. Michael E. Soulé and John Terborgh (Washington, D.C.: Island Press, 1999), 39–64.

8. Although the precise criteria that indicate that a species plays a "keystone" role in a community have been widely debated, it is generally felt that as a class, keystone species are those whose impact on the numbers of individuals in other species far outweighs their own numerical abundance; see L. Scott Mills, Michael E. Soulé, and Daniel F. Doak, "The Keystone Species Concept in Ecology and Conservation," *BioScience* 43 (1993): 219–24.

9. Except where otherwise noted, this historical record was developed primarily from conversations from June to October 1999 with numerous conservation professionals throughout the region. These include Bill Brumback and Greg Lowenberg (New England Wildflower Society), Ken Kimball (Appalachian Mountain Club), Peter Nye, Al Hicks, and Barbara Loucks (New York Department of Environmental Conservation), Kathy Schneider and Steve Young (New York Natural Heritage Program), Liz Thompson (Vermont Nature Conservancy), Tim Simmons (Massachusetts Department of Fish and Wildlife), Bob Eriksen and Jim Sciascia (New Jersey Division of Fish, Game and Wildlife), Marilyn Jordan (Long Island Chapter, The Nature Conservancy), Susi VonOettingen and Michael Amaral (U.S. Fish and Wildlife Service), Joe Kosack (Pennsylvania Game Commission), and Rick Enser (Rhode Island Department of Environmental Management). We also consulted additional written summaries for individual states: James E. Cardoza, Gwilym S. Jones, Thomas W. French, and David B. Halliwell, "Exotic and Translocated Vertebrates of Massachusetts," 2d ed., Fauna of Massachusetts Series No. 6 (Westborough: Massachusetts Division of Fisheries and Wildlife, 1993); Pennsylvania Game Commission, "Pennsylvania's Wildlife Conservation History," www.state.pa.us/PA_Exec/PGC/history/hstindex.htm, 1999, visited 1 August 1999.

10. Keith Kloor, "Lynx and Biologists Try to Recover after Disastrous Start," *Science* 285 (1999): 320–21.

11. Lisa Rathke, "Peregrine Falcon Restoration Effort Deemed a Success," *Burlington Free Press*, 30 July 1999, 5C.

12. C. B. Knisley and J. M. Hill, "Translocation of the Northeastern Beach

Tiger Beetle, *Cicindela dorsalis dorsalis*, to Sandy Hook New Jersey, 1997," final report to the U.S. Fish and Wildlife Service, New Jersey Field Office, 1998.

13. Michael Amaral, Andrea Kozol, and Tom French, "Conservation Status and Reintroduction of the Endangered American Burying Beetle," *Northeast Naturalist* 4 (1997): 121–32; Michael Amaral, personal communication, August 1999.

14. Cedric E. Alexander, Lawrence E. Garland, Ronald J. Regan, and Charles H. Willey, "Moose Management Plan" (Waterbury, Vt: Vermont Agency of Natural Resources, Department of Fish and Wildlife, 1992).

15. Zadoch Thompson, *Natural History of Vermont* (1853; reprint Rutland, Vt: Tuttle, 1982); Robert W. Fuller, "The 1974 Fisher Trapping Season in Vermont" (Burlington: University of Vermont, 1975).

16. Edward B. Walker, personal communication, July 1999.

17. Edward B. Walker, "Fisher Stocking in Vermont" (Montpelier, Vt.: Agency of Natural Resources, Department of Forests and Parks, 1958).

18. Edward B. Walker, personal communication, July 1999.

19. Fuller, "The 1974 Fisher Trapping Season."

20. Thompson, *Natural History of Vermont*.

21. James J. DiStefano, Kimberly J. Royar, Diane M. Pence, and James E. Denoncour, "Marten Recovery Plan for Vermont" (Waterbury, Vt.: Agency of Natural Resources, Department of Fish and Wildlife, 1990).

22. Robert W. Fuller, "Proposed Endangered and Threatened Mammals," in *The Endangered and Threatened Species of Plants and Animals in Vermont*, ed. Sally Laughlin (Montpelier, Vt.: Agency of Environmental Conservation, 1987), 42–54.

23. U.S. Department of Agriculture, Forest Service Wildlife and Fisheries staff, "Challenge Cost-share Program Report for 1990: Partnership in Wildlife and Fisheries Management" (Washington, D.C.: U.S. Forest Service, 1991).

24. Mark H. Davis, "Reintroduction of the Pine Marten into the Nicolet National Forest, Forest County, Wisconsin," M.S. Thesis, University of Wisconsin, Stevens Point, 1978; Sally J. Churchill, Lynn A. Herman, Margaret F. Herman, and James P. Ludwig, "Final Report on the Completion of the Michigan Marten Reintroduction Program," Ecological Research Service Report, Iron River, Michigan, 1981; Larry F. Fredrickson, "Pine Marten Reintroduction into the Black Hills of South Dakota, 1979–1988," PR Project W-75-R-30, Study No. 7518, 1989; Marjorie A. Strickland and Carmen W. Douglas, "Marten," in *Wild Furbearer Management and Conservation in North America*, ed. Milan Novak, James A. Baker, Martyn E. Obbard, and Bruce Malloch (Toronto: Ontario Trappers Association and Ontario Ministry of Natural Resources, 1987), 531–46.

25. William E. Berg, "Reintroduction of Fisher, Pine Marten, and River Otter," in *Midwest Furbearer Management*, Proceedings of a Symposium at the Forty-third Midwest Fish and Wildlife Conference, Wichita, Kansas, ed. Glen C. Sanderson, 1982, 159–73.

26. DiStefano et al., "Marten Recovery Plan."

27. Sharman Buechner, "Evaluation of the Green Mountain National Forest in Vermont as Potential Sites for Pine Marten Reintroduction," Senior Thesis, University of Vermont, Burlington, Vermont, 1986.

28. Arthur W. Allen, "Habitat Suitability Index Models: Marten," U.S. Department of the Interior, Fish and Wildlife Service, FWS/OBS-82/10.11 (Washington, D.C.: U.S. Fish and Wildlife Service, 1982); Arthur F. Ritter, "Marten Habitat Evaluation in Northern Maine Using LANDSAT Imagery," in *Proceedings of the New England Fish and Wildlife Conference*, ed. Mark Sayre (Augusta: Maine Department of Inland Fisheries and Wildlife, 1985).

29. Francois Sarrazin and Robert Barbault, "Reintroduction: Challenges and Lessons for Basic Ecology," *Trends in Ecology and Evolution* 11 (1996): 474–76.

30. Berg, "Reintroduction of Fisher"; Churchill et al., "Michigan Marten Reintroduction Program."

31. Robert M. Pramuk and James Denoncour, "White Rocks National Recreation Area Management Objectives and Direction" (Rutland, Vt.: U.S. Forest Service, Green Mountain National Forest, 1985).

32. Berg, "Reintroduction of Fisher."

33. Robert T. Brooks, "Assessment of Two Camera-based Systems for Monitoring Arboreal Wildlife," *Wildlife Society Bulletin* 24 (1996): 298–300.

34. Kimberly J. Royar, "Monitoring of Reintroduced Marten Populations in Vermont" (Waterbury, Vt.: Agency of Natural Resources, Fish and Wildlife Department, 1996).

35. Fredrickson "Pine Marten Reintroduction"; Brooks, "Assessment of Two Camera-based Systems"; Charlene M. Gieck, "Wisconsin Department of Natural Resource Pine Marten Recovery Plan," Wisconsin Bureau of Endangered Species, Draft No. 3, 1986; Bruce E. Kohn, William A. Creed, and James E. Ashbrenner, "History and Status of Wisconsin's Fisher Population," Wisconsin Department of Natural Resources, Research Management Findings No. 23, 1989; Paul W. Rego, "A Proposal to Reintroduce Fishers to Northwestern Connecticut," Connecticut Department of Wildlife Bureau, 1987.

36. Royar, "Monitoring of Reintroduced Marten Populations."

37. Brooks, "Assessment of Two Camera-based Systems."

38. Trina Marruzzi, personal communication, March 1999.

39. William B. Krohn, Kenneth D. Elowe, and Randall B. Boone, "Relations among Fishers, Snow, and Martens: Development and Evaluation of Two Hypotheses," *The Forestry Chronicle* 71 (1995): 97–107.

40. Brad Griffith, J. Michael Scott, James W. Carpenter, and Christine Reed, "Translocation as a Species Conservation Tool: Status and Strategy," *Science* 245 (1989): 477–80; Donald A. Falk, Constance I. Millar, and Margaret Olwell, *Restoring Diversity: Strategies for Reintroduction of Endangered Plants* (Washington, D.C.: Island Press, 1996); Richard P. Reading, Tim W. Clark, and Brad Griffith, "The Influence of Valuational and Organizational Considerations in the Success of Rare Species Translocations,"*Biological Conservation* 79 (1997): 217–25; C. Magdelena Wolf, Brad Griffith, Christine Reed, and Stanley A. Temple, "Avian and Mammalian Translocations: Update and Reanalysis of 1987 Survey Data," *Conservation Biology* 10 (1996): 1142–54; C. Magdelena Wolf, Theodore Garland, and Brad Griffith, "Predictors of Avian and Mammalian Translocation Success: Reanalysis with Phylogenetically Independent Contrasts," *Biological Conservation* 86 (1998): 243–55; Philip J. Seddon and Pritpal S. Soorae, "Guidelines for Subspecific Substitutions in Wildlife Restoration Projects," *Conservation Biology* 13 (1999): 177–84.

41. Paul Paquet, James R. Stritholt, Reed F. Noss, N. Staus, Carlos Carroll, and G. Heilman, Jr., "Wolf Reintroduction Feasibility in the Adirondack Park, New York," report of the Conservation Biology Institute, Corvallis, Oregon, 1999.

8. Making It Happen (pages 182–210)

1. Howard Zahniser, *Where Wilderness Preservation Began: The Adirondack Writings of Howard Zahniser* (Utica, N.Y.: North Country Books, 1992), 41.

2. For example, when Diamond Occidental sold 790,000 acres in 1988, pre-

cipitating the debate about the future of the Northern Forest, the sale resulted in some two hundred new owners, some of whom liquidated all standing timber to pay off mortgages. Phyllis Austen, "Cracks in the Timber Empire: Goldsmith's Raid Changed Forest Landowning, Perhaps Forever," *The Maine Times*, 13 March 1997, 4–7.

3. John W. Hakola, *Legacy of a Lifetime: The Story of Baxter State Park* (Woolrich, Maine: TBW Books, 1981), 117.

4. Suppression of wildfires in status 1 lands was loosely considered because the issue is not very significant in the Northeast (unlike the West where the codes were developed). Moreover, this would have prevented state and federally designated wilderness areas from being assigned to the highest management status (Frank Biasi, GIS Coordinator, Eastern Resource Office of the Nature Conservancy, personal communication, June 1998).

5. Categorizing Maine's public lands into the top three status categories revealed that the state has approximately 5.12 percent public land in total, with less than 2 percent in status 1 and 2 combined, and just less than 1 percent in status 1 "wilderness" lands. Data provided by Dan Morse of the GIS Office, Eastern Conservation Science of the Eastern Resource Office of the Nature Conservancy, Boston, Massachusetts from regional GIS data (see sources for map 8.1).

6. Press release of the Conservation Fund, 9 December 1998.

7. Reed F. Noss and Allen Y. Cooperrider, *Saving Nature's Legacy: Protecting and Restoring Biodiversity* (Washington, D.C.: Island Press, 1994), 174.

8. The northeastern states have long led the country in making important connections among agriculture, ecology, economy, and community. Farms in the Northeast tend to be smaller by the nature of the landscape and soils; smaller plots, in turn, ensure that farmers are closer to the land, and that positive developments like community-based agriculture and organic farming can continue to grow. Geography points the way. There is a strong network of state chapters of the Northeast Organic Farmers Association, whose mission is to help consumers, gardeners, and farmers work together for cleaner food and a safer, healthier environment. Pennsylvania hosts the venerable Rodale Institute, as well as the headquarters of the biodynamic movement, begun in the 1940s. The Federation of Cooperatives in Waterville, Maine, cultivates and supplies northern-specific plants and works with a network of small organic farmers. The University of New Hampshire has a farm dedicated to organic agricultural research. Located in the Berkshire Mountains of Massachusetts, where community-supported agriculture (CSA) was founded, is the E. F. Schumacher Society's headquarters in Great Barrington, which has regional programs in micro-lending, community land trusts, local currencies, and consumer-supported farming.

9. "$76 m Purchase Lets States Preserve 300,000 Forest Acres," *Boston Globe*, 10 December 1998, 1.

10. Conservation Fund, 1998. The press release announced that organizational goals included retaining 70 percent as active timberland, protected from other forms of development through easement.

11. See, for example, *Burlington Free Press* Readers' Forum, 7 January 1999 and 14 January 1999: "Need More Protection," "Restore the Land," and "Wildlife Not Snowmobiles."

12. Acreage figures were obtained from the GIS Office, Eastern Resource Office of the Nature Conservancy, Boston, Massachusetts, which used data from the Vermont Chapter of the Nature Conservancy and the Spatial Analysis Lab at the University of Vermont. Provisions of the easement were obtained from Vermont Land Trust, "Champion International Lands, Guide to the Working

Forest Easement," http://www.vlt.org/CIForestGuide.html, 1999, visited 22 October 1999.

13. Thomas T. Struhsaker, "A Biologist's Perspective on the Role of Sustainable Harvest in Conservation," *Conservation Biology* 12 (1998): 930. See also, for example, Ian Bowles, "Logging and Tropical Forest Conservation," *Science* 280 (1998): 1899–1900.

14. Reed F. Noss, "Maintaining Ecological Integrity in Representative Resource Networks" (Washington, D.C.: World Wildlife Fund, 1993), 26.

15. E. O. Wilson, *The Diversity of Life* (New York: Norton, 1992), 347.

16. The precautionary principle asserts that if harm is threatened, and if there is uncertainty about that harm, then precautionary actions must be taken. By the 1970s, the policy had been incorporated into Swedish and German environmental laws. The precautionary principle was woven into most of the U.S. environmental legislation written in the 1970s. Derailed by the opposing concept of "risk assessment," which encouraged a narrow focus on single species or chemicals *and* a burden of proof on the opponent of the action, precautionary provisions were seriously weakened or eliminated in the United States by the end of the 1980s. By the early 1990s, "the principle had all but disappeared from public discourse." Because of the increasing awareness of complex and sometimes unforeseen systemic problems from pollution and environmental destruction (CO_2 in the atmosphere, species extinctions, and the like) scientists have started a vigorous effort to bring back the precautionary principle and make it operational in U.S. and international law. The 1998 Wingspread Conference, convened by the Science and Environmental Health Network, focused on this issue, as did the International Forum on Food and Agriculture, which convened in 1998 in Vancouver, and produced a powerful statement on the precautionary principle. See Peter Sauer, "Reinhabiting Environmentalism: Picking up Where Leopold and Carson Left Off," *Orion* (Summer 1999): 30–41.

17. This quote attributed to Theodore Roosevelt is inscribed on a wall in the American Museum of Natural History in New York. He may, however, have been quoting Thoreau, as the words are also attributed to him, with "tolerable" in place of "healthy."

18. Wilson, *The Diversity of Life*, 351.

19. Scott Russell Sanders, "Staying Put," *Orion* (Winter 1992): 48.

20. Wallace Kaufman, "Environmentalists Outside the True Church," *Orion* (Summer 1999): 52.

21. See, for example, Green Mountain National Forest Opinion Survey, 1995, conducted by Robert Manning of the School of Natural Resources at University of Vermont, and a similar White Mountain National Forest opinion poll conducted in the fall of 1998. In the Vermont poll of 1,500 households, 82 percent favored banning clear-cutting, 82 percent did not want timbering if it marred scenic beauty, and 80 percent wanted to protect all remaining undisturbed forest. The Forest Service did not release the poll until the summer of 1998.

22. *America's Wildlife at the Crossroads* (Washington, D.C.: International Association of Fish and Wildlife Agencies, 1999), 3.

23. Land Trust Alliance, *1998 National Land Trust Census* (Washington, D.C.: Land Trust Alliance, 1998).

24. Ibid.

25. Riparian buffers were not studied as a distinct discipline until the 1970s, and this critical area remains an emerging field of study. Land trusts should not adopt the narrow, traditional buffers favored by loggers without updating their knowledge in this field and also remembering how little we do know about the

ecology of riparian areas. Some useful literature, as summarized by Ralph Tiner, wetland ecologist with the U.S. Fish and Wildlife Service, and Ralph Correll, Senior Scientist with the Smithsonian Environmental Research Center, for a River Buffer Workshop at the 1998 Land Trust Rally sponsored by the Land Trust Alliance, includes: C. Scott Findlay and Jeff Houlihan, "Anthropogenic Correlates of Species Richness in Southeastern Ontario," *Conservation Biology* 11 (1997): 1000–1004; John C. Kilgo, Robert A. Sargent, Brian R. Chapman, and Karl V. Miller, "Effect of Stand Width and Adjacent Habitat on Breeding Bird Communities in Bottomland Hardwoods," *Journal of Wildlife Management* 62 (1998): 72–83; Edward S. Corbett, Keith Mussallem, and James A. Lynch, "Best Management Practices for Controlling Non-point Source Pollution on Forested Watersheds," *Journal of Soil and Water Conservation* 40 (January/February 1985): 164–67; James A. Lynch and Edward S. Corbett, "Evaluation of Best Management Practices for Controlling Non-point Pollution from Silvicultural Operations," *Water Resources Bulletin* 26 (February 1990): 41–52; A. J. Castelle, A. W. Johnson, and C. Conolly, "Wetland and Stream Buffer Size Requirements—A Review," *Journal of Environmental Quality* 23 (1994): 878–82; Mary Jo Croonquist and Robert P. Brooks, "Effects of Habitat Disturbance on Bird Communities on Riparian Corridors," *Journal of Soil and Water Conservation* 48 (January/February 1993): 65–70; David L. Correll, "Buffer Zones and Water Quality Protection: General Principles," *Proceedings from International Conference on Buffer Zones, Quest Environmental*, Hertfordshire, U.K., 1996.

26. Jim Northup, "Joseph Battell, Once and Future Philanthropist," *Wild Earth* (Summer 1999): 18.

27. Much of this section is taken from Emily Bateson and Nancy Smith, "Just Buy It: Sweet Water Trust Saves Wildlands in New England," *Wild Earth* (Summer 1998): 28–34.

28. See, for example, Hakola, *Legacy of a Lifetime*.

29. For example, the Packard Foundation has launched a five-year, $175-million initiative to conserve at least 250,000 acres of California habitat. The Merck Family Fund and the Sudbury foundation announced in 1998 that they would take $1.5 million and $1 million out of their endowments, respectively, to help fund land protection in the Northern Forest. The John Merck Fund and interested family members have also provided considerable funds to the St. John purchase, as have the Lennox Foundation and the Libra Foundation. A handful of family foundations, including Davis Family Foundation, Friedman Family Foundation, the Orchard Foundation, the NLT Foundation, and the Dolphin Trust, have stretched beyond their guidelines and joined forces to help fund the Nature Conservancy's St. John River purchase, an informal collaboration that may well add $1 million of wild lands money to that important project.

30. Lynda Gorov, "Spreading the Wealth," *Boston Globe*, 28 November 1999, A1+.

31. Vice President Al Gore as quoted in Bill McKibben, *Hope, Human and Wild* (Boston: Little, Brown, 1995), 1.

32. Wallace Stegner, as quoted in Peter Forbes, Ann Forbes, and Helen Whybrow, eds., *Our Lands, Ourselves: Readings on People and Place* (San Francisco: Trust for Public Land, 1999), 76.

33. Other sources of funding information include: The Trust for Public Land, *Doing Deals: A Guide to Buying Land for Conservation*, 1995; and *The Land Trust Alliance Exchange*, a quarterly periodical of the Land Trust Alliance. For information about both publications, contact the Land Trust Alliance, 1319 F St. NW, Suite 501, Washington, DC, 20004–1106. For updated information about funding

for wilderness and wildlife conservation, also call the National Wildlife Federation or your state chapter of the Nature Conservancy.

34. See *Rachel's Environment and Health Weekly* 672 (October 1999).

35. In Fiscal Year 1999, a total of $328,467,000 was appropriated by Congress to augment wildlife refuges, national forests, and national parks and other federal monuments. Seven million dollars came to the Northeast for acquisition of significant lands: to the Silvio Conte National Wildlife Refuge along the Connecticut River, Lake Umbagog National Wildlife Refuge in New Hampshire, and the Green Mountain National Forest in Vermont. Although the New England congressional delegation and regional advocates fought hard for this important funding, $7 million dollars represents only 2 percent of the LWCF appropriations. Such funding is inadequate to meet the challenge facing the Northern Forest today.

36. Teaming with Wildlife is one good funding mechanism to support nongame wildlife conservation programs, neglected historically. A component of the National Wildlife Federation's work has been to seek funding of state fish and wildlife programs to reverse wildlife declines while populations are still large enough to carry the genetic diversity and flexibility to recover without intensive and expensive recovery programs. Presently, less than 10 percent of state fish and wildlife funding is targeted to the conservation of 86 percent of our nation's wildlife species, the "nongame" species.

37. For Supplemental Environmental Projects information, contact USEPA, Office of Enforcement and Compliance Assurance (2248A) EPA-300-B-98-001, or contact EPA Region 1's SEP BANK Program, OES Regulatory Office, Boston, Massachusetts.

38. Current state bond information can be found on the Web site of the Trust for Public Lands: www.tpl.org/toolbox, or through the Land Trust Alliance in Washington, D.C.

39. Fears that the $50 million bond will not stretch very far are not unfounded. Three million dollars appropriated for Maine land acquisition in 1998 as a stopgap measure before the bond quickly received $11 million worth of quality acquisition proposals. Other political and legal hurdles remain in a state long dominated by the forest products industry. For example, a state statute prohibits expenditure of state funds for land on which the primary use value has been or will be as commercially harvested forestland. MRSA Title V, Chapter 353, Section 6200, lists commercial timberland as a nonqualifying expenditure for land acquisition.

40. Taken from information supplied by Evergreen Capital Advisors, Princeton, New Jersey. Evergreen has worked with towns on installment-purchase agreements.

41. Northup, "Joseph Battell," 18.

42. From Clause 3 of Battell's Last Will and Testament, as cited in ibid., 19.

43. Vermont Forestry Department press release from 1915, as cited in ibid., 18.

44. Robert Braile, "Despite Wish, Vermont Parcel 'Primeval' No More," *Boston Globe*, 15 July 1999, 1+.

45. *The Maine Sportsman*, March 1999, 13; *The Maine Times*, 27 May 1999, 12; and *The Maine Times*, 9 April 1999, 18, respectively.

46. Wilson, *The Diversity of Life*, 311.

47. Joe Choiniere, "Lamentation on a Great and Windy Hill," *Sanctuary: The Journal of the Massachusetts Audubon Society* (July/August 1999): 6.

48. Much of the material in the two subsections on forever wild easement protection is taken from Nancy Smith, "Forever Wild Easements in New England," *Wild Earth* (Fall 1997): 72–77.

The perpetuity of carefully drafted conservation easements held by land trusts is supported by state statutes, the Uniform Conservation Easement Act (which is a basis for some state statutes), IRS regulations, charitable trust law, and case law. Under the IRS regulations governing charitable gifts, conservation easements cannot be extinguished by a qualified charitable trust without a court order, and then only under the doctrine of changed circumstances or eminent domain. Easements are at least as permanent as other forms of land protection. The permanence of conservation easements compares very well to the constitutional or statutory basis of permanence of publicly owned fee land. For example, wilderness areas and national wildlife refuges are created by an act of Congress that would not be easily overturned. In addition to wilderness areas, state and federal lands throughout the Northeast have special designations for small natural heritage sites, for example, the research natural areas on national forests. Many of these are administrative designations and can be changed again through the administrative process, so these have no statutory safeguards. In New York State's Adirondack Park, forever wild land is constitutionally guaranteed. It would take a two-thirds vote of two successive legislatures to amend Article 14 to undo the forever wild status of land so protected, and then the issue would go to a statewide ballot in the fall. However, those lands can be administratively designated either "wilderness" or "wild forest," and an increasing lobbying effort is aimed at moving lands into the latter category, thus allowing extensive motorized recreation.

49. Not all easements are created equal. Many easements on farm and forestland *only* preclude housing development, and do not promote good management practices in any meaningful way. Owners who have donated their lands to groups who promise to protect it through easement have at times been disappointed as a result. It can be misleading on a regional level as well. As discussed in the text, conservation maps generally show all easement properties regardless of management that may not reflect good conservation, thus leading people to believe the region is better protected than it actually is.

50. Michael DiNunzio, Director of Research and Education, the Adirondack Council, personal communication, August 1999.

51. Very large private holdings can achieve similar double protection by creating a form of nonprofit corporation with a board of trustees that holds the property subject to a trust instrument that sets out specific management conditions. A compatible easement is then held and enforced by a local land trust. It was in this manner that philanthropist Bessie Phillips protected more than 5,000 acres around the Rangely Lakes and the Kennebago River in western Maine, inspiring a regional protection effort that continues through the local land trust to this day. Easements can also be co-held in some instances to further cover long-term contingencies. Another method short of an easement, used extensively by the National Fish and Wildlife Foundation when it gives grants for habitat protection, is to require a notice that runs with the deed and requires that the foundation be notified if the land is sold for nonconservation purposes, at which point they must get their money back. This approach, clearly, is not nearly as rigorous or specific as an easement, but does provide some historical record that the property was purchased for conservation, alerts the foundation if it is ever sold, and through the money-back provision adds some incentive for the buyer to conserve the land over time. Sweet Water Trust's draft model Forever Wild Easement is available upon request.

52. Wilson, *The Diversity of Life*, 351.

9. Stewardship and Sustainability (pages 213–233)

The authors would like to thank John Elder, professor at Middlebury College; Darby Bradley, president of the Vermont Land Trust; and David Donath, president of the Woodstock Foundation, for their thoughtful observations and comments. We appreciate the assistance we received from Preston Bristow and Pam Knights with the Vermont Land Trust; Farley Brown with Vermont Coverts; Lars Botzojorns, Heather M. Freeman, and Susan Morse with Keeping Track; Sarah Albert; David M. Clarkson; Jeffrey P. Roberts; Barbara Slaiby; Jacquelyn L. Tuxill; and the Woodstock Historical Society. The illustrations are included courtesy of the Woodstock Foundation and the Vermont Land Trust.

1. Vaclav Havel, quoted in *Our Land, Ourselves: Readings on People and Place*, ed. Peter Forbes, Ann Forbes, and Helen Whybrow (San Francisco: Trust for Public Land, 1999), v.

2. George Perkins Marsh, *Man and Nature; or, Physical Geography as Modified by Human Action*, ed. David Lowenthal (New York: Charles Scribner, 1864; reprint Cambridge: Harvard University Press, 1965); see also David Lowenthal, *George Perkins Marsh: Versatile Vermonter* (New York: Columbia University Press, 1958). David Lowenthal has recently completed a revised biography of Marsh, which will be published in the spring of 2000.

3. Marsh-Billings-Rockefeller National Historical Park is the only national park to focus on conservation history and the evolving nature of land stewardship in America. Opened in June 1998, Vermont's first national park preserves and interprets the historic Marsh-Billings-Rockefeller property in Woodstock. The park is named for George Perkins Marsh, one of the nation's first global conservation thinkers, who grew up on the property, and for Frederick Billings, an early conservationist who established a progressive dairy farm and professionally managed forest on the former Marsh farm. Frederick Billings's granddaughter, Mary French Rockefeller, and her husband, conservationist Laurance S. Rockefeller, sustained Billings's mindful practices in forestry and farming on the property over the latter half of the twentieth century. In 1983, they established the Billings Farm and Museum to continue the farm's working dairy and to interpret rural Vermont life and agricultural history. The Billings Farm and Museum is operated as a private nonprofit educational institution by the Woodstock Foundation, Inc. Marsh-Billings-Rockefeller National Historical Park was created in 1992, when the Rockefellers gifted the estate's residential lands and forestlands to the people of the United States. Today, the park interprets the history of conservation with tours of the Marsh-Billings-Rockefeller mansion and the surrounding 550-acre forest. Working in partnership, the park and museum present historic and contemporary examples of conservation stewardship and explain the lives and contributions of George Perkins Marsh, Frederick Billings and his descendents, and Mary and Laurance S. Rockefeller. A number of publications presenting more detail on the park and its history include: John Elder, "Inheriting Mt. Tom," *Orion* (Spring 1997): 27–32; Rolf Diamant, David A. Donath, and Nora J. Mitchell, "Conservation with a Human Face: Re-considering Stewardship," *History News* (Summer 1997): 22–24; H. Eliot Foulds, Katharine Lacy, and Lauren G. Meier, *Land Use History for Marsh-Billings National Historical Park* (Boston: National Park Service, 1994).

4. Christopher McGrory Klyza and Stephen C. Trombulak, *The Story of Ver-*

mont: A Natural and Cultural History (Hanover, N.H.: University Press of New England, 1999); John Elder, *Reading the Mountains of Home* (Cambridge: Harvard University Press, 1998); Tom Wessels, *Reading the Forested Landscape: A Natural History of New England* (Woodstock, Vt.: The Countryman Press, 1997); Christopher McGrory Klyza and Stephen C. Trombulak, eds., *The Future of the Northern Forest* (Hanover, N.H.: University Press of New England, 1994); William Cronon, *Changes in the Land: Indians, Colonists, and the Ecology of New England* (New York: Hill and Wang, 1983).

5. Elder, "Inheriting Mt. Tom," 27–28.

6. The term "cultural landscape," first used by geographers in the early twentieth century, is now used widely in historic preservation to recognize the value of the landscape as a record of the past and for its associative cultural value today (see Bernd von Droste, Harald Plachter, and Mechtild Rossler, eds., *Cultural Landscapes of Universal Value* [Stuttgart, Germany, and New York: Gustav Fischer Verlag Jena, 1995]). This term is used in international literature and, as of 1992, cultural landscapes could be nominated to the World Heritage List according to revised guidelines for the World Heritage Convention. "Working landscape" has been used to describe places where active management such as forestry or agriculture is an important characteristic. The term "protected landscape" is also used in international literature, primarily by the World Conservation Union (IUCN) (see P. H. C. Lucas, *Protected Landscapes: A Guide for Policy-makers and Planners* [London: Chapman and Hall, 1992]).

7. Bill McKibben, *Hope, Human and Wild: True Stories of Living Lightly on the Earth* (Boston: Little, Brown, 1995).

8. John Terborgh and Michael Soulé, "Why We Need Large-scale Networks and Megareserves: How to Design Them," *Wild Earth* (Spring 1999): 66–72.

9. *Wild Earth* (Spring 1999): 1; Steve Gatewood provides updates on the Wildlands Project in several current issues of *Wild Earth;* see also Reed F. Noss, "The Wildlands Project: Land Conservation Strategy," *Wild Earth* (Special Issue, 1992): 10–25.

10. William Vitek, "Rediscovering the Landscape," in *Rooted in the Land: Essays on Community and Place*, ed. William Vitek and Wes Jackson (New Haven: Yale University Press, 1996), 3.

11. Wendell Berry, "In Distrust of Movements," *Orion* (Summer 1999): 16.

12. Ibid.

13. Brian Donahue, *Reclaiming the Commons: Community Farms and Forests in a New England Town* (New Haven: Yale University Press, 1999), 8.

14. Wes Jackson, *Becoming Native to this Place* (Lexington: University Press of Kentucky, 1994), 3.

15. John Murray, "On Stewardship," in *Sacred Trusts: Essays on Stewardship and Responsibility*, ed. Michael Katakis (San Francisco: Mercury House, 1993), 265.

16. William Cronon, "The Trouble with Wilderness; or Getting Back to the Wrong Nature," in *Uncommon Ground: Toward Reinventing Nature*, ed. William Cronon (New York: Norton, 1995), 89.

17. Gary Synder, *The Practice of the Wild* (New York: North Point Press, 1990), 7.

18. Elder, *Reading the Mountains*, 29.

19. Thomas Davis, "What Is Sustainable Development?," Menominee Sustainable Development Institute, http://www.menominee.com/sdi/articles/whatis.htm, visited 26 October 1999.

20. World Commission on Environment and Development, *Our Common Future* (New York: Oxford University Press, 1988).

21. The Rio Declaration describes the principles of sustainability and Agenda 21 is the plan of action agreed to by national governments at the Earth Summit held in Rio in 1992 (see gopher://gopher.un.org//11/conf/unced/English for a copy of the Rio Declaration and Agenda 21 report). For information on Earth Summit +5, a special session to review and appraise the implementation of Agenda 21 held in New York, 23–27 June 1997, see http://www.un.org/esa/earthsummit/ga97info.htm.

22. "Sustainable Agriculture Research & Education Program, Northeast Region," University of Vermont, http://www/uvm/edu/nesare/what_is.html, visited 30 October, 1999.

23. Agricultural economist John Ikerd, quoted in "1,000 Ways to Sustainable Farming," http://1000ways.baka.com, visited 30 October, 1999.

24. Elizabeth Henderson, keynote address at the Northeast Organic Farmers Association (NOFA) — Vermont Winter Conference, Randolph, Vermont, 21 February, 1998.

25. Alan Gussow, *Sense of Place: The Artist and the American Landscape* (Washington, D.C.: Island Press, 1997), 27–28.

26. These case studies are drawn primarily from a project called the Stewardship Initiative. To explore the evolution of stewardship and to gather contemporary examples of conservation, the Marsh-Billings-Rockefeller National Historical Park, in collaboration with the Woodstock Foundation and the Conservation Study Institute, conducted a series of interviews with practitioners in the Northeast, across the country, and around the world. This Stewardship Initiative began in the summer of 1997 and was conducted with a consortium of organizations, coordinated by Jacquelyn Tuxill. The project team for the Stewardship Initiative included staff from Marsh-Billings-Rockefeller National Historical Park, the Woodstock Foundation, the Conservation Study Institute, the Watershed Center of Bristol, VT, and the Quebec-Labrador Foundation's Atlantic Center for the Environment, based in Ipswich, Massachusetts as well as advisors affiliated with the Vermont Land Trust, Middlebury College, and the U.S. Environmental Protection Agency. The goal of this project was to examine current innovative stewardship practice and to explore the role that stewardship can play in shaping the future of communities and landscapes. Then, based on this understanding of conservation today, the project developed interpretive exhibits for the park and museum, and sought ways to contribute to this new and innovative vision of stewardship. Selection of case studies was guided by a set of criteria that included (1) respect for nature and people, including history, cultural traditions, and the built environment; (2) attention to the health of ecosystems and the needs and values of people and their communities; (3) a strong "sense of place," derived from both natural features of the landscape and human interaction with it; (4) an appreciation for the past linked with a sense of responsibility toward the future; and (5) an understanding that local places and actions have relevance in the larger world. The project team interviewed representatives from over fifty organizations, from the Dudley Street Neighborhood Initiative near Boston to the Menominee Tribal Enterprises in Wisconsin, from Shelburne Farms in Vermont to Campfire in Zimbabwe. This survey of stewardship practitioners was not intended to be comprehensive; rather, the goal was to encompass a small number of organizations that collectively represent a reasonable sample of current innovative stewardship work. For additional information, see Philip Huffman, "Stewardship Initiative Update, 1999," newsletter prepared by Marsh-Billings-Rockefeller National Historical Park, the Woodstock Foundation, and the Conservation Study Institute.

27. Richard Wolkomir, "Following the Footsteps of Fox and Bear," *Smithsonian* (January 1997):42.

28. Ibid.: 36.

29. Susan Morse, director, Keeping Track, interview with Jacquelyn L. Tuxill on 21 December 1997; and from "Keeping Track" brochure and mission statement, Keeping Track, Inc., P.O. Box 848, Richmond, VT 05477.

30. Lars Botzojorns, executive director, Keeping Track, interview with Nora J. Mitchell on 28 April 1999.

31. Wolkomir, "Following the Footsteps," 34–43.

32. Farley Brown, program coordinator for Vermont Coverts, panel discussion on Forest Stewardship at Shelburne Farms, Vermont, 12 October 1999. These 1998 land use statistics are from the Vermont Agency of Natural Resources, Department of Forests, Parks and Recreation. It estimates that of the 78 percent of Vermont that is forested, 75 percent is owned by private, non-industrial owners, 10 percent by industrial owners, and 15 percent by public agencies.

33. David Dobbs, "The Picnic Initiative," *American Forests* (Summer 1999):7–9; David M. Clarkson, "Forest Fragmentation in Vermont, WHIG Model" (Text of a presentation, at Annapolis, Maryland, conference in November 1999).

34. Clarkson, "Forest Fragmentation."

35. Dobbs, "The Picnic Initiative," 8.

36. Ibid.

37. Ibid., 9. See also Richard L. Knight and Peter B. Landres, eds., *Stewardship Across Boundaries* (Washington, D.C.: Island Press, 1998); David Dobbs and Richard Ober, *The Northern Forest* (White River Junction, Vt.: Chelsea Green, 1998).

38. Henry David Thoreau, quoted in Wolkomir, "Following the Footsteps," 42.

39. Marsh, *Man and Nature*, 15.

40. John Elder, "Interview," *Orion Afield* (Spring 1999): 28.

41. Ibid.

42. David Orr, "Re-ruralizing Education," in *Rooted in the Land*, 231.

43. Vermont Land Trust, "Woodlawn Farm Conserved as Part of Mettowee Valley Conservation Project," http://www.vlt.org/family.html, visited 23 October 1999.

44. Ibid.

45. Vermont Land Trust, "Vermont Land Trust Homepage," http://www.vlt.org/, 2000, visited 2 January 2000.

46. "Vermonter of the Year Preserves State's Future," www.burlingtonfreepress.com/voy.htm, visited 26 October 1999.

47. Vermont Land Trust, "The Nature Conservancy of Vermont and the Vermont Land Trust Acquire the Third Largest Private Forest Holding in the State," http://www.vlt.org/forestry.html, visited 24 October 1999.

48. Ibid.

49. Background information on the Champion Lands project can be found at Vermont Land Trust, "Vermont Champion Lands Project," http://www.vlt.org/forestry/html and http://www.vlt.org/CIQ&A.html, visited 24 October 1999. Also, see articles in *VLT Quarterly Reports* (Spring 1999): 3–4; (Fall 1999): 14; (Winter 1999): 1–3.

50. Vermont Land Trust, "Vermont Champion Lands Project."

51. More details about the forest easement, as well as a copy of the document itself, can be found on the Vermont Land Trust Web site: http://www.vlt.org/CIForestEasement.html and http://www.vlt.org/CIForestGuide.html, visited on 24 October 1999.

52. Vermont Land Trust, "Champion Lands Have New Owners," http://www.vlt.org/forestry.html, visited 24 October 1999.

53. Orr, "Reruralizing Education," 231.

54. Vitek, "Rediscovering the Landscape," 1.

55. Cronon, "The Trouble with Wilderness," 89.

56. Elder, "Inheriting Mt. Tom," 31.

57. Will Rogers, "Foreword," in *Our Land, Ourselves*, xiii.

10. Vermont Family Forests (pages 234–255)

1. Vermont Division of Historic Preservation, "Prehistoric Cultural Heritage: Vermont Historic Preservation Plan," prepared by University of Vermont, Consulting Archeology Program (Montpelier, Vt.: Agency of Development and Community Affairs, Divison of Historic Preservation, 1991), 47.

2. Charles W. Johnson, *The Nature of Vermont: Introduction and Guide to a New England Environment*, rev. ed. (Hanover, N.H.: University Press of New England, 1998), 55.

3. Christopher McGrory Klyza and Stephen Trombulak, *The Story of Vermont: A Natural and Cultural History* (Hanover, N.H.: University Press of New England, 1999), 88.

4. Ibid., 89.

5. Hal Salwasser, Douglas W. MacCleery, and Thomas A. Snelgrove, "An Ecosystem Perspective on Sustainable Forestry," in *Defining Sustainable Forestry*, ed. Gregory Aplet, Nels Johnson, Jeffrey T. Olson, and V. Alaric Sample (Washington, D.C.: Island Press, 1993).

6. Vermont Agency of Natural Resources, *Environment 1999: An Assessment of the Quality of Vermont's Environment* (Waterbury, Vt.: Vermont Agency of Natural Resources, 1999), 2.

7. Vermont Department of Forests, Parks, and Recreation, "Vermont Forest Resource Harvest Summary: 1996" (Waterbury, Vt.: Vermont Department of Forests, Parks, and Recreation, 1997).

8. Thomas S. Frieswyk and Anne M. Malley, *Forest Statistics for Vermont: 1973 and 1983*, Resource Bulletin NE-87 (Broomall, Penn.: USDA Forest Service, Northeastern Forest Experiment Station, 1985), 50.

9. Richard H. Widmann and Thomas W. Birch, *Forest-land Owners of Vermont: 1983*, Resource Bulletin NE-102 (Broomall, Penn.: USDA Forest Service, Northeastern Forest Experiment Station, 1988), 54.

10. Northern Forest Lands Council, *Finding Common Ground* (Concord, N.H.: Northern Forest Land Council, 1994), 42; Robert S. Seymour and Malcolm L. Hunter, "New Forestry in Eastern Spruce-Fir Forests: Principles and Applications to Maine," Miscellaneous Publication 716, College of Forest Resources (Orono: University of Maine, 1991).

11. Wendell Berry, *Another Turn of the Crank* (Washington, D.C.: Counterpoint, 1995), 57.

12. William B. Leak, Dale S. Solomon, and Paul S. DeBald, *Silvicultural Guide for Northern Hardwood Types in the Northeast*, rev. ed., Research Paper NE-603 (Broomall, Penn.: USDA Forest Service, Northeastern Forest Experiment Station, 1987), 20.

13. Frieswyk and Malley, *Forest Statistics for Vermont*, 77.

14. National Wildlife Federation and Rainforest Alliance, "SmartWood Certification Program: Northeast Regional Guidelines for the Assessment of Natural Forest Management" (Montpelier, Vt.: National Wildlife Federation, 1997).

11. A Conversation at the Edge of Wilderness (pages 256–262)

This article first appeared in *Wild Earth* vol. 8, No. 4 (POB 455, Richmond, VT 05477) and is reprinted with permission.

1. See Christopher McGrory Klyza, "Lessons from the Vermont Wilderness," *Wild Earth* (Spring 1994): 75–79.
2. William Cronon, "The Trouble with Wilderness; or, Getting Back to the Wrong Nature," in *Uncommon Ground: Toward Reinventing Nature*, ed. William Cronon (New York: Norton, 1995), 85; Bill Devall and George Sessions, *Deep Ecology* (Salt Lake City: Gibbs Smith, 1985), 122.
3. Cronon, "The Trouble with Wilderness," 89.
4. See Aldo Leopold, *A Sand County Almanac* (New York: Oxford University Press, 1949).
5. Dave Foreman, Andy Holdsworth, and Jack Humphrey, "Sky Island/Greater Gila Nature Reserve Network Proposal," draft presented at Wildlands Project Science Workshop, 20 November 1997; Michael Soulé and Reed Noss, "Rewilding and Biodiversity: Complementary Goals for Continental Conservation," *Wild Earth* (Fall 1998); 18–28.
6. Leslie Marmon Silko, "Landscape and History in the Pueblo Imagination," in *Family of Earth and Sky: Indigenous Tales of Nature from Around the World*, ed. John Elder and Hertha Wong (Boston: Beacon, 1994), 251.

12. Some Lessons from Wilderness, East and West (page 263–271)

1. Robin Winks, "The Rockefellers and National Parks," *Wild Earth* (Summer 1998): 23–27.
2. See, for instance, "Public Opinion on and Attitudes toward the Reintroduction of the Eastern Timber Wolf to Adirondack Park," Responsive Management under contract to Defenders of Wildlife, 1996.
3. William D. Newmark, "Legal and Biotic Boundaries of Western North American National Parks: A Problem of Congruence," *Biological Conservation* 33 (1985): 197–208.
4. See, for example, Thomas L. Fleischner, "Ecological Costs of Livestock Grazing in Western North America," *Conservation Biology* 8 (1994): 629–44; George Wuerthner, "Some Ecological Costs of Livestock Grazing," *Wild Earth* (Spring 1992): 10–14; George Wuerthner, "Subdivisions and Extractive Industries," *Wild Earth* (Fall 1997): 57–62; George Wuerthner, "Should We Saddle Up with the Cowboys?" *Wild Earth* (Fall 1998): 68–72.

Contributors

Emily Bateson has been the Associate Director of Sweet Water Trust's Wildlands Program in Boston since 1997. From 1981 to 1996, she was the Science and Policy Director and then Land Project Director for the Conservation Law Foundation, a New England–based environmental law and advocacy organization. She is currently on the board of the Hubbard Brook Research Foundation. Previous publications include: "Dam Confusing," *Conservation Matters*, Summer 1996; "Take Back Your Beaches," *Conservation Matters*, Winter 1995–1996; "Just Buy It," co-authored with Nancy Smith, *Wild Earth*, Summer 1998; and "Sustaining Our Forest—Crafting Our Future" in *The Future of the Northern Forest* (1994).

David Brynn works as the Addison County Forester in Vermont. He is the founder and director of Vermont Family Forests. In his spare time, he and his wife Louise and daughters Devon and E. Callie conserve a thirty-two acre family forest in Bristol, Vermont.

Alicia Daniel, following an irresistible pull north, migrated from Texas in 1987 to become the Associate Director of the Field Naturalist Program at the University of Vermont. Passionate about wild animals and geology, she landed in the Botany Department and quickly expanded her world to include the love of plants. When she isn't roaming the boundaries of and teaching connections between the earth and life sciences and landscape and literature, Alicia divides her time raising daughter Camille with her husband Jim and working with the Winooski Valley Park District and Keeping Track to ensure that wildlife habitat and corridors are included in regional planning maps.

John Davis is Biodiversity Program Officer at the Foundation for Deep Ecology in San Francisco. Prior to that, he edited the *Earth First! Journal* and later was the founding editor of *Wild Earth*, which he edited from 1991 to 1997. He is the editor of the *Earth First! Reader* (1991). Davis currently splits his time between California and the Adirondacks in New York, where he is working with The Nature Conservancy and *Wild Earth* to protect a wildway linking the Adirondack foothills with Lake Champlain.

Rolf Diamant is Superintendent of the Marsh-Billings-Rockefeller National Historical Park in Woodstock, Vermont. Vermont's first national park interprets the theme of conservation stewardship and the many stories of "people taking care of places." Within the park is one of the country's oldest planned and continuously managed forests. He is co-author of *A Citizen's Guide to River Conservation* (World Wildlife Fund/CF). Rolf was a Beatrix Farrand Fellow at the College of Environmental Design at the University of California, Berkeley (BS 1973, MLA 1975) and was a Loeb Fellow in Advanced Environmental Studies at the Graduate School of Design at Harvard University (1985–1986).

John Elder teaches English and environmental studies at Middlebury College, where he has been a member of the faculty since 1973. His latest book, *Reading the Mountains of Home* (Harvard, 1998), explores some of the ways in which Robert Frost's poem "Directive" might help to map an environmental history of the Green Mountains.

Thor Hanson is a naturalist and writer from the Pacific Northwest. He learned about northeastern landscapes while pursuing a Master's degree at the University of Vermont's Field Naturalist Program. His work and studies have taken him from East Africa to Alaska, and he is currently employed as land steward for the San Juan County Land Bank in Washington. Thor writes whenever he can, and his articles on travel and natural history have appeared in newspapers and periodicals across the country.

Christopher McGrory Klyza is associate professor of political science and environmental studies at Middlebury College in Middlebury, Vermont. He is the author of *Who Controls Public Lands?* (1996), the co-author of *The Story of Vermont* (1999), and the coeditor of *The Future of the Northern Forest* (1994). He serves on the board of directors of Vermont Family Forests and the Watershed Center, two conservation groups based in Bristol, Vermont.

Robert T. Leverett is the Executive Director of Friends of Mohawk Trail State Forest, Massachusetts, a co-founder of the Eastern Native Tree Society, and the chairman of the special advisory board of the 500 Year Forest Foundation of Lynchburg, Virginia. Leverett is the principal architect of the Ancient Eastern Forest Conference Series and an advisor and contributor to the Eastern Old Growth Forest Information Clearinghouse, Georgetown, Kentucky. He is well known for his discoveries of and writings about old-growth forests in the eastern United States. He has been called by *Wild Earth* the East's leading old-growth forest evangelist.

Bill McKibben is the author of *The End of Nature*, which has appeared in twenty languages and was recently republished in a tenth anniversary edition by Anchor Press. He writes for the *New Yorker*, the *New York Review of Books*, *Natural History*, *Outside*, the *Atlantic*, *Harpers*, and a wide variety of other national publications. He lives in the central Adirondacks, near the great gorge of the Hudson.

Nora Mitchell is the Director of the National Park Service's Conservation Study Institute, a national program based at the Marsh-Billings-Rockefeller National Historical Park in Vermont. The Institute provides a forum to discuss the history and practice of conservation and future directions in the field. Institute programs encompass training, research, and building networks within the conservation community. During her twenty-year career with the NPS, Nora has authored numerous articles and contributed to national and international programs on landscape conservation. She holds Masters degrees from the University of Montana and Tufts University, and a doctorate in Landscape Studies from Tufts University.

Kimberly Royar has worked as a District Wildlife Biologist for the Vermont Fish and Wildlife Department since 1981. Prior to that she was employed for six years by the U.S. Forest Service in Maine, New Hampshire, and Virginia. Currently, she is the chairperson of Vermont's furbearer program and a member of the bear management team. She participated as one of the leaders in Vermont's marten reintroduction and monitoring program.

Jamie Sayen is author of *Einstein in America* (1985). He has been a wilderness activist in northern New England for over a decade. He is founder and now publisher of *The Northern Forest Forum*. He founded and served as Executive Director of the Northern Appalachian Restoration Project from 1992 to 1997. He has served on the New Hampshire Ecological Reserves Steering Committee since 1995. He is currently writing a book about wilderness and large land sales in northern New England.

Nancy Smith is the Executive Director and Wildlands Program Director of Sweet Water Trust in Boston, a foundation dedicated to the conservation of wild nature. Sweet Water Trust's priority is to work with partners to help acquire land and conservation easements for the creation of protected ecological areas based on sound conservation science. From 1989 to 1995 she also served as president of the Sheffield Land Trust in western Massachusetts, and is currently on the board of the Environmental League of Massachusetts. Previous publications include: "Just Buy It," co-authored with Emily Bateson, *Wild Earth*, Summer 1998; and "Forever Wild Easements," *Wild Earth*, Fall 1997.

Stephen C. Trombulak is the Albert D. Mead Professor of Biology and Environmental Studies at Middlebury College. He is a conservation biologist, with special interest in the design of ecological reserve systems and the application of conservation biology to natural resource policies. He has authored several papers in ecology and conservation, is the co-editor of the book *The Future of the Northern Forest* (1994), and is the co-author of the book *The Story of Vermont* (1999). He is currently on the Board of Governors for the Society for Conservation Biology.

Index